Evidence, Explanation, and Realism

Evidence, Explanation, and Realism

Essays in the Philosophy of Science

Peter Achinstein

OXFORD
UNIVERSITY PRESS

2010

Oxford University Press, Inc., publishes works that further
Oxford University's objective of excellence
in research, scholarship, and education.

Oxford   New York
Auckland   Cape Town   Dar es Salaam   Hong Kong   Karachi
Kuala Lumpur   Madrid   Melbourne   Mexico City   Nairobi
New Delhi   Shanghai   Taipei   Toronto

With offices in
Argentina   Austria   Brazil   Chile   Czech Republic   France   Greece
Guatemala   Hungary   Italy   Japan   Poland   Portugal   Singapore
South Korea   Switzerland   Thailand   Turkey   Ukraine   Vietnam

Published by Oxford University Press, Inc.
198 Madison Avenue, New York, New York 10016

www.oup.com

Oxford is a registered trademark of Oxford University Press.

Library of Congress Cataloging-in-Publication Data
Achinstein, Peter.
Evidence, explanation, and realism : essays in the philosophy of science / Peter Achinstein.
    p. cm.
ISBN 978-0-19-973525-9   1. Science—Philosophy.   I. Title.
Q175.A263 2010
501—dc22   2009029404

9 8 7 6 5 4 3 2 1

Printed in the United States of America
on acid-free paper

Acknowledgments

This book is dedicated to my wife, Linda Brown, whose deep care, loving encouragement, and philosophical acumen sustained me and the project. I have been most fortunate over the years in directing the work of graduate students with very considerable talent, some of whom honor me by showing how to employ various ideas of mine in new areas, others by arguing that such a task is for dreamers only. In any case, I want here to thank two of my favorites who have a special association with this book: Victor DiFate and Richard Richards. I invited both, who know my work well, to suggest various essays they would like to see in the volume. The lists of the three of us matched pretty closely. In addition I owe a good deal of thanks to Victor for invaluable help with the page proofs.

Two other individuals deserve special appreciation: Peter Ohlin, philosophy editor at Oxford University Press, for suggesting this entire project to me, and Morton Lowengrub, Provost at Yeshiva University, for moral and financial support for the volume. Many other individuals who have been helpful in particular ways are identified in the articles themselves.

Contents

Introduction

The essays in this volume represent three major areas of philosophy of science that I have explored over a period of more than forty years: evidence, explanation, and realism. They have appeared in journals or books; some have been reprinted in collections; three were selected for inclusion in *The Philosopher's Annual*, the editors' choice of the best ten essays in philosophy that year.

Philosophy of science, like many other disciplines, has become a field with several fairly narrow subspecialties, where questions are raised about how to understand the concepts and foundations of some particular scientific theory and where practitioners in one area often do not engage those in another. This is in stark contrast with what I take to be a glorious past, when Isaac Newton could formulate a very general scientific methodology under the title "Rules for the Study of Natural Philosophy"; William Whewell, who explicitly rejected Newtonian methodology, could formulate his own methodology in a chapter called "Of Certain Characteristics of Scientific Induction"; John Stuart Mill, who in turn rejected Whewell's ideas, could champion a very general methodology in chapters such as "Preliminary Observations on Induction in General" and "Of the Four Methods of Experimental Inquiry"; Pierre Duhem could title one of the sections of a classic work "What Is the True Nature of a Physical Theory and the Operations Constituting It?"; and in the twentieth century, Carl G. Hempel could write influential articles such as "Studies in the Logic of Explanation" and "Studies in the Logic of Confirmation."

Broadly speaking, my essays are in this tradition. They are based on the idea that one can say something very general, informative, and even true about the topics selected. Admittedly, in pursuing generality, there is always a danger of the sort noted by Niels Bohr when he was asked to say what the difference is between a physicist and a philosopher. "The physicist," he said, "learns more and more about less and less until he knows everything about nothing. The philosopher learns less and less about more and more until he knows nothing about everything." Whether the essays in this volume succeed in avoiding this fate, the reader must decide.

In addition to the generality of its approach, the tradition has another feature of importance. It is based on the idea that although particular causal factors, including historical, psychological, and sociological ones, can be invoked in understanding both how scientists came to develop and defend their ideas in the way they did and how these ideas influenced other scientists and traditions, these factors can be separated from the "logic" of the arguments they used and the methodologies they championed. One can examine and criticize Newton's four rules of reasoning, as Whewell did, from a general philosophical or logical viewpoint, while recognizing the historical and perhaps psychological fact that Newton promulgated these rules, among other reasons, because he sought to convince Cartesian physicists of the truth of his law of universal gravitation, and while recognizing that these rules had a profound effect on how later scientists argued for their own scientific theories.

By contrast with some members of this tradition, the approach I take is historical in this sense. The best way to proceed to understand a concept such as evidence, explanation, or realism in the sciences involves not only producing an "abstract" definition but also, very importantly, showing how that definition applies to actual scientific cases. The essays I have selected include ones that are historically oriented in this sense. For example, in exploring the meaning and truth of scientific realism, I proceed by asking whether Jean Perrin's argument in 1908 for the existence of molecules establishes the truth of scientific realism, as he himself thought.

Although the essays focus on three different topics, they form a natural set because, on my view, the topics are importantly related. The definition I offer for evidence invokes a concept of explanation, and that for scientific realism relies on a suitable concept of evidence. Briefly, to take the third concept first, scientific realism is a doctrine committed to the idea that "unobservables" (e.g., molecules, electrons) exist and can be known to exist and that it is one of the aims of science to provide true theories about them, as well as about the observable parts of the world. I argue that scientific antirealists, such as nineteenth-century positivists and some twentieth-century writers, rejected these claims and that, contrary to their views, scientific realism can be established by invoking suitable empirical evidence. So an important question arises: what is evidence? On my account, evidence for a hypothesis or theory is supposed to provide a good reason for believing that the hypothesis or theory is true. In accordance with the definition I arrive at, which reflects this idea, some fact is evidence that a hypothesis is true only if, given that fact, the probability is high that there is an explanatory connection between the hypothesis and the fact. I explain this definition and show its advantages over alternative accounts, which, unlike the present account, are subject to various types of counterexamples.

This will prompt the question of how to understand "explanatory connection" and, more generally, the idea of explanation. My general account of explanation begins by first considering acts of explaining—what it means for someone to explain something to someone. An explanation, in the sense of the product of such an act, is then defined as an ordered pair, one of whose members is an act-type "explaining q," where q is a certain type of indirect question, and whose other member is a proposition that provides an answer to the question q. A correct explanation is one in which the propositional member of the ordered pair is true. And there is an "explanatory connection" between propositions A and B if and only if either the fact that A is true correctly explains why B is true, or the reverse is the case, or the fact that some third proposition C is true correctly explains why both A and B are true. Although the concept of explanation is defined by reference to a type of explaining act, the resulting concepts, as well as that of a correct explanation, are, I argue, objective concepts—in the sense that whether something is an explanation, and whether it is a correct explanation, does not depend on, or vary with, anyone's beliefs or knowledge or on whether anyone is explaining anything to anyone. This objective concept of explanation will yield objective concepts of evidence and scientific realism. I also argue that there is another important way of evaluating an explanation—resulting in what I call a "good explanation"—which is not objective in this way. Whether an explanation is a good one does depend on particular epistemic situations, which can vary from one context to another. The "objective" and "contextual" ways of evaluating explanations are different, and both are used to generate important types of evaluations, but the most basic concept of evidence I introduce, as well as the ideas underlying scientific realism, require a noncontextual concept of "correct explanation."

Of the fifteen essays that follow, one is from 1965, and the rest are from the late 1970s to the present. (Excluded are essays written mostly in the 1980s and published in my *Particles and Waves* [1991] that deal with wave-particle debates in physics in the nineteenth century.) I have made a few changes in some of the essays included in the present book to conform to later formulations of the views expressed. In some cases, I have added an addendum for this purpose.

Part I

EVIDENCE AND INDUCTION

1

Concepts of Evidence

"Concepts of Evidence." This chapter contains an article by that title from Mind *(1978), 22–45, a selection from* The Book of Evidence *(Oxford University Press, 2001), 160–166 (both reprinted by permission), and an addendum to the* Mind *article for the present volume. The article in* Mind*, which was the first of my works developing a theory of evidence, gives counterexamples to standard probability and nonprobability definitions of evidence, introduces various concepts of evidence, and defines the most basic one, "potential evidence," in terms of probability and a concept of "correct explanation," and the others in terms of it. The selection from my book shows how to define the concept of "correct explanation" required. The addendum briefly summarizes various changes and additions in the later book. The original paper was selected for reprinting in* The Philosopher's Annual *for 1978.*

1. THREE CONCEPTS

Alan's skin has yellowed, so on Monday he sees the doctor, who examines him and declares that he has jaundice, i.e., the visible expression of an increased concentration of bilirubin in the blood (which I shall abbreviate as an i.c.b.). Some tests are made as a result of which on Friday, although Alan's yellowness remains, the doctor declares that Alan does not have an i.c.b. but that his yellow skin was produced by a dye with which he was working. On Friday which of the following propositions, if any, should the doctor affirm?

    i. Alan's yellow skin was evidence of an i.c.b. and still is.
    ii. Alan's yellow skin was but no longer is evidence of an i.c.b.
    iii. Alan's yellow skin is not and never was evidence of an i.c.b.

The doctor might be tempted to assert (i) on the ground that Alan's yellow skin is typically the kind of skin associated with an i.c.b. On the other hand, (ii) might be tempting to say since the doctor now has additional information which makes the original evidence efficacious no longer. Finally, he might be tempted to assert (iii) on the ground that false or misleading evidence is no evidence at all. He might say that Alan's yellow skin is not and never was (real or genuine) evidence of an i.c.b., though on Monday he mistakenly thought it was.

I believe that these three responses represent conflicting tendencies in the way we actually speak about evidence, and that a different but related concept of evidence can be associated with each.

I begin with a notion which I shall call *potential* evidence. The presence of Alan's yellow skin is potential evidence of an i.c.b. since yellow skin of that sort is generally associated with an i.c.b. That 35 percent of those sampled in this district said they would vote for the Democratic candidate is potential evidence that roughly 35 percent of all those voting in the district will vote for him since samples of that size are usually accurate. Without here trying to define this concept let me indicate several of its features.

First, e can be potential evidence that h even if h is false.[1] Secondly, potential evidence is objective in the sense that whether e is potential evidence that h does not depend upon anyone's beliefs about e or h or their relationship. That Alan has yellow skin is potential evidence that he has an i.c.b. even if no one believes that it is or knows or believes that he has yellow skin or an i.c.b. In these two respects potential evidence is akin to the concept Hempel seeks to define in "Studies in the Logic of Confirmation"[2] and to one Carnap calls the classificatory concept of confirmation which he defines using his theory of probability.[3]

Although Hempel and Carnap in addition allow e as well as h to be false, I am inclined to think that if there is a concept of potential evidence in use it is one that requires e to be true. This, then, is the third feature I attribute to this concept. That Alan has yellow skin is potential evidence

---

1. In what follows the evidence sentences that will be considered are, or are transformable into, ones of the form

    (ϕ) The fact that e (or that e) is evidence that h

in which e and h are sentences. However, when speaking schematically about such evidence sentences I shall follow the usual custom and simply write "e is evidence that h." This does not mean that I am subscribing to the view that evidence sentences of form (ϕ) should be construed as relating sentences, or indeed anything at all. This paper will not be concerned with the "logical form" of ϕ-sentences, although the reader is referred to my "Causation, Transparency, and Emphasis," *Canadian Journal of Philosophy* 5 (1975), 1–23, and "What Is an Explanation?" *American Philosophical Quarterly* 14 (1977), 1–15, where such questions about causation and explanation sentences are discussed, the answers to which have a bearing on ϕ-sentences.

2. Reprinted in Carl G. Hempel, *Aspects of Scientific Explanation* (New York, 1965).

3. Rudolf Carnap, *Logical Foundations of Probability* (2nd ed., Chicago, 1962), p. xvi.

that he has an i.c.b. only if he does in fact have yellow skin. The concept that Hempel and Carnap seek to analyze which has no such requirement could be described as "doubly potential" ("e would be potential evidence that h if e were true"). Finally, although both of these authors allow e to entail h (as a "limiting" case), I doubt that there is such a concept of evidence in use. The fact that Alan has yellow skin is not evidence that he has skin; it is too good to be evidence.

Can a concept of evidence with these characteristics be defined, and if so will it support proposition (i)? Various definitions of potential evidence will be examined in later sections, after which this question will be addressed.

I turn now to a second concept, *veridical* evidence, that sanctions proposition (iii) above. e is veridical evidence that h only if e is potential evidence that h and h is true. However, this is not yet sufficient. Suppose that Alan's having yellow skin is potential evidence of an i.c.b. and that Alan in fact has an i.c.b. But suppose that Alan's yellow skin did not result from an i.c.b. but from the chemical dye with which he was working. We would then conclude that his having the yellow skin he does is not (veridical) evidence of an i.c.b. Veridical evidence requires not just that h and e both be true but that e's truth be related in an appropriate manner to h's. Alan does not have the yellow skin he does *because* he has an i.c.b. but because he has been working with a yellow dye. More generally, I shall speak of an *explanatory connection* between e's being true and h's being true and say that

> (1) e is veridical evidence that h if and only if e is potential evidence that h, h is true, and there is an explanatory connection between e's being true and h's being true.

At the moment, I shall not try to define the notion of an explanatory connection. I do so in section 8 (excerpted from my *The Book of Evidence*). Before then, some further comments concerning (1) are in order. The concept of evidence characterized here does not require that h's being true correctly explain e's being true; the converse is also possible. That Jones has a severe chest wound can be veridical evidence that he will die, even though the hypothesis that he will die does not explain the fact that he has a severe chest wound. Rather the reverse explanation is correct: he will die because he has a severe chest wound. Alternatively, there may be some common explanation which correctly explains why both e and h are true. The fact that hydrogen and oxygen combine in a simple ratio by volume may be evidence that nitrogen and oxygen do too. (Gay-Lussac indeed took it to be so.) In this case h does not explain e, nor conversely. Still both h and e are explained by appeal to the fact that the pairs of substances involved are gases and gases combine in simple ratios by volume. (Or at a deeper level both h and e are explained by appeal to Avogadro's hypothesis.)

If we can assume—as I shall do here—that whether there is an explanatory connection between the truth of e and h does not depend on what anyone believes (except, of course, where e and h themselves describe beliefs or intentional actions), then veridical evidence, like potential evidence, is an objective concept of evidence. Moreover, it is a concept in accordance with which proposition (iii) should be asserted. If Alan does not have an i.c.b. (i.e., h is false) then by (i) the fact that he has yellow skin is not and never was (veridical) evidence that he has an i.c.b.

Turning to a third concept of evidence, we speak not only of something's being evidence that h but also of something's being *so-and-so*'s evidence that h. On Monday the doctor's evidence that Alan has an i.c.b. was that Alan has yellow skin. I take this to involve at least the claim that on Monday the doctor believed that Alan's yellow skin is potential evidence of an i.c.b. However, this is not sufficient if on Friday Alan's yellow skin is potential evidence of an i.c.b.; for the fact that Alan has yellow skin is not on Friday the doctor's evidence that Alan has an i.c.b., even if on Friday the doctor believes that it is potential evidence. Accordingly, one might be tempted to say that the fact that Alan has yellow skin is the doctor's evidence that Alan has an i.c.b. only if the doctor believes that this fact is *veridical* evidence of an i.c.b. More generally,

> (2) e is X's evidence that h only if X believes that e is veridical evidence that h; i.e., X believes that e is potential evidence that h, that h is true, and that there is an explanatory connection between the truth of h and e.[4]

However, (2) may be too strong in requiring that X believe that h is true and that there is an explanatory connection between h and e. Suppose that on Monday the doctor is unsure about whether Alan has an i.c.b. He thinks it probable but he does not know whether to believe it, so he orders tests. Later when the tests reveal no i.c.b. and Alan indignantly asks the doctor "what was your evidence that I have an i.c.b.?" the doctor might reply: "the fact that you have yellow skin." Even if on Monday the doctor was not sure whether to believe that Alan has an i.c.b. at least he believed that this is probable and that it is probable that this explains his yellow skin. Accordingly, (2) might be weakened as follows:

> (2′) e is X's evidence that h only if X believes that e is potential evidence that h, that it is probable that h is true, and that it is probable that there is an explanatory connection between the truth of h and e.

---

4. 'X's evidence that h' like 'X's explanation' is ambiguous. It can mean (roughly) 'what X takes to be evidence that h'—as in (2) above—or 'what X takes to be evidence that h *and* is evidence that h', which is a combination of (2) with either 'e is potential evidence that h' or 'e is veridical evidence that h'.

Neither (2) nor (2′), however, supplies a sufficient condition. For e to be X's evidence that h it is necessary in addition that

(3) X believes that h is true or probable (and does so) *for the reason that e.*

The fact that Alan is receiving a certain medical treatment T may be (veridical) evidence that he has an i.c.b. (since treatment T is given only to such people). Even if Alan's doctor knows and therefore believes that the fact that Alan is receiving treatment T is (veridical) evidence that he has an i.c.b., this fact is not the *doctor's* evidence that Alan has an i.c.b. His reason for believing this is not that Alan is receiving treatment T. Accordingly, I would add condition (3) to (2) or (2′) to obtain sufficient conditions. (2) and (3) can be said to characterize a strong sense of "X's evidence," (2′) and (3) a weak one.

Both (2) and (2′) (with (3) added) sanction proposition (ii). When we say that Alan's yellow skin was but no longer is evidence of an i.c.b. we may be understood to be referring to *someone's* evidence, in this case the doctor's. We may mean that on Monday the fact that Alan has yellow skin was the doctor's evidence that Alan has an i.c.b., but on Friday it is no longer so. On Friday due to other facts he has learned the doctor no longer believes (it probable) that Alan has an i.c.b. This concept of evidence is thoroughly subjective. Whether e is X's evidence that h depends entirely on what X believes about e, h, and their relationship, and not on whether in fact e is potential or veridical evidence that h.

This subjectivity means that one cannot draw an inference from the fact that e is X's evidence that h to the claim that e is at least some good reason to believe h, or even for X to believe h. It is commonly supposed that evidence bears some relationship to what it is reasonable to believe. Although this may be expressed in a variety of ways perhaps the following simple formulation will suffice for our purposes:

A Principle of Reasonable Belief. If, in the light of background information b,[5] e is evidence that h, then, given b, e is a good reason for believing h.[6]

This principle is satisfied by the two objective concepts of evidence. If, in the light of the background information (b) that yellow skin of that type is typically associated with an i.c.b., the fact that Alan has yellow skin is

5. The role of background information here and its relationship to evidence statements will be discussed in section 5.

6. Note that this is not a principle relating evidence to what anyone is justified in believing. e can be a good reason for believing h even though Smith, say, is not justified in believing h for the reason e (since, e.g., he is not justified in believing e). The present formulation is stronger than the one in the original paper, in order to bring it in line with more expanded positions in *The Book of Evidence.*

potential (or veridical) evidence that he has an i.c.b., then, given b, the latter fact is a good reason for believing that Alan has an i.c.b. The subjective concept, on the other hand, does not satisfy this principle. The fact that Max has lost ten fights in a row may be *his* evidence that his luck will change and he will win the eleventh. But this fact is not a good reason at all, even for Max, to believe this hypothesis.

To summarize, then, the three concepts of evidence here characterized provide a way of answering the question of whether the fact that Alan has yellow skin is evidence that he has an i.c.b. It is potential evidence since that kind of skin is typically associated with an i.c.b. It is not veridical evidence since the hypothesis is false and his yellow skin is correctly explained not by his having an i.c.b. but by the fact that he was working with a dye. On Monday but not on Friday it was the doctor's evidence that Alan has an i.c.b., since on Monday but not on Friday the doctor believed that Alan has an i.c.b. for the reason that he has yellow skin, which he believed was veridical evidence of an i.c.b.

If potential evidence can be defined, then so can the other two concepts via (1), (2), and (3). Of various definitions of potential evidence that appear in the literature two general types will be discussed here because each by itself is not sufficient but if appropriately altered and combined the result may be. The first and most popular type defines evidence in terms of probability, the second in terms of explanation.

2. THE PROBABILITY DEFINITION

According to one probability definition e is potential evidence that h if and only if the probability of h given e is greater than the prior probability of h:

(1a) e is potential evidence that h if and only if $p(h/e) > p(h)$.

Or, if b is background information,

(1b) e is potential evidence that h if and only if $p(h/e \ \& \ b) > p(h/b)$.

A definition of this sort is offered by many writers.[7] However, despite its widespread acceptance it cannot possibly be correct if "evidence" and "probability" are being used as they are in ordinary language or science. For one thing, neither (1a) nor (1b) requires that e be true; and this, as noted earlier, seems to be necessary for evidence. That Alan has yellow

---

7. E.g., Carnap, *Logical Foundations of Probability*, p. 463; Mary Hesse, *The Structure of Scientific Inference* (Berkeley, 1974), p. 134; Richard Swinburne, *An Introduction to Confirmation Theory* (London, 1973), p. 3.

skin is not evidence that he has an i.c.b., if he does not have yellow skin. However, even with the addition of a truth-requirement the resulting definition is unsatisfactory. I shall concentrate on (1b), since this is the most prevalent form of the definition, and note two types of counterexamples. The first shows that an increase in probability is not sufficient for evidence, the second that it is not necessary.

The lottery case. Let b be the background information that on Monday 1,000 lottery tickets were sold and that John bought 100 and Bill bought 1. Let e be the information that on Tuesday all the lottery tickets except those of John and Bill have been destroyed but that one ticket will still be drawn at random. Let h be the hypothesis that Bill will win. The probability that Bill will win has been increased approximately tenfold over its prior probability. But surely e is not evidence that Bill will win. If anything it is evidence that John will win.

Reverting to the principle of the previous section which relates potential (as well as veridical) evidence to a good reason for belief, assume for the sake of argument that in the light of b, e is potential evidence that (h) Bill will win. Then according to the principle of reasonable belief, given b, e is a good reason for believing h. But surely it is not. In the light of the background information that on Monday John bought 100 and Bill bought 1 of the 1,000 lottery tickets sold, the fact that on Tuesday all of the tickets except those of John and Bill have been destroyed but one ticket will still be drawn at random is not a good reason at all for believing that Bill will win. Someone who believes that Bill will win for such a reason is believing something irrationally.

Events often occur which increase the probability or risk of certain consequences. But the fact that such events occur is not necessarily evidence that these consequences will ensue; it may be no good reason at all for expecting such consequences. When I walk across the street I increase the probability that I will be hit by a 2001 Cadillac, but the fact that I am walking across the street is not evidence that I will be hit by a 2001 Cadillac. When Michael Phelps goes swimming he increases the probability that he will drown, but the fact that he is swimming is not evidence that he will drown.

What these examples show is that for e to be evidence that h it is not sufficient that e increase h's (prior) probability. The next example shows that it is not even necessary.

The paradox of ideal evidence.[8] Let b be the background information that in the first 5,000 spins of this roulette wheel the ball landed on

---

8. The expression is Karl Popper's, *Logic of Scientific Discovery* (London, 1959), p. 407, but I am changing his example to suit my purposes here.

numbers other than 3 approximately 35/36ths of the time. Let e be the information that in the second 5,000 spins the ball landed on numbers other than 3 approximately 35/36ths of the time. Let h be the hypothesis that on the 10,001st spin the ball will land on a number other than 3. The following claim seems reasonable:

$$p(h/e\&b) = p(h/b) = 35/36.$$

That is, the probability that the ball will land on a number other than 3 on the 10,001st spin is unchanged by e, which means, according to (1b), that e is not evidence that h. But it seems unreasonable to claim that the fact that the ball landed on numbers other than 3 approximately 35/36ths of the time during the second 5,000 spins is not evidence that it will land on a number other than 3 on the 10,001st spin, even though there is another fact which is also evidence for this. More generally, e can be evidence that h even if there is other equally good evidence that h. To be sure, if we have already obtained the first batch of evidence there may be no need to obtain the second. But this does not mean that the second batch is not evidence that h.

In the light of these examples perhaps it will be agreed that "e is evidence that h" cannot be defined simply as "e increases h's probability." But it may be contended that a related concept can be so defined, namely, "e increases the evidence that h." Thus,

e increases the evidence that h if and only if $p(h/e\&b) > p(h/b)$.

However, increasing the evidence that h is not the same as increasing the probability of h. To increase the evidence that h is to start with information which is evidence that h and add to it something which is also evidence that h or at least is so when conjoined with previous information. But to do this it is neither sufficient nor necessary to increase h's probability. The lottery example shows that it is not sufficient, while the paradox of ideal evidence shows that it is not necessary. In the lottery example there is no increase in evidence that Bill will win, since in the first place there is no evidence that he will win, and the combined new and old information is not evidence that he will win, even though the probability that he will win has increased. In the paradox of ideal evidence there is an increase in evidence that the ball will land on a number other than 3 on the 10,001st spin, but there is no increase in the probability of this hypothesis.

At this point a second definition of evidence in terms of probability might be offered.

(2) e is potential evidence that h if and only if $p(h/e) > k$ (where k is some number, say 1/2).

Some writers, indeed, claim that the concept of evidence (or, confirmation) is ambiguous and that it can mean either (1) or (2).[9] One of these meanings is simply that given e, h has a certain (high) probability.

This proposal has the advantage of being able to handle both the lottery case and the paradox of ideal evidence. In the lottery case, although h's probability is increased by e, the probability of h given e and b is not high. (It is 1/101.) Therefore, by (2), e&b is not evidence that Bill will win. On the other hand it is evidence that John will win, since p(John will win/e&b) = 100/101. And this is as it should be.

The paradox of ideal evidence is also avoided by (2) since the fact that (e) the ball landed on numbers other than 3 approximately 35/36ths of the time during the second 5,000 spins makes the probability very high that it will land on a number other than 3 on the 10,001st spin. In this case p(h/e) > k, and therefore, by (2), e is evidence that h, even though p(h/e&b) = p(h/b).

However, (2) is beset by a major problem of its own.

The Wheaties case (or the problem of irrelevant information).[10] Let e be the information that this man eats the breakfast cereal Wheaties. Let h be the hypothesis that this man will not become pregnant. The probability of h given e is extremely high (since the probability of h is extremely high and is not diminished by the assumption of e). But e is not evidence that h. To claim that the fact that this man eats Wheaties is evidence that he will not become pregnant is to make a bad joke at best.

Such examples can easily be multiplied. The fact that Jones is drinking whisky (praying to God, taking vitamin C, etc.) to get rid of his cold is not evidence that he will recover within a week, despite the fact that people who have done these things do generally recover within a week (i.e., despite the fact that the probability of recovering in this time, given these remedies, is very high). It may well be for this reason that some writers prefer definition (1) over (2). On (1) e in the present examples would not be evidence that h because p(h/e) = p(h), i.e., because e is probabilistically irrelevant for h. I would agree that the reason that e is not evidence that h is that e is irrelevant for h, but this is not mere probabilistic irrelevance (as will be argued later).

A defender of (2) might reply that in the Wheaties example we can say that the probability of h given e is high only because we are assuming as

9. See Carnap, *Logical Foundations of Probability*, pp. xv–xx; Wesley C. Salmon, "Confirmation and Relevance," in G. Maxwell and R. Anderson, Jr. (eds.), *Minnesota Studies in the Philosophy of Science* vol. 6 (Minneapolis, 1975), p. 5; Hesse, *Structure of Scientific Inference*, pp. 133–134.

10. Salmon, *Statistical Explanation and Statistical Relevance* (Pittsburgh, 1971), uses a similar example against the D–N model of explanation, but not as an argument against (2).

background information the fact that no man has ever become pregnant; and he may insist that this background information be incorporated into the probability statement itself by writing "p(h/e&b) > k". In section 5 contrasting views about the role of background information with respect to probability (and evidence) statements will be noted, only one of which insists that such information always be incorporated into the probability statement itself. However, even if the latter viewpoint is espoused the Wheaties example presents a problem for (2) if we agree that information that is irrelevant for h can be added to information that is evidence that h without the result being evidence that h.

Suppose that b is evidence that h and that p(h/b) > k. There will be some irrelevant e such that p(h/e&b) = p(h/b), yet e&b is not evidence that h. Thus let h be the hypothesis that this man will not become pregnant. Let b be the information that no man has ever become pregnant, and let e be the information that this man eats Wheaties. We may conclude that p(h/e&b) > k, which, as demanded above, incorporates b into the probability statement. But although b is evidence that h we would be most reluctant to say that e&b is too.[11]

Before leaving probability definitions one further comment is in order. In a paper entitled "Bayes' Theorem and the History of Science" (*Minnesota Studies in the Philosophy of Science*, vol. 5, ed. R. Stuewer) Salmon has suggested that the notion of evidence that confirms a hypothesis can be understood in terms of Bayes' theorem of probabilities, a simple form of which is p(h/e) = p(h) × p(e/h)/p(e). According to this theorem, to determine the probability of h on e we must determine three quantities: the initial probability of h (p(h)), the "likelihood" of h on e (p(e/h)), and the initial probability of e (p(e)). Salmon criticizes a view of evidence which says that if a hypothesis entails an observational conclusions e which is true, then e is evidence that h. This view, he points out, considers only one of the probabilities above, namely, p(e/h) = 1. To determine whether e is evidence that h one must also consider the initial probabilities of h and e.

This may be a valid criticism but it does not avoid the previous problems. Suppose that Bayes' theorem is used to determine the "posterior" probability of h, that is, p(h/e), by reference to the initial probabilities of h and of e and the likelihood of h on e. We must still determine what, if anything, this has to do with whether e is evidence that h. If definitions (1) or (2) are used to determine this we confront all of the previous

---

11. An analogous problem arises for those who defend the D–N model of explanation. Kinetic theory entails the ideal gas law, but so does kinetic theory conjoined with laws from economic theory. Not wishing to say that this enlarged set explains the ideal gas law, the D–N theorist requires an elimination of the irrelevant laws in the D–N explanans.

difficulties even though we have used Bayes' theorem in calculating p(h/e). Thus let e be the information that this man eats Wheaties, and let h be the hypothesis that this man will not become pregnant. Assume the following probabilities, which do not seem unreasonable: p(h) = 1, p(e/h) = 1/10, p(e) = 1/10. Then by Bayes' theorem, p(h/e)= 1. Using definition (2) we must conclude that e is evidence that h.

3. THE EXPLANATION DEFINITION

It is not my claim that probability is irrelevant for evidence but only that the particular probability definitions (1) and (2) of the previous section—the standard definitions—will not suffice. Let me turn then to a very different proposal which appeals to the concept of explanation:

> (1) e is potential evidence that h if and only if e is true and h would correctly explain e if h were true.

This definition can be closely associated with at least two views. One is Hanson's account of retroductive reasoning, which takes the form

> Some surprising phenomenon P is observed
>
> P would be explicable as a matter of course if h were true
>
> Hence, there is reason to think that h is true.[12]

The fact that phenomenon P has been observed is then potential evidence that h; it is so because h would correctly explain P if it were true. (1) is also closely associated with the hypothetico-deductive account of theories according to which if hypothesis h is a potential explanans of e (which, on this view, means roughly that h contains a lawlike sentence and entails e), then if e turns out to be true e is confirming evidence for h. Sympathy with (1) might then lead to the following simple definition of veridical evidence:

> (2) e is veridical evidence that h if and only if h correctly explains e (i.e., e is potential evidence that h, and h is true).[13]

Despite the emphasis in recent years on the role of explanation in inference from evidence, neither (1) nor (2) provides a necessary or a

12. N. R. Hanson, *Patterns of Discovery* (Cambridge, 1958), p. 72.

13. (2) might be associated with a view, in addition to the above, that in any inductive inference one infers that a hypothesis correctly explains the evidence. This is Gilbert Harman's view in "The Inference to the Best Explanation," *Philosophical Review*, 64 (1965), 88–95. Later he revised it by requiring only that h correctly explains something, and also by stressing the global nature of inference, namely, that one infers to the best overall system.

sufficient condition for potential or veridical evidence. Neither provides a necessary condition since, as noted earlier, e may be evidence that h even if h does not, and would not if true, correctly explain e. The fact that Jones has the chest wound he does may be potential or veridical evidence that he will die, even though the hypothesis that he will die does not, and would not if true, correctly explain why he has that chest wound. The explanation condition if necessary at all should be changed to require only some explanatory connection between h and e.

Nor do these definitions provide sufficient conditions. Suppose my car won't start this morning. The hypothesis

> h: At precisely 2.07 last night 5 boys and 2 girls removed the 18.9 gallons of gas remaining in my tank and substituted water

would if true correctly explain why my car won't start this morning; indeed, suppose that h is true and that it does correctly explain this. In either case the fact that (e) my car won't start this morning is not evidence that h is true. There is too much of a gulf between this e and h for e to be evidence that h, even if h does or would if true correctly explain e. What this gulf amounts to I shall try to say later.

It is worth noting here that the earlier principle of reasonable belief is violated. According to this principle, if the fact that my car won't start this morning were evidence that h, then this fact would be a good reason for believing h. But (given the "normal" background information one might imagine for such a case) the fact that my car won't start this morning is far too meager a reason to believe the very specific hypothesis h. Indeed, innumerably many hypotheses in addition to h can be invented which if true would correctly explain why my car won't start. The hypothesis that

> h': At precisely 3.05 last night 2 monkeys removed the remaining 3.7 gallons of gas in my tank and substituted crushed bananas

if true would explain why my car won't start. Is the fact that my car won't start evidence that h' is true? Does this fact provide any reason to believe such a hypothesis?

4. A NEW PROPOSAL

Although neither the probability nor explanation definitions are adequate, if these are combined in a certain way the outcome may be more successful. Here are my proposals:

> (1) e is potential evidence that h if and only if (a) e is true, (b) e does not entail h, (c) p(h/e) > k, (d) p(there is an explanatory connection between h and e/h&e) > k.

(2) e is veridical evidence that h if and only if e is potential evidence that h, h is true, and there is an explanatory connection between the truth of h and e. (This is simply (1) of section 1.)

For e to be potential evidence that h we require, in addition to e's being true and not entailing h, the satisfaction of two probability conditions. One is that the probability of h given e be high. The other is that the probability that there is an explanatory connection between h and e, given that h and e are both true, be high; that is, that it be probable, given h and e, that h is true because e is, or conversely, or that some hypothesis correctly explains both. Veridical evidence requires, in addition to this, that h be true and that there be an explanatory connection between the truth of h and e.

In section 1 the following features of potential evidence were cited: (i) e can be potential evidence that h even if h is false; (ii) potential evidence is objective, that is, whether e is potential evidence that h does not depend on whether anyone believes e or h or anything about their relationship; (iii) e is potential evidence that h only if e is true; (iv) e is potential evidence that h only if e does not entail h. Features (i), (iii), and (iv) are obviously satisfied by (1) above, as is feature (ii) provided that the concept of probability used in conditions (1c) and (1d) is construed as an objective one.

To assess these definitions let us reconsider the counterexamples to the previous probability and explanation definitions.

The lottery case. The fact that all the lottery tickets except those of John and Bill have been destroyed, that of the original 1,000 tickets John has 100 and Bill has 1, and that one ticket will be drawn at random, does not make it probable that Bill will win. Hence by condition (1c) this fact is not potential (and therefore not veridical) evidence that Bill will win. On the contrary, as previously indicated, it ought to be potential evidence that John will win. And indeed it is on definition (1), since given the fact in question it is probable that John will win (1c); and given the same fact and the fact that John will win it is probable that a correct explanation of why John will win is that all the 1,000 lottery tickets except those of John and Bill have been destroyed, that of the 101 remaining tickets John has 100 and Bill 1, and that one ticket will be chosen at random (1d). Definition (1) above gives us a reasonable analysis of this case in a way that the probability definition (1) of section 2 does not.

The paradox of ideal evidence. The fact that (e) the roulette ball has landed on numbers other than 3 approximately 35/36ths of the time during the second 5,000 spins ought to be potential evidence that (h) it will land on a number other than 3 on the 10,001st spin, even if the probability of this hypothesis has not increased over its prior probability. Definition (1) gives us what we want, since the probability of h on e is high. And given that h and e are both true it is probable that both h and e are correctly explained by the hypothesis that on the roulette wheel there are 36 places of equal size for the ball to land, 35 of which show numbers other than 3.

The Wheaties case. The fact that (e) this man eats Wheaties should not be (potential or veridical) evidence that (h) this man will not become pregnant, even though the probability of h given e is high. And it is not evidence on definition (1) since condition (d) is violated. Given that h and e are both true it is not probable that there is an explanatory connection between h and e; it is not probable that this man will not become pregnant because he eats Wheaties, or that he eats Wheaties because he will not become pregnant, or that there is some hypothesis that correctly explains both his eating Wheaties and his not becoming pregnant. His eating Wheaties and his not becoming pregnant are not only probabilistically independent, they are (probably) explanatorily independent.

However, we might alter the example as follows. Let e' be the information that this man who wants to become pregnant believes that he never will and as a consequence becomes anxious and eats Wheaties to reduce his anxiety. In this case, it might be urged, given both h and e' it is probable that h does correctly explain e': it is probable that this man believes what he does, becomes anxious and eats Wheaties because in fact he will not become pregnant. Then by definition (1) e' is potential evidence that h. Assuming that h is true and that there is such an explanatory connection between e' and h, then e' is also veridical evidence that h, by definition (2). Is this reasonable?

A claim that it is not might be made on the ground that we do, after all, have extremely good evidence for h, namely, that this man is indeed a *man*, not a woman. And this is both potential and veridical evidence that there will be no pregnancy. However, the fact that there is other evidence whose support for h is stronger than that given by e' does not by itself mean that e' is not evidence that h. Here it is important to recall the distinction between something's being evidence that h and its being *someone's* evidence that h. In our earlier example at the end of section 1, the fact that Alan is receiving treatment T might be (potential or veridical) evidence that he has an i.c.b. without its being the *doctor's* evidence. (The fact that Alan is receiving this treatment may not be the doctor's reason for believing that he has an i.c.b.) Similarly, the fact that this man, who wants to become pregnant, is anxious because he believes he never will and eats Wheaties to reduce his anxiety can be evidence that he will not become pregnant without its being *anyone's* evidence for this. No one who believes that this man will not become pregnant may do so for the reason just given.

The case of the stalled car. The fact that (e) my car won't start this morning is not potential evidence that (h) at precisely 2.07 last night 5 boys and 2 girls removed the 18.9 gallons of gas remaining in my tank and substituted water. This is so because condition (1c) is not satisfied. The gulf mentioned earlier which prevents e from being evidence that h is a probabilistic one: it is not the case that h is probable given e.

The proposed definition of potential evidence thus avoids the counter-examples to previous definitions. Will it sanction evidence statements that we are usually prepared to make? Is the fact that all the observed crows have been black potential evidence that all crows are black? Is the fact that hydrogen and oxygen combine in a simple ratio by volume potential evidence that nitrogen and oxygen do too (as Gay-Lussac thought)? Is the fact that electrons produce tracks in cloud chambers potential evidence that they carry a charge? Is the fact that Alan has yellow skin potential evidence that he has an i.c.b.? Whether these claims can be made depends on whether certain probability statements can be asserted. The fact that Alan has yellow skin is potential evidence that he has an i.c.b. only if it is probable that he has an i.c.b., given that he has yellow skin, and it is prob-able that there is an explanatory connection between his having yellow skin and his having an i.c.b., given that he has both. And whether these probability claims can be made depends on what background information is being assumed, and on the general relationship between probability statements and background information. What view we take of this rela-tionship will determine what evidence statements we can assert, as will be shown next.

5. BACKGROUND INFORMATION

Two views about the role of background information are possible. One is that probability statements should be relativized to the background information to which any appeal is made. The other is that no such rela-tivization is necessary. According to the former view the background in-formation must be incorporated into the probability statement itself. If appeal is made to b in determining that the probability of h on e is r then we should write "$p(h/e\&b) = r$." In the case of evidence, we could say that the conjunction of e and b is evidence that h, provided that the definitions of section 4 are satisfied. Or we can continue to say that e is evidence that h, provided that we relativize the evidence statement to the background information by writing "e is evidence that h, given b," and reformulate the definitions of section 4 as follows:

(1) e is potential evidence that h, given b, if and only if (a) e and b are true, (b) e does not entail h, (c) $p(h/e\&b) > k$, (d) p(there is an explanatory connection between h and $e/h\&e\&b) > k$

(2) e is veridical evidence that h, given b, if and only if e is potential evidence that h, given b; h is true; and there is an explanatory connection between the truth of h and e.

In what follows I will discuss that version of the relativization view given by (1) and (2). According to it the fact that Alan has yellow skin can be shown to be potential evidence that he has an i.c.b., given the doctor's background information on Monday (which includes the fact that people with that kind of skin usually have an i.c.b. and usually have that kind of skin because they have an i.c.b.). However, the fact that Alan has yellow skin is not potential evidence that he has an i.c.b., given the doctor's background information on Friday (which includes the results of tests).

By contrast to the relativization view, one might claim that background information need not be construed as a part of the probability statement itself, but only as information to which one appeals in *defending* or *justifying* that statement. Thus

(3) The probability that Alan has an i.c.b., given that he has yellow skin, is high

might be defended by appeal to the empirical fact that

(4) In most cases people with (that kind of) yellow skin have an i.c.b.

But on this view the fact that (3) is defensible by appeal to the empirical fact that (4) is true shows that (3) itself is an empirical statement. It does not show that (3) is an incomplete version of the (perhaps) *a priori* statement that

The probability that Alan has an i.c.b., given that he has yellow skin and that in most cases people with (that kind of) yellow skin have an i.c.b., is high.

On Monday the doctor defends (3) by appeal to (4). On Friday he has accumulated new information, which includes the results of tests, and he then defends the negation of (3) by appeal to this new information. By contrast, the relativist must say that on Monday the doctor is asserting a probability statement of the form "$p(h/e\&b_1) > k$," while Friday he is asserting one of the form "$p(h/e\&b_2) < k$." And these are not incompatible statements.

Returning to evidence, a non-relativist with regard to background information can accept the definitions of evidence as these are given in section 4, and need not relativize them to the background information by writing either "e&b is evidence that h" or "e is evidence that h, given b." He can consider statements of the form

> (5) The fact that Alan has yellow skin is potential evidence that he has an i.c.b.

to be complete, even though appeals to background information will be made in defending (5) or its denial. On Monday, on the basis of the information available to him, the doctor affirms (5); on Friday, on the basis of the new information, he denies (5). The relativist, on the other hand, regards (5) as incomplete. If (5) if relativized to the background information on Monday it is true, and if relativized to the background information on Friday it is false.

I shall not here try to arbitrate between these views. Perhaps each reflects different tendencies in the way we speak about probability and evidence. Perhaps one is more dominant than the other in linguistic practice or is more advantageous for other reasons. But which of these views about background information we employ will affect what claims about potential and veridical evidence we are prepared to make.

Thus, in section 1 it was asked whether there is a concept of potential evidence according to which

> (6) Alan's yellow skin was evidence of an i.c.b. (on Monday) and still is (on Friday)

is true, despite the fact that on Friday the doctor's tests prove negative. Using (1), a background-relative concept of potential evidence, (6) might be understood by reference to

> (7) The fact that Alan has yellow skin is potential evidence that he has an i.c.b., given the background information of the doctor on Monday.

And (7) is as true on Friday as it is on Monday, since it is true timelessly. Of course if (6) is relativized to the information of the doctor on Friday then it is false timelessly. But the relativist who wants to explain the sense in which (6) is true can use definition (1) and relativize his evidence statement to the doctor's information on Monday.

The non-relativist will not be able to regard (6) as true, if construed as it has been so far. He will say that whereas on Monday he believed (5) to be true, on Friday he realizes that it is false; but he cannot assert that (5) was true on Monday and remains true on Friday, as (6) suggests.

Nevertheless, the non-relativist can resurrect (6) by claiming that it is true if it is construed as making a *general* claim rather than a particular one, namely,

> (8) Having the kind of yellow skin which Alan has is (timelessly) evidence of (having) an i.c.b.

And he can provide the following set of necessary and sufficient conditions for statements of this type, using as a guide the previous definition of potential evidence:

> (9) Having F is potential evidence of having G (for A's) if and only if (a) "X is F" does not entail "X is G"; (b) the probability of something's (an A's) having G, given that it has F, is high; (c) the probability that there is an explanatory connection between something's (an A's) having F and its having G, given that it has both, is high.

Using (9) the non-relativist can argue that (8) is true and therefore that a sense of potential evidence can be provided which sanctions (6). There is then a certain analogy between the relativist's and the non-relativist's response to (6), since according to both (6) has different interpretations. The relativist argues that (6) is true if construed as (7) but false if construed as

> The fact that Alan has yellow skin is potential evidence that he has an i.c.b., given the background information of the doctor on Friday.

The non-relativist argues that (6) is false if construed as (5) but true if construed as (8).

6. THE LOCH NESS MONSTER AND SEVERED HEAD CASES

Two objections to the definitions of section 4 will now be considered.

There is a well-known photograph taken by a London surgeon in 1934 which purports to depict the Loch Ness monster.[14] Even if the existence of the monster is very improbable despite the photograph, isn't the existence of the photograph evidence that the monster exists? If so there is a violation of the condition for potential evidence that p(h/e) be high. Those who favor the "increase in probability" condition for evidence may cite examples such as this in defense of their position and in criticism of mine. Let us examine this criticism.

14. This photograph as well as three others taken between 1934 and 1960 are reproduced in David James, *Loch Ness Investigation* (London).

We are being asked to consider the claim that

(1) The existence of this photograph which purports to depict the Loch Ness monster is evidence that the monster exists.

Someone who believes that (1) is true might defend it by providing information about the surgeon who took the picture, from what position, at what time of day, and so on. He might also point out how the camera used works and that photographs are generally reliable; that is, usually when a photograph depicts what seems clearly to be X and the photographer has not made efforts to be deceptive, then an X exists.[15] But if this is how he defends (1) then, I think, he should not accept the claim that the existence of the monster is very improbable despite the photograph. On the contrary, he should believe that it is probable. (Indeed, this is what Sir Peter Scott claimed about later photographs taken in 1972.) New information can cancel the negative effects of background information. Even if the existence of the Loch Ness monster is improbable on the background information, a suitable photograph can make its existence very probable.

However, two other situations are possible. First, we may not know the reliability of the photographer, the conditions under which the photograph was taken, or indeed whether it is a genuine photograph (rather than a clever drawing). If so, and if there are independent reasons for doubting the existence of X, then we may be very unsure of the truth of claim (1). We should then assert not that the existence of this photograph *is* evidence that a monster exists, but that it *may be* evidence (we don't yet know), or that it is evidence that there *may be* a monster (a claim to which I will return in a moment). Second, we may know that the photographer was unreliable or that the conditions under which he took the photograph were. Given this and other background information, the existence of the Loch Ness monster is very improbable, let us suppose. But given the unreliability of the photographer and photographic conditions would we make claim (1)? I seriously doubt it.

The importance of the subjective concept of evidence should not be minimized here. A question such as "Is there any evidence that there is a Loch Ness monster?" might be understood as "Is there anything that people take to be evidence that the monster exists?" To which the answer is: emphatically yes! It is not that those who believe that the monster exists are unable to appeal to any facts as their reason for so believing. Quite the reverse. The existence of this photograph, among other things, is their evidence.

15. A non-relativistic notion of evidence is here being assumed in accordance with which this background information is being used to defend (1). However, the same argument could proceed with a relativized notion by relativizing (1) to this background information.

Finally, when the probability of h given e is low, although e is not evidence that h is true it can be evidence that h *may be* true (or that h is possible). One might claim that the existence of the surgeon's photograph is evidence that there may be a monster. The fact that Joe is one of 50 finalists in the state lottery is not evidence that he will win $1 million—that is too strong a claim to make. But it can be evidence that he may win $1 million or that his winning is a possibility. The fact that Bob is playing one round of Russian roulette is not evidence that he will die but that he may die, that his dying is a possibility. Such evidence claims, although different from the ones we have been considering, can be understood, I think, by altering the concept of potential evidence so as to require not high probabilities but non-negligible ones. That is,

> e is evidence that h may be true (or that h is possible) if and only if (a) e is true; (b) e does not entail h; (c) the probability of h given e is not negligible; (d) the probability that there is an explanatory connection between h and e, given h and e, is not negligible.

The fact that (e) Bob is playing one round of Russian roulette is evidence that h may be true, where h is the hypothesis that Bob will die. This is so since the probability of h, given e, is not negligible; and given that h and e are both true, the probability is not negligible that there is an explanatory connection between Bob's dying and his playing one round of Russian roulette.

The second objection to definitions of section 4 will be dealt with more briefly. We saw that the requirement of an explanatory connection between e and h for e to be veridical evidence that h allows us to preclude certain unwanted cases. In view of the following gruesome example, however, it may be wondered whether this requirement is too strong.

Henry drops dead from a heart attack. Afterward his head is severed by a fiendish decapitator.[16] Isn't the fact that his head has been severed from his body veridical evidence that Henry is not living, even though there is no explanatory connection between his decapitation and his not being alive? If so the explanatory requirement is not necessary for veridical (or potential) evidence.

The latter conclusion is too hasty. There are various reasons one may not be alive, not all of which need be reasons for which one died. Anyone whose head has been severed from his body is not alive because, among other things, his brain is unable to receive oxygen from the rest of his body. Consider an analogous case. Tom's TV set is not working because

---

16. Brian Skyrms, "The Explication of 'X knows that p,'" *Journal of Philosophy*, 64 (1967), 373–389, uses this kind of case as a counterexample against certain causal analyses of "X knows that p."

one of the tubes burned out. Later Tom accidentally drops the set breaking the remaining tubes. Now among the reasons the set is not working is that all the other tubes are broken (although this is not among the reasons that it stopped working in the first place). There is an explanatory connection between the fact that these other tubes are broken and the fact that the set is not working; indeed, the former is veridical evidence that the latter is true.

7. THE DESIRABILITY OF EVIDENCE

I shall now briefly turn to the question of why evidence is desirable. When one has a hypothesis h why should one seek evidence that h?

The answer, which is straightforward, is that one wants one's hypothesis to be true or at least probable, and one wants a good reason for believing it. To have evidence is to satisfy both desires, at least on the theory of evidence in section 4. If e is veridical evidence that h, then h is true, and if e is (only) potential evidence that h then h is probable given e. Moreover, given background information b, if e is potential or veridical evidence that h, then, following the principle of reasonable belief, given b, e is a good reason for believing h. According to the theory of section 4 evidence that h provides a good reason for believing h only if (a) h is probable given e, and (b) there is probably an explanatory connection between h and e, given h and e. The Wheaties example provides a case satisfying (a) but not (b), while the case of the stalled car satisfies (b) but not (a). And in neither case does e provide a good reason for believing h. The fact that this man eats Wheaties is not a good reason for believing that he will not become pregnant. And the fact that my car won't start this morning is not a good reason for believing the very specific hypothesis h of section 3.

On the other hand, the alternative definitions of evidence that I rejected do not jointly satisfy the twin desires of truth/probability and good reasons for believing. The "increase in probability" definition spawns the lottery case in which the hypothesis that Bill will win is not probable (though its probability is increased over its prior probability), nor in this case does the information cited provide a good reason for believing that Bill will win. The "high probability" definition, although it satisfies the desire for probability, generates the Wheaties case in which, as we have just seen, the "evidence" provides no reason for believing the hypothesis. Finally, the explanation definition satisfies neither the truth/probability desire nor that for a good reason for believing, as is shown by the case of the stalled car.[17]

17. My thanks are due to Stephen Barker, Robert Cummins, and Dale Gottlieb for valuable comments on material in sections 1–7. This work was supported by the N.S.F.

8. CORRECT EXPLANATION

Since the original paper in *Mind* was published in 1978, my thoughts on evidence (and its relationship to explanation) have expanded, particularly in the *Nature of Explanation* and in *The Book of Evidence*. In the present section and the two that follow I excerpt material on correct explanation from *The Book of Evidence*, pp. 160–166, and in the Addendum I summarize a few changes in the definitions of evidence and other concepts in that book.

The concept of an explanatory connection (used for "potential evidence") is defined by reference to that of a correct explanation: There is an explanatory connection between h and e if and only if either h correctly explains why e is true, or e correctly explains why h is true, or some true hypothesis correctly explains why h is true and why e is true. What is this concept of correct explanation?

First, whatever else it is, it is (or, for potential evidence we need) a concept of correct explanation that is objective, rather than subjective. Whether some h correctly explains some e does not depend upon what anyone knows or believes. In this respect the concept needed is like that which Hempel attempts to explicate by means of his deductive-nomological (D–N) model of explanation.[18] A D–N explanation of a particular event is a deductive argument in which the premises contain laws and statements describing "initial conditions," and the conclusion is a sentence describing the event to be explained. Whether some argument is a correct D–N explanation does not depend upon whether anyone knows or believes the truth of the premises or conclusion or knows or believes that the conclusion follows deductively from the premises. Without accepting Hempel's D–N model, I am accepting his idea that there is an objective concept of correct explanation.

Second, the required concept of explanation is that of a *correct* one, not necessarily one that is good or appropriate for one context of inquiry but not another. In this respect the concept of correct explanation is like that of causation. If John's taking medicine M caused his symptoms S to be relieved, then it did so whether or not the context of inquiry calls for a deeper or more detailed causal story (such as one that indicates how M causes relief, or what caused John to select M). In this respect also the concept required is similar to one that Hempel's D–N model attempts to explicate: whether a D–N explanation is correct does not depend upon the context of inquiry. Its correctness is not determined

---

18. Carl G. Hempel. *Aspects of Scientific Explanation* (New York, 1965). part 4.

by standards that can vary with the knowledge and interests of different inquirers.

Third, on pain of circularity, the required concept of correct explanation must not itself be understood or explicated in terms of evidence. In this respect also the concept of correct explanation needed is like that of Hempel's D–N model. Whether an argument satisfies the D–N conditions for being a correct explanation does not depend on the satisfaction of any requirement of evidence. For example, it is not required that there be evidence that supports the premises or conclusion of a D–N argument.

Unfortunately, Hempel's D–N model of explanation is subject to numerous counterexamples and other objections that make it impossible to employ for purposes of defining evidence.[19] In any case the model requires a deductive connection between the explanatory sentences and the sentence describing what is to be explained. As noted in section 2 [omitted here], we want to consider cases where e is evidence that h, yet there is no such deductive connection between h and e, or between some other hypothesis H and both h and e, where H correctly explains h and e.[20]

What can we say further, then, about the concept of correct explanation needed for potential evidence? One option is to say nothing further, but to treat "correct explanation" as a more basic concept than evidence, simply asserting that it has the three features noted above: it is objective, noncontextual, and not to be understood in terms of evidence. This is the usual procedure of philosophers such as Whewell, Peirce, Hanson, Harman, and Lipton, who champion retroductive (explanatory) reasoning, or "inference to the best explanation." Their idea is to say that reasoning from evidence to hypothesis involves reasoning that the hypothesis supplies an explanation, or the best explanation, of something (which may include the evidence). But they provide little if any clarification of the concept of explanation they invoke. Their view does seem to require a concept of explanation that is objective, noncontextual, and not to be understood in terms of a nonexplanatory concept of evidence.

In other writings I have proposed an account of explanation that can be used for present purposes. The account is complex, but I will attempt to simplify appropriate parts of it for presentation here.[21] I will then show that it generates a concept of explanation of a type needed for evidence, and I

---

19. A review of these problems can be found in my *The Nature of Explanation*, chapter 5 (See chapter 8 in the present volume.)

20. Hempel's alternative model for nondeductive cases, the inductive statistical (I-S) model, will not suit our purposes, since it does not provide a notion of *correct* explanation. An I-S explanation may satisfy Hempel's criteria—it may be a good inductive-statistical explanation—without correctly explaining the event it purports to explain.

21. For details see *The Nature of Explanation*, chapters 1–3.

will contrast this concept with Hempel's D–N explanation and indicate its advantages. It is not my claim that my particular account of explanation is required to understand evidence. Everything I have said so far about evidence could be accepted without endorsing this account of explanation. My claim is only that the account supplies a concept that will suffice for evidence.

9. EXPLANATION AND CONTENT

I begin with a category of *content-giving sentences for a content-noun*. Here are some examples:

(1) The *reason* John's symptoms were relieved is that he took medicine *M*.

The *excuse* was that Sam got sick.

The *danger* in climbing the Matterhorn in the afternoon is that the ice will melt.

The *penalty* for trespassing is that the person convicted will be subject to a $1,000 fine.

These sentences contain content-nouns (ones in italics) together with that-clauses, or, more generally, nominals, that give content to the noun. In sentence (1) "reason" is a content-noun and "that he took medicine *M*" is a nominal that gives the content of the reason. Content-nouns are abstract nouns ("reason," "explanation," "excuse," "danger") rather than nouns for physical objects, properties, or events. They can be used to form content-giving sentences, such as ones above, with this form:

The + content-noun + {prepositional phrase} + form of *to be* + nominal {that-phrase}

The nominals are noun phrases with a verb or verb derivative. They include that-clauses, infinitive phrases ("the purpose of the flag is *to warn drivers of danger*"), and many others.

Content-giving sentences are to be contrasted with ones that contain a content-noun but do not give a content to that noun. For example,

The reason John's symptoms were relieved is difficult to grasp.

The excuse was unacceptable.

The penalty for trespassing is severe.

These sentences do not say what the reason, excuse, or penalty is.

A content-giving sentence such as (1) above may be equivalent in meaning to another, such as,

(2) The reason John's symptoms were relieved is his taking medicine *M*.

I shall say that sentences (1) and (2) express the same proposition, and that this proposition is a content-giving proposition for a concept expressed by the noun "reason."

Sentences (1) and (2) contain an answer to the question "Why were John's symptoms relieved?" That answer is given by the content of the reason ("that he took medicine *M*"). The proposition expressed by sentences (1) and (2) above will be said to be a content-giving proposition *with respect to that question*.

A question such as "Why were John's symptoms relieved?" presupposes various propositions, for example,

John had symptoms.

His symptoms were relieved.

(3) John's symptoms were relieved for some reason.

A *complete presupposition* of a question is a proposition that entails all and only the presuppositions of that question. Of the three propositions just given, only (3) is a complete presupposition of the question "Why were John's symptoms relieved?" Sentence (3) can be transformed into a *complete answer form* for the question "Why were John's symptoms relieved?":

(4) The reason that John's symptoms were relieved is_____

by dropping "for some reason" in (3) and putting the expression "the reason that" at the beginning and "is" followed by a blank at the end to yield (4). (For more details and a generalization of this to various types of questions, see my *The Nature of Explanation*, 28ff.)

We can now say that

> *p* is a *complete* content-giving proposition with respect to question Q if and only if (a) *p* is a content-giving proposition (for a concept expressed by some noun N); (b) *p* is expressible by a sentence obtained from a complete answer form for Q (containing N) by filling in the blank; (c) *p* is not a presupposition of Q.

Finally, Q will be said to be a *content-question* if and only if there is proposition that is a complete content-giving proposition with respect to Q. By these definitions, (1) and (2) express complete content-giving propositions with respect to the content-question "Why were John's symptoms relieved?"

If Q is a content-question (whose indirect form is *q*), and *p* is a complete content-giving proposition with respect to Q, *then p provides an explanation of q*. Thus the proposition expressed by

(1) The reason John's symptoms were relieved is that he took medicine *M*

provides an explanation of why John's symptoms were relieved. Any explanation that is offered is, or can be transformed into, one that answers some content-question by supplying a complete content-giving proposition with respect to that question. Thus, an explanation of the relief of John's symptoms that appeals to his taking medicine M can be construed as answering the content-question "Why were John's symptoms relieved?" by furnishing a complete content-giving proposition with respect to that question, namely, (1). The latter provides an explanation of the relief of John's symptoms.

The following simple condition holds for *correctness* of such explanations:

(5) If p is a complete content-giving proposition with respect to Q, then p provides a correct explanation of q if and only if p is true.

So, for example, since (1) expresses a complete content-giving proposition with respect to the content-question

Q: Why were John's symptoms relieved?

Proposition (1), assuming it is true, provides a correct explanation of why John's symptoms were relieved. Condition (5) for correctness of explanations has considerably more bite than it might seem. For example, compare (1) with

(6) John took medicine M.

Even if (6) is true, that will not suffice to guarantee that (6) provides a correct explanation of why John's symptoms were relieved. (His symptoms might not have been relieved *because* he took M.) (6) is not a complete content-giving proposition with respect to Q. By contrast, if (1) is true, then, since it does express a complete content-giving proposition with respect to Q, it provides a correct explanation of q.

A correct explanation may or may not be a (particularly) good one. Nor must a good explanation be correct. Goodness in explanations is a broader concept than correctness, and unlike the latter is context-dependent.[22] Whether (1) provides a good explanation of why John's symptoms were relieved depends on the "appropriateness" of the answer it provides, which is determined by the knowledge and interests of those for whom the answer is provided. If the context is one in which the intended audience already knows that medicine M is the agent that produced relief but not how it did so, then although (1) provides a correct explanation of why John's symptoms were relieved, it is not a good one. Moreover, there are contexts of evaluation in which correctness is not required. Explanations

22. See *The Nature of Explanation*, chapter 4, and chapter 7 in the present volume.

such as the Ptolemaic or Newtonian ones of the observed motions of the planets may be good ones in virtue of their comprehensiveness, precision, or predictive qualities, even though they are incorrect. What is needed for the concept of (potential and veridical) evidence is not a contextual concept of good explanation but a noncontextual one of correct explanation.

In section 8 I indicated three criteria that need to be satisfied by any concept of correct explanation employed for potential evidence. First, it must be objective rather than subjective. Whether h correctly explains e cannot depend upon what anyone knows or believes. Second, it must be noncontextual. It cannot depend upon standards of goodness appropriate in one context of evaluation but not another. Third, the concept must not itself be understood in terms of evidence. I maintain that the concept of correct explanation given in (5) satisfies these conditions.

10. BUT IS IT CIRCULAR?

A pair of circularity charges may be leveled against this account. One involves circularity in the account of explanation itself. Even if "explanation" is not defined by reference to evidence, it is defined by reference to concepts dangerously close to that of explanation itself, that is, by reference to the concept of a content-noun, where the latter category includes the noun "explanation." This charge of circularity I reject, since the category of content-nouns, and more generally of content-giving propositions, is characterized, as I have done in the previous section, without appeal to any concept of explanation.

The second and more serious charge of circularity, or at least triviality, concerns condition (5) in the previous section for being a *correct* explanation. On this condition, whether

   (1) The reason that John's symptoms were relieved is that he took medicine M

is a correct explanation of why John's symptoms were relieved depends not only on whether (1) is a complete content-giving proposition with respect to the question but also on whether (1) is true. But whether (1) is true is just what we want a definition of "correct explanation" to tell us how to determine. And condition (5) in the previous section doesn't do that at all!

My response to this is to agree that (5) does not provide a way of determining whether a proposition such as (1) is true. What (5) does, which is not trivial, is to say that if some proposition p is a complete content-giving proposition with respect to Q, then it provides an explanation of q that is correct if and only if p is true. This cannot be said for propositions generally, even if they are true and provide answers to Q. It is possible for the proposition "John took medicine M" to be both true and to provide an answer to "Why were John's symptoms relieved?" without that proposition's being a correct explanation of why his symptoms were relieved. But it is impossible for the complete content-giving proposition (1) to be true without its also being a correct explanation of why John's symptoms were relieved. (5) does not, however, provide conditions for determining whether (1) is true. In this respect it is not, and is not intended to be, a definition of "correct explanation."

There is an analogy between my procedure here and what Hempel does in his account of D–N explanation. He offers conditions for being a *potential* explanation (which may be a correct or an incorrect explanation). The conditions—such as the requirement of lawlike sentences in the explanans and a deductive relationship between explanans and explanandum—do not invoke any notion of explanation itself. To give the further condition for a *correct* D–N explanation he simply adds that the sentences in the explanans must be *true*. In an analogous fashion I define the notion of explanation in terms of content-giving propositions and so forth, without invoking any notion of explanation itself. The further condition I give for a *correct* explanation is simply that the relevant content-giving proposition must be *true*.

The difference between what Hempel does and what I do is this. Hempel's explanans sentences do not include ones such as (1) above. He banishes from an explanans any terms such as "reason," "causes," and "explanation" (itself). This idea is required by what (in *The Nature of Explanation*) I call the NES (No Entailment by Singular sentences) requirement. (See chapter 8 in the present volume.) NES, to which Hempel is committed, precludes from an explanans any singular sentences (ones describing particular events), including (1), that by themselves, without the necessary laws, entail the explanandum.

Hempel's NES requirement, however, leads to serious counterexamples in which, although the explanans is true (and satisfies all of Hempel's conditions, including NES), it does not *correctly* explain the explanandum. Suppose it is a law of nature that anyone who eats a pound of arsenic dies within 24 hours. Suppose Ann eats a pound of arsenic at time T and dies within 24 hours. The following explanation of this event satisfies all of Hempel's conditions for being a correct D–N explanation:

At time T, Ann ate a pound of arsenic

Anyone who eats a pound of arsenic dies within 24 hours
    Therefore,

Ann died within 24 hours of T.

Suppose, however, Ann was killed not by the arsenic but by being hit by a truck, which had nothing to do with the arsenic. Then the above explanation is incorrect—it does not give a correct reason that Ann died within 24 hours of T—despite the fact that the sentences in the explanans are true, the explanans contains a true law, the explanans deductively implies the explanandum, and NES is satisfied. (The only singular sentence in the explanans, the first sentence in the argument, does not by itself deductively imply the explanandum.)

This problem arises because of the occurrence of an intervening cause. The only way to avoid it is, I suggest, to include in the explanans a sentence such as

The reason that Ann died within 24 hours of T is that she ate a pound of arsenic at T

The cause of Ann's death within 24 hours of T is her eating a pound of arsenic at T.[23]

These sentences, if true, would correctly explain why Ann died within 24 hours of T. They express complete content-giving propositions with respect to the content-question "Why did Ann die within 24 hours of T?" So, in accordance with my condition (5) of the previous section, if they are true they provide correct explanations. But these sentences violate Hempel's NES requirement. They are singular sentence that by themselves, without the need of laws, entail the explanandum sentence "Ann died within 24 hours of T."

I have described a concept of explanation that meets three criteria required for potential evidence. It is objective, noncontextual, and not itself defined in terms of evidence. Nor is the account circular in the sense of defining explanation by reference to itself. The general notion of ("potential") explanation is defined by reference to complete content-giving propositions, without appeal to any notion of explanation. But conditions for correctness in such explanations will need to include the requirement of the truth of propositions that violate NES: the truth of complete content-giving propositions that contain terms such as "reason" and "cause."

---

23. Other attempts to avoid the problem are unsuccessful; see my *The Nature of Explanation*, chapter 5.

ADDENDUM: OTHER CHANGES TO "CONCEPTS OF EVIDENCE"

1. *Potential Evidence*. This is the basic concept in the sense that the others are defined in terms of it. The definition in the paper is this: e is potential evidence that h, given b, if and only if (1) p(h/e&b) > k; (2) p(there is an explanatory connection between h and e/h&e&b) > k; (3) e and b are true; and (4) e does not entail h. The latest definition retains conditions (3) and (4) but replaces (1) and (2) with this:

   (A) p(there is an explanatory connection between h&e/e&b) > 1/2

   The new definition is stronger than the earlier one in two respects. First, it replaces the vague idea of k (the threshold for "high" probability) with a specific number 1/2. The reason for this is that on my view evidence requires a good reason for belief, which, as I argue in *The Book of Evidence* (pp. 115ff), requires probability greater than 1/2. Second, condition (A) above requires the probability of an explanatory connection between h and e to be greater than 1/2, *given e and b alone* (rather than given h and e and b, as in (2) above). The argument behind this idea is presented beginning on page 152 of my book. In addition I prove that (A) obtains if and only if the product p(there is an explanatory connection between h and e/h&e&b)×p(h/e&b) is greater than 1/2. Accordingly, the new condition (A) entails the earlier conditions (1) and (2), but not conversely.

2. *Veridical Evidence*. In the paper the definition is this: e is veridical evidence that h, given b, if and only if (i) e is potential evidence that h, given b; (ii) h is true; and (iii) there is an explanatory connection between h and e. In the book two concepts of veridical evidence are suggested, depending on whether condition (iii) must be satisfied. This allows one to deal with various strange examples, including the "severed head" case, in which e is potential evidence that h, and h is in fact true, but there is no explanatory connection between h and e. In the severed head case, Henry drops dead of a heart attack and later is decapitated. Is the fact that (e) he was decapitated evidence that (h) he died? In the weaker sense it is, and in the stronger sense it isn't, since there is no explanatory connection between h and e.

3. *ES-evidence*. In the book I introduce a fourth concept of evidence: ES-(epistemic-situation) evidence. It is relativized to a type of abstract situation in which one knows or believes that certain propositions are true, and one is not in a position to know or

believe that others are, even if such a situation does not in fact obtain for any person. This type of objective evidence I define in terms of "veridical evidence," as follows: e is ES-evidence that h (with respect to an epistemic situation ES) if and only if e is true and anyone in ES is justified in believing that e is (probably) veridical evidence that h. Using the example in my original paper, we would say that, relative to an epistemic situation ES of the sort the doctor was in on Monday, the fact that Alan's skin had yellowed (e) is ES-evidence that (h) Alan had an i.c.b. Anyone in that ES would be justified in believing that e is (probably) veridical evidence that h (even though in the case in question it turned out not to be veridical evidence).

4. *Probability.* In chapter 5 of my book I introduce a concept of "objective epistemic probability" needed to define "potential evidence." It is construed as a measure of how reasonable it is to believe a proposition. On this conception, reasonableness of belief admits of degrees and is subject to the formal rules of mathematical probability. Certain physical and/or mathematical facts or states of affairs may make it reasonable to degree r to believe something, independently of the beliefs of particular individuals or of epistemic situations. Suppose that this coin, which has two sides marked heads and tails, is balanced; it will be tossed randomly three times; there are 8 possible outcomes in 3 tosses, 3 of which involve exactly 2 heads. These facts make it reasonable to the degree 3/8 to believe that the coin will land heads exactly twice. That there is this degree of reasonableness is an objective, nonphysical, normative fact determined by the physical and mathematical facts of the case. It is abstract in the sense that it is divorced from particular individuals and types of epistemic situations. In the book I indicate how this concept of probability is different from other objective interpretations of probability, including Carnap's logical concept and the propensity interpretation.

2

Why Philosophical Theories of Evidence Are (and Ought to Be) Ignored by Scientists

"Why Philosophical Theories of Evidence Are (and Ought to Be) Ignored by Scientists" is reprinted by permission from Philosophy of Science Association Symposium Proceedings *(PSA 98, published 2000), 180–192. I argue that the answer to the title question is that such theories propose concepts of evidence that (a) are too weak to give scientists what they want from evidence and (b) make the evidential relationship a priori, whereas typically establishing whether e if true is evidence that h requires an empirical investigation.*

1. DISAGREEMENTS ABOUT EVIDENCE

Scientists frequently disagree with one another about whether some fact is evidence that a certain hypothesis is true or, if it is, about how strong that evidence is. I have in mind cases in which they agree that some fact has been observed or established, or some experimental result obtained. They agree on a description of that fact or result. They also agree on the meaning of the hypothesis in question. Their disagreement lies in whether, or the extent to which, what has been observed, or the experimental result, supports, or provides evidence for, the hypothesis. Moreover, they seem to treat this disagreement as an objective matter—one for which there is a right answer, and not one for which different people can have different right answers.

Let me mention two cases, one from the nineteenth century, the other quite recent. In 1883 Heinrich Hertz conducted a series of carefully designed experiments with cathode rays to determine whether they are electrically charged (Hertz 1896). He separated the cathode rays from the ordinary electric current that flows from the cathode to the anode, so that the pure cathode rays would enter an electrometer, the deflection of which would determine the presence of electricity. In his experiments, however, the needle of the electrometer remained at rest when cathode rays were produced. In a second experiment Hertz introduced oppositely electrified plates into the cathode tube. If cathode rays were electrically charged they should be deflected by these plates, as indicated in a changed position of the phosphorescence produced by the rays. But no such change occurred. Hertz took these two experimental results to be evidence, indeed decisive evidence, that cathode rays are not electrically charged.

Fourteen years later J. J. Thomson (1897) repeated the second of Hertz's experiments and got the same results as Hertz, no deflection of the cathode rays. Yet he refused to take this to be evidence—certainly not decisive evidence—that cathode rays are electrically neutral. Thomson hypothesized that if cathode rays are charged particles, then when they pass through the gas in the cathode tube they ionize the gas molecules producing positive and negative charges that will neutralize the charge on the metal plates between which the cathode rays travel. So if the gas in the cathode tube has not been sufficiently evacuated, there will be no deflection of the cathode rays. Indeed, in 1897 Thomson was able to remove a sufficient amount of gas from the tube and demonstrate the electrical deflection of the cathode rays.

Thomson did not dispute that Hertz obtained the results he did, namely, no electrical deflection of the cathode rays. Indeed, Thomson obtained the same results in initial experiments. What he challenged was the claim that these results were evidence that cathode rays are electrically neutral.

My second example involves an archaeological hypothesis about the earliest campfires used for cooking, for light, and as a protection against animals. For 60 years it had been hypothesized that the first campfires were built by Peking Man in caves in Zhoukoudian, China, between 200,000 and 500,000 years ago. The evidence for this hypothesis was the existence of burned animal bones in the same layer of soil as stone tools and the sediment there that looks like wood ash. On July 10, 1998, a group of scientists from Israel, the United States, and China rejected the claim that the existence of the burned animal bones and the existence of sediment together provided strong evidence that campfires existed there (Weiner et al. 1998). This claim was based on the discovery that the sediment in question is not wood ash but fine minerals and clay deposited by water. These scientists claimed that the burned animal bones by themselves do not constitute very good evidence that a fire was started by humans.

In both of these cases there is an agreement between disputants over what has or has not been observed—at least at some important level of description. J. J. Thomson agreed that in the sorts of experiments conducted by Hertz and initially by himself there was no electrical deflection of the cathode rays. The disputants in the campfire case agree that burned animal bones and sediment that looks like wood ash were found in caves in China. The disagreement arises over whether, or to what extent, these observed facts support the hypotheses in question.

I mention cases of this sort because philosophers of science have developed theories or definitions of evidence that are designed to do at least two things for scientists: first, to clarify what it means to speak of confirming evidence; and second, and relatedly, to help scientists determine whether, and to what extent, putative evidence supports a hypothesis. These goals are championed by a range of philosophers who have developed theories of evidence. A corollary—one emphasized by Carnap (1962)—is to develop a theory of evidence that will enable scientists to settle disputes, such as the ones I mentioned, over whether, or to what extent, putative evidence confirms a hypothesis.

By and large, however, philosophical theories of evidence are ignored by scientists. You don't find scientists with disagreements of the sort in question turning to philosophers for help. Why not? Is this just a matter of people in very different fields ignoring one another's work? That may be part of the answer, but I don't think that is the main problem or the most interesting one. I think the problem is deeper and stems from very basic, but questionable, assumptions philosophers usually make about evidence.

Before indicating what these offending assumptions are, let me say that the notion of evidence I am concerned with is an objective, not a subjective, one: whether e is evidence that h, and how strong that evidence is, does not depend on what anyone believes about e, h, or their relationship. Not all philosophers who talk about evidence recognize, or are interested in, an objective sense of evidence. Subjective Bayesians, for example, reject such a notion. But a range of philosophers accept the idea, including objective Bayesians such as Carnap (1962), hypothetico-deductivists, satisfaction theorists such as Hempel (1965), bootstrappers such as Glymour (1980), and others as well.

The first of the two fundamental assumptions philosophers of the sort I have in mind usually make is that evidence is a very weak notion. You don't need very much to have evidence that something is the case. The second is that the evidential relation is a priori not empirical. It is a logical, or semantic, or mathematical relation that can be established by "calculation." These assumptions need to be explained, illustrated, and, I think, rejected.

2. THE WEAKNESS ASSUMPTION

I will illustrate this assumption by reference to three standard theories of evidence. The first theory is a Bayesian one: for a fact e to be evidence that a hypothesis h is true it is both necessary and sufficient that e increase h's probability over its prior probability. So, for example, since my buying one ticket in a million-ticket lottery increases the probability that I will win, this fact is evidence that I will. To be sure, it is not a lot of evidence–it's certainly not decisive—but it is *some*. According to the *New York Times*, there is one elevator accident per 6 million rides. Using this as a basis for a probability judgment, since my riding this elevator today raises the probability that I will be involved in an elevator accident today it is evidence that I will. Not a lot, but some, perhaps a tiny bit of evidence. Such a notion of evidence is, I think you will agree, very weak. To be sure, the bigger the probabilistic boost e gives to h, the stronger the evidence, on this view. But the fact remains that for e to be evidence that h, on this view, all that is required is that e raise h's probability.[1]

A second standard theory of objective evidence is hypothetico-deductive. For e to be evidence that h it suffices that e be derivable deductively from h. So, for example, since the rectilinear propagation of light is derivable from the classical wave theory of light it is evidence for that theory. This is a very weak notion of evidence, because it allows the same fact to be evidence for a range of conflicting theories. (The same is true of the previous Bayesian account.) For example, since the rectilinear propagation of light is also derivable from the classical particle theory, it is evidence for that theory as well.

A third approach to objective evidence is a "satisfaction" theory of the sort proposed by Hempel (1965). The basic idea is that an observation report is confirming evidence for a hypothesis if the hypothesis is satisfied by the class of individuals mentioned in that report. To use Hempel's famous example, an observation report that a particular raven observed is black is evidence that all ravens are black. So is the fact that a particular non-black thing observed is a non-raven. Glymour (1980) devises a more complex bootstrap approach that takes Hempel's idea of satisfaction as basic.

---

1. The present notion of evidence is very weak even in certain cases where the probabilistic boost is substantial. Suppose that on Monday I buy one of the 1 million lottery tickets available and you buy 1,000. Suppose that on Tuesday all the lottery tickets except those owned by you and me are destroyed, but one of the remaining tickets will still be selected at random as the winner. This new fact boosts the probability of my winning almost a thousand-fold, from 1/1 million to 1/1,001. On the present view, this new fact is not only evidence that I will win but also much stronger evidence for this than the information available on Monday.

Let me say why I believe such notions of evidence are too weak for scientists to take an interest in. Why do scientists and others want evidence for their theories? What does evidence that h give you? My answer is that it gives you a good reason to believe h. Not necessarily a conclusive one, or the best possible one, but a good one nonetheless. If the results of the biopsy constitute evidence that the patient's tumor is malignant then there is a good reason to believe the patient has cancer. By contrast, if you visit your doctor complaining of a stomach ache persisting for the last few days I don't believe the doctor would or should count this fact by itself as evidence that you have cancer, even if the probability that you do is raised slightly by this symptom. By itself it is not a good reason to believe this hypothesis. Similarly, although the fact that I am entering an elevator increases my chances of being in an elevator accident, it is not evidence that this will be so, even a little bit of evidence, since by itself it fails to provide any reason to believe this hypothesis.

Now I do think that evidence is related to probability but that it is a "threshold" concept with respect to probability. In order for e to be evidence that h there must be a certain threshold of probability that e gives to h, not just any amount greater than zero. What is the threshold? Returning to the idea that evidence provides a good reason to believe, let me state a principle that I find quite intuitive, namely, that if e is a good reason to believe h, then it cannot also be a good reason to believe not-h or some proposition incompatible with h. (It might of course be the case that e is an equally good reason to believe h as to believe not-h. But that does not make it a good reason to believe both or either.) So, for example, the fact that I am tossing this fair coin is not a good reason to believe that it will land heads, because it is an equally good reason to believe it will land tails; i.e., it is not a good reason to believe either hypothesis. If this is right, then h's probability on e must be greater than 1/2. If it were less than or equal to 1/2, then, as in the coin-tossing case, e could be a good reason to believe both h and not-h.

Indeed, if I am right, and what scientists seek when they seek evidence is a good reason to believe h, then e can be evidence that h even if e *lowers* h's probability from what it was before. Suppose that the initial information is that Peter is taking medicine M to relieve symptoms S, where M is 95% effective. Suppose there is new information that Peter has just taken another medicine M' to relieve symptoms S, where M' is 90% effective in relieving S and where M' completely cancels M. (Peter decides to take M', let us say, because he has just been told that it has fewer side effects.) Now, I would say that the fact that Peter has taken M' is a good reason to believe, is evidence that, his symptoms S will be relieved, despite the fact that the probability of this hypothesis on this information is less than it was before. So evidence need not raise the probability of a hypothesis and can even lower it.

Does this mean that it is impossible to have evidence for conflicting theories? Yes and no. Yes, it is impossible for the same fact to be evidence for conflicting theories. The fact that I am about to toss this fair coin is not evidence that it will land heads and evidence that it will land tails. It is not evidence—not even a little bit of evidence—that either "theory" is true.

Suppose, however, that we consider a different coin, whose fairness we don't yet know. We give the coin to two tossers. The first conducts an experiment making 100 tosses with the coin resulting in 80 heads. The second conducts an experiment also making 100 tosses but obtaining 80 tails, where the conditions of tossing are approximately the same in both cases. Now the results of the first experiment, we might conclude, constitute evidence that the coin in biased in favor of heads, while the results of the second constitute evidence for the conflicting theory that the coin is biased in favor of tails. This conforms in the following way with my claim that evidence provides a good reason for belief: the results of the first experiment, *if considered by themselves*, would provide a good reason to believe the coin is heads-biased, while the results of the second experiment, *if considered by themselves*, would provide a good reason to believe that the coin is tails-biased. I suggest that this is what is meant by having evidence for conflicting theories, that is, having certain information which, if considered by itself, would be evidence for one theory and having other information which, if considered by itself, would be evidence for a conflicting theory.

What happens when the two bodies of evidence are combined? Will the combination be evidence for both theories? Not necessarily. It may be evidence for neither. In our coin-tossing example, if we consider the two experiments to have equal probative value and we combine their outcomes in the simplest manner, the result would be 200 tosses with this coin, yielding a total of 100 heads and 100 tails. This combined information by itself would not be evidence that the coin is heads-biased and evidence that it is tails-biased. The combined results in this case do not provide a good reason for believing either or both of the bias theories.

Do the combined results provide evidence, and hence a good reason to believe, that the coin is fair (since there were 100 heads out of the 200 total)? In this case, where similarly conducted experiments yield re-markably different outcomes, a reasonable conclusion might be to express puzzlement and say that the combined information by itself does not give us a reason to believe the coin is fair either, or indeed to believe anything about the fairness or bias of the coin.

In brief, it is possible to have evidence, i.e., different bodies of evidence, for conflicting theories, provided that each body is considered in the absence of the other. My claim is only that a single body of information is not evidence for conflicting theories. When it seems otherwise, I suggest, we are considering and isolating parts of that information in such a way that one part in the absence of others would be evidence. The combined results of the two coin-tossing experiments constitute evidence for heads-bias and for tails-bias only in this restricted sense.

Now some philosophers who are objective Bayesians about evidence suggest that there is a concept of evidence according to which e is evidence that h if and only if h's probability on e is sufficiently high, say greater than 1/2. This notion is much stronger than the weak increase-in-probability account. And it has the advantage of ruling out the unwanted lottery, elevator, and stomachache cases. However, even if probability greater than 1/2 is a necessary condition, it is not sufficient. High probability by itself is too weak for evidence, since h's probability may be high with or without e. It may have nothing to do with e. Let e be the fact that Michael Jordan eats Wheaties. (He used to promote Wheaties on TV.) Let h be the hypothesis that Michael Jordan will not become pregnant. Now h's probability with or without e is close to 1. Yet surely the fact that Michael Jordan eats Wheaties is not evidence, or a good reason to believe, that he will avoid pregnancy. For e to be evidence that h, for e to be a good reason to believe h, not only must h's probability on e be sufficiently high, but there must be some other connection between e and h, or the probability of such a connection: e must have "something to do" with h. What that amounts to is a question I discuss elsewhere (see chapter 1), and I will not try to deal with here.

Very briefly, the h-d and "satisfaction" views of evidence are much too weak because, like the two probability views just mentioned, they fail to provide a good reason to believe. The fact that the classical wave theory of light entails rectilinear propagation, and the fact that the latter is observed to be the case, is not enough to provide a good reason to believe that theory. Or put it this way: it provides an equally good reason—and hence not a good one at all—for believing a range of conflicting theories, including particle theories. Shifting to Hempel's satisfaction view, the fact that the hypothesis that all ravens are black is satisfied by the one black raven I have observed is not by itself a good reason to believe that hypothesis. Surely I need a bigger sample. Even more important, it depends crucially on how I selected the raven for observation. If, e.g., I purposely selected it from a cage marked "black birds" then the result does not provide a good reason at all for believing that all ravens are black.

On all of the views of evidence I have cited—the two Bayesian views, hypothetico-deductivism, Hempel's satisfaction theory, and Glymour's bootstrapping conception—it is too easy to get evidence. More important, what you get does not necessarily give you a good reason, or indeed, any reason, to believe a hypothesis. This, then, is the first reason scientists don't and shouldn't take such philosophical accounts of evidence seriously: they are too weak to be taken seriously. They don't give scientists what they want, or enough of what they want, when they want evidence.

3. THE A PRIORI ASSUMPTION

I turn now to the second assumption made by many philosophers who try to provide objective accounts of evidence. That assumption is that the evidential relation is a priori: whether e, if true, is evidence that h, and how strong that evidence is, is a matter to be determined completely by a priori calculation, not by empirical investigation.

I will illustrate this idea with brief references to some philosophical theories, the first one being Carnap's. Carnap (1962) embraces both an increase-in-probability and a high probability concept of evidence. But for Carnap the probability relation is entirely a priori. What h's probability is on e is settleable a priori, by reference to the rules of the "linguistic framework" (as Carnap calls it). The h-d view of evidence also makes the evidential relation a priori, since whether h entails e is a priori. (Even more complex and sophisticated h-d views, which appeal in addition to ideas about simplicity or coherence, are a priori, since whether these additional criteria are satisfied is supposed to be settleable without empirical investigation.) Finally, Hempel's satisfaction and Glymour's bootstrapping criteria again yield concepts in accordance with which one calculates a priori whether e is evidence that h.

What's wrong with this a priori assumption? Let's return to the case of Thomson versus Hertz concerning the electrical character of cathode rays. On the basis of his 1883 experiments in which no deflection of the cathode rays was produced Hertz concluded that his results were evidence, indeed conclusive evidence, that cathode rays are electrically neutral. Thomson in 1897 rejected this claim, not on a priori grounds, but on empirical ones. He assumed, on empirical grounds, that if cathode rays are electrically charged particles, then, since there is gas in the cathode tube, when these charged particles pass through the tube they will ionize the gas molecules producing positive and negative charges that will neutralize the charge on the metal plates between which the cathode rays travel. So if the gas in the tube is not sufficiently evacuated there will be no electrical deflection of the cathode rays. If there is sufficient evacuation there will be deflection, something produced in Thomson's later experiments.

Similarly, recent scientists offered an empirical reason for rejecting the claim that the burned animal bones in the same layer as stone tools and sediment that looks like wood ash is evidence that the first culinary campfires were built by Peking Man in caves in China between 200,000 and 500,000 years ago. The empirical reason was the new discovery that although the sediment looks like wood ash, it is in fact not this but fine minerals and clay deposited by water.

I am not claiming that all evidential statements are empirical. There are cases where enough information, or at least information of the right sort, is packed into the e-statement to make the claim that e is evidence that h a priori. For example, suppose that e reports that there is a fair lottery consisting of 1,000 tickets, one of which will be selected at random, and that Sam owns 950 of these tickets. Suppose h is the hypothesis that Sam will win. Then, I think, the claim that e is evidence that h is an a priori claim. No empirical fact will render it false.

Let me say that an evidence statement of the form "e is evidence that h" is *empirically incomplete* if the truth of the statement depends on empirical facts in addition to those reported in e. The evidential claims in the two scientific examples at the beginning are empirically incomplete: Hertz's claim that the absence of electrical deflection in his cathode experiments is evidence that cathode rays are electrically neutral, and the claim of the earlier archaeologists concerning evidence for the hypothesis about the first campfires. Both evidential claims were falsified by later empirical discoveries.

A priorists about evidence will surely have a reply. Before considering it, however, let me draw an obvious conclusion, albeit a conditional one. If evidential claims, or many of them, are empirical, not a priori, then it is scientists not philosophers who are in the best position to judge whether e, if true, is evidence that h, and how strong that evidence is. If evidential claims are, by and large, empirical, this, I suggest, is and ought to be an important reason why scientists don't consult philosophical theories of evidence when they try to settle disagreements over evidential claims. Philosophical theories would make such disagreements settleable on a priori grounds. Accordingly, scientists may find philosophical theories of evidence wanting because they give a very mistaken idea of how evidential disputes are usually settled.

4. AN A PRIORIST RESPONSE

Now, you may object, give the a priorist a fair chance. Surely he will have a devastating response. Let me choose my favorite a priorist, Rudolf

Carnap. Earlier I claimed that there is a crucial relationship between evidence and a good reason for belief. For Carnap there is a relationship between evidence and what one is justified in believing. This relationship, which is implied by his famous "requirement of total evidence," is this:

> If e is evidence that h, or if e confirms h to degree r, and if e represents one's total (relevant) empirical knowledge, then one is (at least to some extent) justified in believing h on the basis of e, or one is justified in believing h to the degree r on the basis of e.

Now, Carnap's claim is this: If e is the entire set of empirical propositions you know to be true, then whether you are justified in believing h to the degree r on the basis of e is an a priori question. For Carnap whether you are justified in believing h depends solely on what you know to be true. And if you put together everything you know to be true, then you can determine from this by a priori calculation whether, or to what extent, you are justified in believing some further empirical proposition.

Now putting together everything you know to be true, or even everything relevant, is a pretty tall order. Yet for a Carnapian this tall order must be filled if we are to use a concept of evidence and determine a priori whether, or to what extent, we are justified in believing h on the basis of e. But even if we could fill this tall order, this won't suffice because Carnap is mistaken in an important respect. What you are justified in believing depends not only on what you know but also on what someone in your position is capable of knowing or ought to know, even if you don't know it. Suppose that a detective seeing a smoking gun lying next to the victim believes that the victim was shot. It turns out, however, that there are no bullet wounds in the victim's body, something that the detective could have, and should have, discovered by looking more carefully. An amateur or scared bystander seeing the smoking gun may be justified in believing the victim was shot. But I don't think the detective is. It is his job, and part of his training, to examine the scene more closely, even if, for some reason, he fails to realize that someone in his position should examine the situation with more care.

An a priorist might agree with this but argue as follows. Using as an example our hasty detective, let us formulate a set of propositions S about the detective's "situation," namely, his training, his abilities, his responsibilities, and whatever other factors that affect whether he is justified in believing something on the basis of what he observes. The a priorist can modify an earlier Carnapian claim in this manner. Suppose that e represents a person's total (relevant) empirical knowledge, and suppose that the person is in a situation S (his abilities, training, responsibilities, etc.). Then whether, or to what extent, e confirms h for such a person depends just on e, h, and S. Moreover, knowing just e, h, and S one can calculate a priori whether, or to what extent, e confirms h. Instead of writing c(h/e) = r, as Carnap does, we can write $c_s(h/e) = r$, which means that for a person in a situation S the degree of confirmation of h on e is r. And statements of this form are a priori true (or false).

I don't want to pursue the question of whether such evidential statements are, or can always be made to be, a priori but rather whether such evidential statements are of interest to science. I don't see how they could be. They are too particular for that. They are swimming in specificity. In the detective case the evidential statement would include not only facts the detective observed—the fallen victim, the smoking gun—but also facts about the detective's particular situation: his responsibilities, training, intelligence, and so forth. Or, reverting to the case of Hertz's experiments with cathode rays in 1883, if we claim, as does the distinguished historian of physics Jed Buchwald (1994), that Hertz was justified in believing that cathode rays are electrically neutral, and we seek to make the justification a priori, then we will need to introduce more facts than simply ones about Hertz's experimental set-up and his results. We will need to include facts about Hertz's particular situation, including his inability, and that of others in 1883, to evacuate more gas from the cathode tube. What's wrong with such a concept of evidence? Why should it be of so little interest to scientists?

To begin with, using such a concept, you can't ask a question such as "Were Hertz's experimental results evidence that cathode rays are electrically neutral?" You need to ask whether they were evidence for Hertz, or for Thomson, or for someone in either of their situations, or for someone else. Keep in mind this is not what someone takes to be, or believes is, evidence. It is supposed to be a set of facts that makes a person in a certain situation justified in believing the hypothesis, whether or not such a person realizes this or believes the hypothesis. Now even if scientists were to have some interest in answering this question, I think they are much more interested in answering the unrelativized question "Are (or were) Hertz's results evidence that cathode rays are neutral?" Not evidence for Hertz, or for Thomson, or for anyone else. They don't particularly want to know whether Hertz, or Thomson, or someone else was justified in those beliefs on the basis of Hertz's results. They want to know something more general that transcends a particular person or type of person. (More about this in a moment.)

Second, to answer the Carnapian evidential question and produce an evidential claim that is true, and a priori, and that will justify one's beliefs, one needs to include a lot of facts about the particular situation to which it is relativized. To know whether Hertz's experimental results were evidence for Hertz or someone in his situation that cathode rays are neutral one needs to know a lot of facts about Hertz and his situation. This is because, on a Carnapian view, one needs to know whether Hertz, or someone in his situation, was justified in believing the hypothesis on the basis of his results. And one needs to know enough about the situation to render such a justification a priori. Such facts about an individual's situation are often difficult to ascertain, and scientists are not usually in a position to know them, and hence to produce true a priori evidence claims of the sort in question.

By contrast, what I think scientists want from evidence is a good reason for believing something, not a Carnapian justification. This notion of "good reason" is not relativized to the circumstances of a particular or type of person. A change in barometric pressure is a good reason to believe in a change in the weather. Your owning 950 of the 1,000 lottery tickets sold is a good reason to believe one of your tickets will win. This is objective—it does not depend on what you or anyone else believes. And it is not, or does not need to be, relativized to anyone. One does not need to know facts about Hertz's training, his intelligence, or his ability, to determine whether the results he obtained in his experiments provide a good reason for believing that cathode rays are electrically neutral. This is something J. J. Thomson determined fourteen years after Hertz's experiments without investigating Hertz's particular epistemic situation in 1883. Moreover, that Hertz's results do not provide a good reason for believing that cathode rays are neutral is a determination that Thomson made empirically, not by a priori calculation.

Finally, suppose one tries to pack enough information into a good reason to believe h to make the fact that it is such a reason a priori. For example, one might try to include enough facts to transform it into a valid deductive argument, or into a valid a priori Carnapian evidential claim. But why do so? Is this the only, or the best, way to discover whether something is a good reason to believe? I don't know whether taking these pills for a headache is a good reason to believe the headache will disappear. Surely a good, indeed the most obvious, way to find out is to conduct a simple appropriate experiment: have one group of headache sufferers take the pills and another group take a placebo.

5. CONCLUSIONS

I have noted two reasons that scientists do and should ignore typical philosophical theories of objective evidence. First, these theories furnish concepts that are much too weak to give scientists what they want from evidence, namely, a good reason to believe. Second, they furnish concepts that make the evidential relation entirely a priori. But frequently scientists try to discover whether evidential claims are true not solely by a priori reasoning but by empirical investigation. This, I think, follows from the idea of providing a good reason to believe. Some fact can be a good reason to believe a hypothesis even if this cannot be demonstrated by a priori calculation. If one seeks to define an a priori concept of evidence based, e.g., on the Carnapian idea of justification, the concept of evidence produced will require too many specific facts about an investigator to be of much interest to scientists generally.

However, not wishing to end on too negative a note, let me close with a challenge to philosophers of science. It is to propose and defend a concept of evidence that is at once empirical and robust. It is empirical because, in general, it renders the question of whether e is evidence that h an empirical question, which scientists can attempt to answer using that concept. It is robust in two ways. It is a strong, not a weak, concept of evidence, and it is one that yields a good general reason to believe something, rather than one that must be tied to specific epistemic situations. If it is empirical and robust in these ways then, I think, it should be of interest to scientists.

REFERENCES

Achinstein, Peter (1985), *The Nature of Explanation*. New York: Oxford University Press.

Achinstein, Peter (2001), *The Book of Evidence*. New York: Oxford University Press.

Buchwald, Jed (1994), *The Creation of Scientific Effects*. Chicago: Chicago University Press.

Carnap, Rudolf (1962), *Logical Foundations of Probability*. Chicago: University of Chicago Press.

Glymour, Clark (1980), *Theory and Evidence*. Princeton, N.J.: Princeton University Press.

Hempel, Carl G. (1965), *Aspects of Scientific Explanation*. New York: Free Press.

Hertz, Heinrich (1896), *Miscellaneous Papers*. London.

Thomson, J. J. (1897), "Cathode Rays," *Philosophical Magazine* 44, 293–316.

Weiner, Steve, Q. Xu, P. Goldberg, J. Liu, and O. Bar-Yossef (1998), "Evidence for the Use of Fire at Jhoukoudian, China," *Science* 281, 251–253.

3

The Grue Paradox

"The Grue Paradox" is reprinted by permission from Yuri Balashov and Alexander Rosenberg, eds., Philosophy of Science: Contemporary Readings *(2002), 307–320. This chapter, written especially for the Balashov and Rosenberg collection, is based on material in* The Book of Evidence. *I offer a new solution to Goodman's important paradox, which must be answered by any account of evidence and inductive reasoning. The present solution is very different from one that Stephen Barker and I proposed in our 1960 article, "On the New Riddle of Induction,"* Philosophical Review *69, 511–522 (to which Goodman replied in the same issue).*

1. GOODMAN'S NEW RIDDLE OF INDUCTION

Nelson Goodman's great paradox[1] begins with the fact that

> e: All the emeralds so far examined are green.

From this fact, by inductive generalization, we ought to be able to conclude that

> h: All emeralds are always green.

Now define "grue" as follows:

> Definition: x is grue at time t if and only if t is prior to A.D. 2500 and x is green at t, or t is A.D. 2500 or later and x is blue at t.[2]

---

1. Nelson Goodman, *Fact, Fiction, and Forecast*, 4th ed. (Cambridge, MA: Harvard University Press 1983).

2. Goodman's original definition is that "grue" applies to all things examined before some specific time T just in case they are green, and to other things just in case they are blue. In our response to Goodman, Stephen Barker and I used the definition in the text (not Goodman's), except that (in 1960) we chose T to be the year 2000, which seems to have created a precedent for other writers on the subject. Since January 1, 2000, is now a memory, I have taken the liberty of pushing the date far into the future.

Since e is true, and since the emeralds so far examined have all been examined prior to 2500, the following is also true:

e′: All the emeralds so far examined are grue.

So by parity of reasoning, from the fact that e′ is true, we ought to be able to conclude that

h′: All emeralds are always grue.

But h′ says that while emeralds before 2500 are green, emeralds beginning in 2500 are blue. And even though it is true all emeralds observed so far are grue (because they are green and it is prior to 2500), this fact does not warrant the inference that all emeralds are always grue, that is, green before 2500 and blue thereafter. That would be absurd! Can this conclusion be avoided?

One approach, suggested first by Carnap, and defended later by Barker and me,[3] is that grue is a temporal property in the sense that a specific time, namely, 2500, is invoked in characterizing the property, whereas this is not so in the case of green. The claim, then, is that induction works only for nontemporal properties, and not for temporal ones. In the present case this means that since h′ attributes a temporal property (grue) to all emeralds, we cannot "project" grue (to use Goodman's term). We cannot make an inductive generalization from e′ to h′. By contrast, since h attributes a nontemporal property (green) to all emeralds, we can make an inductive generalization from e to h.

This solution (which I no longer believe to be adequate) raises two important questions: What is a temporal property? And why should such properties not be projected? My answer to these questions, and my solution to the paradox, will be developed step by step in what follows.

2. A SOLUTION TO GRUE: THE FIRST STEP

To begin with, it is untrue that every property that mentions a specific time cannot be projected. Suppose, for example, that there is a certain necktie produced by Harvard University emblazoned with the letters MCMLVI, and that all the owners of such ties whom we have interviewed were graduated from Harvard in 1956. We might then legitimately infer that all owners of this type of tie were graduated from Harvard in 1956, despite the fact that "were graduated from Harvard in 1956" expresses a temporal property.

---

3. See introductory paragraph.

We need to be more selective with the temporal properties we say cannot be projected. Grue is a very special type of temporal property. It is a disjunctive one having this form:

(1) x has property P at time t if and only if x has property Q_1 at t and t is prior to a specific time T or x has property Q_2 at t and t is T or later.

This is not yet a sufficient characterization. Two provisos must be added. First, the properties Q_1 and Q_2 must be incompatible, for example, green and blue (something cannot have both at once). Second (this will become important later), the properties Q_1 and Q_2 (e.g., green and blue) must not be thought of as disjunctive properties satisfying (1).[4]

Grue, and indeed any property of type (1), is a property of an even more general type that is not necessarily temporal. Consider disjunctive properties with this form:

(2) x has P if and only if x has Q_1 and condition C obtains or x has Q_2 and condition C does not obtain.

Again the properties Q_1 and Q_2 must be incompatible. And they must not be disjunctive properties satisfying (2). In the grue case, Q_1 is green and Q_2 is blue. Condition C is that the time at which x has whatever color it has is before 2500. Goodman's paradox can be generated with respect to any property of type (2), whether temporal or not, if all the Ps examined have been Q_1 and condition C obtains. For example, again let Q_1 be green, let Q_2 be blue, but let condition C be that x's temperature is less than some fixed value M. Suppose that all emeralds so far examined have been green and have been at temperatures below M degrees. Then if we project P with respect to emeralds, we generate a conclusion that entails that at temperatures reaching or exceeding M emeralds are blue. We generate the paradox even when the property P in question is nontemporal.[5]

How can Goodman's puzzle be resolved? Suppose that information e says that all P_1s so far examined are P_2, and hypothesis h states that all P_1s are P_2. Under what conditions can we project P_2 relative to P_1? Let us look at the grue case first.

We *can* project the property grue relative to the property of being an emerald, but only if evidence e reports on times both before and after T (2500), that is, only if e reports that the emeralds examined before T are

---

4. A perceptive discussion of the disjunctive character of grue is found in David H. Sanford, "A Grue Thought in a Bleen Shade: 'Grue' as a Disjunctive Predicate," in Douglas Stalker, ed., *GRUE! The New Riddle of Induction* (Chicago: Open Court, 1994), 173–92.

5. See James Hullett and Robert Schwartz, "Grue: Some Remarks," *Journal of Philosophy*, 64 (1967), 259–71.

grue (and hence green) and that emeralds examined at T or later are grue (and hence blue).

More generally, if P_2 (e.g., grue) is a disjunctive property of types (1) or (2), with Q_1 and Q_2 (e.g., green and blue) as disjuncts, and if P_1 (e.g., being an emerald) is not a disjunctive property of types (1) or (2), and if e reports that all the P_1s examined are P_2 in virtue of being Q_1 and none in virtue of being Q_2, then from e we cannot conclude that all P_1s are P_2.

I will speak of a *selection procedure* as a rule for determining how to test, or obtain evidence for or against, a hypothesis. Consider the following two types of selection procedures for a hypothesis h of the form "All P_1s are P_2":

SP$_1$: Select P_1s to observe at times that are both before and after T. (Or more generally, for properties of form (2), select P_1s to observe at times that satisfy condition C and also ones that fail to satisfy C.)

SP$_2$: Select P_1s to observe at times that are only before T. (Select only P_1s to observe at times that satisfy C.)

Where P_1 and P_2 are properties of the sort described in the previous paragraph, from e (the fact that all observed P_1s are P_2) we can infer h (all P_1s are P_2) only if the selection procedure SP$_1$ is employed, not SP$_2$.

The basic idea derives from an injunction to "vary the instances." A disjunctive property P of the type depicted in (1) and (2) applies to two different sorts of cases: ones in which an item that is P (e.g., grue) has property Q_1 (green) before time T (condition C is satisfied) and ones in which an item that is P has an incompatible property Q_2 (blue) at or after T (condition C is not satisfied). Since property P, when projected, is supposed to apply to items of both types, where these types are incompatible, items of both types need to be obtained as instances of the generalization. That is, SP$_1$ is to be followed, not SP$_2$.

For example, projecting the property grue, in the case of emeralds, requires that some emeralds be examined before 2500 to determine whether they are then green, and that some emeralds be examined after 2500 to determine whether they are then blue. Only if both of these determinations are made, and the emeralds examined before 2500 are green and those examined later are blue, can the resulting information e warrant a generalization to the hypothesis that all emeralds are grue.

Contrast this case with one in which the property green is projected with respect to emeralds. This property is not being construed as one that applies to two different sorts of cases: ones in which a green item has some nondisjunctive property Q_1 before time T and ones in which a green item has some incompatible nondisjunctive property Q_2 after T. So projecting the property green, in the case of emeralds, does not require that some emeralds be examined before T to determine whether they have such a property Q_1 and that some emeralds be examined after T to determine whether they have Q_2. Accordingly, it is not the case that only if both determinations are made and the emeralds examined before T have Q_1 while those examined after T have Q_2 can the resulting information (that all the examined emeralds are green) warrant the conclusion that all emeralds are green. In this case selection procedure SP_2 (as well as SP_1) can be used. One can select emeralds to observe at times that are only before some T, or at times that are before T and after.

The important point is not that grue, unlike green, is a temporal property. That is not enough to prevent grue from being projected. The important point is that grue is a certain type of disjunctive property, while green is not. To project this type of disjunctive property P with respect to some type of item, one needs to vary the instances observed by examining items that satisfy the condition C and items that do not.

3. "I OBJECT. DON'T FORGET BLEEN!" (NELSON GOODMAN)

All of this is subject to what seems like a devastating objection. In characterizing a disjunctive property such as grue as one satisfying condition (1) or, more generally, (2), I indicated that the properties Q_1 and Q_2 must not be disjunctive properties satisfying (1) and (2). But there lies the rub, as Goodman gleefully points out. To illustrate the problem we define "bleen" as follows:

> Definition: x is bleen at time t if and only if t is prior to A.D. 2500 and x is blue at t or t is A.D. 2500 or later and x is green at t.

Now, thinking of grue and bleen as our basic properties, we can characterize the properties green and blue in a way that satisfies conditions (1) and (2):

(3) x is green at t if and only if t is prior to A.D. 2500 and x is grue at t or t is A.D. 2500 or later and x is bleen at t.

(4) x is blue at t if and only if t is prior to A.D. 2500 and x is bleen at t or t is A.D. 2500 or later and x is grue at t.

Looking at the properties green and blue this way and treating grue and bleen as our basic nondisjunctive properties, green and blue become disjunctive properties satisfying conditions (1) and (2). Accordingly, to project green with respect to emeralds we need to examine emeralds both before and after 2500. We must use selection procedure SP_1 and not SP_2. This directly contradicts what was said earlier.

So where do we stand? Can the property grue be projected with respect to emeralds by examining only emeralds before 2500? In gathering
information that will warrant the hypothesis that all emeralds are grue
can we use SP_2 and select emeralds to observe at times that are only before 2500? Similarly, can the property green be projected with respect to
emeralds only by examining emeralds both before and after 2500, that is,
by following only SP_1?

My answer is that *for us*, that is, for normal human beings, green and
blue are not disjunctive properties of types (1) and (2) subject to a temporal condition, while grue and bleen are. What I mean by this is explained
as follows:

(a) For us, the properties green and blue are not defined in the
disjunctive way given above. Our dictionaries do not define the
terms "green" and "blue" in terms of "grue" and "bleen" and a
specific time. Nor do dictionaries in other languages with words
for the properties blue and green. Indeed, the dictionaries I own
do not even contain the words "grue" and "bleen."

(b) When we attempt to ascertain whether something we are
examining is green (or blue) at a certain time t we do not, and
do not need to, ascertain whether it is grue at t and t is before
2500 or whether it is bleen at t and t is 2500 or later. For
example, if it is within five minutes of midnight, one way or the
other, December 31, 2499, but we do not know which, and we
are presented with a colored object, we could examine it and
determine whether it is then green (or blue) without knowing
whether midnight has passed.

By contrast,

(c) For us, the properties grue and bleen are defined disjunctively in
the manner of (1) and (2) and are subject to a temporal condition.
We understand these properties only by reference to such
definitions.

(d) When we attempt to ascertain whether something is grue
(or bleen) at a certain time t we need to ascertain whether it
is green at t and t is before 2500 or whether it is blue at t and
t is 2500 or later. For example, if it is within five minutes of
midnight, one way or the other, December 31, 2499, but we
do not know which, and we are presented with a colored
object, by examining it we could not determine whether it
is then grue (or bleen) without knowing whether midnight
has passed.

We might, however, imagine some extraordinary group of individuals very different from us in the following respects:

(a′) For members of this group the properties grue and bleen are not defined disjunctively in the manner of (1) and (2). Their dictionaries do not define "grue" and "bleen" in terms of "green" and "blue" and a specific time. Indeed, their dictionaries do not even contain the words "green" and "blue."

(b′) When members of this extraordinary group attempt to ascertain whether something they are examining is grue (or bleen) at a certain time t, they do not, and do not need to, ascertain whether it is green at t and t is before 2500 or whether it is blue at t and t is 2500 or later. For example, if it is five minutes before or after midnight, December 31, 2499, but they do not know which, if they are presented with a colored object they could determine whether it is then grue (or bleen) without knowing whether midnight has passed.

(c′) For them, the properties green and blue are defined in the manner of (3) and (4). They understand these properties only by reference to such definitions.

(d′) When they attempt to ascertain whether something is green (or blue) at a certain time t they need to ascertain whether it is grue at t and t is before 2500 or whether it is bleen at t and t is 2500 or later. If it is five minutes before or after midnight, December 31, 2499, but they do not know which, and they are presented with a colored object, by examining it they could not determine whether it is then green (or blue) without knowing whether midnight has passed.

It may be useful to draw an analogy with a different sort of case involving a disjunction that is nontemporal but is different from ones that can spawn Goodman's paradox. Suppose there is an extraordinary group of persons who have a word in their language for male robins and a different word for female robins, but no word for robins. (Perhaps they regard male robins and female ones as belonging to different species.) Using their words for "male robin" and "female robin" we can then define our word "robin" for them, as follows:

x is a robin if and only if x is a male robin or a female robin.

This is how they will understand the word "robin," which is new for them. Moreover, when members of this group attempt to ascertain whether something is a robin they will determine whether it is a male robin, and if it is not, whether it is a female robin. If it is one or the other it is a robin; if it is neither it is not a robin. For them, but not us, "robin" is a sex-linked term.

In the case of grue, what we are imagining is that for members of the extraordinary group the properties green and blue are disjunctive ones subject to a temporal condition, while grue and bleen are not. We have no idea how they do what they do, in particular how they determine whether something is grue at a certain time t without knowing whether t is before 2500 or later. Nor do we have any idea why, in order to determine whether something is green at a certain time t they need to know whether t is before or after 2500. We are imagining simply that these things are so.

My claim is that if there were (or could be) such extraordinary people, they would be justified in projecting the property grue with respect to emeralds after examining emeralds before 2500; they would not need to wait until 2500 to examine emeralds then as well. They would be justified in using selection procedure SP_2. And if there were such extraordinary people they would be justified in projecting the property green with respect to emeralds only by examining emeralds both before and after 2500, that is, by using SP_1.

However, the claim is not that there *are* people such as the extraordinary ones being imagined. Nor is it that there *could be*, in some robust sense of "could be." It may not be physically possible. The claim is only that it is *logically* possible.[6] There is no contradiction (or at least I have not found one) in imagining the existence of extraordinary persons satisfying conditions (a')–(d'). Accordingly, there is no contradiction in supposing the existence of extraordinary persons who are justified in projecting the property grue with respect to emeralds after examining only emeralds before 2500. However, we are not such extraordinary people and there is no reason to believe that any such people exist or, physically speaking, could exist.

4. A CONTRAST WITH GOODMAN'S SOLUTION

In offering his own solution, Goodman, like me, allows the possibility (whether logical or physical) that persons exist who are justified in projecting the property grue with respect to emeralds after examining emeralds only before 2500.

---

6. Here I disagree with Judith Thomson, who claims that it is not even logically possible. See Judith Jarvis Thomson, "Grue," *Journal of Philosophy*, 63 (1966), 289–309.

Briefly, Goodman's solution is based on the idea that the term "green" is much better *entrenched* than "grue." The term "green" (as well as other terms true of the same class of things) has been used much more frequently than "grue" (or other co-extensive terms) in hypotheses of the form "All As are Bs" that have actually come to be adopted. Goodman's question is this: When is a hypothesis of the form "All As are Bs" projectible, that is, when is it confirmed by instances consisting of reports that particular As are Bs?

Suppose that two conflicting hypotheses "All As are Bs" and "All As are Cs" are such that all their examined instances are true. But suppose that the term B is much better entrenched than the term C. Then, according to Goodman, the hypothesis "All As are Cs" is not projectible. It receives no confirmation from its instances. Thus, although all the examined instances of the hypothesis "All emeralds are grue" are true, that hypothesis does not receive confirming support from those instances. The reason is that this hypothesis is "overridden" by the conflicting hypothesis "All emeralds are green," which (up to now) has equal numbers of examined instances but uses the better entrenched term "green" and conflicts with no hypotheses with still better entrenched terms. Under these circumstances examined instances of green emeralds confirm the hypothesis that all emeralds are green, whereas examined instances of grue emeralds fail to confirm the hypothesis that all emeralds are grue.

On this solution it is at least logically, if not physically, possible that persons exist for whom examined instances of grue emeralds confirm the hypothesis that all emeralds are grue, whereas examined instances of green emeralds fail to confirm the hypothesis that all emeralds are green. For such persons "grue" would be a better entrenched term than "green." It would be used more frequently than "green" by such persons in hyotheses of the form "All As are Bs" that have actually come to be adopted by such persons. So, for such persons, the hypothesis "All emeralds are green" would be overridden by the hypothesis "All emeralds are grue," which (until now) has equal numbers of examined instances but uses what is for them the better entrenched term "grue" and conflicts with no hypotheses with still better entrenched terms.

Goodman's solution appeals to entrenchment. Although all the emeralds examined so far are both green and grue, "green" is a much better entrenched term. It appears much more frequently than "grue" in hypotheses of the form "All As are Bs" that we have come to accept. This claim I do not want to deny. My question, however, is why this is so. Why have we accepted generalizations of the form "All As are green" or "All green things are B" much more frequently than "All As are grue" and "All grue things are B"? My solution offers an answer. (Goodman simply accepts that this is so.)

The answer is that for us grue is a disjunctive property of types (1) and (2) of section 2, whereas green is not. (For us, conditions (a)–(d) of section 3 hold.) Accordingly, for us, to generalize from examined instances of grue to hypotheses of the form "All As are grue" and "All grue things are B" (where A and B are not for us disjunctive properties of types (1) and (2)), we need to examine As (for "All As are grue") and grue things (for "All grue things are B") both before and after 2500. Since for us grue is a disjunctive property of type (2), in order to generalize we need to vary the instances and examine both things that satisfy the condition C of a property of type (2) and things that fail to satisfy C. Since green is not for us a disjunctive property of types (1) and (2), in order to generalize from examined instances of green to hypotheses of the form "All As are green" and "All green things are B" (where A and B are not for us disjunctive properties of types (1) and (2)) we do not need to examine As (for "All As are green") and green things (for "All green things are B") both before and after 2500, or ones that satisfy some corresponding condition C and others that fail to.

Accordingly, my solution is not based on the idea of entrenchment, which is really an idea about terms used in generalizations we have come to accept. It is based on the idea that for us, because grue is a disjunctive property of a certain sort, whereas green is not, in order to generalize from examined cases of emeralds that are grue we need to examine emeralds that satisfy one side of the disjunction and emeralds that satisfy the other.

5. EVIDENCE

So far I have talked about generalizing from examined cases of green or grue to all cases (projecting these properties). Goodman, Carnap, and others who write about the grue paradox are concerned with the question of what counts as confirming evidence for a hypothesis. So, finally, on my solutions, is the fact that

(e) All emeralds examined so far are green

evidence that

(h) All emeralds are always green?

To answer, we need to distinguish several concepts of evidence used in the sciences. In *The Book of Evidence* (hereafter, BE), I distinguish four such concepts, which I call (1) subjective, (2) ES (epistemic situation), (3) potential, and (4) veridical. Very briefly, (1) e is some person's (or

group's) subjective evidence that h if the person (or group) believes that
e is evidence that h, and if that person's reason for believing h true or
probable is that e is true. That 24 hours ago Ann ate a pound of arsenic
is my subjective evidence that she is now dead. It is what I take to be
evidence; and my reason for believing she is dead is that she ate the arsenic. (2) e is ES-evidence that h, relative to a type of epistemic situation
(a situation in which one knows or believes certain things), if anyone in
that epistemic situation would be justified in believing that e is evidence
that h. Relative to an epistemic situation containing the knowledge that
arsenic is lethal, the fact that Ann ate the arsenic is ES-evidence that she
is dead. (3) e is potential evidence that h if e provides a good reason to
believe h, irrespective of epistemic situations. No matter what is assumed
known or believed, the fact that Ann ate the arsenic is a good reason to
believe she is dead, since arsenic is lethal. (4) e is veridical evidence that
h if e is potential evidence that h, and h is true.[7]

Only the first concept is subjective: whether e is (subjective) evidence
that h depends upon what some person or group in fact believes about
e, h, and their relationship. The other types are objective. ES-evidence is
relativized to a *type* of epistemic situation, not to the specific one of some
individual or group; no one need be in an epistemic situation of that type.
Finally, like the concepts of "sign" and "symptom," at least on one standard
use of these, potential and veridical evidence are not relativized to any
actual or potential epistemic situation.

In BE, as well as in chapter 1 in the present volume, I provide definitions for each of these concepts (which need not be given here). I argue
that although potential evidence is the most basic concept (the others can
be defined by reference to it), veridical evidence is what scientists seek.
In the characterization of subjective evidence as what one believes to be
evidence, the evidence one believes it to be is veridical; an analogous claim
can be made for ES-evidence.

Our question, then, is whether information e above (concerning
examined emeralds) is evidence that h (all emeralds are always green).
Consider the simplest case first, subjective evidence. We green speakers
(the normal folks who satisfy (a)–(d) of section 3 with respect to green
and grue) believe that e is (veridical) evidence that h and that h is true;
our reason for believing that h is true is that e is. In short, the fact that e
is true is our subjective evidence that h is true. Similarly, if grue speakers
existed (extraordinary but imaginary beings who satisfy (a′)–(d′)), the fact

---

7. A stronger concept of veridical evidence requires in addition that there be an explanatory connection between e and h, that is, that h correctly explain e, or that e correctly
explain h, or that something correctly explain both h and e. See *BE*, chapter 8.

that all the emeralds examined so far are green (and hence grue) would be
their subjective evidence that all emeralds are always grue.

In section 3 I claimed that a grue speaker is justified in projecting the
property grue, while a green speaker is justified in projecting the property green. This is a case of ES-evidence, where the epistemic situation is
understood as including a speaker's knowledge of definitions and of how
to ascertain whether something is grue or green. A grue speaker's ES-
evidence that all emeralds are always grue would be that all emeralds so
far examined are grue. A green speaker's ES-evidence that all emeralds are
always green is that all emeralds so far examined are green.

Is e potential evidence that h? Whether it is depends on the selection
procedure used. I have characterized a selection procedure as a rule for
determining how to test, or obtain evidence for or against, a hypothesis.
In the case of our hypothesis h a selection procedure might include a
rule for selecting emeralds to observe. If, for example, such a rule called
for selecting emeralds only from a box containing green objects, then e
would not be potential evidence that h. But a selection procedure for our
hypothesis h may also include a rule for how to determine whether an
emerald is green at a given time t.[8] Many such rules are possible, but let
me concentrate on two.

SP(green)$_1$: Determine whether an emerald is green at a time t
simply by looking at it at t, in good light, at a distance
at which it can be seen clearly (etc.), and ascertaining
whether it looks green.

SP(green)$_2$: Determine whether an emerald is green at t by looking at
it at t and ascertaining whether it looks grue at t (the way
our imagined grue speaker does) and t is prior to 2500 or
whether it looks bleen at t and t is 2500
or later.

Suppose that all the emeralds selected for observation so far (before
2500) have been determined to be green. Is that fact potential evidence
that all emeralds are always green? That depends not only on which selection procedure was used to select emeralds for observation but on which
one was used to determine whether an emerald is green. Suppose that
SP(green)$_2$ was used (e.g., by genuine grue speakers, who could not use
SP(green)$_1$). Someone following SP(green)$_2$ and examining only emeralds

---

8. The statement e can be understood in two ways: all the emeralds examined so far have
been determined to be green; all the emeralds examined so far are in fact green (whether
or not this has been determined). In what follows I confine my attention to the first. For a
discussion of the second, see *BE*, chapter 9.

before the year 2500 to determine whether they look grue and hence are green would need to wait until 2500 to examine emeralds to determine whether they look bleen after 2500 and hence are green. Such a person would need to do this in order to "vary the instances" to obtain genuine potential evidence that all emeralds are always green. If SP(green)$_2$ is really the selection procedure that was used for determining whether an emerald is green, then e is not potential evidence that h. By contrast, someone following SP(green)$_1$ and examining only emeralds before 2500 would not need to wait until 2500 to examine emeralds to determine whether they look bleen after 2500 and hence are green. The date 2500 plays no role in following SP(green)$_1$ the way it does in following SP(green)$_2$. If e were obtained by following SP(green)$_1$, e would be potential evidence that h.

Now, as Goodman loves to do, let us compare the situation with respect to the grue hypothesis. The question is whether

e′: All emeralds examined so far are determined to be grue

is potential evidence that

h′: All emeralds are always grue.

We need to say what selection procedure is being used. By analogy with the previous ones for green emeralds we have

SP(grue)$_1$: Determine whether an emerald is grue at t simply by looking at it at t in good light (etc.) and ascertaining whether it looks grue.

SP(grue)$_2$: Determine whether an emerald is grue at t by looking at it at t and ascertaining whether it looks green at t, where t is prior to 2500, or whether it looks blue at t and t is 2500 or later.

If SP(grue)$_2$ is used in obtaining the result e′, then e′ is not potential evidence that h′. Someone (such as us) following this selection procedure and examining only emeralds before 2500 to determine whether they look green and hence are grue would need to wait until 2500 to examine emeralds to determine whether they look blue and hence are grue. Such a person would need to do this in order to "vary the instances" to obtain genuine potential evidence that all emeralds are always grue. Using SP(grue)$_2$, examining emeralds only before 2500 would not suffice.

By contrast, a genuine grue speaker following SP(grue)$_1$ and examining emeralds only before 2500 would not need to wait until 2500 to examine emeralds to determine whether they look blue and hence are grue. Using SP(grue)$_1$, examining emeralds only before 2500 and determining that all of them are grue would allow e′ to be potential evidence that h′.

In short, (e) the fact that all emeralds observed so far are green is potential evidence that (h) all emeralds are always green, if selection procedure
SP(green)$_1$ is used, but not SP(green)$_2$. And (e') the fact that all emeralds
observed so far are grue is potential evidence that (h') all emeralds are
always grue, if selection procedure SP(grue)$_1$ is used, but not SP(grue)$_2$. It
should be emphasized that this is not to relativize the concept of potential evidence to a particular person or to a type of epistemic situation. If
SP(green)$_1$ is used e is potential evidence that h, and if SP(grue)$_1$ is used
e' is potential evidence that h', independently of who believes what. Nor
are e and e' just potential evidence for persons in epistemic situations of
certain types.

Now, as a matter of fact, there are no grue speakers, that is, extraordinary persons who satisfy conditions (a')–(d') of section 3 for defining and
identifying grue and green properties. There are just ordinary, everyday
people like us, who satisfy conditions (a)–(d). So, even if it is logically
possible that a selection procedure such as SP(grue)$_1$ is followed in determining whether an emerald is grue, and that a selection procedure such
as SP(green)$_2$ is followed in determining whether an emerald is green,
this will never happen (we confidently believe). In any real-life situation
in which selection procedures involve actual observations of emeralds,
SP(green)$_1$ and SP(grue)$_2$ will be followed, in which case the fact that all
observed emeralds are determined to be green will be potential evidence
that all emeralds are always green, and the fact that all observed emeralds
are determined to be grue will not be potential evidence that all emeralds
are always grue. If (as we also confidently believe) the green hypothesis is
true, then the fact that all observed emeralds are determined to be green
is veridical evidence for this hypothesis. If the hypothesis turns out to be
false, then the fact about the observed emeralds is not veridical evidence
that all emeralds are always green.

4

The War on Induction

Whewell Takes on Newton and Mill
(Norton Takes on Everyone)

"The War on Induction" is an expanded version of a Philosophy of Science Association symposium paper presented at the 2008 PSA meeting. I consider and reject William Whewell's attack on the inductivism of Isaac Newton and John Stuart Mill, and John Norton's attack on any system of universal inductive rules. I also explain how a system of inductive rules of the sort proposed by Newton and Mill should be understood.

1. INTRODUCTION

For some time now induction, particularly inductive generalization, has been under siege. A frontal attack, based on the sort of skepticism attributed to Hume, is made by Popper (1959), according to which no inductive generalization can be rationally justified. But other nonskeptical attacks are meant to be just as devastating. For example, it is claimed that good scientists do not use inductive generalization, and that if and when they *appear* to be using such reasoning they are really employing something else, such as "deductive reasoning" (again, Popper), or "inference-to-the-best-explanation" (Harman 1965, Lipton 1991), or statistical reasoning invoking "severe testing" (Mayo 1996). It is also claimed that inductive generalization, as typically characterized, is too incomplete, too vague, or too puerile to adequately express complex and sophisticated scientific reasoning (Whewell 1967). At best it occurs only when one can directly observe instances of a low-level empirical generalization, and it is not applicable to more theoretical science. Finally, some have claimed that although there is such a thing as inductive generalization, contrary to what inductivists believe, it is not subject to formal and universal rules of the sort usually proposed (Norton 2005).

I want to argue that induction, as traditionally formulated by inductivists such as John Stuart Mill and Isaac Newton, can withstand these attacks. Or at least these inductivists can put up a better fight than their opponents might imagine. I will look at a historically important controversy between William Whewell, on the one hand, and Newton and Mill, on the other. Admittedly, all three claim to be endorsing inductive generalization. But Whewell claims that Newton and Mill really got it wrong. The latter are usually thought of as the more typical inductivists, deserving of philosophical scorn, while Whewell is currently more popular with a disparate group who classify him as one of their own, either as a hypothetico-deductivist, or a defender of inference to the best explanation, or a Quinean holist, or even a Kantian a priorist. I propose to defend Mill and Newton against this formidable opponent. I will also defend Mill and Newton against a more recent formidable opponent, John Norton, who goes even further than Whewell in his rejection of inductivists such Mill and Newton.

Mill (1872, p. 188) offers a classic definition of induction:

> Induction, then, is that operation of the mind by which we infer that what we know to be true in a particular case or cases, will be true in all cases which resemble the former in certain assignable respects. In other words, Induction is the process by which we conclude that what is true of certain individuals of a class is true of the whole class, or that what is true at certain times will be true in similar circumstances at all times.[1]

Isaac Newton never explicitly defines "induction" in his works but, like Mill, considers it to be a necessary component of scientific reasoning to general propositions:

> In . . . experimental philosophy, propositions are deduced from the phenomena and are made general by induction. The impenetrability, mobility, and impetus of bodies, and the laws of motion and the law of gravity have been found by this method. (Newton, 1999)

The closest Newton comes to a definition of induction is in rules 3 and 4 in the opening section of book 3 of the *Principia*:

> *Rule 3*: The qualities of bodies that cannot be intended and remitted and that belong to all bodies on which experiments can be made should be taken as qualities of all bodies universally.

> *Rule 4*: In experimental philosophy propositions gathered from phenomena by induction should be considered either exactly or very nearly true

---

1. Later in the text (pp. 386ff.) Mill makes it clear that inductive conclusions can include not just universal generalizations but also what he calls "approximate generalizations" (of the form "Most As are Bs" or "X% of As are Bs"). Indeed, he even allows inductive conclusions to be about the next A to be examined.

notwithstanding any contrary hypotheses, until yet other phenomena make such propositions either more exact or liable to exception.

Newton treats rule 3 as an inductive rule applicable to "qualities of bodies that cannot be intended and remitted."[2]

These two inductive rules are to be used in conjunction with two causal rules:

> *Rule 1*: No more causes of natural things should be admitted than are both true and sufficient to explain their phenomena.
>
> *Rule 2*: Therefore, the causes assigned to natural effects of the same kind must be, so far as possible, the same.

Newton explicitly invokes all four of these rules in deriving the law of universal gravitation in book 3 of the *Principia*. Very briefly, his derivation starts with six phenomena pertaining to the Keplerian motions of the planets and their satellites that he claims have been astronomically established. Arguing from propositions established in book 1 showing that such motions are produced by an inverse square attractive force, and then using his causal rules of reasoning 1 and 2, he concludes that this force is the same force in each case that causes the Keplerian motions of all the planets and their moons. In accordance with his rule 3 of inductive generalization, he infers that all bodies in the universe are subject to this force. Finally, by rule 4, since the law is derived from phenomena by induction, it should be considered true, or at least approximately true, until new phenomena are discovered that show that the law needs modification.

Whewell takes on both Newton and Mill in his works. Chapter 13 of his *The Philosophy of the Inductive Sciences* is devoted to showing what is wrong with each of Newton's four rules and how to substantially reformulate them in Whewellian terms. However, a far greater criticism is reserved for his contemporary Mill in sections of the book that develop his own doctrines of "colligation" and "consilience." I will discuss Whewell's arguments against Newton and Mill, as well as Norton's arguments against all three.

2. WHEWELL VERSUS NEWTON (MOSTLY)

With respect to Newton's first rule, Whewell's complaint is that it is either trivial and uninteresting, or interesting but stifling to science, or else

---

2. The "intension and remission" phrase is a controversial one that commentators differ about; in his first version of the rule Newton omits the phrase and writes simply: "The laws (and properties) of all bodies on which it is possible to institute experiments are laws (and properties) of all bodies whatsoever." (See McGuire 1968, pp. 233–260; and Achinstein 1991, pp. 35–37.)

it is quite simply Whewell's own rule of "consilience," i.e., a rule requiring us to find a cause that explains various classes of phenomena, not just the ones we started with. It is trivial, Whewell says, if it is simply construed as telling us to search for true causes, i.e., ones that exist (should we search for causes that don't exist?), and uninteresting because it doesn't tell how to do this. It is stifling to science if, as Whewell thinks Newton's rule 1 is usually interpreted, it requires us to look for causes only among those "with which we are already familiar." And it is correct only if construed as conforming to Whewell's own ideas of consilience.

I think Newton would and should have a fit with this. His first rule does not say simply "look for true causes," although I suppose it is committed to at least that much. It is clear from Newton's formulation, from his brief discussion following that formulation, and from his actual use of that rule in deriving the law of gravity that Newton has something more in mind, namely, a principle of simplicity: don't infer as true more causes than are needed. Indeed, immediately after formulating the rule, Newton writes: "Nature does nothing in vain, and more causes are in vain when fewer suffice. For nature is simple and does not indulge in the luxury of superfluous causes." Nor, contrary to Whewell, does Newton restrict inferred causes to ones of a type already known to operate—he simply says that if one suffices, don't postulate two, and that effects of the same kind should be assigned to the same cause, not that these causes must be ones already known.

Whewell has the following objection to Newton's rule 2: it doesn't tell us much, since it doesn't tell us how to determine whether effects are "of the same kind." For example, Whewell asks, why take planetary motions to be motions of the same kind as that of

1. bodies "moving freely [i.e., not propelled by a contact force] in a curvilinear path," as Newton did, rather than as that of
2. bodies "swept round by a whirling current," as Descartes did?

Newton has, I would think, two replies. One is a tu quoque. Whewell himself, when he characterizes what he calls the "consilience of inductions," writes that

> But the evidence in favor of our induction is of a much higher and more forcible character when it enables us to explain and determine cases of a *kind different* from those which were contemplated in the formation of our hypothesis. (his emphasis, not mine)

Whewell, like Newton, does not tell us how to determine whether cases are of the same kind or a different one. But this is because the question is an empirical one, not one to be settled a priori in advance for all cases.

This reply is one with which Whewell should agree. Newton's second response would be to reject Whewell's loaded descriptions of the observed effects such as (1) and (2)—"loaded" in that they presuppose something important about the cause being inferred. In the astronomical case, Newton's same "effects," from which he infers a common cause, concern observed Keplerian facts about the orbits of the planets and their satellites and (contra Whewell) not claims such as (1) and (2) about what is, or is not, producing those orbits (whether the cause is a whirling current, or is not a contact force). The effects, *as described by Newton*, are logically compatible with Newton's central force cause, as well as with Cartesian vortices. Which of these causes to infer is an empirical issue. All Newton is claiming, using his rules 1 and 2, is that the orbital Keplerian "effects" being the same all have the same cause, *whatever that is*.

Finally, let me mention what Whewell mainly objects to about Newton's rules 3 and 4. According to Whewell, Newton makes it seem that, independently of any other considerations, anytime we find a common property of bodies in the ones examined, we can generalize to all bodies. But, Whewell insists, "the assertion of the universality of any property of bodies must be grounded upon the reason of the case, and not upon any arbitrary maxim" (such as Whewell takes Newton's rule 3 to be). Whewell's point here is an important one. I believe he is saying, more generally, that inductive generalization is not governed by a formal rule that allows you to infer that all As are Bs simply when all the As you have observed are Bs. In Bacon's words, this is "puerile induction."

Let me discuss this objection by turning to Mill, whom Whewell regards as an even more unenlightened opponent than Newton, at least about scientific methodology. Mill is more explicit about how to respond to Whewell's claim than is Newton, but I think both would respond in the same way.

Recall Mill's definition of induction as "the process by which we conclude that what is true of certain individuals of a class is true of the whole class." Mill does not say, and indeed he explicitly denies, that any induction so defined is justified. Whether it is, he says, depends on "the number and nature of the instances." For Mill, and I think Newton as well, whether a particular inductive inference from "all observed As are Bs" to "all As are Bs" is justified is an empirical issue, not an a priori one. Mill writes that we may need only one observed instance of a chemical fact about a substance to validly generalize to all instances of that substance, whereas many observed instances of black crows are required to generalize about all crows (Mill 1872, pp. 205–206). This is due to the empirical fact that instances of chemical properties of substances tend to be completely uniform, whereas bird coloration, even in the same species, tends not to be.

In making an inductive generalization to a law of nature, Mill requires that we vary the instances and circumstances in which they are obtained in a manner described by his "four methods of experimental inquiry." Whether the instances and circumstances have been varied, and to what extent, is an empirical question, not determined a priori by the fact that all the observed members of the class have some property.

I think it is reasonable to say that Newton, like Mill, is not claiming that any induction from "all observed As are Bs" to "all As are Bs" is valid. For one thing, he never says this. For another, his inductive rule 3 has restrictions, namely, to inductions about bodies and their qualities that "cannot be intended and remitted." On one interpretation offered by Newton commentators, this rule cannot be applied to qualities such as colors or temperatures of bodies. Moreover, Newton, like Mill, defends his third rule by appeal to a principle of uniformity of nature:

> We [should not] depart from the analogy of nature, since nature is always simple and ever consonant with itself.

Newton does not say how he knows nature is "ever consonant with itself," or indeed what this entails. Mill is more explicit, though not completely so. Perhaps a little bit charitably, given his discussion on pages 200–206 of *A System of Logic*, I would take him to be saying at least, and perhaps not more than, this: there are uniformities in nature, i.e., general laws governing various types of phenomena—laws that are inductively and validly inferred, perhaps using Mill's "four methods of experimental inquiry." That such laws exist is for Mill an empirical claim. Suppose that phenomena governed by such laws bear a similarity to others which by induction we infer are governed by some similar set of laws. Then we can use the fact that one set of phenomena is so governed to strengthen the inference to laws regarding the second set. Whether this is Newton's idea as well, indeed whether it is even all of what Mill has in mind, I can't say. But I believe at least that neither Newton nor Mill regarded inductive inferences as subject to a purely formal rule allowing one to validly infer that for any sample and population the former matches the latter.

3. ENTER NORTON

John Norton (2005) argues that there are no valid universal rules of inductive inference at all. He claims that particular inductive inferences are warranted by and only by empirical facts, and not at all by being shown to satisfy some formal schema or template in the manner of formal deductive inferences. I think it is safe to say that he has in his sights

Newton's methodological rules and Mill's ideas about induction, among many others. Indeed, I think that Norton would equally reject Whewell's rules pertaining to consilience and coherence, though he would probably agree with a number of Whewell's charges against Newton and Mill. So while Norton is a friend of particular inductions, he is also a foe of any general inductive principles.

Again I want to take up the challenge to defend Newton and Mill. To begin with, what is the difference between formal rules of the type Norton has in mind in deductive logic and rules of the sort Newton and Mill propose? Are the latter formal in any sense? They can certainly be given what I would regard as a reasonably formal expression. For example, one of Mill's definitions of an inductive inference might be written like this: an inference from a sentence of the form "all observed As are Bs" to one of the form "all As are Bs." However, as I have already emphasized, what is not the case, and what Mill explicitly denies, is that any argument representing an inference of this form that has true premises will have a conclusion that is true or probably true. Mill makes it clear that there are numerous arguments of this form that are really bad.

Similarly, one might express Newton's causal rule 2 as an inference from "e1 and e2 are effects of the same kind" to "e1 and e2 have the same cause." However, what is not the case, as Newton recognizes, is that any argument of this form with a true premise will have a conclusion that is true or probably true. Just think of simple cases, such as uniform motion in a straight line, which can be caused by a pair of forces or by the absence of a force.

Are there any analogies in deductive logic? Consider a type of argument form in deduction called the syllogism. One standard way to define a syllogism is as a deductive argument with two premises and a conclusion, each of which has one of the four categorical forms, A, E, I, and O; the argument contains three terms, a different pair of which occurs in each of the three propositions. Put this way, a syllogism may be valid or invalid, as can readily be determined by a Venn diagram. In other words, there are good and bad syllogisms, all having a formal structure satisfying the formal rule defining a syllogism. Of course, you could define a syllogism as a *valid* argument satisfying the formal definition, in which case there wouldn't be any invalid syllogisms. But then you could do the same for "inductive generalization," defining it as a valid inference of the form "all observed As are Bs, so all As are Bs." Then there would be no invalid inductive generalizations. No one, certainly not Mill, wants to do that.

So I'll just keep the original definition I gave for the syllogism, and point out that for our purposes the important difference between this case and the inductive and causal ones is that whether a syllogism is valid can be

determined entirely by a priori formal means. Whether an inductive generalization, or a causal inference, is valid or reasonable cannot be. In view
of this, how should we understand inductive rules of the sort proposed by
Newton and Mill? One suggestion is to say that while rules of deduction
are exceptionless, rules of induction are just rules of thumb. They have
numerous exceptions, but at the outset at least, when we can't think of
any exceptions at the moment, they are generally to be followed. (This
is Paul Feyerabend's one concession to rationality.) If so, we might write
Mill's idea of inductive generalization as: if all the As you have observed
have been Bs, then, pending exceptions, it is reasonable at the outset at
least to assume that all As are Bs. Similarly, we might think of Newton's
causal rule 2 as something like this: if effects are of the same kind, then,
pending exceptions, it is reasonable at the outset at least to assume they
have the same cause.[3] This would make the rules in question pretty weak
and rather vague—features of rules that I think both Newton and Mill
would prefer to avoid.

I want to suggest a very different way to regard the rules of Newton
and Mill. Let me begin with Mill. When Mill characterizes induction as
"the process by which we conclude that what is true of certain individuals
of a class is true of the whole class," what is he doing? For one thing, as
I have said, he is giving a definition of "induction" or "inductive generalization." And as he himself emphasizes, the definition permits both good
and bad inductions. For another, as I have also said, he is claiming that
whether the induction is good or bad depends on empirical considerations involving the size and variation of the sample, as well as on other
information available. But he is doing something else as well. For Mill,
one of the main aims of science is to "discover and prove" causal laws that
enable one to explain and predict phenomena. Such discovery and proof
requires making inductions to causal generalizations, which is what laws
are for him. Accordingly, in giving what Norton calls a "formal inductive
template" what Mill is doing, among other things, is identifying and characterizing an important type of scientific reasoning. He is not justifying
any particular instance of reasoning of that form by saying that it has that
form—any more than in deductive logic one justifies a particular syllogism by saying that it has the form of a syllogism.

Similarly, when Newton introduces his four methodological rules, he is
at least implicitly claiming that causal reasoning of the sort expressed in

---

3. Newton himself gives some credence to such an interpretation in writing his second
rule as "the causes assigned to natural effects of the same kind must be, so far as possible,
the same." The "so far as possible" clause might suggest this kind of Feyerabendian rule of
thumb interpretation.

rules 1 and 2 and inductive reasoning of the sort expressed in rules 3 and 4 are crucial in establishing propositions in empirical science. To be sure, it would have been possible for Newton the scientist to argue for his law of gravity without explicitly invoking any of his four methodological rules. By invoking them, however, one of the things I take Newton to be doing is attempting to give us a better understanding of, as we might put it, the "logic" of his argument. And that, indeed, might help us to understand the argument and convince us that it is a good one, that its conclusion does in fact follow from the Newtonian "phenomena" cited, and how it does, which indeed was one of Newton's primary concerns.

Look, e.g., at Newton's initial discussion of proposition 5 of book 3.[4] In this discussion he claims that the revolutions of the moons of Jupiter about Jupiter, of the moons of Saturn about Saturn, and of Mercury and Venus and the other known planets are phenomena of the same kind as the revolution of our moon about the earth and therefore (by rule 2) depend on causes of the same kind, especially since it has been proved that the forces on which those revolutions depend are directed toward the centers of Jupiter, Saturn, and the sun, and decrease according to the same ratio and law (in receding from Jupiter, Saturn, and the sun) as the force of gravity (in receding from the earth). Rule 2, to which Newton alludes, is his second rule of reasoning, according to which "the causes assigned to natural effects of the same kind must be, so far as possible, the same." Newton is here characterizing what he is doing as arguing from the same kind of effects to the same unique cause. John Norton is right in saying that the empirical force of the argument comes when Newton argues that these are the same type of effects, namely, that these are all Keplerian motions. Newton is saying that in view of this he can infer that they have causes of the same kind, especially since he has already proved in book 1 that such motions must be governed by central inverse square forces. He is also saying that he is simply arguing from effects of the same kind to causes of the same kind, in accordance with his second rule, which he thinks will help to explain what he is doing. If you want to attack Newton the physicist, argue against his empirical idea that these motions are all Keplerian or that such motions are produced by central inverse-square forces. If you want to attack Newton the methodologist, you need to show that he wasn't making an inference from effects to causes, or that pointing this out in the way that he does is of little if any value.

---

4. Proposition 5 states the moons of Jupiter gravitate toward Jupiter, the moons of Saturn toward Saturn, and the planets toward the sun, and by the force of gravity they are always drawn back from rectilinear motions and kept in curvilinear orbits.

If you think in the latter way, possibly a loose analogy with musicology might help you. The classical sonata has a rather definite formal structure that music theorists teach. It usually has three movements (an allegro, slow movement, and closing presto). In the first movement there is the introductory section, the exposition, the development, the recapitulation, and the coda. And so forth. Simply following this form will not make the resulting sonata good or bad. And, I suppose, it is possible to play a Mozart sonata well without knowing its structure. However, the musicologist helps us to understand what is going on in the sonata by explicitly invoking the formal structure and applying it to the particular sonata. So, perhaps, Newton is helping us to see the formal structure of his argument by appeal to his rules the way the musicologist is helping us to understand the Mozart sonata.

4. IS THERE A BIGGER PAYOFF?

I suggest that this is at least part of what is going on when Newton and Mill propose their methodologies. Norton and the rest of you may agree, but say: "Big deal! We'll give you that. Induction is still local and not formally warranted."

There is, I think, a good deal more here. Newton and Mill are attempting to present very general rules that constitute their "scientific method" for proving propositions in science. Both explicitly reject the hypothetico-deductive method, according to which you prove or confirm a hypothesis by deriving observational predictions from it which are found to be true. What Newton wants instead are what he calls "deductions from the phenomena" that are made general by induction. What Mill wants in cases that involve multiple causal hypotheses is, I think, close to Newton. Mill calls it the "deductive method." It has three steps: first, a series of causal-inductive arguments to the causal laws in question (this requires the use of Mill's methods to determine causation); second, what Mill calls "ratiocination," which involves explaining various phenomena and deriving new predictions from the set of causal laws; third, experimental verification of these predictions. Some comments are in order.

1. The set of rules Mill offers—his methods for determining causation and his "deductive method"—is both universal and abstract, perhaps sufficiently so to merit Norton's epithet "formal template." The same is true, I think, for Newton's rules.

2. Such rules have a bite to them. They are not trivial or uninformative. They tell scientists what to do and not to do in

attempting to prove causal hypotheses in a system. And they go against various other such methodologies, including in particular that of Whewell, since, as Mill notes, Whewell omits the first causal-inductive step. On occasion such rules are explicitly cited against scientists who flout them, as in the case of Newton himself criticizing Descartes' physics for flouting induction from observed phenomena, or Lord Brougham at the beginning of the nineteenth century excoriating Thomas Young for defending the wave theory of light on the basis of no Newtonian inductions to the assumptions of the wave theory and no experimentally confirmed predictions,[5] or in our own time criticisms of string theory by physicists citing methodological grounds similar to those of Newton and Mill.[6]

3. Although these methods are formulated universally and can be expressed in formal terms, they require the use of empirical assumptions to carry out in such a way that the resulting theoretical system is "proved." The causal-inductive inferences in the first step of Mill's "deductive method" need to be justifiable in the light of what is known, the derivations must be correct, and the experiments and instruments used must be appropriate. So even if step 2 can be accomplished by a priori "calculation," steps 1 and 3 need to be secured empirically. Admittedly, the set of rules is not "formal" in the way that formal rules of deductive inference are. But simply because the validity of an inference to the truth or probability of the system of hypotheses cannot be decided entirely a priori by reference to formal structure, it does not follow that the formal structure of the inference pattern plays no justificatory or explanatory role.

There is analogy here between what Mill is doing in the case of inductive inference and what, in the next century, Hempel (1965) did with the concept of scientific explanation. Hempel formulated a set of conditions, which included both formal ones (he called them "logical") and material ones (he called them "empirical") for his two models of explanation: deductive-nomological and inductive-statistical. Both have formal requirements pertaining to types of premises (singular and general), empirical character, and type of logical connection between premises and conclusion. And both have material conditions involving requirements of truth and/or empirical confirmation. For Hempel both sorts of requirements must be satisfied to have

5. See Achinstein (1991).
6. See Woit (2006) and Smolin (2006).

a correct or justified scientific explanation. What Mill is claiming for scientific inference is that satisfying the formal requirements of his "deductive method," which calls for causal-inductive inferences of certain forms, calculation, and derivations of certain types, is a necessary condition for proving the truth of the theoretical system "beyond reasonable doubt." He is also claiming that satisfying the material requirements of his conditions—i.e., making empirically justified causal-inductive inferences and empirically established predictions—is another necessary condition for proof "beyond reasonable doubt."

4. None of this means that in constructing an empirical "proof" of the sort Mill or Newton had in mind one must explicitly invoke or appeal to the three steps outlined by Mill in his "deductive method," or to the four rules of Newton at the beginning of the third book of his *Principia*. But the same is true in a deductive proof: in constructing such a proof one need not invoke or appeal to any of the formal principles of deduction that logicians love to classify and explicitly use. One cannot conclude from this that the principles, in either the deductive or the inductive case, have no justificatory force.

5. Finally, none of this precludes peaceful coexistence with physically indeterministic systems of the sort John Norton describes. In his dome example a point mass is initially motionless at the apex and can slide at any time in any radial direction without any disturbance at the apex. The physics of the situation as described by Newton's equations of motion admits various solutions in such a way that we can say only what is possible, not what will happen or will probably happen. And this is not a matter of our ignorance, but of the world. If so, and if, following Newton's own methodology, we agree that Newton's equations of motion are established inductively, then we have a situation in which, using inductively supported laws, we show that we cannot predict with certainty or probability what the motion of the point mass will be. It's not that induction fails for this example. It works very well. It tells us that the particular physical situation is such that it is impossible to predict with certainty or probability when, where, or if the point mass will move; it gives us only possibilities. Of course, if you are a "crazy Bayesy" you will demand a degree of belief, i.e., a probability, for every proposition. Newton was a bit crazy, but neither he, nor Mill, nor John Norton is a Bayesian.

5. WHEWELL VERSUS MILL: ARE INDUCTIVE PREMISES RESTRICTED TO SIMPLE OBSERVATIONS?

I will return now to Whewell and deal with several important charges leveled by him against Mill (and implicitly against Newton as well) that were not discussed earlier. I will also examine Mill's actual and possible replies. Understanding this debate between Whewell and Mill goes a long way toward understanding later skepticism about the role or importance of inductive generalization.[7]

Whewell writes:

> Induction is familiarly spoken of as the process by which we collect a *general proposition* from a number of *particular cases*; and it appears to be frequently imagined that the general proposition results from a mere juxtaposition of the cases, or at most, from merely conjoining and extending them. But if we consider the process more closely . . . we shall perceive that this is an inadequate account of the matter. The particular facts are not merely brought together, but there is a new element added to the combination by the very act of thought by which they are combined. There is a conception of the mind introduced in the general proposition, which did not exist in any of the observed facts.[8]

Whewell claims that to think of inductive generalization as something that merely goes from particular cases to a general proposition, or from the composition of a sample to that of a population, is to omit an extremely important aspect of such reasoning, that is, "the act of *invention* which is requisite in every inductive inference."

For example, when in book 3 of the *Principia* Newton makes an inductive generalization to his universal law of gravity from the six phenomena he cites plus his theorems proved in book 1, one of the most important parts, the part that represents the heart of the discovery, is the attribution of a central inverse-square force continually drawing the planets and their satellites away from rectilinear motion. The existence of such a force for each planet and satellite was not a simple observation, but itself a conclusion that required the mind to impose the conception of a central inverse-square force on observed planets and satellites. This process, in which "we bind together facts by superinducing upon them a new conception," Whewell calls "colligation." It is, he thinks, required in a scientific induction; it is crucial for understanding what goes on when an induction is made; it is something omitted in standard accounts of inductive reasoning, such as those given by Newton and Mill; and without

---

7. For vehement skepticism, see Peirce (1960) and Hanson (1958).
8. Whewell (1967, vol. 2, p. 213).

it inductions are restricted to simple observational generalization of the "all crows are black" variety.

I take Whewell to be saying, then, that it is only by recognizing that the mind imposes a conception on what is observed that we can understand how inferences can be made to unobservables. Mill's inductions, which do not introduce such an idea, are confined to generalizations about observables.

I will examine two related claims Whewell makes and Mill's responses to them. The first, discussed in the remainder of this section, involves Whewell's charge against Mill that inductive premises of the sort invoked by Newton (in which it is claimed that an inverse-square force acts on each of the planets) cannot be established by simple observation. The second, to be treated in the following section, involves Whewell's claim, contra Mill, that inductive premises are not mere descriptions of the data.

There is no incompatibility between Whewell's ideas about colligation and Mill's definition of induction, nor between Whewellian colligation and Newton's inductive rule 3. One can accept Mill's definition and Newton's rule 3 (given in section 1), while subscribing to Whewell's view that in determining what is true of certain individuals or at certain times, or what qualities observable bodies have, the mind introduces a conception (e.g., inverse-square force) not in the facts. One could even claim, with Whewell, that when an inductive generalization is made in science this step is often the most original and important. Perhaps recognizing that each of the known planets and satellites is drawn away from rectilinear motion by an inverse-square force was the most original and difficult part for Newton; perhaps generalizing to all bodies was simple. Admitting this, however, does nothing to weaken Mill's definition of induction or Newton's rule 3. Nor does it mean that the general proposition inductively inferred is unimportant. Newton's claim that all bodies in the universe are subject to the same inverse-square attractive force— induced from the claim that all the planets and their satellites are subject to such a force—is one of the boldest and most original scientific claims ever made. Nor does saying that Mill's definition of induction and Newton's rule 3 are compatible with Whewell's ideas about colligation mean that either Mill or Newton would have to accept those ideas. (In the next section I will return to this.)

When Whewell claims that Newton imposed a conception of an inverse-square force acting on bodies in the solar system, and that Kepler imposed a conception of an ellipse on the observed positions of Mars (a claim Mill focuses on in his discussion), one of the things Whewell may be saying is this: Newton could not observe this force in the way that one can feel an impact on one's own body, and Kepler could not observe the elliptical path of Mars in the way that one can observe the elliptical path of a model train around the track. Newton's force and Kepler's elliptical path had to be inferred from other observations, together with various empirical assumptions, using a good deal of mathematics. This can be granted without in any way denying that Newton made an inductive generalization from an inverse-square force operating on known planets and satellites to its operating on all bodies, or that Kepler made an inductive generalization from a fact about the orbit of Mars to a claim about the orbits of all the planets. Inductive generalization, as defined by Mill and as employed by Newton, does not require that the facts from which such a generalization is inferred be "directly observable" without inference.

Nevertheless, Whewell has a legitimate complaint against Mill. Although Mill's *definitions* of induction do not require inferences only from what is "directly observable," some of Mill's discussions of the definitions, for example his discussion of Kepler, suggest otherwise.[9] In the latter case Mill makes it sound as if he is saying that the fact that the successive positions of Mars lie on an ellipse can be determined by "direct observation" without inference. This is certainly not true in the case of Kepler (as Whewell himself emphasizes). Since the Martian orbit with respect to the sun had to be determined from observations made not on the sun but on the moving earth, Kepler in fact attempted to calculate directions of sides in an earth-sun-Mars triangle on the basis of observations of the earth-Mars line. Establishing an elliptical orbit for Mars was an intricate task, involving *among other things* inferences from the positions of Mars observed from the earth. If, despite his definition of induction, Mill believed that induction can be made only from facts themselves ascertained solely by observation without inference, then Whewell's complaint in this regard would be legitimate.

Despite passages from Mill that seem to suggest such a simple view of induction, Mill does not in fact believe this is so. He writes that

> in many branches of science single facts have to be proved, as well as [general] principles; facts as completely individual as any that are debated in a court of justice. . . . A remarkable example of this is afforded by astronomy.[10]

9. For example:
The object of Kepler was to determine the real path described by each of the planets, or let us say by the planet Mars. . . . To do this there was no other mode than that of direct observation; and all which observation could do was to ascertain a great number of the successive places of the planet, or rather, of its apparent places. That the planet occupied successively all these positions, or at all events, positions which produced the same impressions on the eye, and that it passed from one of these insensibly, without any apparent breach of continuity; this much the senses, with the aid of proper instruments, could ascertain. (Mill 1872, 191–192).

10. Mill (1872, p. 187).

Mill's examples are the magnitudes of particular bodies in the solar system, their mutual distances, the shape of the earth, and its rotation. He writes:

> scarcely any of them [is] accessible to our means of direct observation: they are proved directly by the aid of inductions founded on other facts which we can more easily reach.

He cites the determination of the distance of the moon from the earth—summarizing the "circuitous process" by which this was determined. Mill's point here is that these "particular facts" are themselves inferred from others using inductions.[11] Once established, however, they can then form the basis for inductive generalizations.

On Newton's view many of the "phenomena" which form the basis for an inductive generalization are not directly observed but are themselves inferred from other phenomena. For example, Newton's phenomenon 3 states that

> The orbits of the five primary planets—Mercury, Venus, Mars, Jupiter, and Saturn—encircle the sun.

Newton infers this proposition from the observed phases of these planets.

6. WHEWELL VERSUS MILL: ARE INDUCTIVE PREMISES MERE DESCRIPTIONS OF THE DATA?

A second, related claim that Whewell makes against Mill is that inductive premises are not mere descriptions or summaries of the data. According to Whewell, Kepler's ascription of an "elliptical orbit" to Mars is an induction. According to Mill, it is not but simply a summary of the observed data, which he calls a description.

I suggest that the disputants here are referring to different things. Mill is counting the following claim as a description and not an inductive generalization:

> M: All observed points of Mars lie on an ellipse.

11. Mill (1872, p. 186) writes that:
the process of indirectly ascertaining individual facts is as truly inductive as that by which we establish general truths. But it is not a different kind of induction; it is a form of the very same process: since . . . whenever the evidence which we derive from observation of known cases justifies us in drawing an inference respecting even one unknown case, we should on the same evidence be justified in drawing a similar inference with respect to a whole class of cases.

Mill calls this a summary of separate observations. More generally, if we note that all the observed data points in a given experiment lie on a given curve, Mill is saying, we are simply summarizing the observed data by "obtaining a representation of the phenomena as a whole, by combining, or as we may say, piecing these detached fragments together." For Mill this is not an inductive conclusion because the claim is not that all the points—both observed and unobserved—lie on the curve. Indeed, as far as the descriptive or summarizing claim is concerned, there are many different representations of the observed data points; many different curves are satisfied by these points.[12]

What Whewell is claiming is an inductive conclusion is not M as shown previously but

W: The orbit of Mars is an ellipse.

Whewell makes it clear that by the "orbit of Mars" he means the orbit consisting of both observed and unobserved points in the orbit.[13] Accordingly, Whewell is not claiming that Mill's (M) is an inductive conclusion, nor is Mill denying that Whewell's (W) is an inductive conclusion (since it is a generalization from observed points to all points). Mill wants to call (M) a description of observed facts, whereas Whewell rejects this because it does not recognize that Mars moves in an orbit.

There are several points of disagreement here. One, mentioned earlier, is that Mill's talk of "describing" and "summarizing" the observed data makes it sound as if the description or summary can always be directly read off the data without reasoning or calculation. Whewell, by contrast, rejects this idea: the description of the observed positions of Mars as lying on an ellipse is "given, not by the phenomena, but by the mind." Mill (1872, p. 199) responds by agreeing with Whewell's claim that Kepler's statement that the observed positions lie on an ellipse "was not the sum of the observations *merely*; it was the sum of the observations *seen under a new point of view*. But it was not the sum of *more* than the observations."

Whatever Mill intended here, he need not have committed himself to the view that a "description" or "summary" of observed data requires some direct "reading off" of the description from the data—without any

12. "Different descriptions therefore may all be true, but not surely different explanations." Mill (1872, p. 196).

13. "Of course, in Kepler's Induction, of which I speak, . . . all this is included in speaking of the *orbit* of Mars: a continuous line, a periodical motion, are implied by the term *orbit*. I am unable to see what would remain of Kepler's discovery, if we take from it these conditions. It would not only not be an induction, but it would not be a description, for it would not recognize that Mars moved in an orbit." Whewell (1967, p. 248).

reasoning or calculation.[14] Suppose I record some data points from an experiment to determine how a physical quantity y changes with another physical quantity x. I make three observations. One way to describe or summarize the observed data is to give three pairs of numbers, in which the first represents an observed value for quantity x and the second a corresponding observed value for y. For example:

Description 1: The three observed points are (1,7), (2,10), (3,13).

Another way to describe or summarize the observed data is as follows:

Description 2: The three observed points in which the x-values are 1, 2, and 3 all lie on the linear curve y = 3x + 4.

Description 2 requires calculation and reasoning in a way that description 1 does not, or at least it requires more such reasoning and calculation. Description 2 might well be spoken of as summarizing the observations reported in description 1 "under a new point of view"—one that requires the mind to go beyond what is "directly observable." Mill should be willing to concede this point to Whewell.[15]

Even with such a concession, however, there remains a significant difference in the approach of Mill and Whewell toward induction as a process of reasoning. Mill wants to claim that (M) represents a crucial step in the inductive process—one in which Kepler represents the observed positions of Mars using a concept (such as that of an elliptical orbit) *in a way that does not make a generalized claim*: it does not make a claim about the unobserved positions of Mars or about Mars's continuing

---

14. Hanson (1958, p. 84) accuses both Mill and Whewell of misdescribing Kepler's inference, which Hanson takes to be one from "explicanda" to "explicans":

> Of this monumental reasoning from *explicanda* to *explicans*, could any account be more ludicrous than that of J. S. Mill, who argued that Kepler's law is just "a compendious expression for the one set of directly observed facts"? Mill had no real experience of theoretical astronomy. . . . Whewell is rightly uneasy about Mill's account. His alternative account, however, turns on Kepler's having got the hypothesis as a "colligating concept." This is little better than the modern hypothetico-deductive account which has it that Kepler succeeded "by thinking of general hypotheses from which particular consequences are deduced which can be tested by observation."

> Hanson, I suggest, oversimplifies both Mill and Whewell.

15. Laura Snyder (2006, p. 63) insists that for Whewell, the "selection of an appropriate conception" for the data involves inferences and is "not a matter of mere observation." Mill, I suggest, will agree by saying that certain "conceptions" (i.e., descriptions of the data) will require inferences (for example, description 2), while others will not and can be more or less just "read off" from the data (perhaps description 1). Mill's point, however, will be (or should be) that inferences such as the one used to obtain description 2 are not inductive generalizations.

to take an elliptical path.[16] Whewell, by contrast, seems to be denying this step in the induction. Given the observed positions of Mars, he appears to be saying that what Kepler did was apply the concept ellipse to the orbit of Mars, i.e., to the unobserved as well as the observed positions. In other words, Mill claims that Kepler's reasoning involves these steps:

(1) Here are the observed (relative) positions of Mars.
(2) All of these positions lie on an ellipse.
(3) Therefore, all the positions of Mars lie on an ellipse; i.e., the orbit is elliptical.

For Mill, step 2 is not an inductive generalization since it makes no commitment concerning the unobserved points. It is simply one (of possibly many) representation of the data in (1). By contrast, Whewell seeks to omit step (2), going directly from (1) to (3), since, on his view, the mind supplies the concept "elliptical orbit," which it imposes on all the points whether observed or unobserved. Mill is saying that it is possible to represent the observations by using the concept ellipse, as he does in step (2), without making an inductive generalization. If Whewell is denying this, then, on this issue, I side with Mill: (2) does not entail or presuppose (3); (2) is establishable without observing any elliptical orbit.

Moreover, representing the observed positions noted in (1) as Mill does in (2) allows Mill to characterize inductive reasoning as "a process by which we conclude that what is true of certain individuals in a class is true of the whole class." Going directly from step (1) to step (3), as Whewell does, allows him to characterize induction as a process of going from facts about particulars, *whether or not these facts are represented by propositions of the form "all observed As are Bs,"* to a general proposition. Whewell (1967, pp. 239–240) says that he agrees with Mill when the latter characterizes induction as "the operation of discovering and forming general propositions" and also as "generalization from experience." What Whewell wants to do, however, is include among inductions inferences from particulars, *however the latter are characterized*, to a general proposition. Mill will insist that such inferences can be called inductive only when the information about the particulars is, or can be, put in the form of a "description," such as (2).

16. Mill (1872, p. 192) makes it clear that the latter two claims, by contrast to claim (M), are inductions:

> The only real induction concerned in the case consisted in inferring that because the observed places of Mars were correctly represented by points in an imaginary ellipse, therefore, Mars would continue to revolve in that same ellipse; and in concluding (before the gap had been filled by further observations) that the positions of the planet during the time which intervened between two observations, must have coincided with the intermediate points of the curve.

Is this simply a difference in terminology—Mill using the term "induction" only for cases that are, or can be, put into the form he wants and Whewell using the term more broadly? It is a difference in terminology, but one that, I think, reflects a difference in viewpoint about induction. Unless one is able to express an inductive inference to a generalization so as to include a premise such as (2), Mill is saying, we may be unable to see the connection between a premise such as (1) and the conclusion (3). Why should these observed relative positions of Mars justify the claim that the Martian orbit is elliptical? The answer is supplied by premise (2).

Even more important, Mill would say, characterizing induction the way Whewell has done, and even imposing Whewell's crucial "consilience" condition for defending the conclusion of an induction, will not suffice to produce an argument whose premises justify its conclusion. Without the establishment of a descriptive premise such as (2) we can construct invalid arguments that are inductive in Whewell's sense and that seem to satisfy his requirements. Here are two examples:

(A) Mars has been observed to exhibit phases, like the moon.
    Therefore,
    The Martian orbit is elliptical.
(B) Bodies have been observed to fall toward the earth with approximately uniform acceleration. .
    Therefore,
    All bodies in the universe attract each other in accordance with an inverse-square force.

In both cases the premise concerns "particulars" that have been observed. The premise and conclusion are true. And Whewell's requirements for a good induction appear to be satisfied (the conclusion can be used to explain and predict a range of facts in addition to the ones reported in the premise). The problem, Mill would say, is that in each case the premise does not warrant the conclusion. What is missing in both is a suitable description of numerous instances of items satisfying the general conclusion (e.g., in (B) instances of bodies attracting each other with an inverse-square force).

7. HOLISM

This leads to the most important difference between Mill and Whewell regarding induction. Whewell seems committed to some fairly strong form of *holism* regarding inductive reasoning; Mill is not. For Whewell, a conclusion drawn from phenomena using inductive reasoning will not be an isolated one but will be part of a larger system of hypotheses and described phenomena, which will need to be considered in determining the merits of the particular inductive conclusion. Consilience requires not just that the conclusion drawn from a set of phenomena explain those phenomena, but that it explain and/or predict a range of different sorts of phenomena, particularly ones of a type not used to generate that conclusion in the first place. And such explanations and predictions will normally require the use of numbers of hypotheses in addition to the one that may be of interest.[17]

Now there are two holistic positions Whewell might be taking regarding the role of consilience with respect to inductive reasoning:

1. The premises of an inductive argument provide a strong reason to believe the conclusion of the argument if and only if there is a system containing the premises and conclusion that is consilient, that is, that can explain and predict a range of phenomena of different types.

2. ("Duhem-Quine holism") That which is justified is not an individual hypothesis but an entire system of hypotheses. And that which justifies is not an individual phenomenon (or its description) but an entire system of phenomena. If and only if consilience is satisfied with respect to this set of phenomena, then it is the system that is justified. The inductive inference is from the set of phenomena to the system of hypotheses, not from an individual phenomenon to a single hypothesis.

Both of these positions have consequences that an inductivist such as Mill will reject. The first position results in arguments being counted as good or justified ones which seem clearly not to be so—e.g., (A) and (B) in the previous section. These are arguments in which the premises do not supply a good reason for believing the conclusion even though there is a system of hypotheses containing the premises and conclusion that is consilient.

The second position results in entirely rejecting inductive arguments of the sort Mill and Newton have in mind. On this position one cannot

---

17. Such a system tends to change over time as new phenomena are observed and new hypotheses introduced. If in the process the resulting system can explain and predict the new phenomena, and do so in ways that are not complex or ad hoc, then Whewell regards the system as having the highest degree of believability. In other writings I have referred to this as Whewell's "coherence" condition. It is, as Whewell himself notes, essentially "consilience over time," since it introduces the idea that a set of hypotheses must be judged not just "statically" on the basis of how successful they are at the moment, but "dynamically" as well, by considering the history of success of the developing system. This is very different from the "static" evaluations of Newton and Mill. However, in what follows I will consider only "static" evaluations, requiring consilience at a given time.

make a valid inductive inference from any ("isolated") phenomenon or set to some ("isolated") hypothesis. Consider a passage from book 3 of Newton's *Principia* in which he explicitly endorses an inductive inference from the fact ("phenomenon") that bodies on or near the earth gravitate toward the earth, that the moon gravitates toward the earth, that our sea gravitates toward the moon, and that the planets gravitate toward one another, to the proposition that all bodies gravitate toward one another. On position (2) such an inference cannot be made, since it is not holistic. This position amounts to a rejection of Newton's inductive rule 3, and indeed of any inductive generalization that is not a generalization to an entire system of hypotheses (in Newton's case, e.g., a generalization to a set of hypotheses including, in addition to the universal law of gravity, his three laws of motion and perhaps his claims regarding space and time in book 1). Position (2) amounts to a rejection of inductive generalization as customarily understood.

Inductivists such as Mill and Newton can accept a much weaker but I think more plausible position which might be called "modest (or very modest) holism":

3. (Modest holism): Whether and how much an induction involving the claim that all observed As are Bs supports the inductive conclusion that all As are Bs usually depends on empirical facts not reported in the inductive premise—facts that may be assumed within some system that can be appealed to in defending the inductive generalization.

Is this altogether too modest? Who would deny it? Well, Carnap (1962) would, for example. For him, whether and how much inductive premises support or confirm an inductive conclusion is an a priori matter that depends on a logical relationship between premises, conclusion, and the linguistic system in which these are expressed. Of course, the modest holism position seems far too modest for Whewell.

Finally, given Whewell's holism, construed in either of the stronger senses, and given Mill's rejection of it, I think we can better understand one of the most interesting but intractable elements in the debate between the two. Earlier I mentioned that Mill declared inductive generalization to be a necessary first stage in a process he called the "deductive method." The second stage of the process he calls "ratiocination," which involves combining the laws inductively inferred and producing deductive explanations and predictions. The third stage, verification, involves empirical testing of the predictions generated.

Now Mill claims that Whewell omits the first stage in the process, the induction to the laws in the system. He simply has the scientist making a conjecture by imposing some conception on nature. As far as reasoning is concerned, Mill claims, Whewell simply has the second and third stages, the ratiocination and the verification, and even if we impose the Whewellian idea of consilience on the resulting scientific theory, an argument to its truth or probability will be unjustified. Mill claims that without the inductive step (in his sense) there may be an incompatible set of hypotheses which also explain and predict the phenomena and are equally consilient. This is Mill's famous "competing hypothesis" objection, and it is one that Newton also urged against hypothetico-deductivists. Their claim is that with the first inductive step (which for both Mill and Newton could include reasoning generalizing from effects to causes) we eliminate, or at least render improbable, alternative explanations; without it we don't. Whewell's claim is that consilience suffices for this purpose. Indeed, Whewell adds, he knows of no theory in the history of science which was consilient (over time) that turned out to be false.

I won't try to resolve this "competing hypothesis" debate here. But I will mention one of Whewell's favorite examples, the classical wave theory of light, which he claimed must be true because it completely satisfies his criterion. Mill refused to accept this theory at a time when it was almost universally accepted by physicists. He did so because there was no causal-inductive argument to the existence of the luminiferous ether needed to support the waves. And he remarked (1872, p. 328):

> an hypothesis of this kind is not to be received as probably true because it accounts for all the known phenomena, since this is a condition sometimes fulfilled tolerably well by two conflicting hypotheses; while there are probably many others which are equally possible, but which, for want of anything analogous in our experience, our minds are unfitted to conceive.

Nor, Mill believes, will this problem be solved by adding the further Whewellian condition of consilience. Historically, of course, Mill turned out to be right: the quantum theory of light was just such a theory that mid-nineteenth-century minds were "unfitted to conceive." Whether Mill was logically or methodologically right here, I'll leave for another occasion.

REFERENCES

Achinstein, P. (1991), *Particles and Waves* (New York: Oxford University Press).

Achinstein, P., ed. (2005), *Scientific Evidence: Philosophical Theories and Applications* (Baltimore: Johns Hopkins University Press).

Carnap, R. (1962), *Logical Foundations of Probability*, 2nd ed. (Chicago: University of Chicago Press).

Hanson, N. R. (1958), *Patterns of Discovery* (Cambridge, England: Cambridge University Press).

Harman, G. (1965), "The Inference to the Best Explanation," *Philosophical Review* 74.

Hempel, C. G. (1965), *Aspects of Scientific Explanation* (New York: Free Press).

Lipton, P. (1991), *Inference to the Best Explanation* (London: Routledge).

Mayo, D. (1996), *Error and the Growth of Experimental Knowledge* (Chicago: University of Chicago Press).

McGuire, J. E. (1968), "The Origins of Newton's Doctrine of Essential Qualities," *Centaurus* 12, 233–260.

Mill, J. S. (1872), *A System of Logic, Ratiocinative and Inductive*, 8th ed. (London: Longmans).

Newton, I. (1999), *The Principia: Mathematical Principles of Natural Philosophy*, trans. Cohen and Whitman (Berkeley: University of California Press).

Norton, J. (2005), "A Little Survey of Induction," in Achinstein (2005).

Peirce, C. (1960), *Collected Papers*, Hartshorne and Weiss, eds. (Cambridge, Mass.: Harvard University Press).

Popper, K. (1959), *The Logic of Scientific Discovery* (New York: Basic Books).

Smolin, L. (2006), *The Trouble with Physics: The Rise of String Theory, the Fall of a Science, and What Comes Next* (New York: Houghton Mifflin).

Snyder, L. (2006), *Reforming Philosophy: A Victorian Debate on Science and Society* (Chicago: University of Chicago Press).

Whewell, W. (1967), *The Philosophy of the Inductive Sciences* (New York: Johnson Reprint Corp.; reprinted from the 1847 ed.).

Woit. P. (2006), *Not Even Wrong: The Failure of String Theory and the Search for the Unity in Physics* (New York: Basic Books).

5

Waves and the Scientific Method

"Waves and Scientific Method" is reprinted by permission from
Philosophy of Science Association Symposium Proceedings *(1992),*
193–204. I show how nineteenth-century physicists argued for the wave
theory of light, and explain how their reasoning is best understood in
inductive-probabilistic terms.

1. INTRODUCTION

In 1802 a youthful Thomas Young, British physician and scientist, had the
audacity to resuscitate the wave theory of light (Young 1802). For this he was
excoriated by Henry Brougham (1803) in the *Edinburgh Review*. Brougham,
a defender of the Newtonian particle theory, asserted that Young's paper
was "destitute of every species of merit" because it was not based on inductions from observations but involved simply the formulation of hypotheses
to explain various optical phenomena. And, Brougham continued:

> A discovery in mathematics, or a successful induction of facts, when once
> completed, cannot be too soon given to the world. But . . . an hypothesis is a
> work of fancy, useless in science, and fit only for the amusement of a vacant
> hour. (1803, p. 451)

This dramatic confrontation between Young and Brougham, it has been
claimed, is but one example of a general methodological gulf between
19th-century wave theorists and 18th-and 19th-century particle theorists. The wave theorists, it has been urged by Larry Laudan (1981) and
Geoffrey Cantor (1975), employed a method of hypothesis in defending
their theory. This method was firmly rejected by particle theorists, who
insisted, with Brougham, that the only way to proceed in physics is to
make inductions from observations and experiments.

In Achinstein (1991), I argue, contra Laudan and Cantor, that 19th-
century wave theorists, both in their practice and in their philosophical

reflections on that practice, employed a method that is different from the method of hypothesis in important respects; moreover, there are strong similarities between the method the wave theorists practiced and preached and that of 19th-century particle theorists such as Brougham and David Brewster. In this chapter, I will focus just on the wave theorists. My aims are these: to review my claims about how in fact wave theorists typically argued for their theory; to see whether, or to what extent, this form of reasoning corresponds to the method of hypothesis or to inductivism in sophisticated versions of these doctrines offered by William Whewell and John Stuart Mill; and finally to deal with a problem of anomalies which I did not develop in *Particles and Waves* and might be said to pose a difficulty for my account.

2. THE METHOD OF HYPOTHESIS AND INDUCTIVISM

According to a simple version of the method of hypothesis, if the observed phenomena are explained by, or derived from, an hypothesis, then one may infer the truth or probability of that hypothesis. Laudan maintains that by the 1830s an important shift occurred in the use of this method. An hypothesis was inferable not simply if it explained known phenomena that prompted it in the first place, but only if it also explained and/or predicted phenomena of a kind different from those it was invented to explain. This version received its most sophisticated formulation in the works of William Whewell, a defender of the wave theory. In what follows I will employ Whewell's version of the method of hypothesis as a foil for my discussion of the wave theorist's argument.

Whewell (1967, pp. 60–74) offered four conditions which, if satisfied, will make an hypothesis inferable with virtual certainty. First, it should explain all the phenomena which initially prompted it. Second, it should predict new phenomena. Third, it should explain and/or predict phenomena of a "kind different from those which were contemplated in the formation of . . . [the] hypothesis" (p. 65). If this third condition is satisfied Whewell says that there is a "consilience of inductions." Whewell's fourth condition derives from the idea that hypotheses are part of a theoretical system the components of which are not framed all at once, but are developed over time. The condition is that as the theoretical system evolves it becomes simpler and more coherent.

Since both Laudan and Cantor claim that the wave theorists followed the method of hypothesis while the particle theorists rejected this method in favor of inductivism, it will be useful to contrast Whewell's version of the former with Mill's account of the latter. This contrast should be of special interest for two reasons. Both Whewell and Mill discuss the wave theory, which Whewell supports and Mill rejects; and each criticizes the other's methodology.

One of the best places to note the contrast in Mill is in his discussion of the "deductive method" (which he distinguishes from the "hypothetical method" or method of hypothesis) (Mill 1959, pp. 299–305). Mill asserts that the deductive method is to be used in situations where causes subject to various laws operate, in other words, in solving typical problems in physics as well as other sciences. It consists of three steps. First, there is a direct induction from observed phenomena to the various causes and laws governing them. Mill defines induction as "the process by which we conclude that what is true of certain individuals of a class is true of the whole class, or that what is true at certain times will be true in similar circumstances at all times" (p. 188). This concept of inductive generalization is used together with his four famous canons of causal inquiry to infer the causes operating and the laws that govern them. The second part of the deductive method Mill calls "ratiocination." It is a process of calculation, deduction, or explanation: from the causes and laws we calculate what effects will follow. Third, and finally, there is "verification": "the conclusions [derived by ratiocination] must be found, on careful comparison, to accord with the result of direct observation wherever it can be had" (p. 303).

Now, in rejecting the method of hypothesis, Mill writes:

> The Hypothetical Method suppresses the first of the three steps, the induction to ascertain the law, and contents itself with the other two operations, ratiocination and verification, the law which is reasoned from being assumed instead of proved. (p. 323)

Mill's major objection to the method of hypothesis is that various conflicting hypotheses are possible from which the phenomena can be derived and verified. In his discussion of the wave theory of light, Mill rejects the hypothesis of the luminiferous ether on these grounds. He writes:

> This supposition cannot be looked upon as more than a conjecture; the existence of the ether still rests on the possibility of deducing from its assumed laws a considerable number of actual phenomena. . . . most thinkers of any degree of sobriety allow, that an hypothesis of this kind is not to be received as probably true because it accounts for all the known phenomena, since this is a condition sometimes fulfilled tolerably well by two conflicting hypotheses; while there are probably many others which are equally possible, but which, for want of anything analogous in our experience, our minds are unfitted to conceive. (p. 328)

With Whewell's ideas about prediction and consilience in mind, Mill continues:

> But it seems to be thought that an hypothesis of the sort in question is entitled to a more favourable reception if, besides accounting for all the facts

previously known it has led to the anticipation and prediction of others which experience afterwards verified. . . . Such predictions and their fulfill-ment are, indeed, well calculated to impress the uninformed, whose faith in science rests solely on similar coincidences between its prophecies and what comes to pass. . . . Though twenty such coincidences should occur they would not prove the reality of the undulatory ether. . . . (pp. 328–329)

Although in these passages Mill does not discuss Whewell's ideas about coherence and the evolution of theories, it is clear that Mill would not regard Whewell's four conditions as sufficient to infer an hypothesis with virtual certainty or even high probability. The reason is that Whewell's conditions omit the first crucial step of the deductive method, the induc-tion to the causes and laws.

If Laudan and Cantor are correct in saying that nineteenth-century wave theorists followed the method of hypothesis and rejected inductiv-ism, then, as these opposing methodologies are formulated by Whewell and Mill, this would mean the following: Nineteenth-century wave theo-rists argued for the virtual certainty or high probability of their theory by first assuming, without argument, various hypotheses of the wave theory; then showing how these will not only explain the known optical phe-nomena but will explain and/or predict ones of a kind different from those prompting the wave hypotheses in the first place; and finally arguing that as the theory has evolved it has become simpler and more coherent. Is this an adequate picture? Or, in addition, did wave theorists employ a crucial inductive step to their hypotheses at the outset? Or do neither of these methodologies adequately reflect the wave theorists' argument?

3. THE WAVE THEORISTS' ARGUMENT

Nineteenth-century wave theorists frequently employed the following strategy in defense of their theory.

1. Start with the assumption that light consists either in a wave
   motion transmitted through a rare, elastic medium pervading the
   universe, or in a stream of particles emanating from luminous
   bodies. Thomas Young (1845) in his 1807 Lectures, Fresnel (1816)
   in his prize essay on diffraction, John Herschel (1845) in an 1827
   review article of 246 pages, and Humphrey Lloyd (1834) in a 119-
   page review article,[1] all begin with this assumption in presentations
   of the wave theory.

1. Reprinted in Lloyd (1877). In what follows page references will be to this.

2. Show how each theory explains various optical phenomena, including the rectilinear propagation of light, reflection, refraction, diffraction, Newton's rings, polarization, and so on.

3. Argue that in explaining one or more of these phenomena the particle theory introduces improbable auxiliary hypotheses but the wave theory does not. For example, light is diffracted by small obstacles and forms bands both inside and outside the shadow. To explain diffraction particle theorists postulate both attractive and repulsive forces emanating from the obstacle and acting at a distance on the particles of light so as to turn some of them away from the shadow and others into it. Wave theories such as Young and Fresnel argue that the existence of such forces is very improbable. By contrast, diffraction is explainable from the wave theory (on the basis of Huygens's principle that each point in a wave front can be considered a source of waves), without the introduction of any new improbable assumptions. Similar arguments are given for several other optical phenomena, including interference and the constant velocity of light.

4. Conclude from steps 1 through 3 that the wave theory is true, or very probably true.

This represents, albeit sketchily, the overall structure of the argument. More details are needed before seeing whether, or to what extent, it conforms to Whewell's conditions or Mill's. But even before supplying such details we can see that the strategy is not simply to present a positive argument for the wave theory via an induction to its hypotheses and/or by showing that it can explain various optical phenomena. Whether it does these things or not, the argument depends crucially on showing that the rival particle theory has serious problems.

To be sure, neither Whewell's methodology nor Mill's precludes comparative judgments. For example, Whewell explicitly claims that the wave theory is more consilient and coherent than the particle theory. And Mill (who believed that neither theory satisfied his crucial inductive step) could in principle allow the possibility that new phenomena could be discovered, permitting an induction to one theory but not the other. I simply want to stress at the outset that the argument strategy of the wave theorists, as I have outlined it so far, is essentially comparative. The aim is to show at least that the wave theory is better, or more probable, than the rival particle theory.

Is the wave theorist's argument intended to be stronger than that? I believe that it is. Thomas Young, both in his 1802 and 1803 Bakerian lectures (reprinted in Crew 1900), makes it clear that he is attempting to show that hitherto performed experiments, and analogies with sound, and passages in Newton, provide strong support for the wave theory, not merely that the wave theory is better supported than its rival. A similar attitude is taken by Fresnel, whose aim is not simply to show that the wave theory is better in certain respects than the particle theory, but that it is acceptable because it can explain various phenomena, including diffraction, without introducing improbable assumptions; by contrast, the particle theory is not acceptable, since it cannot. Even review articles are not simply comparative. Although he does compare the merits of the wave and particle theories in his 1834 report, Humphrey Lloyd makes it clear that this comparison leads him to assert the truth of the wave theory. In that theory, he claims:

> there is thus established that connexion and harmony in its parts which is the never failing attribute of truth. . . . It may be confidently said that it possesses characters which no false theory ever possessed before. (1877, p. 79)[2]

Let us now look more closely at the three steps of the argument leading to the conclusion. Wave theorists who make the assumption that light consists either of waves or particles do not do so simply in order to see what follows. They offer reasons, which are generally of two sorts. First, there is an argument from authority: "Leading physicists support one or the other assumption." Second, there is an argument from some observed property of light. For example, Lloyd notes that light travels in space from one point to another with a finite velocity, and that in nature one observes motion from one point to another occurring by the motion of a body or by vibrations of a medium.

Whatever one might think of the validity of these arguments, I suggest that they were being offered in support of the assumption that light consists either of waves or of particles. This is not a mere supposition. Argument from authority was no stranger to optical theorists of this period. Young in his 1802 paper explicitly appeals to passages in Newton in defense of three of his four basic assumptions. And Brougham, a particle theorist, defends his theory in part also by appeal to the authority and

---

2. Herschel in his (1845) does not take as strong a position as Lloyd, although there are passages in which he says that the wave theory is confirmed by experiments (e.g., pp. 473, 486). In his later work he is even more positive. For example:

> It may happen (and it has happened in the case of the undulatory doctrine of light) that such a weight of analogy and probability may become accumulated on the side of an hypothesis that we are compelled to admit one of two things; either that it is an actual statement of what really passes in nature, or that the reality, whatever it be, must run so close a parallel with it, as to admit of expression common to both, at least as far as the phenomena actually known are concerned. (Herschel 1987, pp. 196–197).

success of Newton. Moreover, the second argument, if not the first, can reasonably be interpreted as an induction in Mill's sense, i.e., as claiming that all observed cases of finite motion are due to particles or waves, so in all probability this one is too.[3]

I suggest, then, that wave theorists offered grounds for supposing it to be very probable that light consists either of waves or particles. I will write their claim as

$$p(W \text{ or } P/O\&b) \approx 1, \tag{1}$$

where W is the wave theory, P is the particle theory, O includes certain observed facts about light including its finite motion, and b is background information including facts about modes of travel in other cases. ($\approx$ means "is close to.")

This is the first step in the earlier argument. I will postpone discussion of the second step for a moment, and turn to the third. Here the wave theorists assert that in order to explain various optical phenomena the rival particle theorists introduce improbable auxiliary hypotheses. By contrast, the wave theorists can explain these phenomena without introducing auxiliary hypotheses, or at least any that are improbable. Why are the particle theorists' auxiliary hypotheses improbable? And even if they are, how does this cast doubt on the central assumptions of the particle theory?

Let us return to diffraction, which particle theorists explained by the auxiliary hypothesis that attractive and repulsive forces emanate from the diffracting obstacle and act at a distance on the light particles, bending some into the shadow and others away from it. By experiment Fresnel showed that the observed diffraction patterns do not vary with the mass or shape of the diffracting body. But known attractive and repulsive forces exerted by bodies do vary with the mass and shape of the body. So Fresnel concludes that the existence of such forces of diffraction is highly improbable. Again it seems plausible to construe this argument as an inductive one, making an inference from properties of known forces to what should be (but is not) a property of the newly postulated ones. Fresnel's experiments together with observations of other known forces provide inductive reasons for concluding that the particle theorists' auxiliary assumption about attractive and repulsive forces is highly improbable.

---

3. Although Mill defines induction as involving an inference from observed members of a class to the whole class, he clearly includes inferences to other unobserved members of the class. He writes: "It is true that (as already shown) the process of indirectly ascertaining individual facts is as truly inductive as that by which we establish general truths. But it is not a different kind of induction; it is a form of the same process . . . ." (Mill 1959, p. 186).

Even if this is so, how would it show that other assumptions of the particle theory are improbable? It would if the probability of the auxiliary force assumption given the other assumptions of the particle theory is much, much greater than the probability of this auxiliary assumption not given the rest of the particle theory, i.e., if

$$p(A/P\&O\&b) \gg p(A/O\&b), \tag{2}$$

where A is the auxiliary assumption, O includes information about diffraction patterns and Fresnel's experimental result that these do not vary with the mass or shape of the diffractor, b includes information about other known forces, and $\gg$ means "is much, much greater than." If this condition is satisfied, it is provable that the other assumptions of the particle theory have a probability close to zero,[4] i.e.,

$$p(P/O\&b) \approx 0. \tag{3}$$

Although wave theorists did not explicitly argue for (2) above, they clearly had grounds for doing so. If by the particle theory P light consists of particles subject to Newton's laws, and if by observational results O light is diffracted from its rectilinear path, then by Newton's first law a force or set of forces must be acting on the light particles. Since the light is being diffracted in the vicinity of the obstacle, it is highly probable that this obstacle is exerting a force or forces on the light particles. That is, with the assumptions of the particle theory, auxiliary hypothesis A is very probable. However, without these assumptions the situation is very different. Without them the fact that other known forces vary with the mass and shape of the body exerting the force, but diffraction patterns do not, makes it unlikely that such forces exist in the case of diffraction. Or at least their existence is much, much more likely on the assumption that light consists of particles obeying Newton's laws than without such an assumption, i.e., (2) above. An important part of the argument here is inductive, based as it is on information about other mechanical forces.

From (1) and (3) we infer:

$$p(W/O\&b) \approx 1, \tag{4}$$

that is, the probability of the wave theory is close to 1, given the background information and certain optical phenomena, including diffraction.

---

4. For a proof see Achinstein 1991, pp. 85–8. It might be noted that the introduction of an auxiliary assumption with very low probability does not by itself suffice to show that the other assumptions of the theory are highly improbable.

Now we can return to the second step of the original argument, the one in which the wave theorist shows that his theory can explain a range of optical phenomena, not just the finite velocity of light and diffraction. What inferential value does this have? The wave theorist wants to show that his theory is probable not just given some limited selection of optical phenomena but given all known optical phenomena. This he can do if he can explain these phenomena by deriving them from his theory. Where $O_1, \ldots, O_n$ represent known optical phenomena other than diffraction and the constant velocity of light—including rectilinear propagation, reflection, refraction, and interference—if the wave theorist can derive these from his theory, then the probability of that theory will be at least sustained if not increased. This is a simple fact about probabilities.

Accordingly, the explanatory step in which the wave theorist derives various optical phenomena $O_1, \ldots, O_n$ from his theory permits an inference from (4) above to:

$$p(W/O_1, \ldots, O_n \& O \& b) \approx 1, \tag{5}$$

i.e., the high probability of the wave theory given a wide range of observed optical phenomena. This is the conclusion of the wave theorist's argument.

If the explanation of known optical phenomena sustains the high probability of the wave theory without increasing it, does this mean that such phenomena fail to constitute evidence for the wave theory? Not at all. According to a theory of evidence I have developed (see chapter 1), optical phenomena can count as evidence for the wave theory even if they do not increase its probability. I reject the usual increase-in-probability account of evidence in favor of conditions that require the high probability of the theory T given the putative evidence O_i, and the high probability of an explanatory connection between T and O_i, given T and O_i. Both conditions are satisfied in the case of the wave theory.

In formulating the steps of the argument in the probabilistic manner above, I have clearly gone beyond what wave theorists say. For one thing, they do not appeal to probability in the way I have done. More importantly perhaps, while they argue that auxiliary hypotheses of the particle theorists are very improbable, they do not say that these assumptions are much more probable given the rest of the particle theory than without it. The following points are, I think, reasonably clear. (i) Wave theorists suppose that it is very likely that the wave or the particle theory is true, an assumption for which they have arguments. (ii) They argue against the particle theory by criticizing auxiliary assumptions of that theory, which introduce forces (or whatever) that violate inductively supported principles.

(iii) Wave theorists argue that their theory can explain various optical phenomena without introducing any such questionable assumptions. (iv) Their reasoning, although eliminative, is different from typical eliminative reasoning; their first step is not to canvass all possible theories of light, but only two, for which they give arguments; their reasoning is not of the typical eliminative form "these are the only possible explanations of optical phenomena, all of which but one lead to difficulties." Reconstructing the wave theorists' argument in the probabilistic way I have done captures these four points. Whether it introduces too many fanciful ideas is a question I leave for my critics.

Is the argument Whewellian or Millian? It does satisfy the first three of Whewell's conditions. It invokes the fact that various optical phenomena are derived from the wave theory. These include ones that prompted the theory in the first place (rectilinear propagation, reflection, and refraction), hitherto unobserved phenomena that were predicted (e.g., the Poisson spot in diffraction), and phenomena of a kind different from those that prompted it (e.g., diffraction, interference, polarization). The argument does not, however, satisfy Whewell's fourth condition. It does not appeal to the historical tendency of the theory over time to become simpler and more coherent. But the latter is not what divides Whewell from Mill. Nor is it Whewell's first three conditions, each of which Mill allows for in the ratiocinative part of his deductive method. Mill's claim is only that Whewell's conditions are not sufficient to establish the truth or high probability of an hypothesis. They omit the crucial first step, the inductive one to the hypothesized causes and laws.

As I have reconstructed the wave theorists' argument, an appeal to the explanatory power of the theory is a part, but not the whole, of the reasoning. There is also reasoning of a type that Mill would call inductive. It enters at two points. It is used to argue that light is most probably composed either of waves or of particles (e.g., the "finite motion" argument of Lloyd). And it is used to show that light is probably not composed of particles, since auxiliary hypotheses introduced to explain various optical phenomena are very improbable. This improbability is established by inductive generalization (e.g., in the case of diffraction, by inductively generalizing from what observations and experiments show about diffraction effects, and from what they show about forces). My claims are that wave theorists did in fact employ such inductive reasoning; that with it the argument that I have constructed is valid; and that without it the argument is invalid, or at least an appeal to Whewell's explanatory conditions is not sufficient to establish the high probability of the theory (though this last claim requires much more than I say here; see Achinstein 1991, Essay 4).

4. EXPLANATORY ANOMALIES

One objection critics of my account may raise is that it does not do justice to explanatory anomalies in the wave theory. That theory was not able to explain all known optical phenomena. Herschel (1845), e.g., notes dispersion as one such phenomenon—the fact that different colors are refracted at different angles. Now the wave theorist wants to show that his theory is probable given all known optical phenomena, not just some favorable subset. But if dispersion is not derivable from the theory, and if there is no inductive argument from dispersion to that theory, then on the account I offer, the wave theorist cannot reach his desired conclusion. He can say only that his theory is probable given other optical phenomena. And he can take a wait-and-see attitude with respect to the unexplained ones. This is essentially what Herschel himself does in the case of dispersion.[5]

Let me now say how wave theorists could in principle deal with such anomalies that relate to the probabilistic reconstruction I offer. The suggestion I will make is, I think, implicit in their writings, if not explicit. And interestingly, it is a response that combines certain Whewellian and Millian ideas. In what follows, I restrict the anomalies to phenomena which have not yet been derived from the wave theory by itself or from that theory together with auxiliary assumptions whose probability is very much greater given the wave theory than without it.

As Cantor notes in his very informative book *Optics after Newton*:

> Probably the central, and certainly the most repeated, claim [by the 1830's] was that in comparison with its rival the wave theory was more successful in explaining optical phenomena. (Cantor 1983, p. 192)

Cantor goes on to cite a table constructed in 1833 by Baden Powell, a wave theorist, listing 23 optical phenomena and evaluating the explanations proposed by wave and particle theories as "perfect," "imperfect," or "none." In the no-explanation category there are 12 entries for the particle theory and only 2 for the wave theory; while there are 18 "perfects" for the wave theory and only 5 for the particle theory.

Appealing, then, to the explanatory success of the wave theory, a very simple argument is this:

---

5. Herschel writes: "We hold it better to state it [the difficulty in explaining dispersion] in its broadest terms, and call on the reader to suspend his condemnation of the doctrine for what it apparently will not explain, till he has become acquainted with the immense variety and complication of the phenomena which it will. The fact is, that neither the corpuscular nor the undulatory, nor any other system which has yet been devised, will furnish that complete and satisfactory explanation of all the phenomena of light which is desirable" (Herschel 1845, p. 450).

Optical phenomena $O_1, \ldots, O_n$ can be coherently
   explained by the wave theory.
O is another optical phenomenon.   (6)
   So probably
O can be coherently explained by the wave theory.

By a "coherent" explanation I follow what I take to be Whewell's idea: either the phenomenon is explained from the theory without introducing any additional assumptions, or if they are introduced they cohere both with the theory and with other known phenomena. In particular, no auxiliary assumption is introduced whose probability given the theory is very high but whose probability on the phenomena alone is low. Or, more generally, no such assumption is employed whose probability on the theory is very much greater than its probability without it.

Commenting on argument (6), the particle theorist might offer a similar argument to the conclusion that the particle theory can also explain O. But this does not vitiate the previous argument. For one thing, by the 1830s, even though Powell's table was not constructed by a neutral observer, it was generally agreed that the number of optical phenomena known to be coherently explainable by the wave theory was considerably greater than the number explainable by the particle theory. So the wave theorist's argument for his conclusion would be stronger than the particle theorist's for his. But even more importantly, the conclusion of the argument is only that O can be coherently explained by the wave theory, not that it cannot be coherently explained by the particle theory. This is not eliminative reasoning.

Argument (6) might be construed in Millian terms as inductive: concluding "that what is true of certain individuals of a class is true of the whole class," and hence of any other particular individual in that class (Mill 1959, p. 188; see note 3 here). Mill's definition is quite general and seems to permit an inference from the explanatory success of a theory to its continued explanatory success. Indeed, in his discussion of the wave theory he notes that "if the laws of propagation of light accord with those of the vibrations of an elastic fluid in as many respects as is necessary to make the hypothesis afford a correct expression of all or most of the phenomena known at the time, it is nothing strange that they should accord with each other in one respect more" (Mill 1959, p. 329). Mill seems to endorse this reasoning. What he objects to is concluding from it that the explanation is true or probable.

Argument (6) might also be construed as exhibiting certain Whewellian features. Whewell stresses the idea that a theory is a historical entity which changes over time and can "tend to simplicity and harmony." One of the important aspects of this tendency is that "the elements which we require for explaining a new class of facts are already contained in our system." He explicitly cites the wave theory, by contrast to the particle theory, as exhibiting this tendency. Accordingly, it seems reasonable to suppose that it will be able to coherently explain some hitherto unexplained optical phenomenon. The important difference between Whewell and Mill in this connection is not over whether the previous explanatory argument (6) is valid, but over whether from the continued explanatory success of the wave theory one can infer its truth. For Whewell one can; for Mill one cannot.

Let me assume, then, that some such argument as (6) was at least implicit in the wave theorists' thinking and that it would have been endorsed by both Mill and Whewell. How, if at all, can it be used to supplement the probabilistic reconstruction of the wave theorists' argument that I offer earlier in the chapter? More specifically, how does it relate to the question of determining the probability of the wave theory given all the known optical phenomena, not just some subset?

The conclusion of the explanatory success argument (6) is that the wave theory coherently explains optical phenomenon O. This conclusion is made probable by the fact that the wave theory coherently explains optical phenomena $O_1, \ldots, O_n$.

Accordingly, we have:

$$p(W \text{ coherently explains optical phenomenon } O / \\ W \text{ coherently explains optical phenomena } O_1, \ldots, O_n) > k \qquad (7)$$

where k is some threshold of high probability, and W is the wave theory. If we construe such explanations as deductive, then

$$\text{"}W \text{ coherently explains } O\text{" entails that } p(W/O\&O_1, \ldots, O_n) \geq \\ p(W/O_1, \ldots, O_n) \qquad (8)$$

So from (7) and (8) we get the second-order probability statement

$$p(p(W/O\&O_1, \ldots, O_n) \geq p(W/O_1, \ldots, O_n)/W \text{ coherently} \\ \text{explains } O_1, \ldots, O_n) > k \qquad (9)$$

But the conclusion of the wave theorists' argument is

$$p(W/O_1, \ldots, O_n) \approx 1, \qquad (10)$$

where $O_1, \ldots, O_n$ includes all those phenomena for which the wave theorist supplies a coherent explanation (I suppress reference to background information here). If we add (10) to the conditional side of (9), then from (9) we get

$$p(p(W/O\&O_1,\ldots,O_n) \approx 1/W \text{ coherently explains } O_1,\ldots,O_n$$
$$\text{and } p(W/O_1,\ldots,O_n) \approx 1) > k. \tag{11}$$

This says that, given that the wave theory coherently explains optical phenomena $O_1, \ldots, O_n$, and that the probability of the wave theory is close to 1 on these phenomena, the probability is high that the wave theory's probability is close to 1 given O—the hitherto unexplained optical phenomenon—together with the other explained phenomena. If we put all the known but hitherto unexplained optical phenomena into O, then we can conclude that the probability is high that the wave theory's probability is close to 1 given all the known optical phenomena.

How is this to be understood? Suppose we construe the probabilities here as representing degrees of reasonableness of belief (see addendum to chapter 1). Then the first-order probability can be understood as representing how reasonable it is to believe W; while the second-order probability is interpreted as representing how reasonable it is to believe it is so reasonable. This, of course, does not permit the wave theorist to conclude that $p(W/O\&O_1, \ldots, O_n) \approx 1$, i.e., that the probability of the wave theory on all known optical phenomena—explained and unexplained—is close to 1. But it does permit him to say something stronger than simply that his theory is probable given a partial set of known optical phenomena. It goes beyond a wait-and-see attitude with respect to the unexplained phenomena.

REFERENCES

Achinstein, P. (1983), *The Nature of Explanation*. New York: Oxford University Press.
Achinstein, P. (1991), *Particles and Waves*. New York: Oxford University Press.
Brougham, H. (1803), *Edinburgh Review* 1, 451ff.
Cantor, G. (1975), "The Reception of the Wave Theory of Light in Britain," *Historical Studies in the Physical Sciences* 6, 109–132.
Cantor, G. (1983), *Optics after Newton*. Manchester: Manchester University Press.
Crew, H. (ed.) (1990). *The Wave Theory of Light*. New York: American Book Co.
Fresnel, A (1816), "Memoir on the Diffraction of Light," reprinted in Crew (1900), 79–144.
Herschel, J. (1845), "Light," *Encyclopedia Metropolitana*.
Herschel, J. (1987), *A Preliminary Discourse on the Study of Natural Philosophy*. Chicago: University of Chicago Press.
Laudan, L. (1981), " The Medium and its Message," in *Conceptions of the Ether*, G. Cantor and M. Hodge (eds.). Cambridge: Cambridge University Press.

Lloyd, H. (1834), "Report on the Progress and Present State of Physical Optics," *Reports of the British Association for the Advancement of Science*, 297ff.

Lloyd, H. (1877), *Miscellaneous Papers*. London: Longmans, Green.

Mill, J. (1959), *A System of Logic*. London: Longmans, Green.

Whewell, W. (1967), *The Philosophy of the Inductive Sciences*, vol. 2. New York: Johnson Reprint.

Young, T. (1802), "On the Theory of Light and Colors," reprinted in *Crew* (1900), 45–61.

Young, T. (1845), *A Course of Lectures on Natural Philosophy and the Mechanical Arts*. London: Taylor and Walton.

Part II

EXPLANATION

6

An Illocutionary Theory of Explanation

"An Illocutionary Theory of Explanation" is reprinted by permission from my The Nature of Explanation *(Oxford University Press, 1983), 1, 6–19, 23–28, 42–56. I argue that one must understand the concept of explanation in terms of an illocutionary act of explaining, for which I provide a general account. Material in section 3 on "Understanding and content" presupposes definitions introduced in chapter 1, section 9.*

1. CONDITIONS FOR AN ACT OF EXPLAINING

Explaining is what Austin calls an illocutionary act.[1] Like warning and promising, it is typically performed by uttering words in certain contexts with appropriate intentions. It is to be distinguished from what Austin calls perlocutionary acts, such as enlightening someone, or getting someone to understand, or removing someone's puzzlement, which are the effects one's act of explaining can have upon the thoughts and beliefs of others.

The illocutionary character of explaining can be exposed by formulating a set of conditions for performing such an act. To do so I shall consider sentences of the form "S explains q by uttering u," in which S denotes some person, q expresses an indirect question, and u is a sentence. (I will assume that any sentence of this form in which q is not an indirect question is transformable into one that is.)[2]

The first condition expresses what I take to be a fundamental relationship between explaining and understanding. It is that S explains q by uttering u only if

(1) S utters u with the intention that his utterance of u render q understandable.

---

1. J. l., Austin, *How To Do Things with Words* (Oxford, 1962). Austin includes "explain" on his list of "expositives," pp. 160–161.
2. In Section 5, the field will be broadened to include cases in which u is not a complete sentence.

This expresses the central point of S's act. It is the most important feature which distinguishes explaining from other illocutionary acts, even ones that can have indirect questions as objects. If by uttering u I am asking you, or agreeing with you about, why the tides occur, by contrast to explaining it, I will not be doing so with the intention that my utterance render why the tides occur understandable. (I shall return to the concept of understanding in section 2 after formulating the remaining conditions.)

To explain q is not to utter just anything with the intention that the utterance render q understandable. Suppose I believe that the words "truth is beauty" are so causally efficacious with you that the mere uttering of them will cause you to understand anything, including why the tides occur. By uttering these words I have not thereby explained why the tides occur, even if I have satisfied (1). The reason is that I do not believe that "truth is beauty" expresses a correct answer to the question "Why do the tides occur?" More generally, assuming that answers to questions are propositions, we may say that S explains q by uttering u only if

(2) S believes that u expresses a proposition that is a correct answer to Q. (Q is the direct form of the question whose indirect form is q.)

Often people will present hints, clues, or instructions which do not themselves answer the question but enable an answer to be found by others. To the question "Why do the tides occur?" I might respond: "Look it up in chapter 10 of your physics text," or "Newton's *Principia* has the answer," or "Think of gravity." Some hints, no doubt, border on being answers to the question. But in those cases where they do not, it is not completely appropriate to speak of explaining. By uttering "Look it up in chapter 10 of your physics text" I am not explaining why the tides occur, though I am uttering something which, I believe, will put you in a position to explain this.

These conditions are not yet sufficient. Suppose that S intends that his utterance of u render q understandable not by producing the knowledge that u expresses a correct answer to Q but by causing people to come to think of some nonequivalent sentence u' which, like u, S believes expresses a proposition that is a correct answer to Q. In such a case, although S utters something which he believes will cause others to be able to explain q, S does not himself explain q by uttering u. For example, to an audience that I believe already knows that the tides occur because of gravitational attraction, I say

u: The tides occur because of gravitational attraction of the sort described by Newton.

Although I believe that u does express a correct answer to Q (Why do the tides occur?), suppose that I utter u with the following intention: that this utterance will render q understandable not by producing the knowledge of the proposition expressed by u that it is a correct answer to Q, but by causing my audience to look up the more detailed and precise answer actually supplied by Newton, which I don't present. This is like the situation in which I give the audience a hint that in this case is a correct answer, but is not the answer in virtue of which I intend q to be understandable to that audience.

To preclude such cases we can say that S explains q by uttering u only if

> (3) S utters u with the intention that his utterance of u render q understand-able by producing the knowledge, of the proposition expressed by u, that it is a correct answer to Q.

In the case of the tides, I do not intend that my utterance of u render q understandable by producing the knowledge *of the proposition expressed by u* that it is a correct answer to Q, but by producing such knowledge with respect to another proposition. So, according to condition (3), in such a case by uttering u I am not explaining why the tides occur.

Suppose, by contrast, I know that my audience is familiar with the answer supplied by Newton, but its members have no idea whether this answer is correct. Since the audience knows what sort of gravitational attraction Newton describes, I might explain why the tides occur, simply by uttering u. In this case I intend to render q understandable by producing the knowledge, of the proposition expressed by u, that it is a correct answer to Q. It is possible for me to have this intention with respect to u since I know that the audience is aware of the sort of gravitational attraction described by Newton.

Let us change the example once more. Suppose I believe that the audience does not know that the tides are due to gravitational attraction. I now proceed to utter u above with the intention that my utterance of u will render q understandable by the following combination of means (which I regard as jointly but not separately sufficient for rendering q understandable): (i) producing the knowledge, of the proposition expressed by u, that it is a correct answer to Q; and (ii) causing others to look up some different, more detailed, proposition (supplied by Newton) which is also a correct answer to Q. By uttering u am I explaining why the tides occur?

One might be inclined to say that I am *both* explaining q by uttering u *and* giving a clue about where to find another answer to Q. If this is correct, then (3) should be understood in a way that allows S to intend to render q understandable by a combination of means that includes producing the knowledge, of the proposition expressed by u, that it is a correct answer to Q. On the other hand, in the case just envisaged one might be tempted to say that I am doing something that falls between explaining and giving clues but is not exactly either. If this is correct, then (3) should be understood in a way that requires S to intend to render q understandable *solely* by producing the knowledge, of the proposition expressed by u, that it is a correct answer to Q. I am inclined to regard the latter interpretation of (3) as preferable, but I will not press the point. (This, of course, does not preclude S from explaining q by formulating a number of different propositions whose conjunction constitutes an answer to Q, or from engaging in several acts in which different, though not necessarily competing, answers to Q are provided.)

In section 5, some further conditions (involving restrictions on q and u) will be suggested whose formulation requires concepts to be introduced later. For the present I shall treat these three conditions as not only necessary but jointly sufficient. If so, then the same honor can be accorded to (3) by itself, since (3) entails both (1) and (2).

Although "explain" may be used in describing an act governed by these conditions, it can also be employed in a more restricted way to cover only correct explainings. We can say that Galileo explained why the tides occur, even though he did so incorrectly, or that he failed to explain this, even though he tried. When one has correctly explained q by uttering u one has performed the illocutionary act of explaining q and in doing so one has provided a correct answer to Q. In what follows, however, when reference is made to acts of explaining I shall mean acts for which this is not a requirement. (See chapter 1, section 8, for an account of "correct explanation.")

2. UNDERSTANDING AND KNOWLEDGE-STATES

Explaining q has been defined as uttering something with the intention of rendering q understandable (in a certain way). A theory of explaining, however, that invokes an undefined notion of understanding does not take us far enough. Much of the discussion that follows is devoted to formulating an account of understanding that will complement the conditions for explaining and allow us to develop the concept of an explanation (product) and that of a good explanation later (see chapter 7).

Since explaining involves an intention to render q understandable—where q is an indirect question—I shall be concerned with cases of understanding where q is also an indirect question. Such understanding I take to be a form of knowledge.[3] One understands q only if one knows a correct answer to Q which one knows to be correct. Using quantificational notation, we can say that a necessary condition for the truth of sentences of the form "A understands q" is

(1) (∃x)(A knows of x that it is a correct answer to Q).

If A satisfies this condition, I shall say that A is in a *knowledge-state* with respect to Q. This condition involves a *de re* sense of knowing. (In the *de re*, by contrast with the *de dicto*, sense, from "A knows of x that it is P," and "x = y," we may infer "A knows of y that it is P.") I am construing an answer to a question as a proposition, and *de re* knowledge of a proposition as involving an "acquaintance" with it (a knowledge of its content). There are several points to be made about knowledge states. First, being in such a state is not simply knowing that there is some proposition that is a correct answer to Q. It is not defined simply as

A knows that (∃x)(x is a correct answer to Q),

for this could be true even if A fails to know any correct answer to Q.

Second, being in a knowledge-state with respect to Q entails that Q has a correct answer; therefore, so does understanding q. If there is no correct answer to Q, if, e.g., Q is based on a false presupposition, then understanding q is an impossibility. One cannot understand why helium is the lightest element, since it isn't.

Finally, it is not sufficient that A know of (i.e., be acquainted with) an answer to Q which happens to be correct. A speaker who claims that he does not understand how a certain accident occurred might ask: Was it caused by the slippery road, did the driver fall asleep, was there a blowout, or what? Suppose that, unbeknownst to the speaker, the slippery road did cause the accident. The mere fact the he knows of an answer that happens to be correct is not sufficient to say that he understands. What he does not know of this answer is that *it is correct*, and this is necessary for understanding. Condition (1) is a strong one for understanding, and it might be denied. If A knows of no answers to Q at all, or only incorrect ones, then we might be willing to follow (1) and deny that A understands q. But (1) makes the stronger claim that A knows of some answer to Q that it is correct. Suppose that the police believe, but do not know, that the accident was caused by the slippery road. And suppose that their belief is correct. If (1) is a necessary condition for understanding, we cannot say that the police understand what caused the accident. This

---

3. Not all forms of understanding are amenable to the "understand q" context or are forms of knowledge—e.g., "understand that" in the sense roughly of "take it as a fact that."

seems odd, since they can produce what they believe to be, and is, a correct answer to Q.

Nevertheless, I suggest that this refusal is justified. If the police suspect, but do not yet know, that the accident was caused by the slippery road, then, although they are well on the way toward understanding what caused the accident, they are not yet in the position of someone who does understand it. Their failure to be in this position derives not from the fact that they have yet to find a correct answer, but from the fact that they have yet to achieve a required epistemic state with respect to that answer, namely, one of knowing that it is correct. To be sure, if the police believe correctly, but do not know, that the accident was caused by the slippery road, then it could be misleading to deny that they understand what caused the accident. This is because we would not be giving the whole truth, only part of it, regarding their epistemic situation. To avoid misleading the audience what might be said is that the police do not yet understand what caused the accident, although they believe it was the slippery road.

On the other hand, our definition of a knowledge-state may be accused of being too weak for understanding. Suppose that A once heard a correct answer to Q which he can no longer remember. However, he knows that the answer he heard is correct. Therefore, he is in a knowledge-state with respect to Q, despite the fact that he cannot remember a correct answer to Q. But surely if A is to be said to understand q he cannot be in this position.

My reply is that in the case envisaged A is not in a knowledge-state with respect to Q, although he once was. At one time, but not now, he was acquainted with a correct answer to Q. He does now know that the answer he once knew is correct. His situation can be described by saying that

> $(\exists x)$(A knew of x that it is a correct answer to Q), and A knows that
> $(\exists x)$(x is a correct answer to Q).

But it is not the case that

> $(\exists x)$(A knows of x that it is a correct answer to Q).

3. UNDERSTANDING AND CONTENT

We are now in a position to return to understanding. It is my contention that A understands q only if A knows a correct answer to Q *which is a complete content-giving proposition with respect to* Q. (For a definition of this concept see chapter 1, section 9.) That is, A understands q only if

> (1) $(\exists p)$(A knows of p that it is a correct answer to Q, and p is a complete content-giving proposition with respect to Q).

Thus, one who knows of the proposition

(2) The reason that Nero fiddled is that he was happy

that it is a correct answer to

(3) Why did Nero fiddle?

satisfies this condition for understanding why Nero fiddled, since (2) is a complete content-giving proposition with respect to (3). By contrast, one who knows the truth of

(4) The reason that Nero fiddled is difficult to grasp

does not thereby understand why Nero fiddled. For one thing, (4) is not a correct answer to (3). For another, (4) is not a complete content-giving proposition with respect to (3).

Let me mention four other cases in which (1) is violated. First, consider the question

(5) How high is the Matterhorn?

and the proposition

(6) The height of the Matterhorn is 14,700 feet.

Someone might know of (6) that it is a correct answer to (5). Moreover, proposition (6) is expressible by a sentence obtained from a complete answer form for (5)—"The height of the Matterhorn is _____"—by filling the blank with a number plus a term for a distance. Nevertheless, (6) is not a complete content-giving proposition with respect to (5), since it is not a content-giving proposition (for the concept expressed by "height"). (The sentence "The height of the Matterhorn is 14,700 feet" violates all the conditions for content-giving sentences given in section 9.) Therefore, someone could not be said to understand how high the Matterhorn is in virtue of the fact that he knows of (6) that it is a correct answer to (5). By contrast, one who knows of (6) that it is a correct answer to (5) can be said to know how high the Matterhorn is. In general, knowing q, by contrast with understanding q, does not require knowledge of content-giving propositions.

Second, consider the question

(7) What execution is now occurring?

and the proposition

(8) The execution now occurring (alternatively: the event now occurring that is an execution) is the one that is being covered by the Associated Press.

Someone might know of (8) that it is a correct answer to (7). Yet it seems wrong to conclude that, in virtue of this, such a person understands what execution is now occurring. And, indeed, (1) thwarts such a conclusion, since (8) is not a complete content-giving proposition with respect to (7).

For a third violation of (1), consider the question

(9) What caused the explosion?

and the true proposition

(10) The cause of the explosion is what caused the explosion.

For the sake of argument, let us suppose that (10) can be counted as a correct answer to (9). Proposition (10) is expressible by a sentence obtained from a complete answer form for (9)—"The cause of the explosion is _____"—by filling the blank; and "cause" is a content-noun. But surely we would deny that someone who knows of (10) that it is a correct answer to (9) in virtue of this fact understands (or even knows) what caused the explosion. Such a denial is indeed justified by condition (1) for understanding. Proposition (10) is not a complete content-giving one with respect to (9). For one thing, it is not expressible by a content-giving sentence for "cause." ("What caused the explosion" in (10) is not a nominal.) For another, (10) is presupposed by (9).

Suppose that knowing of p that it is a correct answer to Q does not suffice for understanding q. Can we conclude that q is not understandable? Of course not. (9) is understandable—one can understand what caused the explosion. The point is just that one cannot understand this in virtue of knowing of (10) that it is a correct answer to (9). Indeed, condition (1) does not even preclude someone from understanding (7), namely, what execution is now occurring. "The event now occurring that is an execution is the killing of the prince" expresses a complete content-giving proposition with respect to (7). One who knows of this proposition that it is true satisfies condition (1) for understanding. We cannot, of course, conclude that such knowledge entails understanding, since condition (1) is not being claimed to be sufficient. (See the last part of section 6.)

Finally, it might be objected, it will be possible for p to be a complete content-giving proposition with respect to Q when p and Q are expressed in one way but not another. Consider

(11) What person was elected U.S. president in 1980?

On my account the proposition expressed by the sentence

(12) The person who was elected U.S. president in 1980 is Reagan

is not a complete content-giving proposition with respect to (11). By contrast, with respect to

(13) What outcome of the 1980 U.S. presidential election obtained?

the sentence

(14) An outcome of the 1980 U.S. presidential election is that Reagan was elected

expresses a complete content-giving proposition. But, it seems, (11) and (13) express the same question, and (12) and (14) the same proposition.

More generally, there will be questions expressed without content-nouns that are expressible using such nouns. Thus, "What number will win the lottery?" can be rephrased as "What will be the *result* of the lottery?"; "Will it rain today" as "What *possibility* concerning its raining today will actually obtain?"; and so forth.

My response is twofold. First, if a question and answer are expressible in such a way that the latter is shown to be a complete content-giving proposition with respect to the former, then we do have a candidate for understanding. But, second, I am dubious that these cases are illustrations of this. In particular, e.g., I am dubious that interrogative sentences (11) and (13) express the same question. (13) is broader than (11); it can be answered in ways not open to the latter, e.g., by

An outcome of the 1980 U.S. presidential election is that the Democrats lost control of the Senate.[4]

To be sure, there are cases in which an interrogative sentence beginning with "what" which lacks a content-noun is transformable into an equivalent interrogative with such a noun. ("What execution is now occurring?" we took to be equivalent to "What event is now occurring that is an execution?") But what I am now claiming is that this is not universally the case. When such transformations are made the new interrogative will not always be equivalent to the old. Thus, "The result of the lottery will be that the state will go broke" expresses an answer to "What will be the result of the lottery?" but not to "What number will win the lottery?" and "A possibility concerning its raining today that will actually obtain is that my airplane flight will be delayed" is an answer to "What possibility concerning its raining today will actually obtain?" but not to "Will it rain today?"

---

4. Even if we try to make (13) more specific by writing "What outcome involving the U.S. presidency (or what presidential outcome) obtained in the 1980 presidential election?" we get similar results. "An outcome involving the U.S. presidency (or a presidential outcome) that obtained in the 1980 election is that Jimmy Carter lost" is an answer to this question but not to (11).

4. ELLIPSES

My contention is that A understands q only if

(1) (∃p)(A knows of p that it is a correct answer to Q, and p is a complete content-giving proposition with respect to Q).

In accordance with this, one cannot understand how high the Matterhorn is simply in virtue of knowing of "The height of the Matterhorn is 14,700 feet" that it is a correct answer to "How high is the Matterhorn?" Still, there are situations in which we might speak of understanding how high the Matterhorn is. If John knows that it is sufficiently high to require equipment and a guide for climbing we might well say that he understands how high the Matterhorn is. In such a case we are treating "John understands how high the Matterhorn is" as elliptical for something like

(2) John understands what significance the height of the Matterhorn has for the prospective climber.

The constituent question in (2) is

(3) What significance does the height of the Matterhorn have for the prospective climber?

John knows of the proposition

(4) The significance of the height of the Matterhorn for the prospective climber is that this height is sufficient to require equipment and a guide for climbing

that it is a correct answer to (3). But (4) is a complete content-giving proposition with respect to (3). Therefore, by (1), John satisfies a necessary condition for understanding with respect to (3).

Bobby who knows nothing about physics sees a certain instrument for the first time and is informed that it is a bubble chamber. Does he now understand what instrument this is simply in virtue of knowing of the proposition

This instrument is a bubble chamber

that it is a correct answer to the question

What instrument is this?

No, but if he is now informed that this instrument is used in physics to record the tracks of subatomic particles, then we might conclude that now he understands what instrument this is. If so, our claim is elliptical for

Bobby understands what the function of this instrument is.

The constituent question here is one for which there is an answer that is a complete content-giving proposition, namely,

The function of this instrument is to record the tracks of subatomic particles.

More generally, "A understands q" may be elliptical for "A understands q'" where condition (1) is satisfied with respect to Q' but not Q.

Another case of this sort involves questions of the form "What is (an) X?" (where X is a type of thing or substance). Do I understand what copper is in virtue of knowing of the proposition

(5) Copper is a metal

that it is a correct answer to the question

(6) What is copper?

If so, then we have a violation of condition (1) since proposition (5) is not a complete content-giving proposition with respect to (6). (All the conditions for content-giving sentences are violated.) It might be concluded that this result is welcome, since one cannot be said to understand what copper is simply in virtue of knowing (5). But suppose I know of the proposition

(7) Copper is the metal of atomic number 29 which has the melting point 1083° C, is reddish in color, is malleable and ductile, etc.

that it is a correct answer to (6). It might now be concluded that, in virtue of this wealth of knowledge, I understand what copper is. Yet (7), like (5), is not a complete content-giving proposition with respect to (6).

This case can be accommodated by construing "understanding what (an) X is" as elliptical for (something like) "understanding what fact about X is important (in the context in question)," or perhaps for "understanding what significance or importance X has (in the present context)." On such a construction, one who knows of the proposition

(8) A fact about copper that is important (in the context) is that copper is the metal of atomic number 29 which has the melting point 1083° C, etc.

that it is a correct answer to

(9) What fact about copper is important?

might be said to understand what copper is, in virtue of (8)'s being a complete content-giving proposition with respect to (9). Moreover, there will be contexts in which a fact about copper that is important (or in which what significance copper has) is that it is a metal. In such contexts it will be possible to say that one who knows the relevant information understands what copper is. (The relativity of understanding is an idea that will be explored in section 5.)

Finally, there are cases in which, although we may be reluctant to speak of understanding q, there is something about the situation—some related q'—that we do understand, even though "understanding q" is not elliptical for "understanding q'." Mary intends to leave her money to a certain university. Do I understand what university Mary intends to aid in virtue of knowing of the proposition "The university Mary intends to aid is Johns Hopkins" that it is a correct answer to "What university does Mary intend to aid?"? Not on the account of understanding presented here. Nevertheless, on this account, there is something about the situation that I do understand, namely, what Mary's intention is.

5. EXPLAINING REVISITED

Returning to the concept of an illocutionary act of explaining, we are now in a position to formulate some further conditions. So far no restrictions have been imposed on the indirect question q being explained, or on u, what is uttered by the explainer. (The conditions speak only of S's intentions and beliefs concerning q and u.) Various positions might be advocated. According to one, no restrictions whatever should be imposed on q or u; i.e., condition (3) of section 1 should stand as it is. One can explain anything by uttering anything, so long as one has the right intentions and beliefs. A position at the other end of the spectrum would be that q must always be a why-question and that u should cite causes and laws. The problem we face is how to draw the line between something which is an explaining act (however bad the product), and something which is no such act at all. To some extent this will be arbitrary; I doubt that there is a precise dividing line. However, I do think that the concept of an illocutionary act of explaining is somewhat narrower than that suggested so far. In what follows I shall suggest some restrictions to be added to condition (3) of section 1 that still allow a broad range of explaining acts.

Consider once again the question

(1) How high is the Matterhorn?

I claimed that someone could not be said to understand how high the Matterhorn is simply in virtue of the fact that he knows of the proposition

(2) The height of the Matterhorn is 14,700 feet

that it is a correct answer to (1). Now I suggest that an analogous claim can be made for explaining: By uttering (2) a speaker S is not explaining how high the Matterhorn is. Unless (1) is being construed as elliptical for something else, it is not the right sort of question to fill the q-position in "S explains q by uttering u." Still, intentions being what they are, it seems possible for some misguided speaker S to utter (2) with the intention described in condition (3) for explaining given in section 1: that of rendering q understandable (Q = (1)) by getting others to know of the proposition expressed by (2) that it is a correct answer to Q. In such a case we would not say that S is explaining q by uttering (2), but that he *intends* to be doing this.

Let us call Q a *content-question* if and only if (∃p)(p is a complete content-giving proposition with respect to Q). A content-question has a complete answer form whose blank can be filled with content-giving expressions that will transform the result into a sentence that expresses a content-giving proposition. A question such as "Why did Nero fiddle?" is a content-question, but one such as "How high is the Matterhorn?" is not. Now I suggest that the q-position in "S explains q by uttering u" can be filled only by interrogatives expressing content-questions, or by interrogatives that in "S explains q by uttering u" are elliptical for ones expressing content-questions. Since (1) is not a content-question, if, by uttering (2), S is said to be explaining how high the Matterhorn is, what is said is either false or else elliptical for something in which the explanatory question is a content-question.

I turn next to a proposal for a restriction on u, what is uttered in an act of explaining q.

> *u-restriction for* Q: what S utters is, or in the context is transformable into, a sentence expressing a complete content-giving proposition with respect to Q.

Suppose that S explains why Nero fiddled, by uttering

> u: Nero was happy.

In the context of S's utterance u is transformable into (what S said in that context can also be expressed by) the sentence

> The reason that Nero fiddled is that he was happy,

which expresses a complete content-giving proposition with respect to the question "Why did Nero fiddle?"

The u-restriction will allow us to exclude a number of kinds of cases. For example, with it S cannot be explaining how Jones escaped from prison, by uttering

> The reason that Nero fiddled is that he was happy

(unless, in the context of utterance, this is to be understood as expressing some different proposition). Nor can S be explaining why Nero fiddled, by uttering "The reason that Nero fiddled is difficult to grasp," or nonsense words like "glip glop."

However, the u-restriction still allows a broad range of cases. Thus it permits S to explain why atoms emit discrete radiation, by uttering

The reason that atoms emit discrete radiation is that God is love,

provided, of course, that the other conditions on explaining are satisfied (in particular, e.g., that S believes that this sentence expresses a correct answer to the question). Will the u-restriction countenance explaining acts involving utterances even more bizarre than this? That depends upon which u's we take as expressing propositions.

I construe propositions broadly to be expressible by that-clauses following a range of psychological verbs (such as "believe," "fear," and "hope") and illocutionary verbs (such as "say," "state," "propose," and "suggest"). Such verbs can be followed by that-clauses that are grammatically or semantically deviant, even though the resulting sentence is neither, and indeed is true, e.g.,

Heidegger believed that *the nothing noths,*
John said that *numbers speak silently.*

I shall say that the emphasized words in these sentences express propositions. More generally, u can be said to express a proposition if and only if it can appear in (many)[5] contexts of the form

(3) Subject term + psychological or illocutionary verb + that + u.

(Here the "that" is to be constructed as associated with the verb, not as modifying u.) Although by this criterion syntactically and semantically deviant utterances can express propositions, not all utterances can. Thus, since

John said (believes, hopes) that *glip glop,*
John said (believes, hopes) that *go table chair,*

are deviant, the emphasized words do not express a proposition. ("John said 'glip glop') (or 'go table chair')" is not deviant, but this is not the relevant context.)

To adopt this criterion is not to be committed to the view that every true sentence of form (3) requires the subject to have *de re* knowledge (by acquaintance) of the proposition expressed by u. If Sam, who knows no physics, is told by a reputable physicist that strangeness is conserved in strong interactions, then it may be true to say that

(4) Sam believes that strangeness is conserved in strong interactions,

5. Obviously, some such contexts will be inappropriate, e.g., "S predicts that yesterday it snowed."

which is a sentence of form (3). But what makes (4) true in this case is not (among other things) Sam's *de re* knowledge of the proposition that strangeness is conserved in strong interactions, since he has none. Rather it is his *de re* knowledge of the sentence "Strangeness is conserved in strong interactions." Sam believes, of this (or some equivalent) sentence, that it expresses a true proposition. In the present case this is sufficient to make (4) true. If Sam understood physics, what could make (4) true is his belief, of the proposition in question, that it is true—which involves acquaintance with the proposition itself. Accordingly, even though propositions are expressible by that-clauses in sentences reporting beliefs (etc.), this does not necessitate an analysis of belief sentences that requires the believer to be acquainted with some proposition.

Nevertheless, if sentences such as "The nothing noths" and "Numbers speak silently" do express propositions, then one ought to be able to have *de re* knowledge by acquaintance with the propositions they express. But how is this possible if these sentences are meaningless? In section 2 (in material omitted here), I suggested that to be acquainted with a proposition p is to be in a certain mental state that can be functionally characterized by typical causes and effects. Typically, such a state is caused by having seen or heard certain sentences that express p whose meaning one knows, and it results in the ability to produce the same or equivalent sentences, of which one knows the meaning and knows that they express p. Now, just as "proposition" is being construed broadly, so is "meaning." Not every syntactically or semantically deviant sentence is utterly without meaning; there are degrees of deviation. A sympathetic reader of Heidegger knows something about the sentence "The nothing noths" that the nonreader does not. Within the Heideggerian corpus it has some meaning (I am inclined to suppose) despite its deviance, and the sympathetic reader knows what this meaning is. Even if for such a person the sentence is sufficiently opaque to lack a truth-value, it is not in the same league, e.g., as "glip glop." On my suggestion, those who suppose that it is should refuse to assent to "Heidegger believed that the nothing noths," but should accept only sentences such as "Heidegger wrote (or said, or believed true, the sentence) 'the nothing noths'" (just as we are willing to assert "John said 'glip glop'" but not "John said that glip glop"). However, it is not my purpose here to argue that this particular Heideggerian sentence (or the sentence "Numbers speak silently") is not complete nonsense; I assume only that a range of syntactically or semantically deviant sentences are not. (For the sake of the argument I will continue to use these sentences.)

With the present understanding of what can express a proposition, the u-restriction for Q allows S to be explaining by making deviant utterances. Heidegger can be explaining something by uttering a sentence of the form

The reason that _____ is that the nothing noths.

And John can be explaining why numbers cannot be heard, by uttering

The reason that numbers cannot be heard is that numbers speak silently.

However, John cannot be explaining why numbers cannot be heard, by uttering

The reason that numbers cannot be heard is that glip glop.

Thus, although the u-restriction (in conjunction with a criterion permitting deviant sentences to express propositions) does exclude various utterances from explaining acts, it is sufficiently broad to allow some that violate rules of syntax or semantics. But this is as it should be. At least in certain cases we do, I think, want to describe the philosopher, the scientist, or the nonspecialist as engaging in an act of explaining, even if we criticize the act, the explanation, or both for insufficient intelligibility. Some will insist that we have allowed too broad a class of explaining acts. Perhaps, but while this may be somewhat arbitrary, I am inclined to stop at this point and treat further restrictions as proposals for *evaluating* explaining acts and their products.

We may now formulate the resulting conditions for explaining, as follows:

"S explains q by uttering u" is true if and only if either
(a) Q is a content-question, the u-restriction for Q is satisfied, and condition (3) of section I holds (i.e., S utters u with the intention that his utterance of u render q understandable by producing the knowledge, of the proposition expressed by u (in that context), that it is a correct answer to Q): *or*
(b) "S explains q by uttering u" is elliptical for "S explains q′ by uttering u," Q′ is a content-question, the u-restriction for Q′ is satisfied, and condition (3) obtains with respect to Q′.

The parenthesized words "in that context" in (a) allow S to explain q by uttering words that do not normally express a proposition, but do so in the explaining context. Thus, S might explain why Othello killed Desdemona by uttering simply "uncontrollable jealousy"—which, in the context, can be taken to express the proposition that Othello was uncontrollably jealous.

Just as the u-restriction permits a wide range of explanatory utterances, though not every concatenation of words, so the restriction of the interrogative to one expressing a content-question also permits a wide range of interrogatives, but not just any. It permits interrogatives with false presuppositions. (Mary can explain why helium is the lightest element.) Indeed, it permits ones with presuppositions expressed by sentences that are grammatically or semantically deviant. (Heidegger can explain why the nothing noths.) But not every interrogative is possible. As noted, one cannot explain how high the Matterhorn is (unless this is elliptical for something else). Nor can one explain why go table chair, since nothing of the form "the reason that go table chair is that_____" expresses a proposition, which is required for q to express a content-question.[6]

6. INSTRUCTIONS

In section 3 the following condition was proposed as a necessary one for understanding: A understands q only if

(1) (∃p)(A knows of p that it is a correct answer to Q, and p is a complete content-giving proposition with respect to Q).

Is this also sufficient for understanding?

What complicates the issues is that often a question can be correctly answered in different ways by providing various kinds and amounts of information. A person might be said to understand q in one way but not another. This idea can be explicated by introducing the concept of *instructions* for a question.

Consider the question

(2) What caused Smith's death?

Each of the following, let us assume, is a correct answer to (2):

(a) The cause of Smith's death was his contracting a disease;

(b) The cause of Smith's death was his contracting a disease involving a bacterial infection;

(c) The cause of Smith's death was his contracting legionnaire's disease.

---

6. My former student Herbert Walker has noted another bizarre case allowed by (a) and (b): one in which the explainer S, believing that u expresses a correct answer to Q, utters u with an intention appropriate for explaining, although S does not know what u means. (Say S reads the answer u to Q in a textbook and then utters u to his students believing that they will come to understand q by this means.) This could be precluded by adding a further condition in (a) and (b) that S has *de re* knowledge of the proposition expressed by u. However, I am inclined to regard this type of case as on or near the borderline, admit it under the liberal concept of explaining given here, and say that it is to be precluded, if necessary, by means of conditions for evaluating explaining acts.

Someone who replies to (2) in one of these ways may be following certain instructions pertaining to (2), e.g.,

Ia: Say in a very general way what caused Smith's death, e.g., whether it was caused by contracting a disease, or by some accident that befell him, or by an act of suicide;

Ib: Follow Ia, and if a disease is cited indicate something about what it involves, e.g., whether it is bacterial or viral;

Ic: Follow Ia, and if a disease is cited identify it by using a common name for it.

Instructions are rules imposing conditions on answers to a question. They govern the proposition that is the answer, and the *act* of answering only insofar as they do this. ("Answer in a low voice" imposes a condition on the act of answering, but not on the proposition that is the answer.) Various instructions are generally possible for one and the same question. Some instructions will be vague, some precise. Some will be appropriate for science, others not. Some will be quite general, others very specific. Talk of "a way of understanding q" will be construed by reference to a set of instructions for Q. Someone who knows that (a) is a correct answer to (2), but does not know that (b) and (c) are, can be said to understand q in a way that satisfies instructions Ia but not Ib or Ic.

More generally, utilizing (1), we can say that *A understands q in a way that satisfies instructions I*, or, more briefly, A understands q_I, only if

(3) $(\exists p)(p$ is an answer to Q that satisfies instructions I, and A knows of p that it is a correct answer to Q, and p is a complete content-giving proposition with respect to Q).

For example, A has fulfilled this condition with respect to question (2) and instructions Ia, if A knows of proposition

(a) The cause of Smith's death was his contracting a disease

that it is a correct answer to

(2) What caused Smith's death?

An answer to question (2) will be said to *satisfy* instructions Ia if and only if that answer says (and does not merely purport to say) in a very general way what really did cause Smith's death, i.e., if it cites a true cause. In such a case, if the instructions have been satisfied then question (2) has been correctly answered. But consider the following instructions for (2):

Id: Give an answer that George accepts.

An answer to (2) satisfies Id if and only if it is an answer to (2) that George accepts. The satisfaction of these instructions, unlike the satisfaction of Ia, does not guarantee that (2) has been correctly answered. In general, some, but not all, questions and instructions are such that if the instructions are satisfied the questions will have been correctly answered. Of course, because of false assumptions, inconsistencies, excessive vagueness, or just sheer irrelevance, some instructions cannot be satisfied at all with respect to a given question. In such a case, understanding q in a way that satisfies I will be impossible.

In section 2, I said that A is in a knowledge-state with respect to Q if $(\exists p)$(A knows of p that it is a correct answer to Q). If condition (3) is satisfied—i.e., if A knows of some complete content-giving proposition with respect to Q which satisfies I that it is a correct answer to Q—I shall say that A is in a *complete knowledge-state with respect to Q_I*. Being in such a state, I am claiming, is at least a necessary condition for understanding q_I. By this criterion, if A knows of (a) (which is a complete content-giving proposition with respect to (2) that satisfies Ia) that it is a correct answer to (2), then A fulfills a necessary condition for understanding what caused Smith's death, in a way that satisfies instructions Ia.

Can a claim of the form

(4) A understands q,

where there is no explicit appeal to any instructions, be construed in terms of understanding q_I? Three possibilities suggest themselves. First, it might be that (4) is true if and only if A understands q in a way that satisfies some instructions or other, i.e.,

$(\exists I)$(I is a set of instructions for Q, and A understands q_I).

But this would render claims about understanding very weak, since their truth would then require only a complete knowledge-state with respect to an answer satisfying the weakest instructions for Q. My knowing that Smith's death was caused by his contracting a disease would always suffice to say that I understand what caused his death. But it seems doubtful that we would want to say that such knowledge is always sufficient for understanding.

This leads to the second proposal, with is that when a speaker utters a sentence of form (4) his claim is always elliptical for

A understands q_I

where I is some contextually implicit set of instructions intended by the speaker, and I may vary from one context of utterance to another. Sentences of form (4) are, I think, sometimes used in this way. We may say that some-one understands something, meaning that he understands it in a way that we have in mind. Let me call this the "implicit-instructions" use of (4).

There is, however, another more likely possibility. Suppose that I hear speaker S assert (4). I may not know what instructions, if any, the speaker S intended, and this may not be clear from the context of his utterance. Moreover, I may have no idea what particular instructions A's under-standing satisfies. Still it seems possible for me to assert (4), because I believe that A understands q in some way that is *appropriate*—even if I do not know what this is.

This leads to the third suggestion. When a speaker utters (4) his claim is elliptical for

(5) ($\exists$I)(A understands q_I, and I is a set of appropriate instructions for Q).

Let me call this the "appropriate-instructions" use of (4). It is, I suggest, the most typical use of (4). Various views are possible about how to de-cide whether I is a set of appropriate instructions for Q. On one, there are universal standards of appropriateness, at least in science. On another, the standards of appropriateness can vary, depending on contextual features of A's situation. (See chapter 7 for an account of the latter.)

Recall now that A is said to be in a complete knowledge-state with respect to Q_1 provided that

(3) ($\exists$p)(p is an answer to Q that satisfies instructions I, and A knows of p that it is a correct answer to Q, and p is a complete content-giving proposition with respect to Q).

If we use (5)—the appropriate-instructions use of "understand"—then on the basis of (3) we may conclude that

A understands q only if ($\exists$I)(I is a set of appropriate instructions for Q, and A is in a complete knowledge-state with respect to Q_1).

On the appropriate-instructions use, then, knowing of a complete con-tent-giving proposition that it is a correct answer to Q is not sufficient for (nonrelativized) understanding; the proposition known must also satisfy appropriate instructions for Q.

7

The Pragmatic Character of Explanation

"The Pragmatic Character of Explanation" is reprinted by permission from Philosophy of Science Association Symposium Proceedings *1984 (1985), 275–292. I distinguish a strong and a weak sense in which the concept of an explanation might be considered pragmatic. I provide a definition of "an explanation"—that is, the product of a potential act of explaining. And I argue that such a product is pragmatic only in a weak sense—one that does not vary from one explainer or audience to another. I also distinguish the concept of a "good explanation," which is strongly pragmatic, from that of a "correct explanation," which is only weakly pragmatic. There is a brief addendum on "correct explanations."*

Some of those, including the present writer, who criticize standard models of explanation, such as Hempel's D–N (deductive-nomological) model or Salmon's S–R (statistical-relevance) model, do so on the grounds that explanation is a "pragmatic" or "contextual" concept—an idea which the standard models seem to reject. Yet the sense in which explanation is, or is not, pragmatic is not always made clear by the critics or champions of the models. Indeed, some critics and some champions may even mean different things by "pragmatic" or "contextual." In this chapter, I want to try to clarify a sense in which explanations might reasonably be considered pragmatic, discuss a couple of theories that are or are not pragmatic in this sense, argue the advantages of a pragmatic account, and briefly note some consequences of this for those seeking models of explanation.

1. HEMPEL'S CHARACTERIZATION OF "PRAGMATIC"

Hempel certainly acknowledges that there is a pragmatic aspect of explanation. He writes:

> Very broadly speaking, to explain something to a person is to make it plain and intelligible to him, to make him understand it. Thus construed, the word

I am indebted to the National Science Foundation for support.

"explanation" and its cognates are *pragmatic* terms: their use requires reference to the persons involved in the process of explaining. In a pragmatic context we might say, for example, that a given account A explains fact X to person P_1. We will then have to bear in mind that the same account may well not constitute an explanation of X for another person P_2, who might not even regard X as requiring an explanation, or who might find the account A unintelligible, or unilluminating, or irrelevant to what puzzles him about X.

Explanation in this pragmatic sense is thus a relative notion: something can be significantly said to constitute an explanation in this sense only for this or that individual. (1965, p. 425)

Now although Hempel recognizes a pragmatic use, or sense, or concept, of explanation, he sees his own task as one of

... constructing a nonpragmatic concept of scientific explanation—a concept which is abstracted, as it were, from the pragmatic one, and which does not require relativization with respect to questioning individuals. ... (1965, p. 426)

I take Hempel to be saying something like this. There are sentences, such as ones of the form

(1) Account A explains fact X to person P,

which make essential reference to some person or type of person who is explaining or being explained to. Such sentences are examples of a *pragmatic* use or concept of explanation. By contrast, there are other sentences, such as ones of the form

(2) Account A explains fact X,

which make no reference to any (type of) explainer or audience. These sentences are examples of a *nonpragmatic* use or concept of explanation. Hempel's D–N and I–S (inductive-statistical) models are meant to provide truth-conditions for certain sentences of this type.

Let me use the term "explanation-sentence" to refer to any sentence containing the terms "explains" or "explanation." I shall say that the terms for persons replacing S and P in sentences with forms such as the following are terms for explainers or audiences:

S explains fact X to P

The explanation of X given by S to P is _____

S gave account A to P as an explanation of _____

S and P may be terms for particular explainers and audiences or for types. For example, we might have "Achinstein explained his theory to philosophers at the 1984 PSA meetings" for a particular explainer and audience, and "the contemporary physicist explains the structure of matter by invoking quarks" for a type of explainer.

Now I shall broaden what I take to be Hempel's characterization by saying that an explanation-sentence is "pragmatic" if (a) it contains terms for a (particular or type of) explainer or audience or if (b) its truth-conditions contain such terms or others defined using such terms. Clause (b) will take into account a view which says that although some explanation-sentences are not explicitly pragmatic they are implicitly so. For example, one might hold the view that an explanation-sentence of the form "Account A explains fact X" is true iff some (type of) explainer S explains (or could explain) fact X to an audience (of type) Y by citing A. On this conception, the explanation-sentence in question would be pragmatic.

Whether this characterization of "pragmatic" captures what Hempel has in mind I will take up later. For the present, let us accept it as a sufficient condition.

Hempel's claim can now be put like this. Admittedly, there are pragmatic explanation-sentences, e.g., ones of the form

Account A explains fact X to person P.

Explainer S explains X to person P by giving account A.

But there are also nonpragmatic explanation-sentences. Most important for our purposes (Hempel will claim) an explanation-sentence of the following form is nonpragmatic:

(2) Account A explains fact X.

I shall say that someone holds a pragmatic theory of explanation with respect to explanation-sentences of a given form if he maintains that explanation-sentences of that form are pragmatic. Someone holds a nonpragmatic theory with respect to explanation-sentences of a given form if he maintains that explanation-sentences of that form are not pragmatic. Hempel holds a pragmatic theory with respect to sentences of form (1) but not of form (2).

I want to raise some questions about nonpragmatic theories of sentences of form (2) and others like it. But before doing so let me turn to someone who claims to be an arch-pragmatist, namely, Bas van Fraassen.

2. VAN FRAASSEN'S PRAGMATISM

In the chapter entitled "The Pragmatics of Explanation" in his book *The Scientific Image*, van Fraassen seems to be arguing in direct opposition to Hempel's nonpragmatic theory of explanation-sentences of form

(2) Account A explains fact X.

Van Fraassen writes:

> The description of some account as an explanation of a given fact or event is incomplete. It can only be an explanation with respect to a certain *relevance relation* and a certain *contrast-class*. These are contextual factors, in that they are determined neither by the totality of accepted scientific theories, nor by the event or fact for which an explanation is requested. (p. 130)

I shall briefly characterize van Fraassen's position by using as an example some Baltimore lore. By the dawn's early light Francis Scott Key is able to see the flag atop Fort McHenry. And he asks:

> Q: Why is our flag still there?

This interrogative, van Fraassen will say, can be used to pose different questions depending on the contrast intended. For example, Key might be asking:

> Why is *our* flag (rather than some other flag) still there?
>
> Why is our flag *still there* (rather than somewhere else)?
>
> Why is our *flag* (rather than something else) still there?

And so forth. The contrast class includes what is presupposed by the question (our flag being there) together with the alternatives (there being some other flag there, our flag being somewhere else, etc.). More generally, van Fraassen claims, in the case of any why-question there is a contrast-class that is usually implicit in the context:

> In general, the contrast is not explicitly described because, *in context*, it is clear to all discussants what the intended alternatives are. (p. 128)

For Key the context will tell us that the likely contrast is between our flag being there and the British flag being there.

Now let's turn to the second contextual concept van Fraassen mentions, the relevance relation. Francis Scott Key's interrogative

> Q: Why is our flag still there?

might be construed (in van Fraassen's terms) as a request for the "events leading up to its being still there." If so, we might answer by appeal to the battle raging throughout the night and the failure of the British to capture Fort McHenry. However, there is another possible (though perhaps less likely) interpretation of this interrogative, that is, as a request for the function or purpose of our flag's being there. What we need to know, says van Fraassen, is what "relevance relation" is being requested—"events leading up to," "function," or something else. And this, as in the case of the contrast class, is to be determined by looking to the context. "Looking to the context" in our example means invoking the intentions, beliefs, and puzzlements of Francis Scott Key. And this is pragmatic.

Now let's apply this to explanation-sentences of the Hemplian type (2). For our example consider:

> (3) The hypothesis that the British failed to capture Fort McHenry during the night's battle explains the fact that our flag is still there.

Recall van Fraassen's words:

> The description of some account as an explanation of a given fact or event is incomplete. It can only be an explanation with respect to a certain *relevance relation* and a certain *contrast-class*.

And the latter are contextual, requiring reference to some particular person. Well, if (3) is incomplete, let us complete it by specifying some relevance relation and contrast-class. We can do so, van Fraassen tells us, by understanding the question being raised as having three components: the topic (in this case "our flag is still there"), the contrast class (in this case let's say: "our flag is still there," "the British flag is there"), and the relevance relation (in this case let's say: "events leading up to"). Although van Fraassen does not do it quite this way we might now reformulate (3) above by writing:

> (4) The hypothesis that the British failed to capture Fort McHenry during the night's battle explains (by citing "events leading up to") why our flag is still there (rather than the British flag being there).

We now have an explanation-sentence which provides the sort of information van Fraassen wants. Is it pragmatic?

It is not explicitly pragmatic, since it contains no terms for an explainer or audience. Is it implicitly so? Do its truth-conditions contain terms for an explainer or audience or others defined by reference to these? Van Fraassen points out, correctly I think, that to determine what relevance relation and contrast-class are being requested appeal is made to the context. We look to the explainer, Francis Scott Key, and what intentions and beliefs he had. But this is not sufficient to show that the truth-conditions for (4) must contain terms for an explainer or audience.

Indeed, Hempel—presumably van Fraassen's arch-foe—could agree that in order to determine what question someone wants to answer, or what event someone wants to explain, essential reference to the intentions and beliefs of the questioner will need to be made. This is no damaging admission for the nonpragmatist, Hempel will say. The important issue is whether once the question being asked has been identified, it can be determined whether the explanation explains without invoking any term for an explainer or audience. So far van Fraassen has offered no reason why this cannot be done. All he has said is that (3) is incomplete. By analogy, Hempel might say, the following sentence is incomplete:

> The hypothesis that the British failed to capture Fort McHenry during the night's battle explains _____.

Suppose we find this incomplete sentence in a history book. To complete it appeal is made, let us say, to the historian's likely intentions and beliefs, and/or perhaps to those of Francis Scott Key. That won't make the resulting completed sentence "pragmatic" in what I have so far taken to be Hempel's sense. Suppose we complete the sentence by identifying the explanandum as

> why our flag (rather than the British) is still there.

Just because we have appealed to pragmatic considerations in identifying the explanandum, Hempel will ask, how does that show that the truth-conditions for the completed explanation-sentence must contain terms for an explainer or audience? Indeed, Hempel will urge us to accept his own truth-conditions for the completed sentence—say those of the D–N or I–S model—which contain no terms for an explainer or audience.

What about van Fraassen's truth-conditions? I find his intentions a bit cloudy at this point. He seems to present two sets of conditions, one set (perhaps) for the concept of a (merely, or minimally) correct explanation, and another for the concept of a good explanation. To give the first set of conditions we have a question Q determined by the topic P, the contrast class X, and the relevance relation R. And we have an answer of the form

> P in contrast to X because A.

Van Fraassen asks: what is claimed in this answer (p. 143)? He gives four conditions. First, that P is true. Second, that the other members of the contrast class are not true. Third, that A is true. And fourth, that A does bear the relevance relation R to P and X—e.g., that the answer A does give the events "leading up to" the event in P. I'm not sure if this is supposed to be a set of sufficient conditions, or only necessary ones, or, indeed, if it is supposed to be a set of conditions for the *truth* of sentences of the above form (the latter is suggested by van Fraassen's question "What is claimed in this answer?")[1] In any case, these conditions, let it be noted, contain no terms for an explainer or audience. Nor does their application to sentences of the form "P in contrast to X because A" require any reference to explainers or audiences once the question Q is given. Nor do the definitions of van Fraassen's technical terms in these conditions ("topic," "contrast class," and "relevance relation") appear to require the concept of an explainer or audience.

What about van Fraassen's second set of conditions for (as he puts it) "evaluating" answers? Again, we have a question Q determined by the topic P, the contrast class X, and the relevance relation R. How good is the answer

P in contrast to X because A?

Van Fraassen proposes three things that must be determined (pp. 146–147):

1. We must determine whether proposition A is "acceptable" or "likely to be true."
2. We must determine whether A shifts the probability toward P more than toward other members of the contrast class X.
3. We must compare "because A" with other possible answers to the explanatory question in three respects:
   a. Is A more probable than other answers given the background information K?
   b. Does A shift the probability toward P more than other answers do?
   c. Does some other answer probabilistically "screen off" A from P? (Is there an answer A' such that $p(P/A'\&A) = p(P/A')$?)

This evaluation of explanations introduces two important new factors: a set of background beliefs K relative to which probabilities are to be determined, and a set of answers to the question Q with which the answer A is being compared. Both factors might be deemed pragmatic or contextual. To determine what background beliefs should be used, and what alternative answers proposition A should be compared with, reference will be made to intentions and beliefs of the explainer or perhaps of the evaluator of the explanation. (Indeed, van Fraassen insists that only part of the background information K is to be used in the evaluation, and that which this is "must be a further contextual factor" (p. 147).)

---

1. In conversation van Fraassen suggests that the answer "P in contrast to X because A" should be understood as relativized to some particular set of assumptions B made in the context. If so his conditions might be construed as truth-conditions for sentences of the form "P in contrast to X because A, given B."

I don't propose here to assess van Fraassen's conditions. (For criticisms see my 1983, chapter 4.) I will simply note what I believe the nonpragmatist's response is likely to be. Just as van Fraassen earlier accused the nonpragmatists of focusing on an incomplete explanation-sentence, so the nonpragmatists will retort "tu quoque" to van Fraassen. All van Fraassen is arguing, the nonpragmatist will say, is that sentences of the following form are incomplete:

"P in contrast to X because A" is a good explanation of q.

The (more) complete form of such explanation-sentences is

(5) "P, in contrast to X, because A" is a good explanation of q relative to alternatives $A_1, \ldots, A_n$, and relative to background information K (or relative to such and such a subset of K).

Now that we have completed the explanation-sentence by relativization to a specific set of alternative hypotheses and to background information we are in a position to use the three conditions van Fraassen presents. These conditions invoke no terms for an explainer or audience. Nor will their application to sentences of form (5) require any such terms. Indeed Hempel himself insists on relativizing inductive-statistical (I–S) explanations to a set of background beliefs K, which, of course, can be different from one explanatory context to the next. This doesn't suffice to make Hempel believe that he is analyzing a pragmatic concept of explanation when he offers his inductive-statistical model.

I conclude that van Fraassen ought not to view his position as a pragmatic one—at least with reference to complete explanation-sentences such as those of forms (4) and (5). To be sure, to obtain such complete sentences to begin with, reference may have to be made to explainers. With this Hempel could agree. But once the sentences are complete no reference to any (particular or type of) explainer or audience needs to be made to understand what they mean, or to determine whether or not they are true.

3. THE ORDERED PAIR THEORY

Let me turn from van Fraassen's theory to one that I elaborate in my book *The Nature of Explanation*. Here I don't plan to present the theory in detail but only to say enough about it to show that it is pragmatic and to argue the advantages of a pragmatic account.

As did Sylvain Bromberger in a seminal essay in 1965, I begin with the concept of an explaining act. The explanation-sentences of concern to me are ones of the form

(6) S explains q by uttering u,

where q is the indirect form of a question Q. Simplifying my view, such sentences are true iff S utters u with the intention of rendering q understandable by producing the knowledge that u expresses a correct answer to the question Q. To develop this one needs to talk about the concept of understanding, which I will not attempt to do here. (See chapter 6) In any case there is no need to do so, for explanation-sentences of the form "S explains q by uttering u" are clearly pragmatic in the Hempelian sense. Such sentences make essential reference to an explainer.

The second stage in my theory consists in an attempt to provide a definition of an explanation itself—i.e., the product of an act of explaining or at least of a potential act of explaining. For certain reasons which we need not explore here I say that an explanation of q can be construed as an ordered pair whose first member is a proposition or set of propositions that constitutes an answer to Q, and whose second member is a type of explaining act, namely, explaining q. So, e.g., if Newton explains why the tides occur by saying that they occur because of the gravitational pull of the moon, then his explanation—whether good or bad, right or wrong—can be construed as the ordered pair

(7) (The tides occur because of the gravitational pull of the moon; explaining why the tides occur).

The second member of this pair invokes the concept of a type of explaining act, to which the account briefly summarized before is applicable. The first member of the pair is a proposition that constitutes an answer to the question cited in the second member. Unlike usual accounts, an explanation need not be restricted to why-questions. There can be an explanation of what event is now occurring in the bubble chamber, of what significance the American election has for Europe, and so forth. The view I develop attempts to characterize in a general way the kinds of questions (which I call content-questions) that can appear in explanations, and also to characterize in a general way what constitutes an answer to a content-question. The present manner of viewing explanations allows us easily to distinguish explanations from other products, whose second members will not be types of explaining acts, but something else. Furthermore, although this account defines explanation by reference to the concept of an explaining act, for something to *be* an explanation it is not required that it be the product of some particular explaining act. The previous ordered pair would be an explanation, on my account, even if neither Newton nor anyone else expressed the proposition that is its first member (i.e., even if no one ever explained why the tides occur by uttering any sentence expressing that proposition).

The latter point is important for the issue of the pragmatic character of explanation, so let me take it just a bit further. Let's consider explanation-sentences of the form

E is an explanation of q,

where there is no implication regarding E's goodness or correctness. On the ordered pair theory, the following is a set of truth-conditions for sentences of this form:

(i) Q is (what I call) a content-question (see chapter 1, section 9);
(ii) E is an ordered pair whose first member is (what I call) a complete content-giving proposition with respect to Q and whose second member is the act-type *explaining q*.

Do these truth-conditions contain terms for an explainer or audience or any terms defined by reference to these? They do not do so explicitly. Nor do the definitions of "content-question" and "complete content-giving proposition." This leaves the act-type "explaining q," which I take to be definable as a type of act whose instances are acts in which explainers explain q. (a is a type of act "explaining q" iff (S) (S performs an act of type a ≡ (∃u) (S explains q by uttering u).) If so then a term for an explainer is invoked in defining one of the concepts in the truth-conditions. And by our previous criterion of "pragmatic," this suffices to make sentences of the form "E is an explanation of q" pragmatic.

Yet there is something different about this case and the ones Hempel may have in mind. For although a term for an explainer is invoked, the truth-value of sentences of the form "E is an explanation of q" will not vary with who, if anyone, is giving or receiving the explanation E mentioned in the explanation-sentence. Earlier I characterized an explanation-sentence as pragmatic if it contains terms for a (particular or type of) explainer or audience or if its truth-conditions contain such terms or others defined using such terms. We might now introduce a second condition, and say that the truth-value of explanation-sentences of that form can vary with a change in the person giving or receiving the explanation mentioned or referred to in the explanation sentence. If both of these conditions are satisfied, let us say that the explanation-sentence is *strongly pragmatic*. If only the first is satisfied, the explanation-sentence is *weakly pragmatic*. By this criterion, sentences of the form

S explains q by uttering u

are strongly pragmatic. (Such sentences contain a term for an explainer, and their truth-value can vary with a change in explainer.) On the ordered pair theory, sentences of the form

E is an explanation of q

are only weakly pragmatic. Truth-conditions for sentences of this form (according to the ordered pair theory) invoke a term for a type of explainer, one who explains q, but the truth-value of sentences of this form does not vary with any change in who is giving E as an explanation of q, or to whom. On the ordered pair theory the concept of an explanation is defined by reference to the concept of an act in which an explainer explains something (thus making "E is an explanation of q" weakly pragmatic). But whether some particular sentence of the form "E is an explanation q" is true will not depend upon who, if anyone, gives the explanation (thus preventing such sentences from being strongly pragmatic). By contrast, according to Hempel's models of explanation, sentences of the form "E is an explanation of q" are neither strongly nor weakly pragmatic.[2]

I am inclined to think that when Hempel uses the term "pragmatic" he has in mind "strongly pragmatic," and that he would not object too strenuously to a "weakly pragmatic" concept of explanation, since the latter can be "objective." But this is speculation on my part.

Let me turn to another, perhaps more important, concept for which the ordered pair theory offers an account, namely, that of a "good explanation." Are sentences of the form "E is a good explanation of q" pragmatic in either sense?

Different evaluations of explanations are possible depending on what ends are to be achieved. The ends might be purely universal ones, e.g., the achievement of truth, empirical adequacy, simplicity, unification, and so on. Or they might be more contextual. The end I am particularly concerned with is one that, by the definition given in the first part of the theory, an explainer has when he performs an act of explaining q, that is, rendering q understandable (in some appropriate way) by producing the

---

2. The two conditions are independent. We have already seen an example satisfying the first but not the second. Here is something satisfying the second but not the first: "The fact that I was delayed in traffic is the correct explanation of why I am late." This sentence contains no terms for an explainer or audience (in the sense indicated earlier: it contains nothing of the form "S explains q to P" or "the explanation of q given by S to P is_____.") Yet its truth-value will vary with a change in the person giving the explanation mentioned. By the definitions here, this explanation-sentence is neither strongly nor weakly pragmatic. (To transform it into a strongly pragmatic explanation-sentence satisfying both conditions we could write: "The fact that he was delayed in traffic is the correct explanation given by Danny Dawdle of why he is late.")

knowledge of the answer one gives that it is a correct answer to Q. An evaluation with this end in view will take into account both universal and contextual criteria. Very roughly, E will be a good explanation for an explainer to give in explaining q to an audience if E is capable of rendering q understandable in an appropriate way to that audience by producing the knowledge of the answer to Q that it supplies that it is correct, or if it is reasonable for the explainer to believe that this obtains. The appropriateness of the understanding will depend on what the audience already knows and is interested in finding out. It will also depend on what it would be valuable for the audience to know—which, especially in the sciences, can bring in universal criteria. (For details see Achinstein 1983, pp. 107–117.)

In the case of such evaluations, which I call "illocutionary," sentences of the form "E is a good explanation of q" will be construed as elliptical for "E is a good explanation for an explainer to give in explaining q to an audience." Explanation-sentences of the latter form are strongly pragmatic. They contain terms for an explainer and audience, and the truth-value of sentences of this form can vary with a change in explainer or audience.

Now I am not claiming that illocutionary evaluations are the only possible ones (see the Addendum). I do insist that they are important, that they are frequently given, and that using them, by contrast to nonillocutionary, nonpragmatic evaluations, will enable us to see why certain scientific explanations are generally judged better than others. Let me illustrate this by invoking a simple example, Rutherford's 1911 explanation of the results of scattering experiments involving alpha particles.

In experiments published in 1909 Geiger and Marsden showed that when alpha particles are directed at a thin metal foil most of them go through the foil with small angles of deflection, but some are scattered through an angle of more than 90°, thus emerging on the side of incidence. In order to explain these surprising results Ernest Rutherford proposed a new theory of the structure of the atom. He assumed that an atom contains a positive charge that is not evenly distributed but is concentrated in a nucleus whose volume is small compared to that of the atom. He also assumed that the positively charged nucleus is surrounded by a compensating charge of moving electrons. Finally, he assumed that each scattering was the result of a single encounter between an alpha particle and a foil atom. Since most alpha particles penetrate the foil without being appreciably scattered, the foil atoms are mostly empty of matter. An alpha particle that is scattered at a wide angle is not scattered by a much less massive electron, but by a positive charge concentrated in the nucleus. From these assumptions, together with classical principles including conservation of energy and momentum, Rutherford derived a formula which gives the number of alpha particles falling on unit area deflected through an angle θ as a function of several other quantities. From this formula it is possible to calculate the number of alpha particles scattered at wide angles such as 150° or 135°.

Is Rutherford's explanation of the scattering results a good one? If we evaluate it in a nonillocutionary way using only criteria that are nonpragmatic, it would, I suppose, get a mixed review. True, it derives the wide scattering angles in a precise way from lawlike, quantitative assumptions; it appeals to microentities; and it offers a cause of the scattering—all of which physicists and philosophers of science tend to regard with favor. But, as later developments in physics show, it is only a crude approximation to what actually occurs in the foil atoms. And it introduces a conception of the atom as involving moving electrons that is incompatible with classical electrodynamics. (Moving electrons should radiate energy and collapse into the nucleus, which clearly they do not.) Furthermore, if we use only nonpragmatic criteria in our evaluation, we will have a difficult time seeing why Rutherford's explanation is better than certain others we might construct that are clearly inferior.

Consider, e.g., the following quantitative hypothesis that Geiger and Marsden could have constructed from their experiments without appeal to Rutherford's theory. (I'll call it the G–M hypothesis.)

The G–M hypothesis: When alpha particles are directed at thin metal foils the atoms comprising the foils cause the alpha particles to be scattered at various angles in accordance with the formula

$$N = Qnt(ze)^2 E^2 / 4r^2 (MV^2)^2 \sin^4 \theta/2$$

(N is the number of alpha particles deflected at angle θ, Q is the total number of alpha particles incident on the foil, n the number of atoms per unit volume in the foil, t the thickness of the foil, z the atomic number of the metal of the foil, e the elementary unit of charge, E the charge of the alpha particle, r the distance from the foil to the detection screen, and M and V the mass and velocity of the incident alpha particle.)

From the G–M hypothesis, together with information about a particular experimental setup indicating the number of alpha particles, the thickness and the atomic number of the foil material, and so forth, the number of alpha particles scattered at various angles, including large ones, can be described in a precise way, using lawlike, quantitative assumptions. Moreover, this explanation is unifying in the sense that it permits the derivation of several different results obtained in the experiments of Gieger and Marsdon. (For example, it permits a derivation of the fact that the number of alpha particles scattered through a given angle is directly proportional to the thickness of the scattering foil, and that the number is inversely proportional to the square of the energy of the alpha particles.) The explanation is causal in the sense that the G–M hypothesis contains a description of something that causes the scattering, namely, the presence of the atoms in the metal foil. And in so doing it appeals to microentities. Yet I think it would be regarded as vastly inferior to Rutherford's explanation. But objective, nonpragmatic values such as derivability from quantitative laws, unification, causation, and microentities will not *by themselves* tell us why Rutherford's explanation is a good one by contrast with the G–M hypothesis. Rutherford's explanation is good, or is as good as it is, not simply because it answers a causal question about the scattering in a quantitative way at a unifying microlevel, but because it does so at the *subatomic level of matter in a way that physicists at the time were interested in understanding the scattering.*

By 1911, the time of Rutherford's paper, the atomic theory of matter was widely accepted in physics, as was the idea that the atom itself is not atomic but has an internal structure. The latter idea emerged from the discovery of radioactivity and the electron, and the results of scattering of beta particles by atoms. It was also thought reasonable to suppose that alpha particle scattering was produced by events at the subatomic level. The question was how to work this out quantitatively using some theory about the structure of the atom. About five years before Rutherford's paper, J. J. Thomson had proposed the "plum pudding" model of the atom according to which the positive electricity in the atom is uniformly distributed throughout the atom and the electrons are held stationary in equilibrium positions by the positive charges surrounding them and the repulsion of other electrons. However, it was impossible to derive the wide scattering angles of alpha particles from the Thomson model.

One of the reasons Rutherford's explanation is highly regarded is that it does derive these angles from a model of the internal structure of the atom—which physicists at the time were seeking. And I think that the major reason the G–M explanation would not be so highly regarded—despite the fact that it derives the wide scattering angles from quantitative hypotheses—is that it does not give an explanation by appeal to subatomic structure. (It simply says that the scattering is produced by atoms, and it provides an empirical formula for the scattering.) But to assess Rutherford's explanation in the manner suggested is to offer an illocutionary evaluation. In the present case we are considering whether Rutherford's explanation (by contrast, say, to G–M) is a good one for Rutherford to have given. To determine this we need to look at the situation of Rutherford and other physicists in 1911. What did they know, and what did they seek to know? Doing this means treating the explanation-sentence "Rutherford's explanation of the alpha scattering is a good one" as strongly pragmatic. We need not, of course, treat it this way only with reference to Rutherford as explainer or a 1911 audience. The explanation-sentence might have a different truth-value if construed as elliptical for one making reference to a contemporary explainer and audience.

Now let me offer a conjecture. Suppose, following in the footsteps of Hempel and Salmon, you formulate a set of objective, nonpragmatic criteria that you think all scientific explanations must satisfy to be evaluated highly. These criteria will be universal in the sense that they are not to vary from one explanation to the next, but are to be ones applicable to all scientific explanations. They are also universal in the sense that they are not to incorporate specific empirical assumptions or presuppositions that might be made by scientists in one field or context but not another. So they might include the use of laws, causal factors, and quantitative hypotheses, the satisfaction of some criterion of unification or simplicity, and so forth. My conjecture is that whatever set of objective, nonpragmatic, universal criteria you propose you will be able to find or construct counterexamples to it, both as a set of necessary conditions and as a set of sufficient conditions. You will be able to find explanations that you will want to evaluate highly, despite the fact that they violate one or more of your favorite criteria. (Although this is not something I have illustrated here, you will evaluate them highly because they satisfy pragmatic criteria that are appropriate to use in the context of evaluation.) And you will be able to find, or at least construct, explanations (as I tried to do with the G–M explanation) that satisfy your criteria yet would not be highly regarded. You can emphasize criteria such as the introduction of laws, causal factors, and unification. But unless you say something more specific about the kinds of laws and causal factors to be used, or what is to be unified, you won't find your criteria sufficient to exclude examples you want excluded. But this "something more," as I tried to illustrate in the Rutherford case, will involve fairly specific empirical assumptions that may be made by certain scientists at certain times but not by others at others times: You want to derive the scattering angles not just from any laws that will do the job, or from any causes no matter how described, but (e.g.) from ones that invoke events occurring within the atom. You desire an explanation that provides unification, but not just any sort of unification. (One that unifies only various results obtained in scattering experiments, as does the G–M hypothesis, may not be of sufficient interest to you.) To determine what this "something more" is requires pragmatic assumptions about the explanatory context.

Now let me consider one major objection the nonpragmatist may offer. It is the one mentioned earlier that he might make against van

Fraassen. Even if you accept the importance of illocutionary evaluations, the nonpragmatist may say, all this shows is that sentences of the form "E is a good explanation of q" are incomplete. In the case of illocutionary evaluations the view I have espoused completes such sentences by writing "E is a good explanation for an explainer to give in explaining q to an audience"—which makes them strongly pragmatic. But there may be ways to complete such sentences that yield the same evaluations but that are not pragmatic.

Let me use the term "instructions" to refer to a set of rules or guidelines an explainer may be following when he explains q to an audience, or that an audience may want followed when q is explained to it. Instructions impose conditions on the answer to the explanatory question. They may incorporate very specific empirical conditions assumed by the explainer or audience. (For example, "Describe the structure of the atom in such a way that the interaction between alpha particles and either positively or negatively charged constituents of the atom produces the scattering.") They may also incorporate some very general conditions. ("Derive the scattering angles from quantitative laws.") Suppose that by appeal to a particular explanatory context—by appeal to the knowledge, beliefs, desires, and values of the explainer and audience—we determine that some set of instructions I is an appropriate one for that explainer to follow in explaining q to that audience. (The instructions themselves will not include reference to any explainer or audience.) We can now take the (allegedly) incomplete sentence "E is a good explanation of q" and complete it by relativizing it to the instructions I (and perhaps also to some set of beliefs K of explainer and/or audience):

(8) E is a good explanation of q relative to instructions I (and K).

We then supply truth-conditions for sentences of this form which are "objective" and are not relativized to explainer or audience. Here is one possibility:

(9) A sentence of form (8) is true iff
   (a) E satisfies instructions I, and E provides a correct answer to question Q; or
   (b) Given K, it is probable that (a) obtains.

I don't wish to defend these conditions but only to use them as an example. By our earlier definition, sentences of the form (8) should be neither strongly nor weakly pragmatic. Such sentences contain no terms for an explainer or audience; their truth-conditions (9) do not contain such terms; and their truth-values will not vary with a change in who is explaining or to whom (as long as instructions I are kept the same). So, the nonpragmatist will admit, just as you need to appeal to the context to determine what question Q is being raised, and what beliefs K can be assumed, so you need to appeal to the context to determine what instructions I are to be followed. But once all these things are determined, then the issue of whether E is a good explanation of q relative to I and K is settleable in an objective, nonpragmatic way (by determining, e.g., whether (a) or (b) of (9) is satisfied).

This reply, I suggest, trivializes the nonpragmatist's position with regard to the evaluation of explanations. The aim of nonpragmatists such as Hempel and Salmon is to provide nonpragmatic criteria of evaluation—criteria whose applicability does not depend on, or vary with, who is explaining or to whom. What I have called "instructions" are rules that incorporate criteria to be used in evaluating explanations. And the nonpragmatist is now agreeing with me that the applicability or appropriateness of some set of instructions will depend upon, and vary with, explainer and audience. But this is too much of an admission. When it comes to evaluating explanations I take the nonpragmatist to be seeking a set of instructions whose appropriateness is not affected by context.

Let me put this in another way. The nonpragmatist should not transform a sentence of the form "E is a good explanation of q" into "E is a good explanation of q relative to instructions I," but into "E is a good explanation of q relative to *appropriate* instructions I." Or better, he should say that sentences of the form "E is a good explanation of q" are true only if there is some set of *appropriate* instructions that E satisfies. In either case the instructions are to be appropriate ones. And if, as previously, the nonpragmatist admits that appropriateness always depends, in part, on context, he is in agreement with the pragmatist. If the very definition of "appropriateness" with regard to instructions requires reference to an explainer and audience (see *The Nature of Explanation*, pp. 112ff), and if the truth-conditions for "E is a good explanation of q" require the satisfaction of appropriate instruction, then "E is a good explanation of q" is strongly pragmatic.

In sum, the situation here is different from that of van Fraassen, who appeals to the context to determine only the question being raised, a set of alternative hypotheses, and the background information. By contrast, the instructions he formulates for evaluating explanations are not pragmatic. Their applicability does not depend on, or vary with, explainer or audience.

4. IMPLICATIONS

Let me comment briefly on the implications of a pragmatic theory of explanation for two contested issues in the philosophy of science.

a. Realism versus Antirealism

Of course, a good deal depends on how you define "realism" and "antire-alism." According to van Fraassen's formulation, the realist aims to give "a literally true story of what the world is like," while the antirealist aims to give "theories that are empirically adequate" (pp. 9, 12), i.e., theories that yield truths about "observables."

The first point I want to make is that, contrary to what might be thought, a pragmatic theory of explanation does not commit one to anti-realism. Consider a theory of the sort I offer for pragmatic explanation-sentences of the form

> E is a good explanation for an explainer to give in explaining q to an audience.

The theory proposes several truth-conditions for sentences of this form, but the important one for the present issue is that E provides a correct answer to question Q or that it is reasonable for the explainer to believe it does. The fact that E provides a correct answer to Q is not by itself sufficient to make E a good explanation of q; further contextual condi-tions need to be satisfied. But these contextual conditions in no way pre-vent a realist construal of "correct answer to Q" as one that, among other things, provides a "literally true story." The contextual conditions do not require that we construe a "correct answer" to be one that simply "saves the phenomena." By reference to the context of Rutherford's 1911 expla-nation, we can determine the need to provide an explanation of the scat-tering that appeals to the inner structure of the atom. We may evaluate Rutherford's explanation highly, in part because it satisfies such contextu-ally determined instructions. But this need to appeal to context does not mean that we must construe Rutherford's explanation nonrealistically.

Indeed, so far as I can see, even van Fraassen's own evaluative theory—which earlier I argued is not pragmatic—does not require an antirealist posi-tion of the sort he himself urges. We are supposed to evaluate the goodness of the explanation "P in contrast with X because A" by determining whether proposition A is "acceptable" or "likely to be true," and by determining cer-tain probabilistic relationships between A, the contrast class X, and the other answers being considered. None of this would seem to require antirealism. And the fact that the contrast class and alternative answers are determined contextually in no way precludes a realistic construal of answer A.

Conversely, pragmatism with regard to explanation does not commit one to realism. A "correct answer to questions Q" might be construed antirealistically as one that "saves the phenomena." Or, perhaps better, one might drop the condition that the explanation provides a correct answer to Q in favor of the condition that the explanation provides an answer to Q that saves the phenomena. This modification is in no way precluded by the need to appeal to contextual facts about an explainer or audience. (There are other more compelling reasons to resist antirealism that I explore in chapter 11. My point is only that the need to invoke explainers and audience is not a compelling reason.)

b. Relativism versus Absolutism

Pragmatism with regard to explanation, particularly strong pragmatism, is a form of relativism. The truth-value of a strongly pragmatic explanation-sentence will vary with explainer and/or audience. But this relativism does not necessarily commit one to particularly virulent forms such as subjectivism or (Feyerabendian) anarchism. For example, it will not be the case that an explanation will be a good one for an explainer to give an audience if it simply satisfies any criteria set by the explainer or audience. For one thing, the explanation must satisfy some truth or confirmation requirement. For another, there may be certain criteria the satisfaction of which by the explanation is valuable for the explainer or audience, despite their own beliefs about these criteria. The form of relativism I would support could agree that the introduction of laws, causes, unification, and so forth, are general methodological criteria valued in science. They are "prima facie" virtues. But in giving assessments of explanations of the sort I have been describing—in giving illocutionary evaluations—they cannot be treated as necessary or sufficient conditions. They are relevant, but they must be combined in appropriate ways with pragmatic information.

REFERENCES

Achinstein, Peter (1983), *The Nature of Explanation*. New York: Oxford University Press.

Bromberger, Sylvain (1965), "An Approach to Explanation." In *Analytic Philosophy*, 2nd Ser. Edited by R. J. Butler. Oxford: Basil Blackwell. Pages 72–105.

Geiger, H., and E. Marsden (1909), "On a diffuse reflection of the α-particles," *Proceedings of the Royal Society* (A) 82, 495–500.

Hempel, Carl G. (1965), *Aspects of Scientific Explanation and Other Essays in the Philosophy of Science*. New York: Basic Books.

Rutherford, E. (1911), "The scattering of α and β particles by matter and the structure of the atom," *Philosophical Magazine* 21, 669–688.

Thomson, J. J. (1904), "On the structure of the atom—an investigation of the stability and periods of oscillation of a number of corpuscles arranged at equal intervals around the circumference of a circle; with application of the results to the theory of atomic structure," *Philosophical Magazine* 7, 237–265.

van Fraassen, Bas (1980), *The Scientific Image*. Oxford: Clarendon.

ADDENDUM TO "THE PRAGMATIC CHARACTER OF EXPLANATION"

Is the Concept of a Correct Explanation "Pragmatic"?

In this chapter, when speaking of evaluating explanations, I focus on illocutionary evaluations. These are "strongly pragmatic" because they are concerned with determining whether E is a good explanation for an explainer to give in explaining q to some type of audience. And whether this is the case will vary with explainer and audience. There is, however, another important kind of evaluation, which I introduced in chapter 1. Its aim is to determine whether an explanation is a correct one, which may be the case even if it is not a good explanation for a certain type of explainer to give to a certain type of audience. For example, the explanation that the reason the soldier died is that he suffered a severe chest wound may be perfectly correct, but it may not be a particularly good, or good enough, explanation of why or how he died for the lieutenant to give in his official report to the division commander.

In terms of material introduced in this chapter, we can say this: E is a correct explanation of q if (i) Q is a content question; (ii) E is an ordered pair (p; explaining q), whose first member p is a complete content-giving proposition with respect to Q, and whose second member is an act-type of explaining; and (iii) p is true. Because a type of illocutionary act is mentioned, this concept of "correct explanation" is pragmatic in the weak sense. But it is not strongly pragmatic, since whether (p; explaining q) is a correct explanation of q does not depend upon who, if anyone, gives the explanation, or upon what audience, if any, is intended. In *The Nature of Explanation*, pp. 103–106, I show how this definition can be readily expanded to cover correct explanations that are not in the form of ordered pairs of the sort in question (e.g., "the soldier died because of a severe chest wound").

This concept of correct explanation is important in my definitions of "potential" and "veridical" evidence, given in chapter 1. Thus, a necessary condition for e to be potential (or veridical) evidence that h, given b, is that the probability be greater than 1/2 that there is an explanatory connection between h and e, given e and b. Such an explanatory connection exists if and only if either h correctly explains e, or e correctly explains h, or something correctly explains why both e and h are true. Whether the latter obtains is not pragmatic in the strong sense. Its truth does not depend upon who, if anyone, is explaining what to whom.

8

Can There Be a Model of Explanation?

"Can There Be a Model of Explanation?" is reprinted by permission from Theory and Decision 13 *(1981), 201–227. Standard models of scientific explanation impose two requirements. One is that no singular sentence or conjunction of such can entail the explanandum. The other is that the only empirical consideration in determining whether the explanans correctly explains the explanandum is the truth of the explanans; all other considerations are a priori. I argue that no model of explanation can satisfy these two conditions.*

1. INTRODUCTION

Since 1948, when Hempel and Oppenheim[1] published their pioneering article, various models of explanation have appeared. But each has had its counterexamples, and observers of the philosophical scene may wonder whether models of the kind sought are really possible. Are their proponents engaged in a fruitless task of inquiry?

Hempel and other modelists are particularly concerned with explanations that answer questions of the form

(1) Why is it the case that *p*?[2]

The sentence replacing '*p*' in (1) Hempel calls the *explanandum*. It describes the phenomenon, or event, or fact, to be explained. The answer to an explanation-seeking why-question of form (1) Hempel calls the *explanans*. It is a sentence, or set of sentences, that provides the explanation. We can speak of the explanans as explaining the explanandum. And we can say that an explanans *potentially* explains an explanandum when, if

1. Carl G. Hempel and Paul Oppenheim, "Studies in the Logic of Explanation," reprinted in Hempel, *Aspects of Scientific Explanation* (New York, 1965), 245–290.
2. See Hempel, *Aspects*, p. 334.

the sentences of the explanans were true, the explanans would correctly explain the explanandum.

Thus, if the explanation-seeking why-question is

Q: Why is it the case that this metal expanded,

then the explanandum is

(2) This metal expanded.

If, in reply to Q, an explainer claims that

(3) This metal was heated; and all metals that are heated expand,

then (3) is the explanans for the explanandum (2). And (3) potentially explains (2) if, given the truth of (3), (3) would correctly explain (2).

A *model* of explanation is a set of necessary and sufficient conditions that determine whether the explanans correctly explains the explanandum (where the explanation-seeking question is of form (1)). It can also be described as a set of conditions that determine whether the explanans potentially explains the explanandum. If the conditions are satisfied by a given explanans and explanandum, then the former correctly explains the latter, provided that the former is true.

In what follows, my concern will be with models as sets of sufficient (rather than necessary) conditions for correct explanations; and as providing such conditions for explanations of particular events or facts rather than of general laws. Most of the counterexamples in the literature have been raised against models construed in this way. I shall argue that one important reason for the failure of these models is that their proponents want to impose requirements which, in effect, destroy the efficacy of their models.

2. TWO REQUIREMENTS FOR A MODEL

The first is that no singular sentence or conjunction of such sentences in the explanans can entail the explanandum.[3] I will call this the

---

3. Or, in a tighter formulation, where the explanans is a set or conjunction of sentences: (i) no subset of these all members of which are singular sentences entails the explanandum; (ii) the explanandum is not entailed by a singular conjunct in a conjunctive equivalent of the explanans. To explicate the latter let S be a sentence containing within it one or more occurrences of some singular sentence (or some compound of singular sentences) P. Delete from S one or more occurrences of P, obtaining a sentence S*. Form a conjunction of S* with P. If this conjunction is equivalent to S it is a conjunctive equivalent of S containing P as a singular conjunct. For example, (a) "(Ga v Ja) & -Ja & (x) (Fx⊃Gx)" is a conjunctive equivalent of (b) "(x) ((Ga v Ja) & -Ja & (Fx⊃Gx))," which contains "(Ga v Ja) & -Ja" as a singular conjunct.

No-Entailment-by-Singular-Sentence requirement, or NES for short. What is the justification for it?

There are, I suggest, three reasons that modelists I have in mind support it. First, it precludes certain 'self-explanations' and 'partial self-explanations'. Suppose we want to explain why a particular metal expanded. Assume that the explanandum in this case is

(1) This metal expanded.

The NES requirement precludes (1) itself from being or, being part of, an explanans for (1). It also precludes from an explanans for (1) sentences such as "This metal was heated and expanded," and "This metal expanded, and all metals that are heated expand," which would be regarded as partial self-explanations of (1).

Second, modelists emphasize the importance of general laws in an explanans. Such laws provide an essential link between the singular sentences of the explanans and the singular sentence that constitutes the explanandum. Intuitively, to explain a particular event involves relating it to other particular events via a law; if the singular sentences of the explanans themselves entail the explanandum laws become unnecessary, on this view.

Third, the NES requirement in effect removes from an explanans certain sentences which involve explanatory connectives such as 'explains', 'because', 'on account of', 'due to', 'reason', and 'causes'. Let me call sentences in which such terms connect phrases or other sentences *explanation-sentences*. Here are some examples:

(2) This metal's being heated explains why it expanded.
     This metal expanded because it was heated.
     This metal expanded on account of its being heated.
     The reason this metal expanded is that it was heated.
     This metal's expanding is due to its being heated.
     The fact that this metal was heated caused it to expand.

NES precludes any of the explanation-sentences in (2) from being, or being part of, an explanans for (1), since each of them is a singular

---

Since this singular conjunct entails "Ga," explanans (b) violates NES for explanandum "Ga." The notion of a singular sentence which Hempel and others use in characterizing their model is often employed in a more or less intuitive way. And when there is an attempt to make this notion more precise, difficulties emerge, as Hempel himself is aware (see ibid., p. 356). Hempel suggests that the concept can be adequately defined for a formalized language containing quantificational notation, but there are problems even here (see my *Law and Explanation* (New York, 1970, pp. 36–37)). However, the kinds of cases I will be concerned with are quite simple and would, I think, be classified by modelists both as singular sentences and as ones to be excluded from the explanations in question. (I am indebted to Hempel for personal correspondence in which he noted a difficulty in an earlier formulation of this footnote.)

sentence that entails (1).[4] Without a condition such as NES one could simply require, e.g., that an explanans for an explanandum p be a singular explanation-sentence of the form 'q explains (why) p' or 'p because q'. Any such explanans, if it were true, would correctly explain the explanandum p. Of course, any of the the six sentences in (2), if true, could be cited in correctly explaining why this metal expanded. Modelists need not deny this. Their claim is that the sentences in (2) do not correctly explain (1) in the right sort of way. They would exclude sentences in (2) from an explanans for (1) because they think that an adequate explanans for (1) must reconstruct the sentences in (2) so that the explanatory connectives in the latter are, in effect, analyzed in nonexplanatory terms. One of the purposes of a model of explanation is to define terms such as 'explains', 'because', 'reason', and 'cause', and not to allow them to be used as primitives within an explanans. By providing some analysis of explanation modelists want to show why it is that this metal's being heated explains why it expanded. There is little enlightenment in saying that this is so because (2) is true.

NES does not exclude all singular explanation-sentences (or all explanatory connectives) from an explanans.[5] But by precluding those that entail the explanandum it does eliminate ones that, from the viewpoint of the modelists, most seriously reduce the possibility of philosophical enlightenment from the resulting explanation. (Whether such modelists would advocate a broader requirement eschewing all explanation-sentences from an explanans is a possibility I shall not discuss.)

NES also excludes certain sentences from an explanans that do not explicitly invoke explanatory connectives but are importantly like those that do which are excluded. Suppose we want to explain why the motion of this particle was accelerated. Our explanandum is

(3) The motion of this particle was accelerated.

Consider the explanans

(4) An electrical force accelerated the motion of this particle.

---

4. To classify them as singular, of course, is not to deny that they have certain implicitly general features which further analysis might separate from the singular ones. Some might claim that NES should be applied only to completely singular sentences—ones with no generality present at all (cf., Hempel). The sentences in (2) must first be reduced. For example, in the case of the last the reduction might be: "this metal was heated; this metal expanded; and whenever a metal is heated it expands." If the latter is now taken to be the reduced form of the explanans, then the reduced explanans contains a singular sentence—"this metal expanded"—which entails the explanandum (1).

5. For example, it permits the following. Explanandum: "An event of type C occurred." Explanans: "An event of type A caused one of type B; whenever an event of type B occurs so does one of type C."

Although (4) itself contains no explicit explanatory connective such as 'explains', 'because', or 'causes', it nevertheless carries a causal implication concerning the event to be explained. It is roughly equivalent to the following explanation-sentences which do have such connectives:

(5) An electrical force caused the motion of this particle to be accelerated. The motion of this particle was accelerated because of the presence of an electrical force.

NES precludes (4) as well as (5) from an explanans for (3), since (4) is a singular sentence that entails (3). Those who support NES would emphasize that (4), no less than (5), invokes an essentially explanatory connection between an explanans-event and the explanandum-event which it is the task of a model of explanation to explicate.

The second requirement, which I shall call the *a priori* requirement, is that the only *empirical* consideration in determining whether the explanans correctly explains the explanandum is the truth of the explanans; all other considerations are *a priori*. Accordingly, whether an explanans potentially explains an explanandum is a matter that can be settled by *a priori* means (e.g., by appeal to the meanings of words, and to deductive relationships between sentences). A model must thus impose conditions on potential explanations the satisfaction of which can be determined nonempirically. A condition such as this would therefore be precluded:

An explanans potentially explains an explanandum only if there is a (true) universal or statistical law relating the explanans and explanandum.

Whether there is such a law is not an *a priori* matter.

The idea is that a model of explanation should require that sufficient information be incorporated into the explanans that it becomes an *a priori* question whether the explanans, if true, would correctly explain the explanandum. There is an analogy between this and what various logicians and philosophers say about the concepts of *proof* and *evidence*.

Often a scientist will claim that a proposition q can be proved from a proposition p, or that e is evidence that h is true, even though the scientist is tacitly making additional empirical background assumptions which have a bearing on the validity of the proof or on the truth of the evidence claim. If all of these assumptions are made explicit as additional premises in the proof, or as additional conjuncts to the evidence, then whether such and such is a proof, or is evidence for a hypothesis, is settleable *a priori*. Similarly, often a scientist who claims that a certain explanans correctly explains an explanandum will be making relevant empirical background assumptions not incorporated into the explanans;

if the latter are made explicit and added to the explanans, it becomes an
a priori question whether the explanans, if true, would correctly explain
the explanandum.

There is an additional similarity alleged between these concepts. A scientist would not regard a proof as correct—i.e., as proving what it purports to prove—unless its premises are true. Nor would he regard *e* as
evidence that *h* (or *e* as confirming or supporting *h*) unless *e* is true. (That
John has those spots is not evidence that he has measles unless he does
have those spots.)[6] And whether the premises of the proof, or the evidence report, is true is, in the empirical sciences at least, not an *a priori*
question. Nevertheless, deductive logicians, as well as inductive logicians
in the Carnapian tradition, believe that they can isolate an *a priori* aspect
of proof and evidence such that the only empirical consideration in determining whether a proof or a statement of the form '*e* is evidence that *h*'
is correct is the truth of the premises of the proof or of the *e*-statement in
the evidence claim; all other considerations are *a priori*. What I have been
calling the *a priori* requirement makes the corresponding claim about the
concept of explanation: The only empirical consideration in determining
whether an explanation is correct is the truth of the explanans.

3. MODELS PURPORTING TO SATISFY THESE REQUIREMENTS

a. The Basic D–N Model

Consider this model as providing a set of sufficient conditions for explanations of particular events, facts, and so on. The explanation-seeking
question is of the form 'why is it the case that *p*?' where *p*, the explanandum, is a sentence describing the event to be explained. The explanans is
a set containing sentences of two sorts. One sort purports to describe particular conditions that obtained prior to, or at the same time as, the event
to be explained. The other are lawlike sentences (sentences that if true are
laws). The model requires that the explanans entail the explanandum and
that the explanans be true.

No singular sentence (or conjunction of such sentences) that entails
the explanandum will appear in the explanans.[7] Any such sentence
which is an explanation-sentence that someone might utter in explaining
something will itself be analyzed as a D–N explanation, i.e., as a deductive
argument in which no premises that are singular sentences entail the

---

6. See chapter 1.
7. This is required in Hempel's informal and formal characterizations of his model. See
his *Aspects*, pp. 248, 273, 277.

conclusion. For example, if someone utters the singular explanation-sentence

(1) This metal's being heated explains why it expanded (caused it to expand, etc.)

in explaining why the metal expanded, a D–N theorist will restructure (1) as an argument such as this

(2) This metal was heated.
    Any metal that is heated expands.
          Therefore,
    This metal expanded.

And he will identify the premises of (2) as the explanans of the explanation and the conclusion as the explanandum. The premise in (2) that is a singular sentence does not entail the conclusion.

The *a priori* requirement also seems to be satisfied by this model. The only empirical consideration in determining whether the explanans correctly explains the explanandum is the truth of the explanans; all other considerations are *a priori*. What are these other considerations? They are whether the explanans (but not the conjuction of singular sentences in it) deductively entails the explanandum and whether it contains at least some sentences that are lawlike. The former is not an empirical question, nor is the latter, as construed by Hempel, since whether a sentence is lawlike depends only on its syntactical form and the semantical interpretation of its terms.[8]

The D–N model as a set of sufficient conditions for particular events is very broad, and one might seek to add further restrictions. Three more limited versions will be noted.

b. The D–N Dispositional Model

In this model,[9] the explanandum is a sentence with a form such as

(3) X manifested P when conditions of type C obtained.

And the explanans contains sentences of the form

(4) X has F, and conditions of type C obtained.

(5) Anything with F manifests P when conditions of type C obtain.

For an explanans consisting of (4) and (5) to provide a correct D–N dispositional explanation of (3) the model requires that F be a disposition-term,

---

8. See Hempel's discussion of lawlikeness, *Aspects*, pp. 271–272, 292, 340. I am here giving a simplified account of the D–N model; the same considerations apply to the more complete account given by Hempel and Oppenheim in section 7 of their classic paper.

9. See Hempel, *Aspects*, 462.

that (5) be lawlike, that (4) and (5) entail (3), and that (4) and (5) be true. The singular sentence in the explanans is not to entail the explanandum. And the satisfaction of all the conditions of the model, save for the truth of the explanans, is determined *a priori*. The only condition in addition to those of the basic D–N model is that F be a disposition-term, something settleable syntactically and/or semantically.

c. The D–N Motivational Model

In this model,[10] the explanandum is a sentence saying that some agent acted in a certain way. The explanans contains a singular sentence attributing a desire (motive, end) to that agent, a singular sentence attributing the belief to that agent that performing the act described in the explanandum is, in the circumstances, a (the best, the only) way to satisfy that desire, and a lawlike sentence relating desires, beliefs, and actions of the kind in question. For example, the explanandum might be a sentence of the form

(6) Agent X performed act A,

and the explanans might contain sentences of the form

(7) X desired G.

(8) X believed that doing A is, in the circumstances, a (the best, the only) way to obtain G.

(9) Whenever an agent desires something G and believes that the performance of a certain act is, in the circumstances, a (etc.) way to obtain G he performs that act.[11]

For an explanans consisting of (7)–(9) to provide a correct D–N *motivational* explanation of (6) the model requires that (9) be lawlike, that (7)–(9) entail (6), and that (7)–(9) be true. In this model, like the others, the singular sentences in the explanans are not to entail the explanandum, and the satisfaction of all the requirements of the model, save for the truth of the explanans, is settleable *a priori*.

d. Woodward's Functional Interdependence Model

This model[12] proposes adding to the basic D–N conditions the following additional necessary condition:

10. See Hempel, *Aspects*, p. 254.

11. I do not for a moment believe that (9) is true. But this is not the problem I want to deal with here.

12. James Woodward, "Scientific Explanation," *British Journal for the Philosophy of Science* **30** (1979), 41–67.

(10) *Condition of functional interdependence*: the law occurring in the explanans for the explanandum *p* must be stated in terms of variables or parameters, variations in the values of which will permit the derivation of other explananda which are appropriately different from *p*. (p. 46)

Suppose that the explanation-seeking question is "Why is it the case that this pendulum has a period of 2.03 seconds?" for which the explanandum is

(11) This pendulum has a period of 2.03 seconds.

Consider the following D–N argument:

(12) This pendulum is a simple pendulum.
　　　 The length of this pendulum is 100 cm.
　　　 The period T of a simple pendulum is related to the length L by the formula $T = 2\pi(L/g)^{1/2}$, where g = 980 cm/sec^2.
　　　　　　　Therefore,
　　　 This pendulum has a period of 2.03 seconds.

The third premise in (12) is a law satisfying Woodward's condition (10). Its variables are the period T and the length L. And variations in the values of these variables will permit the derivation of explananda which Woodward regards as appropriately different from (11). For example, if we change the explanandum (11) to

(13) This pendulum has a period of 3.14 seconds

the law in (12) allows the derivation of (13) if the value of L is changed to 245 cm. Woodward is impressed by the fact that explanations, particularly in science, permit a variety of possible phenomena to be explained. He writes:

> The laws in examples [of this sort] formulate a systematic relation between . . . variables. They show us how a range of different changes in certain of these variables will be linked to changes in others of these variables. In consequence, these generalizations are such that when the variables in them assume one set of values (when we make certain assumptions about boundary and initial conditions) the explananda in the . . . explanations are derivable, and when the variables in them assume other sets of values, a range of other explananda is deriavable. (p. 46)

The satisfaction of condition (10) is settleable *a priori*. If this condition is the only one to be added to those of the basic D–N model, then the resulting model satisfies the *a priori* requirements and NES.[13]

---

13. Woodward does not claim that (10) plus the basic D–N model provides a set of sufficient conditions for correct explanations—a point to which I will return later. But for the moment I want to treat his model as if it did purport to provide such a set.

4. VIOLATION OF THE A PRIORI REQUIREMENT

Despite the claims of these models the *a priori* requirement is not really satisfied (or else we will have to call certain explanations correct which are clearly not so). In order to show this I shall make use of some of the many counterexamples that have been employed against the D–N model. In these examples, the explanans is true, and the other D–N conditions are satisfied. Yet the explanandum-event did not occur because of the explanans-event, but for some other reason, and this can only be known empirically.

Consider this example:

(a) Jones ate a pound of arsenic at time *t*.
Anyone who eats a pound of arsenic dies within 24 hours.
Therefore,
Jones died within 24 hours of *t*.

Assume that the premises of (a) are true. Then it is supposed to be settleable *a priori* whether these premises correctly explain the conclusion. According to the D–N model all we need to determine is whether the second premise is lawlike (let us assume that it is), and whether the conjunction of premises (but not the first premise alone) entails the conclusion (it does). Since these D–N conditions are satisfied, the explanans should correctly explain the explanandum; and assuming the truth of the explanans, this matter is settleable on *a priori* grounds alone, no matter what other empirical propositions are true. However, the matter is not settleable *a priori*, since Jones could have died within 24 hours of *t* for some unrelated reason. For example, he might have died in a car accident not brought on by his arsenic feast, which, given the information in the explanans, could only be determined empirically. Suppose he did die from being hit by a car. Then the explanans in (a) does not correctly explain the explanandum, even though all the conditions of the D–N model are satisfied. Assuming the truth of the premises in (a) it is not settleable *a priori* whether these premises correctly explain the explanandum.

A similar problem besets all the more specialized versions of the D–N model cited above. Thus consider these D–N arguments:

(b) Disposition example
That bar is magnetic, and a small piece of iron was placed near it.
Any magnetic bar is such that when a small piece of iron is placed near it the iron moves toward the bar.
Therefore,
This small piece of iron moved toward the bar.

Suppose, however, that a much more powerful contact force had been exerted on the small piece of iron, and that it moved toward the bar because of this force, not because the bar is magnetic. (Assume that the magnetic force is negligible by comparison with the mechanical force.)

(c) Motivational example
Smith desired to buy eggs and he believed that going to the store is the only way to buy eggs.
Whenever, etc. (law relating beliefs and desires to actions)
Therefore,
Smith went to the store.

But suppose Smith went to the store because he wanted to see his girlfriend who works in the store, not because he wanted to buy eggs.

(d) Functional interdependence example
This pendulum is a simple pendulum.
The period of this pendulum is 2.03 seconds.
The period T of a simple pendulum is related to the length L by the formula $T = 2\pi(L/g)^{1/2}$, where $g = 980$ cm/sec^2.
Therefore,
This pendulum has a length of 100 cm.

A pendulum has the period it has because of its length, but not vice versa. (This type of counterexample is like the others insofar as it invokes an explanans-fact that is inoperative with respect to the explanandum-fact but the case is also different because there is no intervening cause here, although there is in the others.)

With each of the D–N models considered, whether a particular example satisfies the *requirements of the model* (with the exception of the truth-requirement for the explanans) is a settleable *a priori*. Yet in all of these cases, given the truth of the explanans, whether the latter correctly explains the explanandum is not settleable *a priori*. Thus in example (c), even if Smith desired to buy eggs, and he believed that going to the store is the only way to do so, and the lawlike sentence relating beliefs and desires to actions is true, it does not follow that

(1) Smith went to the store *because* he desired to buy eggs and believed that going to the store is the only way to buy eggs.

The explanans of (c) correctly explains the explanandum only if (1) is true. Yet given the truth of the explanans of (c) it is not settleable *a priori*, but only empirically, whether (1) is true.

We could, of course, see to it that the matter is settleable *a priori* by changing the motivational model so as to incorporate (1) into the explanans of (c). Assuming that this enlarged explanans is true, whether the latter correctly explains the explanandum is *a priori*—indeed trivially so. But now, of course, the NES requirement is violated, since (1) is a singular sentence that entails the explanandum of (c).

In example (d), even if the explanans is true and Woodward's condition of functional interdependence is satisfied, it does not follow that

(2) This pendulum has a length of 100 cm *because* it is a simple pendulum with a period of 2.03 seconds and the law of the simple pendulum holds.[14]

The explanans of (d) correctly explains the explanandum only if (2) is true. Yet assuming the truth of the explanans of (d), the truth-value of (2) is not settleable *a priori*, but only empirically. Assuming that there is a lawlike connection between the period and length of a simple pendulum, whether the pendulum has the period it does because of its length, or whether it has the length it does because of its period, or whether neither of these is true, is not knowable *a priori*.[15]

More generally, in the explanans in each of these models some factors are cited, together with a lawlike sentence relating these factors to the type of event to be explained. But given that the factors were present and that the lawlike sentence is true, there is no *a priori* guarantee that the event in question occurred because of those factors. Whether it did is an empirical question whose answer even the truth of the lawlike sentence does not completely determine. And if we include in the explanans a sentence to the effect that the event in question did occur because of those factors we violate the NES requirement.

It might be replied that we should tighten the conditions on the lawlike sentence in the explanans by requiring not simply that it relate the factors cited in the explanans to the type of event in the explanandum, but that it do so in an explicitly explanatory way. Thus in (a) we might require the lawlike sentence not to be simply "Anyone who eats a pound of arsenic dies within 24 hours" but

(3) Anyone who eats a pound of arsenic dies within 24 hours because he had done so.

It is settleable *a priori* whether an explanans consisting of (3) together with "Jones ate a pound of arsenic" is such that, if true, it would correctly explain the explanandum in (a).

---

14. We might be willing to say that this pendulum *must* have a length of 100 cm because it is a simple pendulum with a period of 2.03 seconds, etc. But here the explanandum is different.

15. Woodward recognizes the pendulum example (d) as a genuine counterexample to the D–N model even when supplemented by his functional interdependence condition (p. 55). He believes that a causal condition, which he does not formulate, will need to be added to the D–N model in addition to his condition. This type of proposal will be examined in section 6 when Brody's causal model is discussed.

This solution, however, would not be an attractive one for D–N theorists, since (3) is just a generalized explanation-sentence containing an explanatory connective that such theorists are trying to analyze by means of their model. Moreover, tightening the lawlike sentence in this way will produce many false explanations, since such tightened sentences will often be false even though their looser counterparts are true. For example, (3), construed as lawlike, is false since people who eat a pound of arsenic can die from unrelated causes. And if we weaken (3)—still keeping the explanatory clause—by writing

(4) Anyone who eats a pound of arsenic *can* die within 24 hours because he has done so,

we obtain a sentence that is true but not powerful enough for the job. It is not settleable *a priori* whether an explanans consisting of (4) together with "Jones ate a pound of arsenic at t," if true, would correctly explain why Jones died within $t + 24$, since he could have died for a different reason even though this explanans is true.

Another possible way of tightening the conditions on the lawlike sentence in the explanans is to require that it relate spatio-temporally contiguous events. (This would mean that the explanans would have to describe an event—or chain of events—that is spatio-temporally contiguous with the explanandum-event.) Jaegwon Kim has discussed laws of this sort, and he provides schemas for them which are roughly equivalent to the following:

(5) (x) (t) (t') $(x$ has P at t, and $loc(x, t)$ is spatially contiguous with $loc(x, t')$, and t is temporally contiguous with $t' \rightarrow x$ has Q at $t')$

(6) (x) (y) (t) (t') $(x$ has P at t, and $loc(x, t)$ is spatially contiguous with $loc(y, t')$, and t is temporally contiguous with $t' \rightarrow y$ has Q at $t')$.[16]

'$loc(x, t)$' means the location of x at time t. Kim does not specify a precise meaning for the arrow in (5) and (6), except that it is to convey the idea of "causal or nomological implication" (p. 229, note 19). Under the present proposal, the arsenic explanation (a) would be precluded, since the only law invoked in (a) is not of forms (5) or (6). It does not express a relationship between types of events that are spatio-temporally contiguous. And, indeed, the explanans-event in (a) is not spatio-temporally contiguous with the explanandum-event.

This solution, like the previous one, may succeed in excluding intervening cause counterexamples such as (a). But it would not, I think, be

16. Kim, "Causation, Nomic Subsumption, and the Concept of an Event," *Journal of Philosophy* **70** (1973), 217–236. This is a modification of Kim, whose formulations need a slight repair.

welcomed by D–N theorists. If the arrow in (5) and (6) is to be construed causally as meaning (something like) "causes it to be the case that," then, as with (3), the laws in D–N explanations will be generalized explanation-sentences containing an explanatory connective that D–N theorists seek to define by means of their model. Furthermore, requiring laws of forms (5) or (6) in an explanans will disallow explanations that D–N theorists, and many others, find perfectly acceptable. For example, it will not permit an explanation of a particle's acceleration due to the gravitational or electrical force of another body acting over a spatial distance. It will not permit explaining why a certain amount of a chemical compound was formed by appeal simply to (macro-)laws governing chemical reactions—where the formation of that amount of the compound takes time and is not temporally contiguous with the mixing of the reactants. Nor will the present proposal suffice to preclude all of the previous counterexamples. In particular, the pendulum example (d)—in which the pendulum's length is explained by reference to its period—is not disallowed. Assuming that the arrow in (5) and (6) represents nomological but not causal implication, we can express the following 'law':

$(x)(t)(t')$ (x is a simple pendulum with a period T at time t, and loc(x, t) is spatially contiguous with loc(x, t'), and t is temporally contiguous with $t' \rightarrow x$ has a length L at t' which is related to T by the formula $T = 2\pi(L/g)^{1/2}$).

This, being of form (5), can be used in the explanans in (d), which, when suitably modified, will permit an explanation of the pendulum's length by reference to its period. For these reasons the present proposal does not seem promising.

Our observations regarding the various D–N models can be generalized. Assume that the explanans satisfies the NES requirement. In the explanans we can describe an event of a type always associated with an event of the sort described in the explanandum. We can include a law saying that such events are invariably and necessarily associated. The truth of the explanans event-description and of the law is no guarantee that the explanandum-event occurred because of the explanans-event. It could have occurred because some event unrelated to the one in the explanans was operative whereas the explanans-event was not. And this cannot be known *a priori* from the explanans. We can make it *a priori* by including in the explanans an appropriate singular sentence that entails the explanandum (e.g., an explanation-sentence that says in effect that the explanandum is true because the explanans is, or that the explanans-event caused the explanandum-event). But then the NES requirement would be violated. Or, we can make it *a priori* by using a generalized explanation-sentence. But since this is contrary to the philosophical spirit of such models and will, in any case, tend to produce false explanations, it will not be considered a viable solution. We can also make it *a priori* by requiring laws of form (5) or (6) and construing the arrow causally. But this too does not satisfy the intent of such models, and, in addition, will not permit wanted explanations. On the other hand, if the arrow is understood nomologically but not causally, then whether the explanans, if true, correctly explains the explanandum is, in general, not knowable *a priori*.

To avoid the kind of problem in question we can say that it is an empirical, not an *a priori*, question whether an explanans describing events and containing laws relating these types of events to the explanandum-event correctly explains the latter. Or we can include in the explanans some singular sentence—either an explanation-sentence or something like it (e.g., (4) in section 2)—that entails the explanandum. In the first case the *a priori* requirement is violated, in the second, NES. For this reason, I suggest, D–N models which attempt to provide sufficient conditions for correct explanations in such a way as to satisfy both these requirements will not be successful.

5. EMPIRICAL MODELS

The models I shall now mention satisfy NES but overtly violate the *a priori* requirement. Their proponents seem to recognize that if the former requirement is to be satisfied it is not an *a priori* but an empirical question whether the explanans if true would correctly explain the explanandum. However, I shall argue, the empirical considerations they introduce are not of the right sort to avoid the problem discussed here.

a. Salmon's Statistical-Relevance (S–R) model

This is a model for the explanation of particular events.[17] Salmon construes such an explanation as answering a question of the form

(1) Why is X, which is a member of class A, a member of class B?

Although Salmon does not do so, I shall say that the explanandum in such a case has the form

(2) X, which is a member of class A, is a member of class B,

---

17. Wesley C. Salmon, *Statistical Explanation and Statistical Relevance* (Pittsburgh, 1971).

which is presupposed by (1). The explanans consists of a set of empirical probability laws relating classes A and B, together with a class inclusion sentence for X, as follows:

(3) $p(B/A\&C_1) = p_1$

$p(B/A\&C_2) = p_2$

.
.
.

$p(B/A\&C_n) = p_n$

$X \in C_k \ (1 \leq k \leq n)$.

Salmon imposes two conditions on the explanans. One is that the probability values $p_1, \ldots, p_n$ all be different. (I shall not go into the reason for this.) The other is

(4) *The homogeneity condition*:

$A\&C_1, A\&C_2, \ldots, A\&C_n$ is a partition of A, and each $A\&C_i$ is homogeneous with respect to B.

$A\&C_1, A\&C_2, \ldots, A\&C_n$ is a *partition* of A if and only if these sets comprise a set of mutually exclusive and exhaustive subsets of A. To say that a set A is *homogeneous* with respect to B is to say that there is no way, even in principle, to effect a partition of A that is statistically relevant to B without already knowing which members of A are also members of B. (C is statistically relevant to B within A if and only if $p(B/A\&C)$ $\neq p(B/A)$.) Intuitively, if A is homogeneous with respect to B then A is a random class with respect to B. Unlike the D–N models, Salmon's model does not require that the explanans show that the event in the explanandum was to be expected, but only with what probability it was to be expected.

I shall assume that for Salmon if the explanans (3) and the explanandum (2) are true, then the explanans correctly explains the explanandum, provided that Salmon's two conditions are satisfied.[18] Let's consider a simple example in which the probabilities have the values 0 and 1. There is a wire connected in a circuit to a live battery and a working bulb, and we want to explain why the bulb is lit, or more precisely, what, if anything, the wire does which contributes to the lighting of the bulb. Putting

18. Salmon in his book does not explicitly say this, but this seems to be the most reasonable interpretation of his position. See e.g., his remarks on pp. 79–80 in which he is distinguishing homogeneity from epistemic homogeneity, and in which he compares his model with Hempel's. Salmon might, of course, say that he is supplying conditions only for the concept of a well-confirmed or justified explanation. But I am construing his model in a stronger sense, and in private conversation he assures me that this is the correct interpretation.

this in Salmon's form (1), the explanatory question becomes "Why is this wire, which is a member of the class of things connected in a circuit to a live battery and working bulb, a member of the class of circuits containing a bulb that is lit?" The explanandum is

(5) This wire, which is a member of the class of things connected in a circuit to a live battery and working bulb, is a member of the class of circuits containing a bulb that is lit.

Letting

A = The class of things connected in a circuit to a live battery and a working bulb

B = the class of circuits containing a bulb that is lit

C_1 = the class of things that conduct electricity

C_2 = the class of things that don't conduct electricity

X = this wire,

we can construct the following explanans for (5):

(6) $p(B/A\&C_1) = 1$

   $p(B/A\&C_2) = 0$

   $X \in A\&C_1$.

Salmon's two conditions are satisfied since the probability values are different, and since $A\&C_1$ and $A\&C_2$ is a partition of A and each $A\&C_i$ is homogeneous with respect to B. Roughly, (6) explains why the bulb is lit by pointing out that the probability that the bulb in the circuit will be lit, given that the wire conducts electricity, is 1, that the probability that it will be lit, given that the wire does not conduct electricity, is 0, and that the wire does in fact conduct electricity.

Salmon's model satisfies the NES requirement since the only singular sentence in the explanans will not entail the explanandum. (Otherwise at least one of the probability laws in the explanans would be a priori, not empirical.) However, the homogeneity condition prevents his model from satisfying the a priori requirement.[19] Whether $A\&C_1, A\&C_2, \ldots ,$ $A\&C_n$ is a partition of A, i.e., whether these classes have any members in common and every member of A belongs to one of them, is not in general

---

19. It is possible to construe Salmon's model as requiring the satisfaction of the homogeneity condition to be stated in the explanans itself. If so the model would purport to satisfy the a priori requirement. However, in what follows I shall continue to assume that only sentences of the type in (3) comprise the explanans, and thus that the model is an empirical one. On either construction the same difficulty will emerge.

an *a priori* question (though it happens to be in this example). Nor is the question of whether each $A\&C_i$ is homogeneous with respect to B. For example, it cannot be decided *a priori* whether there is some subclass of the class of electrical conductors such that the probability of the bulb being lit is different in this subclass from what it is in the class as a whole; this is an empirical issue. Accordingly, whether the explanans (6), if true, would correctly explain the explanandum (5) is not settleable *a priori*.

Does the inclusion of the empirical homogeneity condition avoid the kind of problem earlier discussed plaguing the D–N models? Unfortunately not. This can be seen if we change our circuit example a bit. Let A and B be the same classes as before. We now introduce

C_3 = the class of things that conduct heat

C_4 = the class of things that do not conduct heat

I shall make the simplifying assumption that it is a law that something conducts heat if and only if it conducts electricity. Now consider this explanans for (5):

(7) $p(B/A\&C_3) = 1$
       $p(B/A\&C_4) = 0$
       $X \in A\&C_3.$

Although Salmon's two conditions are satisfied, (7) ought not to be regarded as a correct explanation of (5), even if (7) is true. Intuitively, it we took (7) to correctly explain (5) we would be saying that the bulb is lit because the wire conducts heat (where the probability that it is lit, given that the wire does (not) conduct heat, is 1 (0)). But this seems incorrect. The bulb is lit because the wire conducts electricity not heat, though to be sure it does both, and that it does one if and only if it does the other is a law of nature. Admittedly, by our assumption, the class $A\&C_3$ = the class $A\&C_1$. But it is not a class which explains for Salmon, but a sentence indicating that an item is a member of a class. If the class is described in one way the explanation may be correct, while not if described in another way. In sentences of the form

(8) X 's being an $A\&C_i$ (a member of the class $A\&C_i$)—together with such and such probability laws—correctly explains why X, which is a member of A, is a member of B,

the '$A\&C_i$' position is referentially opaque. A sentence obtained from (8) by substituting an expression referring to the same class as 'the class $A\&C_i$' will not always have the same truth-value.

The kind of example here used against Salmon's model[20] is similar to those raised earlier, in the following respect. In the explanans a certain fact about the wire is cited, namely, that it conducts heat, which (under the conditions of the setup) is nomologically associated, albeit indirectly, with the fact to be explained, that is, the bulb's being lit. However, it is not the explanans-fact that is the operative one in this case but the fact that the wire conducts electricity. By invoking the homogeneity condition Salmon in effect recognizes that the question of the explanatory operativeness of the explanans is not an *a priori* matter. The problem is that his homogeneity condition is not sufficient to guarantee that the explanans-fact is operative with respect to the explanandum-fact.

b. Brody's Essential Property Model

Brody construes this model as providing a set of sufficient conditions for explanations of particular events.[21] These conditions are those of the basic D–N model together with the following:

> *Essential property condition*: "The explanans contains essentially a statement attributing to a certain class of objects a property had essentially by that class of objects (even if the statement does not say that they have it essentially) and . . . at least one object involved in the event described in the explanandum is a member of the class of objects." (p. 26)

For example, since Brody thinks that atomic numbers are essential properties of the elements he would regard the following explanation as correct, provided its premises are true, since the D–N conditions plus his essential property condition are satisfied:

(9) This substance is copper.
   Copper has the atomic number 29.
   Anything with the atomic number 29 conducts electricity.
      Therefore,
   This substance conducts electricity.

Brody proposes the essential property condition in order to preclude certain counterexamples to the basic D–N model. Moreover, he regards the satisfaction of this condition as an empirical matter.[22] Brody's model, in

20. A variety of such examples, as well as other trenchant criticism, can be found in John B. Meixner's doctoral dissertation, *Salmon's Statistical Model of Explanation* (Johns Hopkins University, Baltimore, 1976).

21. B. A. Brody, "Towards an Aristotelian Theory of Scientific Explanation", *Philosophy of Science* **39** (1972), 20–31. There is a corresponding model for the explanation of laws, which I won't discuss.

22. See Brody, p. 27.

cases in which the explanans does not say explicitly that the property in question is essential, does not satisfy the *a priori* condition.[23] To know whether (9) is a correct explanation if its premises are true is not an *a priori* matter, since we must know whether having the atomic number 29 is an essential property of copper, and this knowledge is empirical, according to Brody. On the other hand, the NES requirement is satisfied since the singular premises in an explanans will not entail the explanandum.

One might object to Brody's model on grounds of obscurity in the notion of an essential property (which, by the way, he seems to distinguish from mere properties a thing has necessarily). However, the problem I want to raise is not this, and so I shall suppose the model is reasonably clear; indeed I shall stick to atomic number, which is the sort of property Brody claims to be essential to the element which has it.

Consider now the following argument which satisfies Brody's essential property condition plus the other requirements of the D–N model.

(10) Jones ate a pound of the substance in that jar.
       The substance in that jar is arsenic.
       Arsenic has the atomic number 33.
       Anyone who eats a pound of substance whose atomic number is 33 dies within 24 hours.
           Therefore,
       Jones died within 24 hours of eating a pound of the substance in that jar.

Suppose, however, that Jones died in an unrelated car accident, and not because he ate arsenic. Although Brody's essential property condition is satisfied, as are the conditions of the D–N model, the explanans in (10) does not, even though true, correctly explain the explanandum. Brody may in effect recognize that it is not an *a priori* but an empirical question whether a D–N explanans if true correctly explains its explanandum. Nevertheless, the empirical requirement which his model invokes—the essential property condition—is not of the right sort to avoid the kind of problem plaguing this and previous models. Like Salmon's homogeneity condition, Brody's essential property condition is not sufficient to guarantee that the explanans-fact is explanatorily operative with respect to the explanandum-fact.

Both Salmon and Brody seem to recognize that if the NES requirement is to be satisfied it is an empirical, not an *a priori*, question whether

---

23. If the explanans explicitly says that the property is essential, then the model purports to satisfy the *a priori* condition. But I want here to consider a model that explicitly violates this condition. (In either case the model turns out to be unsatisfactory.)

an explanans if true correctly explains an explanandum. Yet the empirical considerations their models deploy are not sufficient to ensure that if satisfied an explanation will be correct if its explanans is true. Can problems of the sort generated by these models be avoided in any way other than by abandoning NES?

6. TWO CAUSAL MODELS

The final two models I shall discuss seem to offer a solution. They satisfy NES, violate the *a priori* requirement, and yet avoid the previous problems. However, whether they provide accounts that would be welcome to most of those seeking models of explanation is quite dubious.

a. Brody's Causal Model

As in the case of his essential property model, Brody regards this as providing a set of sufficient conditions for explanations of particular events. These conditions are those of the basic D–N model together with the

> *Causal condition*: The explanans "contains essentially a description of the event which is the cause of the event described in the explanandum."[24]

To see how this is supposed to work let us reconsider

(1) Jones ate a pound of arsenic at time *t*.
   Anyone who eats a pound of arsenic dies within 24 hours.
     Therefore,
   Jones died within 24 hours of *t*.

The problem we noted with the basic D–N model occurs, e.g., if both premises of (1) are true but Jones died within 24 hours of *t* for some unrelated reason. Brody's causal condition saves the day since in such a case the event described in the first premise of the explanans was not the cause of the event described in the explanandum. Hence, on this model we cannot conclude that the explanans if true correctly explains the explanandum.

The present model, like those in section 5, violates the *a priori* requirement. Whether the explanans if true correctly explains the explanandum is not an *a priori* question, since the causal condition must be satisfied; and whether the explanans-event caused the explanandum-event is, in general, an empirical matter. It is not completely clear whether Brody

24. Brody, p. 23.

wants to exclude from the explanans itself singular causal sentences that entail the explanandum, but I shall consider that version of his model which makes this exclusion. Like the models in section 5, this model, I shall assume, is to satisfy the NES requirement.

Woodward is another modelist who proposes the need for a causal condition to supplement the basic D–N model and his own functional interdependence condition:

> These examples suggest that a fully acceptable model of scientific explana-
> tion will need to embody some characteristically causal notions (e.g., some
> notion of causal priority), or some more generalized analogue of these (e.g.,
> some notion of explanatory priority). (p. 53)

However, unlike Brody, he leaves open the question of how such a causal condition should be formulated.[25]

b. The Causal-Motivational Model

Here, as in the D–N motivational model (section 3), the explanandum is a sentence saying that some agent acted in a certain way.[26] The explanans contains a sentence attributing a desire (motive, etc.) to that agent, and a sentence attributing the belief to that agent that performing the act described in the explanandum is, in the circumstances, a (the best, the only) way to satisfy that desire. Thus the explanandum might be a sentence of the form

Agent X performed act A,

and the explanans might contain sentences of the form

X desired G.
X believed that doing A is, in the circumstances, a (the best, the only) way to obtain G.

Unlike the D–N motivational model, however, a law in the explanans relating beliefs and desires to actions is not required. What is required is the satisfaction of a

Causal condition: X's desire and his belief (described in the explanans) caused X to perform act A.

---

25. In his most recent writings, Salmon too proposes adding a causal condition to his S–R model. Unlike Brody and Woodward, he attempts to define the concept of causation he utilizes, although, by his own admission, the definition is not entirely adequate. See his "Why Ask Why?" *Proceedings and Addresses of the American Philosophical Association* **51** (1977), 683–705.

26. See C. J. Ducasse, "Explanation, Mechanism, and Teleology" *Journal of Philosophy* 22 (1925), 150–55; Donald Davidson, "Actions, Reasons, and Causes" *Journal of Philosophy* 60 (1963), 685–700; Alvin I. Goldman, *A Theory of Human Action* (Englewood Cliffs, N.J.), p. 78.

The counterexample cited earlier against the D–N motivational model is now avoided, since in that example it was not the agent's belief and desire mentioned in the explanans, but some other belief and desire, that caused him to act. As in the case of Brody's causal model, the *a priori* requirement is not satisfied, but NES is.

I shall not here try to defend or criticize these two models.[27] I shall assume for the sake of the argument that each avoids, or can be modified so as to avoid, the kind of problem I have been concerned with. However, each does so by violating NES in spirit, whereas the earlier models satisfy this requirement both in spirit and in letter. In order to apply the present causal models one must determine the truth of sentences such as these:

(2) Jones' eating a pound of arsenic at time *t* caused him to die within 24 hours of *t*.

(3) Smith's desire to buy eggs and his belief that going to the store is the only way to do so caused him to go to the store.

But these are singular explanation-sentences that entail the explanandum. To be sure, neither model requires such sentences to be in the explanans. Still, in each model to determine whether the explanans if true correctly explains the explanandum one has to determine the truth of such sentences. I am not criticizing the models on these grounds. But I believe that many of those who seek models of explanation will want to do so. They will say that in order to know whether the explanans in such a model correctly explains the explanandum one has to determine, independently of the truth of the explanans, the truth of sentences of a sort these modelists want to exclude from the explanans itself. Morever, they will point out that there is not much difference between determining the truth of (2) and (3), on the one hand, and that of

Jones' eating a pound of arsenic at *t* explains why he died within 24 hours of *t* (or Jones died within 24 hours of *t* because he ate a pound of arsenic at *t*)

Smith's desire to buy eggs and his belief that going to the store is the only way to do so explains why he went to the store (or, Smith went to the store because he had this desire and belief)

---

27. A cogent attack on Brody's model can be found in Timothy McCarthy, "On an Aristotelian Model of Scientific Explanation" *Philosophy of Science* 44 (1977), 159–166. See Davidson, "Psychology as Philosophy" in J. Glover (ed.), *Philosophy of Mind* (Oxford, 1976), pp. 103–104, for criticism of the causal-motivational model (which Davidson himself once supported).

on the other. Models which impose these causal conditions, they are likely to say, provide insufficient philosophical clarification for the concept of explanation, even though the explanation-sentence expressing the causal relationship is not itself a part of the explanans.[28] If a central aim of modelists is to define terms such as 'explain', 'because', and 'causes', this excludes their employment as primitive notions in the explanans or, as in the present case, in the conditions of the model.

Regardless of whether we view such criticism as important, the present models are of interest because to avoid the sorts of problems raised in section 4 these models, unlike their D–N ancestors, require establishing the truth of empirical sentences to determine whether the explanans if true correctly explains the explanandum. In this respect they are like Salmon's S–R model and Brody's essential property model. However, unlike the latter, the empirical sentences whose truth they require establishing are themselves singular sentences that entail the explanandum.

7. CONCLUSIONS

Our discussion suggests the following conclusions: (i) If the explanans is not to contain singular sentences that entail the explanandum, then it will be an empirical not an *a priori* question whether the explanans if true correctly explains the explanandum. (ii) This empirical question will involve determining the truth-values of certain singular sentences (either explanation-sentences or something akin to them) that do entail the explanandum; otherwise factors will be citable in the explanans which are not explanatorily operative with respect to the explanandum-event.

Can there be a model of explanation? Specifically, can there be a set of sufficient conditions which are such that if they are satisfied by the explanans and explanandum the former correctly explains the latter? Our discussion suggests that there can be no such model if, like D–N theorists, we insist that it satisfy both the *a priori* and the NES requirements. Moreover, it also suggests that we will not be successful in discovering a model in which (a) the NES requirement is satisfied, and in which (b) it is not an explicit condition of the model that some singular sentence be true that entails the explanandum.

---

28. Indeed, some formulations of the causal-motivational model (e.g., Ducasse's and Goldman's) seem to allow as an explicit part of the explanans a singular explanation-sentence that entails the explanandum. In such cases the NES requirement is violated in letter as well as in spirit.

It does not follow from this that an explanans which appeals to causal factors, laws, dispositions, desires and beliefs, statistically relevant factors, or essential properties cannot correctly explain an explanandum. However, models of explanation of the sort I am considering do not simply list kinds of factors that can be explanatory. Their proponents want to supply sufficient conditions for correct explanations. If it is demanded that these conditions satisfy the NES and *a priori* requirements, or NES plus (b) then I am suggesting that such models will not be forthcoming.

9

Explanation versus Prediction

Which Carries More Weight?

"Explanation vs. Prediction: Which Carries More Weight?" is reprinted by permission from Philosophy of Science Association Proceedings 1994 *(1995), 156–164. Two contrasting views have emerged in the literature to answer this question. One is that successful predictions of a theory always carry more weight in favor of that theory than successful explanations. The other is that the reverse is true. In this chapter I deny both claims. Sometimes a successful prediction provides stronger support; sometimes a successful explanation does. Which obtains has nothing to do with whether it is a prediction or an explanation, but rather with the selection procedure used to generate the evidence. (In my The Book of Evidence, chapter 10 is an expanded version of this essay, in which Patrick Maher's "predictionist" account and Clark Glymour's problem of "old evidence" are also examined.)*

1. THE HISTORICAL THESIS OF EVIDENCE

According to a standard view, predictions of new phenomena provide stronger evidence for a theory than explanations of old ones. More guardedly, a theory that predicts phenomena that did not prompt the initial formulation of that theory is better supported by those phenomena than is a theory by known phenomena that generated the theory in the first place. So say various philosophers of science, including William Whewell (1847) in the 19th century and Karl Popper (1959) in the 20th, to mention just two.

Stephen Brush (1989) takes issue with this on historical grounds. He argues that generally speaking scientists do not regard the fact that a theory predicts new phenomena, even ones of a kind totally different from those that prompted the theory in the first place, as providing better evidential support for that theory than is provided by already known facts explained by the theory. By contrast, Brush claims, there are cases, including general relativity and the periodic law of elements, in which scientists tend to consider known phenomena explained by a theory as constituting much stronger support than novel predictions.[1]

Both the predictionist and the explanationist are committed to an interesting historical thesis about evidence, namely:

> *Historical thesis*: Whether some claim e, if true, is evidence for an hypothesis h, or how strong that evidence is, depends on certain historical facts about e, h, or their relationship.

For example, whether, or the extent to which, e counts as evidence for h depends on whether e was known before or after h was formulated. Various historical positions are possible, as Alan Musgrave (1974) noted years ago in a very interesting article. On a simple predictionist view (which Musgrave classifies as "purely temporal") e supports h only if e was not known when h was first proposed. On another view (which Musgrave attributes to Zahar (1973) and calls "heuristic"), e is evidence for h only if when h was first formulated it was not devised in order to explain e. On yet a third historical view (which Musgrave himself accepts), e is evidence for some theory T only if e cannot be explained by a "predecessor" theory, i.e., by a competing theory which was devised by scientists prior to the formulation of T. These views, and other variations, are all committed to the historical thesis.

Is the historical thesis true or false? I propose to argue that it is sometimes true, and sometimes false, depending on the type of evidence in question. Then I will consider what implications, if any, this has for the debate between Brush and the predictionists.

Before beginning, however, let me mention a curious but interesting fact about various well-known philosophical theories or definitions of evidence. As Laura Snyder (1994) points out in a perceptive paper entitled "Is Evidence Historical?" most such theories, including Carnap's (1962) a priori theory of confirmation, Hempel's (1945) satisfaction theory, Glymour's (1980) bootstrap account, and the usual hypothetico-deductive account, are incompatible with the historical thesis. They hold that

---

1. To what extent Brush wants to generalize this explanationist position is a question I leave for him to answer. There are passages in his writings that strongly suggest a more general position. For example: "There is even some reason to suspect that a successful explanation of a fact that other theories have already failed to explain satisfactorily (for example, the Mercury perihelion) is more convincing than the prediction of a new fact, at least until the competing theories have had their chance (and failed) to explain it" (1989, p. 1127). In what follows I consider a generalized explanationist thesis.

whether, or the extent to which, e is evidence for, or confirms, h is an objective fact about e, h, and their relationship. It is in no way affected by the time at which h was first proposed, or e was first known, or by the intentions with which h was formulated. Defenders of these views must reject both the predictionist and the explanationist claims about evidence. They must say that whether, or the extent to which, e supports h has nothing to do with whether e was first formulated as a novel prediction from h or whether e was known before h and h was constructed to explain it.

Accordingly, we have two extreme or absolutist positions. There is the position, reflected in the historical thesis, that evidence is always historical (in the sense indicated). And there is a contrasting position, reflected in certain standard views, that evidence is never historical. Does the truth lie at either extreme? Or is it somewhere in the middle?

2. SELECTION PROCEDURES

Suppose that an investigator decides to test the efficacy of a certain drug D in relieving symptoms S. The hypothesis under consideration is

h: Drug D relieves symptoms S in approximately 95% of the cases.

The investigator may test drug D by giving it to persons suffering from S and by giving a placebo to other persons suffering from S (the "control group"). In deciding how to proceed, the investigator employs what I will call a "selection procedure," or rule, determining how to test, or obtain evidence for, an hypothesis, in this case determining which persons he will select for his studies and how he will study them.

For example, here is one of many possible selection procedures (SP) for testing h:

SP 1: Choose a sample of 2,000 persons of different ages, sexes, races, and geographical locations, all of whom have symptoms S in varying degrees; divide them arbitrarily into 2 groups; give one group drug D and the other a placebo; determine how many in each group have their symptoms relieved.

Now, suppose that a particular investigator uses this (or some other) selection procedure and obtains the following result:

e: In a group of 1,000 persons with symptoms S taking drug D, 950 persons had relief of S; in a control group of 1,000 S-sufferers not taking D but a placebo none had symptoms S relieved.

The first thing to note about this example is that whether the report e supports hypothesis h, or the extent to which it does, depends crucially on what selection procedure was in fact used in obtaining e. Suppose that instead of SP1 the following selection procedure had been employed:

> SP 2: Choose a sample of 2,000 females age 5 all of whom have symptoms S in a very mild form; proceed as in SP1.

If result e had been obtained by following SP2, then e, although true, would not be particularly good evidence for h, certainly not as strong as that obtained by following SP1. The reason, of course, is that SP1, by contrast with SP2, gives a sample that is varied with respect to two factors that may well be relevant: age of patient and severity of symptoms. (Hypothesis h does not restrict itself to 5-year-old girls with mild symptoms, but asserts a cure-rate for the general population of sufferers with varying degrees of the symptoms in question.)

This means that if the result as described in e is obtained, then whether, or to what extent, that result confirms the hypothesis h depends crucially on what selection procedure was in fact used in obtaining e. That is, it depends on a historical fact about e: on how in fact e was obtained. If e resulted from following SP1, then e is pretty strong evidence for h; if e was obtained by following SP2, then e is pretty weak evidence for h, if it confirms it at all. Just by looking at e and h, and even by ascertaining that e is true, we are unable to determine to what extent, if any, e supports h. We need to invoke "history."

To nail down this point completely, consider a third selection procedure:

> SP 3: Choose a sample of 2,000 persons all of whom have S in varying degrees; divide them arbitrarily into 2 groups; give one group drugs D and D' (where D' relieves symptoms S in 95% of the cases and blocks possible curative effects of D when taken together); give the other group a placebo.

Consider once more result e (which, again, let us suppose, obtains). In this case e supports h not at all. And, again, whether this is so cannot be ascertained simply by examining the propositions e, h, or their "logical" relationship. We need to know a historical fact about e, namely, that the information it (truly) reports was obtained by following SP3.

So far then we seem to have support for the historical thesis about evidence. Can we generalize from examples like this to all cases? Can we say that for any true report e, and any hypothesis h, whether, or to what extent, e is evidence for h depends upon historical facts about how e was obtained? No, we cannot.

Consider another very simple case. Let e be the following report, which is true:

> e = In last week's lottery, 1,000 tickets were sold, of which John owned 999 at the time of the selection of the winner; this was a fair lottery in which one ticket was selected at random.
>
> h = John won the lottery.

In an attempt to obtain information such as e to support h different rules or "selection procedures" might have been followed, e.g.,

> SP 4: Determine who bought tickets, and how many, by asking lottery officials.
>
> SP 5: Determine this by standing next to the person selling tickets.
>
> SP 6: Determine this by consulting the local newspaper, which publishes this information as a service to its readers.

Let us suppose that following any of these selection procedures results in a true report e. (And, as in the symptoms case, we may suppose that following any of these procedures is a reasonable way to establish whether e is true.) But in this case, unlike the drug example, which selection procedure was in fact followed is completely irrelevant in determining whether, or to what extent, e is evidence for h. In this case, unlike the drug example, we do not need to know how information e was obtained to know that e (assuming it is true) is very strong evidence for h. Nor do we need to know any other historical facts about e, h, or their relationship. (In particular, contrary to both the predictionist and explanationist views, we do not need to know when e was first known relative to when h was first formulated; i.e., we do not need to know whether e was explained or predicted. But more of this later when these two historical views are examined more fully.) Accordingly, we have a case that violates the historical thesis of evidence.

Since examples similar to each of these two can be readily constructed, we may conclude that there are many cases that satisfy the historical thesis of evidence, and many others that fail to satisfy it. Is there a general rule for deciding which do and which do not?

Perhaps our two examples will help generate such a rule. In the drug case the evidence report e is historical in an obvious sense: it reports the results of a particular study made at some particular time and place. But this is clearly not sufficient to distinguish the cases, since the evidence report e in the lottery case is also historical: it reports facts about a particular lottery, who bought tickets, and when. So, I submit, what distinguishes the cases is not the historical character of the evidence, but something else.

I shall say that a putative evidence statement e is *empirically complete* with respect to a hypothesis h if whether, or to what extent, e is evidence for, or confirms, h depends just on what e reports, what h says, and the relationship between them. It does not depend on any additional empirical facts—e.g., facts about when e or h was formulated, or with what intentions, or on any (other) facts about the world. In the drug example, e is not empirically complete with respect to h: whether, or to what extent, e supports h depends on how the sample reported in e was selected—empirical information not contained in e or h.[2] By contrast, in the lottery example, e is empirically complete with respect to h: whether, and to what extent, e supports h in this case does not depend on empirical facts in addition to e. To determine whether, and how much, e supports h in this case we do not need any further empirical investigation. To be sure, additional empirical inquiry may unearth new information e′ which is such that both e and e′ together do not support h to the same extent that e by itself does. But that is different. In the drug but not the lottery example information in addition to e is necessary to determine the extent to which e itself supports h. In the drug case we cannot legitimately say whether or to what extent the report e supports the efficacy of drug D unless we know how the patients described in e were selected. In the lottery case information about how purported evidence was obtained is irrelevant for the question of whether or how strongly that evidence, assuming its truth, supports h.

So we have one important difference between the two examples. Is this enough to draw a distinction between cases that satisfy the historical thesis of evidence and those that do not? Perhaps not. There may be cases in which e is empirically incomplete with respect to h, but in which empirical facts needed to complete it are not historical. Consider

e = Male crows are black.

h = Female crows are black.

One might claim that whether, or the extent to which, e supports h in this case depends on empirical facts in addition to e. If, e.g., other species of birds generally have different colors for different sexes, then e does not support h very much. If other species generally have the same color for both sexes, then e supports h considerably more. But these additional facts are not "historical," at least not in the clear ways of previous examples. (I construe "other species of birds generally have different colors for different sexes" to be making a general statement, and not to be referring

---

2. For Carnap (1962) and others, every e is empirically complete with respect to every h. For these writers, whether, and the extent to which, e confirms h is an a priori matter.

to any particular historical period.) If this is granted, then we need to add a proviso to the completeness idea above.

There are cases (including our drug example) in which a putative evidence claim e is empirically incomplete with respect to a hypothesis h, where determining whether, or to what extent, e supports h requires determining the truth of some historical fact. I shall speak of these as historical evidence cases. They satisfy the historical thesis of evidence. By contrast, there are cases in which a putative evidence claim e is empirically complete with respect to hypothesis h (e.g., our lottery case), and there may be cases in which a putative evidence claim e, although empirically incomplete with respect to h, can be settled without appeal to historical facts (possibly the crow example). Cases of the latter two sorts violate the historical thesis of evidence. What implications, if any, does this hold for whether predictions or explanations provide better confirmation?

3. PREDICTIONS VERSUS EXPLANATIONS

Let us return to the original question proposed by Brush. Do predictions of novel facts provide stronger evidence than explanations of old ones, as Whewell and Popper claim? Or is the reverse true? My answer is this: Sometimes a prediction provides better evidence for a hypothesis, sometimes an explanation does, and sometimes they are equally good. Which obtains has nothing to do with the fact that it is a prediction of novel facts or that it is an explanation of known ones.

To show this, let us begin with a case that violates the historical thesis of evidence. Here it should be easy to show that whether the putative evidence is known before or after the hypothesis is formulated is irrelevant for confirmation. Let the hypothesis be

  h = This coin is fair, i.e., if tossed in random ways under normal
      conditions it will land on heads approximately half the time in
      the long run.

  e = This coin is physically symmetrical, and in a series of 1,000
      random tosses under normal conditions it landed on heads
      approximately 500 times.

We might reasonably take e to be empirically complete with respect to h. Accordingly, whether e supports h, and the extent to which it does, does not depend on empirical facts other than e. In particular, it does not depend on when, how, or even whether e comes to be known, or on whether e was known first and h then formulated, or on whether h was conceived first and e then stated as a prediction from it. Putative evidence e supports hypothesis h and does so (equally well) whether or not e is known before or after h was initially formulated, indeed whether or not h is ever formulated or e is ever known to be true.

So let us focus instead on cases that satisfy the historical thesis of evidence. We might suppose that at least in such cases explanations (or predictions) are always better for confirmation. Return once again to our drug hypothesis:

h = Drug D relieves symptoms S in approximately 95% of the cases.

Consider now two evidence claims, the first a prediction about an unknown future event, the second a report about something already known:

e_1 = In the next clinical trial of 1,000 patients who suffer from symptoms S and who take D, approximately 950 will get some relief.

e_2 = In a trial that has already taken place involving 1,000 patients with S who took D (we know that) approximately 950 got some relief.

On the prediction view, e_1 is stronger evidence for h than is e_2. On the explanation view it is the reverse. And to sharpen the cases let us suppose that e_2, by contrast to e_1, was not only known to be true prior to the formulation of h, but that h was formulated with the intention of explaining e_2. Which view is correct? Neither one.

Let us take the prediction case e_1 first. Whether, and to what extent, e_1 (if true) supports h depends on empirical facts in addition to e_1. In this case it depends on the selection procedure to be used in the next clinical trial. Suppose this selection procedure calls for choosing just 5-year-old girls with very mild symptoms who in addition to D are also taking drug D′ which ameliorates symptoms S in 95% of the cases and potentially blocks D from doing so. Then e_1 would be very weak evidence for h, if it supports it at all. This is despite the fact that e_1 is a correct prediction from h, one not used in generating h in the first place. By contrast, suppose that the selection procedure used in the past trial mentioned in e_2 is much better with respect to h. For example, it calls for choosing humans of both sexes, of different ages, with symptoms of varying degrees, who are not also taking drug D′. Then e_2 would be quite strong evidence for h, much stronger than what is supplied by e_1. In such a case, a known fact explained by h would provide more support for h than a newly predicted fact would.

Obviously the situations here can be reversed. We might suppose that the selection procedure used to generate the prediction of e_1 is the one cited in the previous paragraph as being used to generate e_2 (and vice versa). In this situation a newly predicted fact would provide more support for h than an already explained one.

In these cases what makes putative evidence have the strength it does has nothing to do with whether it is being explained or predicted. It has to do with the selection procedure used to generate that evidence.[3] In one situation—whether it involves something that is explained or predicted—we have a putative evidence statement generated by a selection procedure that is a good one relative to h; in the other case we have a flawed selection procedure. This is what matters for confirmation—not whether the putative evidence is being explained or predicted.

4. BRUSH REDUX

Brush is clearly denying a general predictionist thesis. By contrast he cites cases in which scientists themselves regarded known evidence explained by a theory as stronger support for that theory than new evidence that was successfully predicted. And he seems to imply that this was reasonable. He offers an explanation for this claim, namely, that with explanations of the known phenomena, by contrast with successful predictions of the new ones, scientists had time to consider alternative theories that would generate these phenomena. Now, even if Brush does not do so, I want to extend this idea and consider a more general explanationist view that is committed to the following three theses that Brush invokes for some cases:

1. A selection procedure for testing a hypothesis h is flawed, or at least inferior to another, other things equal, if it fails to call for explicit consideration of competitors to h.
2. The longer time scientists have to consider whether there are plausible competitors to h, the more likely they are to find some if they exist.
3. With putative evidence already known before the formulation of h scientists have (had) more time to consider whether there are plausible competitors to h than is the case with novel predictions.

I would challenge at least the first and third theses. In my first example, selection procedure 1 for the drug hypothesis does not call for explicitly considering competitors to that hypothesis. Yet it does not seem flawed on that account, or inferior to one that does. However, even supposing it were inferior, whether a selection procedure calls for a consideration of competitors is completely irrelevant to whether the putative evidence claim is a prediction or a known fact being explained. In the case of a prediction,

3. Cf. Mayo (1991).

no less than that of an explanation, the selection procedure may call for a consideration of competitors.

For example, in our drug case, where h is "Drug D relieves symptoms S in approximately 95% of the cases," and e is the prediction "In the next clinical trial of 1,000 patients suffering from symptoms S who take D, approximately 950 will get some relief," the selection procedure to be used for the next clinical trial might include the rule

> In conducting this next trial, determine whether the patients are also taking some other drug which relieves S in approximately 95% of the cases and which blocks any effectiveness D might have.

Such a selection procedure calls for the explicit consideration of a competitor to explain e, namely, that it will be some other drug, not D, that will relieve symptoms S in the next trial. This is so even though e is a prediction. Moreover, to respond to the third thesis about time for considering competitors, an investigator planning a future trial can have as much time as she likes to develop a selection procedure calling for a consideration of a competing hypothesis. More generally, in designing a novel experiment to test some hypothesis h as much time may be spent in precluding competing hypotheses that will explain the test results as is spent in considering competing hypotheses for old data.

5. THOMSON VERSUS HERTZ

Finally, let me invoke an example more recognizably scientific. It involves a dispute between Heinrich Hertz and J. J. Thomson over the nature of cathode rays.[4] In experiments conducted in 1883 Hertz observed that the cathode rays in his experiments were not deflected by an electrical field. He took this to be strong evidence that cathode rays are not charged particles (as the English physicist William Crookes had concluded), but some type of ether waves. In 1897 J. J. Thomson repeated Hertz's experiments but with a much higher evacuation of gas in the cathode tube than Hertz had been able to obtain. Thomson believed that when cathode rays pass though a gas they make it a conductor, which screens off the electric force from the charged particles comprising the cathode rays.[5] This screening off effect will be reduced if the gas in the tube is more thoroughly evacuated. In Thomson's 1897 experiments electrical deflection of the cathode

---

4. See Achinstein (1991), chapters 10 and 11; also Buchwald (1994), chapter 10.
5. See Thomson (1897), p. 107.

rays was detected, which Thomson took to be strong evidence that cathode rays are charged particles.

Here, however, I want to consider the evidential report of Hertz in 1883, not of Thomson in 1897. Let

e = In Hertz's cathode ray experiments of 1883 no electrical deflection of cathode rays was detected.

h = Cathode rays are not electrically charged.

Hertz took e to be strong evidence for h. In 1897 Thomson claimed, in effect, that Hertz's results as reported in e did not provide strong evidence for h, since Hertz's experimental setup was flawed: He was employing insufficiently evacuated tubes. To use my previous terminology, Thomson was claiming that Hertz's selection procedure for testing h was inadequate.[6]

Here we can pick up on a point emphasized by Brush. Hertz, we might say, failed to use a selection procedure calling for considering a competitor to h to explain his results (that is, that cathode rays are charged particles, but that the tubes Hertz was using were not sufficiently evacuated to allow an electrical force to act on these particles). But—and this is the point I want to emphasize—in determining whether, or to what extent, Hertz's putative evidence e supports his hypothesis h, it seems to be irrelevant whether Hertz's e was a novel prediction from an already formulated hypothesis h or an already known fact to be explained by h. Hertz writes that in performing the relevant experiments he was trying to answer two questions:

> Firstly: Do the cathode rays give rise to electrostatic forces in their neighbourhood? Secondly: In their course are they affected by external electrostatic forces? (Hertz 1896, p. 249)

In his paper he did not predict what his experiments would show. Nor were the results of his experiments treated by him as facts known before

---

6. Lord Rayleigh (1942, pp. 78–79), in a biography of Thomson, made the same claim: "He [Hertz] failed to observe this [electrical] effect, but the design of his experiment was open to certain objections which were removed in a later investigation by Perrin in 1895, directed to the same question. Perrin got definite evidence that the rays carried a negative charge. J. J. Thomson, in a modification of Perrin's experiment showed that if the Faraday cylinder was put out of the line of fire of the cathode, it acquired a charge when, and only when, the cathode rays were so deflected by a magnet as to enter the cylinder." [Note Rayleigh's claim that Perrin (and Thomson) got "definite evidence" that cathode rays carry a negative charge, whereas, by implication, Hertz's experiments did not give "definite evidence" concerning the question of charge.]

he had formulated his hypothesis h. Once he obtained his experimental result he then claimed that they supported his theory:

> As far as the accuracy of the experiment allows, we can conclude with certainty that no electrostatic effect due to the cathode rays can be perceived. (p.251)

To be sure, we might say that Hertz's *theory* itself predicted some such results, even if Hertz himself did not (i.e., even if Hertz did not himself draw this conclusion before getting his experimental results). But even if we speak this way, Hertz did not claim or imply that his experimental results provide better (or weaker) support for his theory because the theory predicted them before they were obtained. Nor did Thomson in his criticism of Hertz allude to one or the other possibility. Whichever it was—whether a prediction or an explanation or neither—Hertz (Thomson was claiming) should have used a better selection procedure. This is what is criticizable in Hertz, not whether he was predicting a novel fact or explaining a known one.

I end with a quote from John Maynard Keynes (1921, p. 305), whose book on probability contains lots of insights. Here is one:

> The peculiar virtue of prediction or predesignation is altogether imaginary. The number of instances examined and the analogy between them are the essential points, and the question as to whether a particular hypothesis happens to be propounded before or after their examination is quite irrelevant.

REFERENCES

Achinstein, P. (1991), *Particles and Waves.* New York: Oxford University Press.

Brush, S. (1989), "Prediction and Theory Evaluation: The Case of Light Bending," *Science* 246, 1124–1129.

Buchwald, J. (1994), *The Creation of Scientific Effects.* Chicago: University of Chicago Press.

Carnap, R. (1962), *Logical Foundations of Probability,* 2nd ed. Chicago: University of Chicago Press.

Glymour, C. (1980), *Theory and Evidence.* Princeton, N. J.: Princeton University Press.

Hempel, C. (1945), "Studies in the Logic of Confirmation," *Mind* 54, 1–26, 97–121.

Hertz, H. (1896), *Miscellaneous Papers.* London: Macmillan.

Keynes, J. M. (1921), *A Treatise on Probability.* London: Macmillan.

Mayo, D. (1991), "Novel Evidence and Severe Tests," *Philosophy of Science* 58, 523–552.

Musgrave, A. (1974), "Logical versus Historical Theories of Confirmation, "*British Journal for the Philosophy of Science* 25, 1–23.

Popper, K. (1959), *The Logic of Scientific Discovery.* London: Hutchinson.

Rayleigh, R. (1942), *The Life of Sir J. J. Thomson.* Cambridge: Cambridge University Press.

Snyder, L. (1994), "Is Evidence Historical?" In *Scientific Methods: Conceptual and Historical Problems*. Edited by P. Achinstein and L. Snyder, Malabar, Fla.: Krieger.

Thomson, J. J. (1987), "Cathode Rays," *The Electrician* 39, 104–108.

Whewell, W. (1847), *The Philosophy of the Inductive Sciences*. New York: Johnson Reprint, 1967.

Zahar, E. (1973), "Why Did Einstein's Programme Supercede Lorentz's?" *British Journal for the Philosophy of Science* 24, 95–123, 223–262.

ACKNOWLEDGMENT   I am indebted to Laura J. Snyder for very helpful discussions, and to Robert Rynasiewicz for trying to convince me of the error of my ways.

10

Function Statements

"Function Statements" is reprinted by permission from Philosophy of Science *44 (1977), 341–367 (selected for Philosopher's Annual 1977). I introduce counterexamples to three standard accounts of functions (good consequence, goal, and etiological theories) and propose a positive account in terms of a means-end relationship and the idea of design, use, or benefit. I also argue that function statements can provide different types of explanations, including noncausal explanations of the presence of the item with the function.*

1. THREE ACCOUNTS

Talk of functions looms large in discussions of teleology. The concern has been mainly with statements of the form "the (or a) function of x is to y," e.g., "the function of the heart is to pump the blood." In recent years analyses of such statements tend to fall into three general categories. Most popular is what I shall call the good consequence doctrine, which appears in various forms in the writings of Canfield (1963), Hempel (1965), Hull (1974), Lehman (1965), Ruse (1973), Sorabji (1964), and Woodfield (1976). The general idea is that doing y is x's function only if doing y confers some good.

Some specify what this good is, others do not. According to Sorabji, there is a sense of "function" for which a necessary condition is that "the performance by a thing of its (putative) function should confer some good" (1964, p. 291).[1] But the goods can vary and particular ones should not be specified as part of an analysis. Woodfield has a similar account. Hempel and Ruse, on the other hand, identify specific goods, adequate

I am indebted to Stephen Barker, Robert Cummins, Dale Gottlieb, and George Wilson for making a number of very helpful suggestions.

1. Sorabji (p. 290) also recognizes a second sense of function which involves the idea of making an effort to obtain a result.

working order for the former, survival and reproduction for the latter. According to Hempel, a function of x in a system S is to y if and only if x does y and x's doing y ensures the satisfaction of certain conditions necessary for S's remaining in adequate, effective, or proper working order. For Ruse, the function of x in S is to y if and only if S does y by using x and y aids in the survival and reproduction of S.

In what follows I shall formulate the doctrine in a general way without mentioning specific goods, although this can be done to obtain particular versions.

> *The Good-Consequence Doctrine:* The (a) function of x (in S) is to y if and only if x does y (in S) and doing y (in S) confers some good (upon S, or perhaps upon something associated with S, e.g., its user in the case of artifacts).

Thus we can say that the function of the heart in mammals is to pump the blood because the heart does pump the blood in mammals and pumping blood confers a good upon mammals. But we cannot say that the function of a poison ivy reaction in humans is to make the skin itch, since the latter confers no good upon humans.

The second doctrine focuses upon the idea of contributing to a goal that something or someone has.

> *The Goal Doctrine:* The (a) function of x (in S) is to y if and only if x does y (in S) and doing y (in S) is or contributes to some goal which x (or S) has, or which the user, owner, or designer of x (or S) has.

For example, a function of my hands is to grasp objects, because my hands do this, and grasping objects is, or at least contributes to, one of the goals which I, their user, have. An appeal may be made here to the notion of a *goal-directed system*, roughly, a system which persists in or tends to achieve some state (the goal) under a variety of disturbing conditions. Those who speak this way would say that the function of the thermostat in a home heating system is to turn the heat on and off, since doing so contributes to a "goal" of the heating system, namely, to maintain a constant temperature. Anyone who refuses to attribute goals to inanimate objects can still espouse the present doctrine, provided that he attributes the goal to an animate user, owner, or designer of the object or system.

Although so far as I know no one has formulated the doctrine in exactly this way, a goal doctrine is suggested by Nagel (1961), as well as more recently by Boorse (1976).[2] According to both authors, in the case of items such as guided missiles the goals are to be attributed to the artifacts themselves; with items such as chairs and fountain pens, according

2. Nagel's analysis seems to come to this: The function of x in S is to y if and only if x is necessary (or sufficient or both) for S to do y and S is a goal-directed system with some goal G.

to Boorse at least, the goal is to be attributed to a "system" consisting of the artifact together with its user (1976, p. 70). In general, however, neither writer would attribute the goal simply to the user or to the designer of the artifact, as my more general formulation permits.

The good-consequence and goal doctrines are quite broad, as I have stated them, and the question of their logical independence might be raised. Specific forms of one doctrine can be independent of either specific or general forms of the other. Something may contribute to a goal that I have even though it does not increase my chances of survival and reproduction (Ruse's specific good); and something may increase my chances of survival and reproduction even though survival and reproduction is not, and fails to contribute to, any goal of mine (e.g., my goal is to die quickly and without descendants). Again a good consequence theorist might refuse to attribute goals to anything but humans and higher animals while nevertheless claiming that various activities can confer a good upon things in addition to humans and higher animals. (Soaking up rainwater is beneficial for plants, he might say, even though it does not contribute to any of their goals, since they have none.)

On the other hand, if we consider these two doctrines in their most general formulations and include an appeal to goal-directed systems, to goods and goals not just for S but for users, owners, and designers of S, and to cases in which doing y either is or contributes to a goal, then the doctrines may well not be independent. It is difficult to imagine a case in which doing y confers a good upon S (or upon its user, owner, or designer) but is not and does not contribute to any goal of S (or its user, etc.), or vice versa.

A third position, the explanation doctrine, which has been defended by Wright (1973, 1976), Ayala (1970), Bennett (1976), and Levin (1976), seems quite different from the other two. The general idea is that function statements provide etiological explanations of the existence or presence of the item with the function. Since Wright's account is simple and general I will use it in what follows.

The Explanation Doctrine: The function of *x* is to *y* if and only if *x* is there because it does *y* (this "because" involves the idea of etiological explanation

---

But this is incomplete as it stands since doing y, on this analysis, need make no contribution to the attainment of G. (For example, a home heating system is, for Nagel, a goal-directed system whose goal is to maintain constant temperature. For the heating system to make the temperature in the house 23° warmer than the outside temperature a thermostat is necessary, let us suppose. But it is not the function of a thermostat in a heating system to make the temperature in the house 23° warmer than the outside temperature.) If we change Nagel's account to require that doing y in S is or contributes to a goal of S then we obtain a view much closer to the goal doctrine. On the other hand, Boorse's account of sentences of the form "x is performing the function z in the G-ing of S at t" does come very close to the goal doctrine.

which Wright understands may include causes and agent's reasons); and *y* is a consequence of *x*'s being there.

For example, the function of that switch is to turn the light on and off since the presence of that switch in this room is etiologically explainable by reference to the fact that it turns the light on and off, and its doing this is a consequence of its being there. When it comes to natural functions Wright invokes the ideas of natural selection and heredity. The function of the human heart is to pump the blood since the heart's presence in humans can be explained, via natural selection and heredity, by the fact that it does pump the blood. (Nature selected in favor of those who get their blood pumped by means of the heart.) And the blood's being pumped is a consequence of the heart's presence. Although it will often be the case, it is not required by this analysis that *x*'s doing *y* confer some good or contribute to some goal of anyone or anything.

The goal and explanation doctrines are meant to apply to the functions of artifacts as well as natural objects and processes. Their proponents advocate a unified analysis. By contrast, some good-consequence theorists, e.g., Ruse, restrict their particular versions of this doctrine to the functions of natural items only, while others, such as Hempel, believe that their doctrine holds generally for all items to which functions are ascribed.

2. COUNTEREXAMPLES

It should not be surprising that counterexamples to each view have been or might readily be proposed. Whether they are completely devastating is a matter that will be taken up in section 5.

If the good-consequence doctrine is meant to apply to artifacts, the following example seems to show that the doctrine fails to provide a necessary condition. Consider a sewing machine which contains a special button designed by its designer to activate a mechanism which will blow up the machine. Activating such a mechanism, we are to suppose, will never have any good consequences whatever for the machine or its user or even its designer. This is so whether we focus on the goods usually mentioned such as survival and reproduction (in the case of user and designer), or proper working order (in the case of the machine), or indeed on any other goods it seems reasonable to consider. It is simply something which the designer designed the button to do.[3] Still, it would seem, the function of that button is to activate a mechanism which will blow up the machine.

---

3. To say that this button activates the exploding mechanism is to imply, of course, that it is capable of doing this, and not that the mechanism is always being activated. In such a

It might be replied that if no good comes of activating such a mechanism at least its designer must have believed that it would. The present doctrine might then be weakened to require in the case of artifacts not that doing y in fact confers some good but only that x's designer believes that it will. Still, although it would be strange and pointless to design such a button if the designer did not believe that activating the exploding mechanism would confer some good, it would not be impossible. And if he did design such a button then its function would be to activate the exploding mechanism.

A second example, proposed by Larry Wright (1973, 1976), purports to show that the present doctrine fails to provide sufficient conditions for functions. Suppose that the second hand in this watch happens to work in such a way that it sweeps the dust from the watch and doing this confers a good upon the watch and its owner since it makes the watch work more accurately. Although the good consequence doctrine is satisfied, it seems not to be the (or even a) function of the second hand in this watch to sweep dust from the watch. As Wright points out, the fact that the second hand does this is a coincidence; and, he argues, if x does y by coincidence then y cannot be the function of x, even if doing y confers a good. We might say that the second hand *functions as* a dustsweeper, but we would not identify this as its function, according to Wright.

The next example seems to impugn the claim that the good-consequence doctrine provides necessary conditions even for nonartifacts. The example, first introduced by Hempel (1965) against a simple consequence view of functions,[4] can also be used against the good consequence doctrine, as Frankfurt and Poole (1966), critics of this doctrine, have noted. The human heart produces heartsounds in the body, and the production of heartsounds is of benefit to the heart's owner, since it aids doctors in diagnosing and treating heart disease. In a human whose beating heart produced no sound, heart disease would be more difficult to detect and treat. Yet, all these authors insist, it is not the (or a) function of the heart to produce heartsounds.

These three examples can also be used against the goal doctrine. We might imagine that neither the designer nor the user of the sewing machine with the self-destruct button has as a goal the activation of the exploding mechanism and that doing this contributes to no goal of the

---

case, however, I take the good-consequence doctrine to be saying that it is the actual activation of this mechanism, and not simply the capability of doing so, that confers a good (at least on certain occasions). But even if on this doctrine the mere capability is to be taken as what confers the good the same example could be used; we can suppose that having such a capability confers no good at all.

4. That is, the view that x's function is to y if and only if y-ing is a consequence of x or x's presence.

designer or user. We might suppose that sewing machines with such but-
tons are the only ones made, that people who buy them use them only for
sewing, and that activating the exploding mechanism is not and does not
contribute to one of their goals. As far as users are concerned activation of
such a mechanism is completely useless and quite dangerous. Indeed, its
nonactivation contributes to one of their goals.

A goal theorist might reply that it is a goal of the designer that the
button on the machine be *capable* of activating the exploding mechanism. In response, however, it seems more appropriate to say that the
designer's goal in such a case is *to design* (or *produce*, or *bring into existence*)
a button with such a capability (see section 6)—a goal which is not identical with activating the exploding mechanism (the putative function of
the button), nor one to which such activation contributes. Moreover, on
the goal theory, if it is a function of x to do y then it is the doing of y, and
not merely having the capability of doing y that is or contributes to the
goal. If the function of the heart is to pump the blood then, on the present
theory, pumping the blood and not merely having the capability to do so
is or contributes to the goal. And, if we modify the goal theory and allow
capabilities as goals we seem to generate altogether too many functions.
The designers may have designed the Cadillac to be capable of traveling
150 miles per hour. Yet it seems incorrect to say that it is a function of the
Cadillac to have this capability. Designers generally imbue their products
with more capabilities than are functions.

A goal theorist might also respond to the sewing machine example by
invoking the idea of a goal-directed system. Yet if we think of the sewing
machine as such a system—to use the jargon of Nagel and other—it is
not a goal of this system to activate the exploding mechanism. This is not
something which the machine, even when it is in use, tends to do or persists in doing under a variety of disturbing conditions. Nor does activating
the exploding mechanism contribute to some other "goal" which might be
attributed to the machine, such as sewing. Should we then speak here of
conditional persistence and say that the exploding mechanism tends to be
activated under a variety of disturbing conditions *if the button is pushed?*
Conditional goals, like capabilities mentioned, will saddle us with a bevy
of unwanted functions. But even if they were allowed on the goal doctrine
this proposal will not work, for a reason which vitiates the previous non-
conditional version as well. This sewing machine (indeed all of them) may
have faulty wiring so that the exploding mechanism will not be or tend to
be activated even if the button is pushed. Still the function of this button
is to activate the exploding mechanism.

For these reasons the conditions of the goal doctrine do not appear to
be necessary for functions. Nor are they sufficient, if we accept Wright's

watch example or the heartsounds example. Let us imagine that one of my goals is always to be prompt for appointments. My watch's second hand sweeps dust from the watch and this, by making it work more accurately, contributes to the goal of promptness which I, the watch's owner, have. Despite this fact it is not the second hand's function to sweep dust from the watch. Similarly, my heart's producing heartsounds does contribute, albeit indirectly, to one of my goals, namely, good health or at least prompt diagnosis and treatment in case of bad health. Yet its producing heartsounds is not a function which my heart has.

When we turn to the explanation doctrine new examples are needed. Part of the problem with this doctrine—at least in Wright's formulation—stems from the vagueness of the "is there because" locution. Wright urges that function statements are explanatory but that what they explain (the "object" of explanation) can vary significantly.[5] On his view a function statement might explain how x came to exist, or how x came to be present, or why x continues to exist, or why it continues to be present, or why it exists where it does, or why it continues to exist where it does, or why it is used, and so forth. Some of his examples involve one of these explanations, others different ones. But they are not necessarily the same. (One might explain how that light switch came to exist without thereby explaining why it is present in that room.) Yet Wright seems to think that if x's doing y explains why x "is there" in any of these ways then his explanation condition for function statements is satisfied.

Consider now a situation in which the manager of the local baseball team adopts a new policy to keep a player on the first team if and only if that player continues to bat over .300. We might imagine a situation in which both of the following statements are true: (a) Jones is there (i.e., on the first team) because he continues to bat over .300; (b) Jones' continuing to bat over .300 is a consequence of his being there (i.e., on the first team, which gives him practice and confidence). In (a) we are not explaining Jones' existence but rather his presence on the first team—something allowable on Wright's analysis. In (b) we are claiming that his continuing to bat over .300 is a consequence of the same state of affairs explained in (a), namely, his presence on the first team. So Wright's conditions appear to be satisfied. Yet it seems false to say that Jones' function (or even his function on the team) is to continue to bat over .300. This may be one of his aims or goals but not his function.[6] If so then Wright's conditions are not sufficient.

5. See Wright (1976), p. 81.
6. I use this example in 1975, but others of this sort abound. Suppose a patient is being kept in a certain room in the hospital because he is sneezing a lot, but it turns out that his sneezing a lot is a consequence of his being kept in that room (which happenes to be full of dust and pollens). Is his function, therefore, to sneeze a lot?

Because of the latitude in the explanation condition it is harder, but
perhaps not impossible, to show that they are not necessary either. The
function of the human heart is, let us say, to pump the blood. If so,
Wright is committed to holding that one can explain etiologically (in
this case presumably causally) why humans came to have hearts, or why
they continue to have hearts, or why human hearts are where they are
in the body, or some such, by appeal to the fact that hearts pump blood.
Whether an explanation of the sort Wright envisages is possible, I shall
not discuss. But let us change the case to consider just my heart. Its
function, I take it, is to pump blood.[7] Yet in this case it is difficult to see
how to construct a Wrightian explanation. Does the fact that my heart
pumps blood causally explain how my heart came to exist, or why it
continues to exist, or why it is present on the left side of my body, or
indeed any of the other possibilities Wright allows? How will natural
selection plus heredity lead causally from the fact that my heart does
pump blood to the fact that it exists or even to the fact that it continues
to exist? Indeed it can continue to exist for years even after it ceases to
pump blood.[8]

There is another type of example, however, which appears to impugn
both of Wright's conditions as necessary conditions. Artifacts can be designed and used to serve certain functions which they are incapable of
performing. The function of a divining rod is to detect the presence of
water, even if such a rod is incapable of doing so. The function of this
paint on the faces of the savages is to ward off evil spirits, even though
there are no such spirits to ward off. Now both of Wright's conditions
commit him to saying that when x's function is to y, then x in fact does
y (or at least that x is *able* to do y under appropriate conditions.)[9] Yet
in these examples x in fact does not do y nor is x able to do y. Late
in his discussion Wright grants the existence of such cases (1976, pp.
112–113), but says they are nonstandard or variant uses of function
sentences. Whether this is so is something I shall want to take up. But at
least he recognizes that such uses exist and that they fail to satisfy either
of his conditions.

I will return to a number of these counterexamples for purposes of
reassessment after introducing some needed distinctions.

---

7. Wright might, of course, say that "that function of my heart is to pump blood" is always just a figurative way of making the *general* claim that the function of the human heart
is to pump blood. But he explicitly rejects such a move; see 1976, p. 88.

8. This is not to deny that one can explain the presence of my heart in my body by
appeal to its function. But as I shall argue in section 7, this is not a causal or etiological
explanation.

9. See Wright (1976), p. 81.

3. THREE TYPES OF FUNCTIONS: A PRELIMINARY DISTINCTION

Suppose that a magnificent chair was designed as a throne for the king; i.e., it was designed to seat the king. However, it is actually used by the king's guards to block a doorway in the palace. Finally, suppose that although the guards attempt to block the doorway by means of that chair they are unsuccessful. The chair is so beautiful that it draws crowds to the palace to view it, and people walk through the doorway all around the chair to gaze at it. But its drawing such crowds does have the beneficial effect of inducing more financial contributions for the upkeep of the palace, although this was not something intended. What is the function of this chair?

In answering this question I suggest that all of this information would be relevant. It would be appropriate to say what the chair was designed to do, what it is used to do, and what it actually does which serves to benefit something. As this example indicates the answers to these questions need not be the same. Accordingly one might distinguish three types (some might want to say senses) of function: design functions, use functions, and service functions. The design function of that chair is to seat the king; its use function is to block the doorway; its service function is to attract visitors to the palace and thus induce more financial contributions.[10]

Before trying to clarify this distinction one additional aspect of function statements should be noted, the possibility of relativization. An item can have a function for someone or within one system or set of activities that is not its function for another. In swimming (for the swimmer) the, or at least one, (use or service) function of the legs is to help keep the body horizontal in the water; in walking their function is to help keep the body vertical; in soccer it is to kick the ball. An item can also have a function at one time or occasion which it does not have at another.[11] If the regal chair was once used to seat the president of United States when he visited the king's palace then this was its (use) function on that occasion even though this was not its function on any other occasion.

In pointing to various possible relativizations I am not saying what some philosophers have said about function statements, namely, that they must always be understood as relativized to some "system" and time.[12] To understand the claim that the function of that mousetrap is to catch

10. Note that, contrary to the explanation doctrine, the latter is a function of the chair even though the chair's existence (presence, etc.) cannot be etiologically explained by reference to its attracting visitors to the palace.

11. Boorse (1976) notes this point.

12. See, e.g., Boorse (1976).

mice one need not identify or be able to identify anyone for whom, or any system within which, or any occasion on which, this is its function. To be sure, this mousetrap may on a given occasion, or within some system, or for some particular person serve a function other than that of catching mice, and if so we may need to identify the occasion, and so forth. But we need not conclude from this that all function statements must be so relativized. Indeed it is the (design) function of that mousetrap to catch mice whether or not it serves that function for anyone, or within any system, or on any occasion.

4. CLARIFICATION

a. Design Functions

The basic idea is that x's design function is what x was designed to do. But this is not yet quite right, since my stopwatch was designed to resist water. Yet that is not its function. Design functions, as well as those of the other two types, involve the important idea of a *means* of doing something. The designer designs x to be or to serve as a means of doing y. This mousetrap was designed by its designer to be a means of catching mice. But my stopwatch was not designed to be a means of resisting water. (I shall have more to say about the concept of means in section 6.) Alternatively, x may be a part of or belong to or otherwise be present in a "system" S which was designed by its designer to do y by means of x. If so we say that the (design) function of x in S is to *enable* S to do y. The function of the gasoline in this engine is to enable the engine to run. So we can write

(1) If x was designed to be or to serve as a means of doing y then x's function (at least one of them) is to do y.

(2) If S was designed to do y by means of x then x's function in (with respect to) S is to enable S to do y.

Should design functions be restricted only to cases in which x (or S) is *designed?* A chemical can be *produced*, a person *appointed*, a rock *placed where it is*, to be or to serve as a means of doing something. If so we can speak of the chemical's, person's, or rock's function, even though these items were not themselves designed. Nevertheless, design was present. Perhaps then (1) can be generalized as follows:

If x was produced (created, established, appointed, placed where it is, etc.) by design to be or to serve as a means of doing y then x's function is to do y.

A similar generalization of (2) would be possible.

However, with the inclusion of these additional activities all done by design we encounter cases in which x might have been designed for one end, produced for another, and placed where it is for a third. Suppose that the Universal Design Company designed a certain type of bolt to serve as a means of bolting a car engine to the frame. The Ford Motor Company purchases this design but produces the bolt in its own shops to serve as a means of bolting the torsion bar to the frame. The bolt is then sent unattached to the dealers who are to install it when they receive the car. The dealers, however, ignoring the previous designs, affix the bolt to the wheel. What is the function of this bolt? Does it have three functions? Each of the agents noted—the designer, the producer, and the placer of the bolt—might well claim that the bolt has only one (proper) function and disagree over what this is.

In reply we might proliferate types of functions still further by talking about production functions, placement functions, and so forth. But the more natural way to settle this dispute is to recognize that function statements do not always need to take the simple form "the function of x is to do y," which philosophers tend to focus upon. We also make statements of the form "the function x was *designed* to serve is to do y," "the function x was *produced* to serve is to do y," "the function x was *placed where it was* to serve is to do y," and so forth. Each of the three protagonists in our bolt story can then be understood as making a different type of function claim. When an agent from the Universal Design Company indicates the function of that bolt he means to indicate the function it was designed to serve; the agent from the Ford Motor Company is talking about the function it was produced to serve; the dealer is speaking of the function it was placed where it was to serve.

My solution to this dispute, then, is to recognize not different types (or senses) of function but different types of function *statements*. Several of the latter can be grouped together under the heading "design function statements," all of which involve the general idea of design in origin or placement. One of their basic forms is this:

(3) The function x was designed (produced, created, established, appointed, placed where it is, etc.—all by design) to serve is to do y,

which is true if and only if x was designed (produced, etc.) to be or to serve as a means of doing y. If x does not itself do y but S does we can write

(4) The function x was designed (produced, etc.) to serve is to enable S to do y,

which will be true if and only if x was designed (produced, etc.) to be or to serve as a means of enabling S to do y.

My claim now comes to this. A sentence of the form

(5) The function of x is to do y (or to enable S to do y)

is ambiguous. Someone who utters it may be making one of a number of different claims about design in origin or placement *some* of which are given by (3) and (4). But not all. The second chapter of Ayer's *Language, Truth, and Logic*, entitled "The Function of Philosophy," states that the function of philosophy is to provide analyses of certain sorts or "definitions in use." When Ayer wrote this he was aware that this is not the function that philosophy is produced or written by most philosophers to serve. Nor is his claim to be taken simply as one about the function of *analytic* philosophy. Rather he is indicating the function that (all) philosophy *ought* to be produced or written to serve. Accordingly, another type of design function statement which someone uttering (5) might mean to be asserting is

The function x ought to be designed (produced, etc.) to serve is to do y (or to enable S to do y),

which is true if and only if x ought to be designed (produced, etc.) to be or to serve as a means of doing y (or of enabling S to do y).

One can, of course, answer a question of the form "What is x's function?" by uttering sentences other than (5), for example, by saying that x is an A (a church, a mousetrap). In such a case x is not designed to be a means of being an A, although the notion of means is not irrelevant here. If that building is a church then its function is to enable Christians to worship together. And the latter claim, which can be understood as being of type (4), will be true if and only if a corresponding means statement is.

b. Use Functions

When someone utters a sentence of form (5) he may mean to be saying something not about x's origin or placement but about its use, e.g.,

The function x is used to serve is to do y (or to enable S to do y),

which will be true if and only if x is used as a means of doing y (or as a means of enabling S to do y). Someone who says that the function of the human hands is to grasp objects may be saying that this is the function they are *used* to serve. And this will be so if and only if the hands are used as a means of grasping objects.

Although what function an item has been designed (or produced, etc.) to serve often coincides with the function it is used to serve, sometimes it does not. Something may have been designed or even placed where it is to serve as a means of doing *y* although it is never in fact used, or although it is used only as a means of doing *z*. The function that trough may have been designed and placed where it is to serve is to water the pigs, even though it is never used or the only function it is used to serve is to water the flowers.[13] Moreover, *x* may be used to serve a given function without this being so by *design*. The function a mosquito's wings are used to serve is to enable the mosquito to fly. We need not say that the mosquito uses them by design or that they were designed or created by design.

Use function, like design function, statements can be prescriptive. Someone who claims that the function of a college education is to arouse intellectual curiosity and not just to get a job might mean that this is the function it ought to be used to serve, not that it is in fact used to serve this. There is a related use of function sentences of form (5). Pointing to the wings on a particular mosquito I might say that the function of those wings is to enable the mosquito to fly, even though in this case the wings are broken or for some other reason the mosquito never flies. My claim, then, could be that

(6) The function those wings are supposed to be used to serve is to enable that mosquito to fly.

And I may make such a claim because I believe something about the function of wings in mosquitos generally, namely, that

(7) The function a mosquito's wings are (generally) used to serve is to enable the mosquito to fly.

The general statement (7) provides a norm on the basis of which the function statement (6) about a particular *x* can be asserted. On the other hand, pointing to those particular broken wings I might also say that they have no function at all, since they cannot be used.

c. Service Functions

One who utters (5) might mean to be claiming something stronger than simply what function *x* was designed or is used to serve, namely,

---

13. In our earlier example the function the regal chair was placed where it is to serve is the same as the function it is used to serve by the guards, namely, to block the doorway. However, if the chair remains where it is long after the guards are all dismissed by the king, then the function it was placed where it is to serve remains the same, but the function it is used to serve may not.

(8) What x in fact does, the performance of which is a function that it serves, is y (or to enable S to do y).

Thus we might say that although the function the regal chair was designed to serve is to seat the king, and the function it is used to serve is to block a doorway, the only thing the chair actually does, the performance of which is a function it serves, is to draw crowds to the palace. We might say this because crowds are in fact drawn to the palace by means of the chair and this is of benefit, while the king is in fact not seated, nor is the doorway really blocked, by means of that chair.[14] More generally, a statement of form (8) is true if and only if

(9) y is in fact done by means of x (or S is in fact enabled to do y by means of x), and either x was designed (produced, etc.) to be or to serve as a means of doing y (enabling S to do y), or x is used as a means of doing y (enabling, etc.), or y's being done confers a good.

A number of points must now be made about the last clause in (9). It would be a mistake, I think, to follow those writers who require only one specific type of good such as survival and reproduction. As Sorabji (1964, p. 293) notes, a certain creature might have an organ which shuts off sensations of pain when lethal damage has been done to its body. We might then identify this as the function of the organ even if shutting off the pain does not increase the creature's chances of surviving and reproducing. Analogous examples are possible against views committed to other specific goods.

Possibly, those who select one type of good such as survival and reproduction do so because they think of this as an ultimate good—as worthy of having for its own sake; other states of affairs can be beneficial only because they contribute to the ultimate good. But even if we distinguish ultimate and intermediate goods it is doubtful that there is a unique ultimate good with which all functions can be associated. Another reason for selecting survival and reproduction as the only good is that the authors that do so are concerned almost exclusively with biology. The function of the nose, they will say, is to breathe, not to hold up eyeglasses, although both are done by means of the (human) nose and their being done confers a good. To this the correct response is that the nose serves or can serve

---

14. Service function statements, however, need not be confined to those in which y is in fact done. Pointing to a particular defective kidney in Jones' body we might say that its function is to remove wastes, and mean that what this kidney is supposed to do, the performance of which is a function it would serve (if it did it), is to remove wastes. This claim would be based on a general service function statement of form (8) about what human kidneys in fact generally do.

a number of different functions not all of which are *biological*. Whether doing *y* is classifiable as a biological function will depend at least in part upon the type of good it confers, upon what, and how; however, I shall not here try to offer criteria for such functions. If holding up eyeglasses is not a biological function of the nose it is nevertheless an important function of the nose in the eyeglass "support system."

Doing *y* need not be of benefit to *x* itself or to its owner or user but to something else. The sickness and subsequent death of various animals in a species may be of no benefit to *them*, but to other members of the species, who will now have fewer competitors for food. So the sickness and death of these animals can have a function for the species, even if not for the animals themselves.

Doing *y* can confer a good upon a person *S* even if doing *y* is not something which *S* knows about or regards as beneficial even if he knows about it. One of the functions of basic training in the army is to teach recruits to obey orders, even if the recruits do not realize that basic training is teaching them to do this and even if they do not want to be taught or regard this as beneficial. One who believes that basic training is of value in this way can make such a function statement.

By contrast, one can also make a service function statement without committing oneself to values, if any, in that statement. Suppose that watching television dulls the mind to the problems of the world and people act as if so dulling the mind is beneficial for them. For the television viewer, one might say, what television does, the performance of which is a function it serves, is to dull the mind. One can make such a statement from the point of view of the television viewer with his set of values. On the other hand, employing one's own more intellectual values one might say that for the television viewer what television does, that is, dull the mind, serves no function at all, since it confers no benefits. The speaker can make explicit which point of view—which set of values— he is employing, or this can be clear from the context. This means that speakers with quite different values can still agree over the truth of those service function statements based on the conferring of a good, provided that they invoke the values of the party in the function statement, not their own.

Finally, it should be clear, I am not maintaining that all function statements, or even all service function statements, commit one to the claim that doing *y* confers a good. We can utter a true service function statement of form (8) by saying that what that button on the sewing machine in fact does, the performance of which is a function it serves, is to activate the exploding mechanism, even if activating this mechanism is of no benefit at all.

5. THE COUNTEREXAMPLES RECONSIDERED

I have claimed that a sentence of the form "the function of x is to do y" is ambiguous and can be used to make a variety of quite different function statements. This does not mean, conversely, that whenever one explicitly makes some design, use, or service function statement one is willing to assert a statement of this form. We can generally do this in the case of artifacts. With natural objects, however, such an inference may be resisted unless the identity of some system in which the object has that function, or of some user of the object, or of some item benefited is made clear either by the context or within the function statement itself by relativization. One might be willing to make the service function statement "one of the things this tree does, the performance of which is a function it serves, is to provide shade," based on the conferring of a good, but be unwilling to conclude that this tree's function is to provide shade. The latter statement should become less objectionable, however, if it is relativized to be making a claim about its function for the homeowner on whose property it lies.

By contrast to the view I have been suggesting, the good consequence, goal, and explanation doctrines say that sentences of the form "the function of x is to do y" (or in the case of some advocates of the first view, that sentences of this form in which x is not an artifact) are always used to make the same type of statement, which is subject to the same analysis. In rejecting these doctrines, however, I do not thereby accept all of the counterexamples to them in section 2. Our discussion in the last two sections will facilitate an assessment of these counterexamples and will also illustrate some of the distinctions I have pressed.

In the case of the sewing machine button, the function it was *designed* to serve is to activate the exploding mechanism, even if this has no good consequences whatever. Accordingly, one might say that the function of this button is to activate the exploding mechanism and be making a design function statement. On the other hand, someone impressed by the fact that the button because of its extreme danger never is or will be used might claim that this button has no function at all; it is "disfunctional." Such a person would be making or rather denying a use function statement.

Wright's watch example is subject to a similar treatment. To be sure, the function the second hand was *designed* to serve is to indicate the seconds and not to sweep the dust from the watch. So one might say, following Wright, that sweeping dust away is not its function. On the other hand, since dust is in fact swept from the watch by means of the second hand and this is beneficial to its owner, we can say that one of the things the second hand does, the performance of which is a function it serves, is to sweep the dust from the watch, and hence that this is one of its functions, even though this is not a function it was designed to serve.

Wright insists that if x does y by coincidence then y cannot be the or a function of x. True, if x is designed to do y then generally if x does y it is not by coincidence.[15] But in the case of service function statements, x may come to perform a beneficial service which it was not designed to perform and in this way is coincidental, yet the performance of this service can be a function that x acquires. Wright also emphasizes the distinction between x's function and what x functions as. Although the watch's second hand functions as a dustsweeper, its function is not to sweep dust away, he claims. I agree that we might say that the second hand functions as a dustsweeper, but I suggest we would speak this way not because this is not a function of the second hand but because it is not a function the second hand was *designed* to serve. The "functioning as" locution seems particularly appropriate when what x is doing contrasts with what it was designed to do or when x was not designed at all. Yet there is no general incompatibility between x's functioning as a y and y being one of x's functions. The heart functions as a blood pump, but pumping blood is one of its functions.

Turning to Hempel's heartsounds example, the claim is made by certain opponents of the good-consequence doctrine that it is not a function of the heart to produce heartsounds, even though this confers a good upon the heart's owner since it aids doctors in diagnosing and treating heart disease. But if it does then I suggest that the critics are mistaken. One of the things which the heart does, the performance of which is a function it serves, is to produce a beating sound, since the production of such a sound is beneficial. Perhaps what confuses these critics is a failure to distinguish what x does which is of greater benefit from what it does which is beneficial but less so (more important vs. less important functions), or what x does which is directly beneficial and what it does which is less directly so. The pumping of the blood is of greater and more direct benefit to the body than the producing of heartsounds. Still in doing both the heart is performing two functions. What may also be moving the critics is the fact that although the heart's pumping the blood is always beneficial to the body in all mammals, the heart's producing heartsounds is of diagnostic

---

15. But this need not be so in all cases. I may design a divining rod to enable me to find water underground. Now I use the rod, and it does jerk downward on several occasions when water is present underground, but only because the rod is magnetic and there happen to be metals also beneath the surface. Accordingly, the rod enabled me to find water underground, but only by coincidence. Still that is the function it was designed to serve.

value mainly in humans, and only for those rich or wise enough to have medical checkups. Accordingly, one can say that what the heart does, the performance of which is and always has been a function that it serves in all mammals, is to pump the blood; one cannot make a claim this strong about the production of heartsounds. Because of these differences the former activity of the heart may be classifiable as more centrally its *biological* function, and this consideration may be weighing heavily in the minds of the critics as well.

The baseball counterexample to Wright's analysis is appropriate if we are making a design function statement. Jones was not *put on the team* to serve the function of continuing to bat over .300. Can a service function statement be made here, e.g., that one of the things Jones does which is a function he performs on the team is to continue to bat over .300? This is inappropriate, I suggest, because continuing to bat over .300 is not something done *by means of* Jones, but simply something which he does (more of this in the next section). On the other hand, we might say that Jones' continuing to bat over .300, or his batting skill, has served a function on the team, namely, that of enabling the team to win consistently. This would be appropriate to say because the team has been enabled to win consistently by means of Jones' continuing to bat over .300, or his batting skill, and winning consistently is of benefit to the team. But note that here the function is attributed not to Jones, as it could be on Wright's analysis, but to his continuing to bat over .300 or to his batting skill; and the function itself is not continuing to bat over .300 but enabling the team to win consistently.

Another counterexample used against Wright involved the divining rod whose function is to detect the presence of water and the paint on the faces of the savages whose function is to ward off the evil spirits, although neither function is or can be performed by these items. Wright's response is that these are nonstandard uses of function sentences. My rejoinder is that one who makes these claims would generally be making not a service function statement but a perfectly ordinary design or use function statement. He might not be claiming that what the divining rod does, the performance of which is a function it serves, is to detect water, but that this is the function it was designed or is used to serve.

6. FUNCTIONS, ENDS, AND MEANS

Functions are intimately related to ends of certain kinds, and the items to which functions are attributed are means to those ends. The latter are doing-ends rather than thing-ends. Although money or fame might be spoken of as ends they cannot be functions. Rather, catching mice, pumping blood, and enabling one to climb mountains are functions. Indeed, Geach (1975) has argued that no ends can be things but that all ends have a propositional structure. If I say that my end is money what I want is to make and retain money, and this should be understood as saying that my end is *that I make and retain money*. I shall not here try to say whether statements reporting ends are referring to objects, activities, propositions, or nothing at all. I am in agreement with Geach, however, that end-statements can be transformed into ones in which the end is given in a propositional form, and that such statements will often clarify the end in question.

Thus earlier we noted that my stopwatch was designed by its designers to resist water, but that resisting water is not one of its functions. The end which the designers want to achieve here is *that this stopwatch resists water*. And this end is not something designed to be achieved *by means of* this stopwatch, but rather by means of certain water-resistant sealing material. (Thus we *could* claim that the function of this material in my stopwatch is to enable the watch to resist water.) Similarly, in the baseball example the end which Jones or his manager wants to achieve is *that Jones continues to bat over .300*. And this end is not something designed to be achieved *by means of* Jones, but, say, by means of constant practice on his part. (Thus we could claim that the function of constant practice on the part of Jones is to enable him to continue to bat over .300.)

Although functions are intimately related to ends the two should not be identified. Functions as well as ends can be given by infinitives and nominalized verb phrases, yet ends but not functions can be given propositionally. My end might be that I make money, but my function (as chief fundraiser, say) is not that I make money or that money be made by me but simply to make money or the making of money. Nevertheless, for any function there is an associated end which can be formulated in a propositional way. And the item with the function is a means to this end. For this to be the case the associated end will need to be a "generalized" one in this sense: its propositional formulation will include no reference to the item x to which the function is attributed. If my function in this organization is to make money for the organization then the associated end is that *money be made for the organization*, not that I make money for the organization or that money be made for the organization by me. And if this is my function then I am the (or a) means by which this generalized end is to be achieved. The association between functions and ends, then, comes to this. If x's function is to do y then that y is done is a generalized end (given in propositional form) for which x is a means.

The ends with which functions are associated can be *pure*, i.e., ends which no one or thing actually desires or intends.[16] The function of the button on the sewing machine is to activate the exploding mechanism even if no one desires or intends *that the exploding mechanism be activated* (the italicized words give the associated end). What, then, makes something an end with which a function can be associated?

Our discussion in section 4 provides an answer. Doing y—or that y is done—is an end with which x's function can be associated if (but not only if)[17] one or more of the following conditions is satisfied:

(1) x was designed (produced, etc.) to be or to serve as a means of doing y.
(2) x is used as a means of doing y.
(3) y is in fact done by means of x and either (1) or (2) or y's being done confers a good.[18]

If that button is designed to serve as a means of activating the exploding mechanism then activating the exploding mechanism (that the mechanism be activated) is an end for which the button was designed, even if no one desires or intends that the mechanism be activated. If bodily wastes are removed by means of the kidneys and this being done confers a good upon their owner, then removal of such wastes is an end served by the kidneys, even if their owner neither desires nor intends this end.

Can the concept of *means* be eliminated from this account in favor of something else? For example, is x a means of doing y when and only when x (or x's presence or occurrence) is *necessary* or *sufficient* for y to be done? Obviously not. It is not necessary since the same end can often be achieved by a variety of means. Nor is it sufficient, since x can be a means of doing y without y's being done. (The electric chair is a means of executing prisoners even if prisoners are not executed.) Nor for the same reason is x a means of doing y when and only when x (or x's presence)

16. Geach (1975, p. 80) speaks of purely teleological propositions as "propositions affirming that something happened to a certain end with no reference to some desire or intention, nor yet to any subject who desires or intends."

17. These conditions do not exhaust the possibilities, since function statements can also be understood prescriptively. But the prescriptive uses are subject to analogous conditions.

18. Woodfield attempts to provide a completely unified analysis of ends by in effect identifying all ends as *goods*. To do this, however, he must assume (a) that if someone designed something to do y then he wants y to be done; and (b) that if someone wants y to be done then he believes that y is a good thing to do (1976, p. 203). Woodfield thinks that there are senses of "want" and "good" which make (a) and (b) true. I disagree. A reluctant designer may have designed this particular machinery to execute the prisoner even though he neither wants the prisoner to be executed nor believes this is a good thing to do, in any sense of "want" or "good."

causes y. Should we then weaken the claim to say that x is a means of doing y when and only when x *can* cause y. This is also too strong, since although ropes are a means by which people climb mountains I doubt that we would say that ropes can cause people to climb mountains. And if we weaken the claim still further by saying that x is a means of doing y when and only when x can be *causally relevant* for y (without necessarily being something that can cause y) we allow too broad a class of means. The strap on the electric chair can be causally relevant for the execution of prisoners insofar as it keeps prisoners in the chair. But it is not a means by which prisoners are executed. Some might want to appeal to the concept of *making possible* (or enabling). The heart makes it possible for the blood to be circulated; ropes make it possible for people to climb mountains. And x can make possible (or enable) the doing of y without being necessary or sufficient for, or causing, y to be done. However, this concept is also too broad for the job. The presence of these straps on the electric chair may make it possible for the prisoner to be executed without being a means by which he is executed.

These brief observations are not meant to demonstrate the impossibility of eliminating talk of means in favor of one or more of these other concepts. If such a reduction can be accomplished, however, I doubt that it will be a simple or straightforward one. Moreover, if the concept of means is not so reducible, I am not suggesting that this is so because it is irreducibly teleological, i.e., associated, e.g., with the concept of an end. Although means are typically associated with ends they are not always or necessarily so. Smith may have been killed by means of his own carelessness, even if Smith's being killed is not an end. (E.g., it is not something which anyone intended or desired, it was not something which anything was designed to be, or was used as, a means of achieving, and it did not confer a good.) In a similar way one can speak of a certain reaction as occurring by means of a catalyst, or of chemical bonds forming by means of electrons, without assuming that the reaction's occurrence or the formation of the bonds is an end. Although functional talk involves both the idea of a means and an end what makes such talk teleological is the commitment not to a means but to an end. In this respect reference to means is on a par with other possible appeals to necessary and sufficient conditions, causation, and making possible.

The fact that functional talk involves not only the idea of a means but that of an end in the way I have suggested explains why we resist such talk in certain instances. There are cases in which y is done by means of x and yet doing y is not x's function since doing y (or that y is done) is not an end. Although the formation of a chemical bond between a sodium atom and a chlorine atom occurs by means of the transfer of an electron from the former atom to the latter, it seems objectionable to say that the function of such a transfer is to form a chemical bond between these atoms. This is because normally we do not regard the formation of such a bond as an end.

In the light of the discussion in this and the previous sections we ought to recognize certain elements of truth in the good-consequence, goal, and explanation doctrines. Conferring a good can be an important consideration in assigning a function to something, though it is neither necessary nor sufficient in general. But it is necessary in cases in which talk of design or use is inappropriate. And if y is done by means of x, then the fact that y's being done confers a good is sufficient for characterizing the doing of y as a function that x serves. The goal doctrine is important because it stresses the idea of a goal and thus brings out the teleological character of function statements. It goes awry, however, in requiring the doing of y to be or to contribute to some goal which x or its user, owner, or designer has. The goals—or more broadly the ends—associated with function statements, even with design or use function statements, can be pure ones. Finally, as will be seen in the next section, the explanation doctrine is correct in its claim that function sentences can be invoked in providing explanations, even of x's existence or presence, although contrary to this doctrine these explanations are not in general causal or etiological.

7. FUNCTIONAL EXPLANATIONS

Do function sentences explain anything, and if so what? This question, I believe, is badly put since it is primarily people who explain by uttering words or sentences. Explaining is an illocutionary act—one typically performed by uttering words in certain contexts with appropriate intentions; and in my 1965 article I have suggested conditions required for its performance (see chapter 6 in this book). Roughly, on my account, a person P explains q by uttering u if and only if P utters u with the intention that his utterance of u render q understandable by producing the recognition that u expresses a correct answer to a question Q which presupposes q. If we assume that any sentence of the form "P explains q by uttering u" is or is transformable into one in which q is an indirect question then Q is the direct form of that question. This does not mean that we cannot explain things such as events, but only that we do so by answering some question about them.

Accordingly, we might ask: When one utters a function sentence what is one explaining? I.e., what does one intend to render understandable in the manner suggested here? To this the reply must be: not necessarily anything. If someone asks what organ's function it is to pump the blood, and I reply that it is the function of the heart to pump the blood, I need not be explaining anything at all but simply identifying an organ. (By analogy, if someone asks "who got sick because he ate spoiled meat?" and I reply "Jones got sick because he ate spoiled meat" I am not explaining why Jones got sick but simply identifying the unfortunate man.) I make this point here only because there are those who seem to think that when one utters a function sentence one is necessarily explaining something.[19]

Still it seems plausible to suppose that one *can* explain by uttering a function sentence, and if so the question is what. A typical view among those who analyze functional explanations is that at most one thing is explained (though there is some disagreement over what this is). By contrast, I want to suggest that a number of different things can be explained by uttering function sentences; i.e., a number of different explanatory questions can be answered.

Most simply, one can utter a function sentence in explaining what function x has. There is a lever on the dashboard of my car whose function puzzles people since when it is pulled nothing seems to happen. I explain its function to them by saying that its function is to open the reserve fuel tank.

One can also utter a function sentence in explaining the doing of y. The latter can be explained in various ways, i.e., on my view, by answering a number of different questions including

(1) How, i.e., by what means, is y done?

(1) can be answered by uttering a function sentence since in identifying x as an item whose function is to do y one identifies a means by which y is done. Some writers say that function sentences are used to provide *causal* explanations of y's occurrence, i.e., that by uttering such sentences one can answer the question

(2) What causes (caused) y to occur?

No doubt in many cases when an answer to (1) is given by a function sentence an answer to (2) is easy to construct. If the reserve fuel tank is opened by means of that lever, than pulling the lever causes the reserve tank to open. But as indicated in section 6 a means by which y is done is not in general a cause of y's being done. (1) and (2) are not identical questions, and if someone explains the doing of y by uttering a function sentence the question he is answering is (1), although his answer to (1)

---

19. Thus Wright: "Merely saying of something x, that it has a certain function is to offer an important kind of explanation of x" (1973, p. 154). And Wimsatt: "That is, to give the function of an adaptation is to explain (in part) why it was selected for . . ." (1972, p. 8).

will often, but not always, contain sufficient information to enable the construction of an answer to (2).

Finally, as a number of writers have claimed, one can utter a function sentence in explaining x's existence, continued existence, presence, location, use, and so forth. Among the ways these can be explained is by answering the question

(3) For what end does x exist (continue to exist, is x present, used, etc.)?

One should distinguish the teleological claim that x does something which serves an end from the stronger teleological claim that it exists (is present, is used, etc.) in order to serve that end. The sun does things which serve various ends, yet it does not exist in order to serve any of them. By contrast, artifacts exist by human design to serve certain ends. Bodily organs are generally regarded not merely as serving certain ends but as existing or being present in order to serve those ends. Since only in some cases is an end served by x an end for which x exists, an answer to (3) can be provided only by certain function statements, that is, by design, use, and those service function statements based on design or use. If x was designed (etc.) to serve as, or is used as, a means of doing y, then x exists (is present, is used) in order to serve the end of doing y. Service function statements based on the conferring of a good can also be used to answer (3) provided that, as with bodily organs, the x in such cases exists in order to do y. Thus it is possible to utter "the function of this lever is to open the reserve fuel tank" and "the function of the heart is to pump the blood" in explaining the existence of these items by answering a question of form (3). To bring out the fact that x in such cases not only serves an end but exists to serve an end one might formulate one's function sentence as "the function for which x exists is to do y."

Some writers who say that function sentences can be used to explain x's existence, presence, and so on believe that such explanations are causal (in the sense of efficient rather than final causation), i.e., that they answer a question such as

(4) What causes x to exist (be present, etc.)?

On this view the answer function sentences provide is that what causes x to exist is the fact that x does y. Against this Robert Cummins (1975) correctly argues that function sentences cannot in general be used to provide causal explanations of x's existence. My heart was not caused to exist by the fact that it pumps my blood. Cummins, however, mistakenly concludes from this that at least in the case of nonartifacts, function sentences cannot be used to explain x's existence or presence. What he overlooks is that one can explain x's existence or presence by answering a question such as (3) in a way that is not causal.

The child who asks why he has a heart or why hearts are present in humans may simply want to know a function for which they exist, in this case, what benefit to the body is accomplished by means of the heart for which it exists. He is not or need not be asking a causal or etiological question about how a heart came to be present in humans, what causes it to remain present in the human species, or to be where it is in the body. Similarly if the earth doctor dissects a Martian's body and discovers an organ different from any he knows, he might ask: "Why do Martians have that organ?" In asking this question he may not want to know how Martians came to have that organ but simply for what end it exists.

To this it might be replied that the doing of y is an end for which x exists only if it is a cause of x's existence. But this cannot be right. It is not the *opening of the reserve fuel tank* which causes this lever to exist, but rather the actions of certain agents (who may have designed the lever or placed it where it is to serve that end). Accordingly, a second reply might be that the doing of y is an end for which x exists only if there is some act or event in which the doing of y is an end where that act or event caused x to exist. Opening the reserve fuel tank is an end for which this lever exists only if agents who designed or positioned the lever to serve that end acted in certain ways. Pumping the blood is an end for which the heart exists, it might be said, only if nature acts in such a way as to select in favor of those in whom the benefit of pumping the blood is achieved by means of the heart. Furthermore, to establish that doing y is an end for which x exists we must discover what caused x to exist or at least make certain causal assumptions.

The validity of this second reply need not be discussed, since even if it is accepted the point I am trying to make is not vitiated. (3) and (4) are different questions, and an answer to (3) is not, and need not contain, an answer to (4). An answer to (3) may contain the information that the doing of y is an end for which x exists without identifying any act or event that caused x to exist, and this is so even if in order to establish the correctness of this answer one must be able to identify or make some assumption about such an act or event. To be sure, having received an answer to a question of form (3) one is often in a position to construct at least some answer to (4). If I am informed that the function for which this lever exists is to open the reserve fuel tank, then knowing that it is an artifact I know that it was some action of an agent that caused it to be present. But if I get much more specific I risk the danger of falsehood. For example, if I assume that it was designed by its designer to serve that end, I may be making a mistake (as in the car bolt example of section 4). Moreover, some answers to a question of form (3) may not put one in a position to answer every or any form of (4). One who is ignorant of the doctrines of natural selection and heredity may be informed about the function of that strange organ in the Martian body and yet be unable to causally explain how the organ came into existence or to say what, if anything, causes it to remain or to exist where it does.

Contemporary philosophers of science tend to adopt the view that to explain x's existence or presence is to cite a cause or causes. Within this tradition opinion then divides over functional explanations. On the one hand there are those who say that function sentences can be used to explain x's existence because they cite causes; on the other hand there are those who deny that function sentences provide causes for, and hence can be used to explain, x's existence. By contrast, I have been defending a position within a more ancient tradition, the Aristotelian, according to which one can explain x's existence—one can explain why x exists, why x is present, why S's have x—not only by answering a question of form (4) but by answering one of form (3), even if an answer to the latter does not contain an answer to the former.

REFERENCES

Achinstein, P. (1977), "What Is an Explanation?" *American Philosophical Quarterly* 14, 1–15.

Achinstein, P. (1975), Review of Michael Ruse's *Philosophy of Biology*, *Canadian Journal of Philosophy* 4, 745–754.

Ayala, F. (1970), "Teleological Explanations in Evolutionary Biology," *Philosophy of Science* 37, 1–15.

Bennett, J. (1976), *Linguistic Behaviour.* Cambridge: Cambridge University Press.

Boorse, C. (1976), "Wright on Functions," *Philosophical Review* 85, 70–86.

Canfield, J. (1963), "Teleological Explanation in Biology," *British Journal for the Philosophy of Science* 14, 285–295.

Cummins, R. (1975), "Functional Analysis," *Journal of Philosophy* 72, 741–765.

Frankfurt, H., and B. Poole (1966), "Functional Analyses in Biology," *British Journal for the Philosophy of Science* 17, 69–72.

Geach, P. (1975), "Teleological Explanation." In *Explanation*. Edited by S. Körner, New Haven: Yale University Press, pages 76–95.

Hempel, C. G. (1965), "The Logic of Functional Analysis." In *Aspects of Scientific Explanation*. New York: Free Press, pages 297–330.

Hull, D. (1974), *The Philosophy of Biological Science.* Englewood Cliffs, N.J.: Prentice Hall.

Lehman, H. (1965), "Functional Explanation in Biology," *Philosophy of Science* 32, 1–20.

Levin, M. E. (1976), "On The Ascription of Functions to Objects, with Special Reference to Inference in Archaeology," *Philosophy of the Social Sciences* 6, 227–234.

Nagel, E. (1961), *Structure of Science.* New York: Harcourt, Brace and World.

Ruse, M. (1973), *The Philosophy of Biology.* London: Hutchinson.

Sorabji, R. (1964), "Function." *Philosophical Quarterly* 14, 289–302.

Wimsatt, W. (1972), "Teleology and the Logical Structure of Function Statements." *Studies in the History and Philosophy of Science* 3, 1–80.

Woodfield, A. (1976), *Teleology.* Cambridge: Cambridge University Press.

Wright, L. (1973), "Functions," *Philosophical Review* 82, 139–168.

Wright, L. (1976), *Teleological Explanations.* Berkeley: University of California Press.

Part III

REALISM, MOLECULES, AND ELECTRONS

11

IS THERE A VALID EXPERIMENTAL
ARGUMENT FOR SCIENTIFIC REALISM?

"Is There a Valid Experimental Argument for Scientific Realism?" is reprinted by permission from The Journal of Philosophy 99 (2002), 470–495. *I define a concept of scientific realism employed by philosophical and scientific defenders and opponents of that doctrine, and I argue against antirealists that Jean Perrin's experimental results with Brownian motion provide the basis for a valid empirical argument for scientific realism.*

Long before atoms could be detected individually, scientists deduced their existence from the way dust motes danced in droplets of liquid; atoms making up the liquid were colliding with and jostling the dust.

—*New York Times*[1]

Wesley C. Salmon[2] claims that there is a valid experimental argument for scientific realism, and that one of the best examples is that provided by Jean Perrin[3] early in the twentieth century. In 1908, Perrin conducted a series of experiments on Brownian motion on the basis of which he claimed that Avogadro's number N, the number of molecules in a substance whose weight in grams equals its molecular weight, is approximately 6×10^{23}. Perrin drew the conclusion that unobservable molecules exist (pp. 213–227).

In memory of Wesley C. Salmon.

For very helpful questions and suggestions, I am indebted to Joseph Berkovitz, Sean Greenberg, Gregory Morgan, and Michael Williams.

1. March 29, 2001, p. A19.

2. *Scientific Explanation and the Causal Structure of the World* (Princeton, N.J: University Press, 1984), pp. 213–227.

3. "Brownian Movement and Molecular Reality," reprinted in Mary Jo Nye, ed., *The Question of the Atom* (Los Angeles: Tomash, 1984), pp. 507–601 (see *Annales de Chimie et de physique* (1909)); and *Atoms* (Woodbridge, CT: Ox Bow, 1990).

By "scientific realism," Salmon means a doctrine committed at least to the claim that unobservable entities exist. (What else, if anything, scientific realism does or should entail is controversial; the question will be taken up in sections 5–7). In seeking an argument to establish the claim that unobservables exist, Salmon writes:

> I decided to try an empirical approach to the philosophical problem [of scientific realism]. Since it seemed unlikely that scientists would have been moved by the kinds of arguments supplied by philosophers, I felt that some insight might be gained if we were to consider the evidence and arguments that convinced scientists of the reality of unobservable entities. Although scientists, by and large, seem committed to the existence of a variety of unobservable entities. . . , the existence of atoms and molecules, as the microphysical constituents of ordinary matter, is the most clear and compelling example. (pp. 213–214)

Salmon proceeds to reconstruct Perrin's argument and to claim that it establishes the existence of molecules experimentally. It is a simple step to scientific realism:

Molecules exist.

Molecules are unobservable entities.

Therefore, unobservable entities exist.

Since the first step is itself the conclusion of an argument based on Perrin's experiments with Brownian motion, we seem to have an experimental argument for scientific realism. Because this argument convinced at least some antirealist scientists of the reality of molecules,[4] Salmon challenges antirealist philosophers to say why they should not follow suit.

In what follows, I want to see how antirealist philosophers respond, or could respond, to Salmon's challenge to accept an experimental argument for scientific realism. First, however, I turn to Perrin's argument itself.

1. PERRIN'S EXPERIMENTAL ARGUMENT

A discovery was made in 1827 by the English botanist Robert Brown that small microscopic particles suspended in a liquid do not sink but exhibit

---

4. For example, in 1909, Friedrich Wilhelm Ostwald, who had previously rejected atomic theory on antirealist grounds, wrote: *"I have convinced myself that we have recently come into possession of experimental proof of the discrete or grainy nature of matter, for which the atomic hypothesis had vainly been sought for centuries, even millennia.* The isolation and counting of gas ions on the one hand . . . and the agreement of Brownian movements with the predictions of the kinetic hypothesis on the other hand, which has been shown by a series of researchers, most completely by J. Perrin—this evidence now justifies even the most cautious scientist in speaking of the *experimental* proof of the atomistic nature of space-filling matter"—quoted in Stephen G. Brush, "A History of Random Processes," *Archive for History of the Exact Sciences*, 5 (1968), 1–36.

rapid, haphazard motion—so-called Brownian motion. In 1908, Perrin conducted a series of experiments involving microscopic particles of gamboge (a gum resin extracted from certain Asiatic trees) in a dilute emulsion. These particles exhibited Brownian motion which was visible using a microscope. The emulsion was contained in a cylinder of known height h. Perrin determined the density D of the material making up the particles, the density d of the liquid, the mass m of the particles (all of them prepared by him to be the same weight), the temperature T of the liquid, and (with microscopes) the number of suspended particles per unit volume at various heights. He performed experiments with different emulsions, particles of different sizes and mass, different liquids, and different temperatures.

Using an argument that I shall note presently, he derived the following equation, which relates the quantities just cited:[5]

$$\frac{n'}{n} = 1 - \frac{Nmg(1-d/D)h}{RT} \tag{1}$$

Employing different experimental values obtained for all the quantities in equation (1) except for N, Perrin used this equation to determine whether Avogadro's number N is really a constant, and if so, what its value is.

He arrived at equation (1) by assuming that the motions of the visible Brownian particles are caused by collisions with the molecules making up the dilute liquid in which these visible particles are suspended. Accordingly, he also assumed that the visible particles will mirror the behavior of the invisible molecules. Finally, he assumed that molecules in a dilute solution of the sort in question will behave like molecules in a gas with respect to their vertical distribution. He then derived the following formula (the law of atmospheres) that governs a volume of gas contained in a thin cylinder of unit cross-sectional area and very small elevation h:[6]

$$\frac{p'}{p} = 1 - \frac{Mgh}{RT} \tag{2}$$

The pressure of a gas is proportional to its density, and hence, Perrin assumed, to the number of molecules per unit volume. So he replaced the ratio of pressures p'/p by the ratio n'/n, where n' and n are the number of

---

5. In addition to the quantities mentioned here, in equation (1), n' and n represent the number of Brownian particles per unit volume at the upper and lower levels; mg is the weight of a particle; R is the gas constant; and N is Avogadro's number.

6. In (2), p' and p are the pressures of the gas at the top and bottom of the cylinder; M is the gram molecular weight of the gas (the mass in grams equal to the molecular weight of the gas); g is the constant of gravitation; R is the gas constant; and T is absolute temperature.

molecules per unit volume at the upper and lower levels. He also replaced M by Nm, where m is a mass of a molecule of gas and N is Avogadro's number. With these substitutions, Perrin obtained

$$\frac{n'}{n} = 1 - \frac{Nmgh}{RT} \tag{3}$$

He now transformed equation (3) into equation (1) by letting n' and n represent the number of Brownian particles per unit volume at the upper and lower levels, and in (3) substituting the expresion $mg(1-d/D)$—the "effective weight" of a Brownian particle—for mg, the weight of a molecule.[7] Strictly speaking, in equation (1), N represents a number for Brownian particles: any quantity of these particles equal to their molecular weight will contain the same number N of particles. Perrin assumed that this number will be the same as Avogadro's number for molecules.

On the basis of various experiments involving different values for the observable quantities n', n, m, h, and T, Perrin used equation (1) to determine a value for Avogadro's number N and discovered that N is indeed a constant, whose approximate value is 6×10^{23}. He concluded that molecules exist:

> Even if no other information were available as to the molecular magnitudes, *such constant results would justify the very suggestive hypotheses that have guided us* [including that molecules exist], and we should certainly accept as extremely probable the values obtained with such concordance for the masses of the molecules and atoms. . . . The objective reality of the molecules therefore becomes hard to deny.[8]

Now for antirealist responses. There are two general kinds I shall consider: first, that Perrin's argument for molecules is invalid; second, that even if valid, it does not suffice to establish scientific realism.

2. THE CIRCULARITY OBJECTION

The first charge is that at the outset Perrin assumes that molecules exist while arguing that they exist. He derives equation (1), which he uses to obtain a value for Avogadro's number N and to see whether N is a constant, from equation (3), which presupposes the existence of molecules. In (3), n', n, and m are quantities associated with invisible molecules

---

7. The effective weight of a Brownian particle is the excess of its weight over the upward thrust caused by the liquid in which it is suspended.

8. *Atoms*, p. 105.

in a gas. He then assumes that a modified version of (3), namely, (1), can be applied to much larger visible Brownian particles suspended not in a gas but in a dilute fluid.

Reply

The argument presented here is only part of Perrin's reasoning, and indeed not the first part.[9] In his book *Atoms*, long before he gets to this argument from Brownian motion, he devotes eighty-two pages to a development of atomic theory, giving chemical arguments in favor of the existence of molecules. His 1909 article begins with a qualitative description of Brownian motion followed by qualitative arguments that Brownian motion is caused by collisions with molecules, and hence that molecules exist. In this article, he writes:

> It was established by the work of M. Gouy (1888), not only that the hypothesis of molecular agitation gave an admissible explanation of the Brownian movement, but that no other cause of the movement could be imagined, which especially increased the significance of the hypothesis.[10]

Gouy performed experiments in which he examined possible external causes of Brownian motion. These included vibrations transmitted to the fluid by passage of heavy vehicles in the street, convection currents produced when thermal equilibrium was not yet attained, and artificial illumination of the fluid. When these and other external sources of motion were reduced or eliminated, the Brownian motion was not altered. Perrin concludes: "these [Brownian] particles simply serve to reveal an internal agitation of the fluid" (p. 511).

Perrin offers a second argument from Brownian motion to molecules (pp. 514–515). Since the Brownian particles are continually accelerating and decelerating, they must be subject to forces exerted upon them, in such a way as to satisfy conservation of momentum. These forces are not present in the particles themselves, nor, as he argued earlier, are they produced by forces external to the fluid. Accordingly, he concludes, they must be produced by the perpetual motions of unobservable particles in the fluid itself.

These arguments for the existence of molecules are presented before Perrin's argument from the law of atmospheres given in section 1. Both involve eliminative-causal reasoning of the following sort:

---

9. For an expanded discussion of issues in this reply, see chapter 12.
10. "Brownian Movement and Molecular Reality," pp. 510–511.

Eliminative-causal argument:

(1) Given what is known, the possible causes of effect E (for example, Brownian motion) are C, C_1, . . . ,C_n (for example, the motion of molecules, external vibrations, heat convection currents). (In probabilistic terms, given what is known, the probability is high that E is caused by one of the Cs cited.)

(2) C_1, . . . ,C_n do not cause E (since E continues when these factors are absent or altered).

So probably

(3) C causes E.

Later, I shall consider whether such an argument is valid for molecules (or anything else). At the moment, I am claiming only that an argument of this type is employed by Perrin, and that it is employed prior to, and in addition to, the argument of section 1. Perrin offers additional arguments for molecules which are also independent of the law of atmospheres argument.[11]

Accordingly, independently of his own law-of-atmospheres experiments on Brownian motion, Perrin presents both experimental and theoretical arguments for the following claim:

H: Chemical substances are composed of molecules, the number N of which in a gram molecular weight of any substance is approximately 6×10^{23}.

Let b represent the information, other than the law-of-atmospheres considerations, on the basis of which Perrin infers H. He is claiming that the probability of H is high, given b, that is,

$$p(H/b) > k \tag{4}$$

where k is some threshold of high probability, say $1/2$.[12]

Now, on the basis of his law-of-atmospheres experiments, using equation (1), Perrin claims that:

H': The calculation of N done by means of Perrin's experiments on Brownian particles, using equation (1), is 6×10^{23}, and this number remains constant even when various values in equation (1) are varied.

---

11. These involve chemical considerations and also the fact that experiments on various phenomena other than Brownian motion yield approximately 6×10^{23} for Avogadro's number, although Perrin claims that for the most part these other methods do not yield the same precision as the determination from Brownian motion. Salmon emphasizes this second part of Perrin's reasoning, which he takes to be an example of "common-cause reasoning." For a discussion of Salmon's particular analysis, see chapter 12.

12. For arguments that k is greater than or equal to $1/2$, see my *The Book of Evidence*.

In H', the number N represents a number for Brownian particles. Perrin can be understood as assuming that, given both H and b, the probability of H' is (substantially) increased over what it is given b alone. That is, the probability that Perrin's experiments will yield result H' for Brownian particles is greater given the assumption that molecules exist, and that their number in a gram molecular weight of a substance is constant and approximately equal to 6×10^{23}, than it is without this assumption. That is

$$p(H'/H\&b) > p(H'/b)$$

It follows that

$$p(H/H'\&b) > p(H/b) \tag{5}$$

assuming that neither $p(H)$ nor $p(H'/b)$ is zero. In short, the probability of the molecular hypothesis H is (substantially) increased by H', the results of Perrin's experiments with Brownian motion. From (4) and (5) we can conclude that the molecular hypothesis H is highly probable given H' and b, that is,

$$p(H/H'\&b) > k$$

Perrin's argument, so represented, does not involve circularity. Even though Perrin derives the law of atmospheres (3) involving molecules from the assumption that molecules exist, and even though he derives H' from the law of atmospheres for molecules, H' itself does not state or presuppose that molecules exist or that Avogadro's number for molecules is 6×10^{23}. H' is established experimentally. On Perrin's view, given b, H' bestows substantial probability on H (which does state that molecules exist and that Avogadro's number for molecules is constant).

3. THE "MULTIPLICITY" OBJECTION

A second objection is that, given Perrin's experimental results, various hypotheses can be shown to receive just as much support as the particular molecular one that he accepts. And these alternatives need not be committed to the existence of molecules. The multiplicity objection comes in two forms.

A. Parallel Antirealist Argument

The idea, a generalization of one offered by Bas van Fraassen,[13] is that, for each argument used by Perrin whose conclusion is that molecules exist,

---

13. *The Scientific Image* (New York: Oxford, 1980).

another argument, at least as good, can be constructed from the same premises which does not conclude that molecules exist, but only that the molecular theory "saves the phenomena." Indeed, an argument of the latter sort is simpler and stronger than the former, since it commits one to much less than does any argument of the former sort. It commits one only to the "empirical adequacy" of the molecular theory, not to its truth, whereas an argument of the former sort is committed to both.

For example, an eliminative-causal argument of the sort attributed to Perrin in section 2 is replaced by the following:

Antirealist eliminative-causal argument
(1) Given what is known, of the theories that attribute a cause for effect E (for example, Brownian motion), the possible candidates for theories that save the phenomena are ones that invoke causes $C, C_1, \ldots, C_n$. (In probabilistic terms, given what is known, the probability is high that at least one of the theories cited saves the phenomena.)
(2) Theories that invoke causes $C_1, \ldots, C_n$ do not save the phenomena (since these theories predict that, under certain observable conditions, effect E will continue, which new information shows to be false).

So probably,

(3) The theory that invokes cause C (for example, molecules) saves the phenomena.

The conclusion is not that the theory that claims that C causes E is true, or that the entities it postulates (for example, molecules) exist or cause E, but simply that it is empirically adequate.

A similar claim is made for any argument that concludes with the truth of a theory postulating the existence of unobservables. For example, with respect to parallel "inference-to-the-best-explanation" arguments, van Fraassen offers two objections (pp. 20–21). The first is that the claim that scientists reason in accordance with realist versions of such arguments (or analogous eliminative-causal ones) is an *empirical* hypothesis "to be confronted with data, and with rival hypotheses" (p. 20). Van Fraassen proposes a rival hypothesis, namely, that scientists reason in accordance with the antirealist version of inference-to-the-best-explanation (or an analogous version of the eliminative-causal argument given previously). Both hypotheses, he seems to be saying, are compatible with the empirical fact that scientists employ explanatory (or eliminative-causal) reasoning. Van Fraassen's second objection is that the realist needs an extra premise for his argument, one that van Fraassen regards as false. For inference-to-the-best-explanation, the extra premise is that "every universal regularity in nature needs an explanation" (p. 21). For causal reasoning, the extra premise would be that every phenomenon in nature has a cause.

Reply

(1) To be sure, the fact that Perrin invokes eliminative-causal reasoning does not by itself establish that he is employing a realist or an antirealist version of such reasoning. Here one needs to examine what he in fact says. His claim is not (simply) that of various theories that attribute a cause for Brownian motion, the ones he cites are the possible candidates for saving the phenomena; it is the stronger claim that these theories are the possible candidates for truth. Nor is his conclusion (simply) that the theory invoking molecules as causes in fact saves the phenomena. It is the stronger claim that such a theory is true, that molecules exist ("the objective reality of the molecules therefore becomes hard to deny"), and that molecules cause Brownian motion. If, as van Fraassen insists, it is an empirical question what form of reasoning a scientist in fact is using, then the best empirical method to determine this is to look at what he actually says.

(2) Perrin does not need an extra premise asserting that every phenomenon in nature has a cause (or that every universal regularity needs an explanation). All he needs is the assumption that Brownian motion has a cause. To be sure, he does not explicitly defend this assumption, although he clearly makes it.[14] Presumably, if required to defend this assumption Perrin would have appealed to the idea that Brownian motion involves accelerations of bodies—both changes in speed and direction—which, in the classical physics that he was assuming—require causes. Perrin had no need to introduce some very general assumption that every universal regularity in nature has a cause or needs an explanation (an assumption not even made in classical mechanics). He simply needed to assume that the Brownian motion of the observable particles of gamboge has a cause.

B. *Multiplicity-of-Causes Objection*

The idea behind this second form of the multiplicity objection is to attack Perrin's particular eliminative-causal argument, which assumes that, given that known observable causes of Brownian motion are eliminated, one can infer an unobservable cause. The problem is that not all possible observable causes have been considered. The objection could be raised as a general criticism of eliminative-causal reasoning ("In general, how do you know you have cited all possible causes of a phenomenon?"). Or it could be raised as a specific one against Perrin ("What reason was there for supposing that Perrin had considered all possible causes of Brownian motion?").

14. See, for example, *Atoms*, pp. 85–86.

Reply

(1) The *general* criticism is based on the assumption that one is justified in employing an eliminative-causal argument only if all but one of the possible causes of the phenomenon have been listed and eliminated. But this is too demanding. One can be justified in employing an eliminative-causal argument if, *given one's background information,* one has considered and eliminated all but one of the possible causes, or at least, all but one of the causes that (on the basis of the background information) have any significant probability of causing the phenomenon in question. The claim that the possible causes cited probably include the actual one can be defended by appeal to the fact that the phenomenon in question is of a certain type that, experience has shown, in other cases is caused by one or the other of the causes cited.

(2) The *specific* criticism is that, even if eliminative-causal reasoning can be reasonable, if properly employed, Perrin did not properly employ it. He did not cite all the (plausible) causal candidates for Brownian motion, given information available to him. To be sure, he cites several candidates and argues that experiments eliminate these. But why suppose that these are the only possible or plausible causes permitted by his background information? And even if they are the only possible *observable* causes, why suppose that the motion of particles is the only possible *unobservable* cause?

Here, I suggest, the burden of proof is on the critic. Perrin cities various known causes of motion in a fluid and argues that experiments, particularly those of Christian Wiener in 1863 and Gouy in 1888 and 1889, show that Brownian motion continues unabated when these causes are altered or eliminated.[15] Perrin, quoting Wiener, concludes that the motion "does not originate either in the particles themselves or in any cause external to the liquid, but must be attributed to internal movements."[16] Since Perrin cited and eliminated various possible causes, it is, I think, up to the critic to say what other possible causes he should have eliminated, given his information (and why these should be assumed to be observable).

---

15. Wiener demonstrated that Brownian motion is not caused by infusoria (one-celled animals found in exposed bodies of water), by electrical forces, by temperature differences, or by evaporation of the fluid. In addition to these, Gouy's experiments eliminated causes pertaining to the size, composition, and density of the Brownian particles. For a discussion of various observable causes of Brownian motion postulated by scientists opposed to molecular theory, see Nye, *Molecular Reality* (London: Macdonald, 1972), pp. 22–27. Nye concludes (p. 27) that in his experiments, "Gouy [in 1889] refuted, point by point, all previous theories of Brownian movement other than the [molecular-] kinetic."

16. *Atoms,* p. 86.

(3) Both the general and the specific criticisms cited here, if valid, could equally well be used against the antirealist version of the eliminative-causal argument. That version cites theories that invoke causes C, C_1, . . . ,C_n as the possible candidates for saving the phenomena and then eliminates all but one of these theories. But, the critic can ask, why suppose that these are the only possible causal theories that will save the phenomena? And the critic can ask Perrin the specific form of this question for Brownian motion. So an antirealist version of eliminative-causal reasoning is no better off than the realist version. My response is simply to reject the critic's claims for the reasons given in replies 1 and 2.

4. THE "LIMITS OF EXPERIENCE" OBJECTION

The general idea here is simple and powerful. By observing nature, we can only make inferences about what is observable in nature, not what is unobservable. Here are claims of two prominent antirealists. First, Pierre Duhem:

> Now these two questions—Does there exist a material reality distinct from sensible appearances? and What is the nature of this reality?—do not have their source in experimental method, which is acquainted only with sensible appearances and can discover nothing beyond them.[17]

Second, van Fraassen:

> I explicate the general limits [of experience] as follows: *experience can give us information only about what is both observable and actual.*[18]

The claim, then, is that any argument from what is observed to the truth of claims about what is unobservable is unjustified. Since Perrin claimed truth for his theory about unobservable molecules, and since his argument is based on observed results of experiments that he and others conducted, his argument is unjustified.

What is the basis for the claim that by observing nature one can make inferences only about what is observable? A simple defense, one indeed suggested by Duhem, is that this is the essence of empiricism; inferring beyond the observable is metaphysics, which is not empirical. Indeed, immediately following the passage quoted here, Duhem claims that the

---

17. *The Aim and Structure of Physical Theory* (Princeton, N.J.: Princeton University Press, 1991), p. 10.

18. *Images of Science,* Paul M. Churchland and Clifford A. Hooker, eds. (Chicago: Chicago University Press, 1985), p. 253.

resolution of questions as to what lies beyond the "sensible appearances" "transcends the methods used by physics; it is the object of metaphysics" (p. 10). But this begs the issue, which in this case is that of characterizing empiricism. Perrin, no less than Duhem, regarded himself as engaged in empirical science, not metaphysics. He believed that empirical arguments could be given for the truth of a theory about unobservable molecules. It will not do simply to claim that his argument is not (entirely) empirical, or that he has gone beyond what empiricism allows.

Van Fraassen regards as extreme a policy that permits inferences beyond the "range of possible additional evidence," that is, inferences to the truth of claims about unobservables.[19] If only evidence can justify a belief, he goes on to say, then belief in the truth of a theory is "supererogatory," since we can have evidence for truth only via evidence for empirical adequacy (p. 255). Van Fraassen's first claim presupposes, or at least strongly suggests, that inferences to the truth of claims about unobservables are inferences beyond what the evidence allows. His second claim is that one can have evidence only for the empirical adequacy, not the truth, of a theory postulating unobservables, or that evidence for truth only amounts to evidence for empirical adequacy. Both claims, I suggest, require justification. Perrin, for example, clearly believed that he had evidence for the truth of propositions about unobservable molecules, not simply for their empirical adequacy; he had evidence that molecules exist, not simply evidence that the molecular theory saves the phenomena. Why was he wrong in this belief?

Let me suggest an argument an antirealist might offer in the spirit of the two quoted passages. Suppose that having observed a great many As and found them all to be B, one infers that all As are B. For example, from the fact that all observed bodies have mass one infers that all bodies, including any unobservable ones, do too.[20] (In Perrin's case, we might consider an inference from "All observed accelerating bodies in contact

---

19. *Images of Science*, p. 254.

20. The points to be made that follow will apply as well to causal reasoning from all observed As (for example, accelerations) are caused by Bs (for example, forces) to all As are caused by Bs. Realists generally extend inductive generalizations and causal reasoning to unobservables. For example, Isaac Newton writes, in his discussion of his inductive Rule 3: "The extension of bodies is known to us only through our senses, and yet there are bodies beyond the range of these senses; but because extension is found in all sensible bodies, it is ascribed to all bodies universally"—*Principia*, I. B. Cohen and Anne Whitman, eds. (Berkeley: University of California Press, 1999), Book 3, p. 795. Other such properties Newton mentions in this discussion are hardness, impenetrability, mobility, inertia, and gravitational attraction. Newton also extends his causal Rule 2 to apply to reasoning from effects to unobservable causes. Antirealists such as Duhem and van Fraassen do not deny the existence of unobservables. Their claim, contrary to Newton's, is that one cannot extend inductive or causal reasoning to unobservables by claiming truth for the conclusions of such arguments.

with other bodies exert forces on them" to "All accelerating bodies, in-cluding molecules (if any exist), in contact with other bodies exert forces on them.") Is an inference of this sort legitimate? Not necessarily. The sample observed may be unrepresentative. Even if we do not know that it is unrepresentative, we may have no positive empirical reason to think it is not biased. Suppose that all the As chosen for observation satisfy a condition C. Then unless we can argue that C is irrelevant—that C does not bias the sample with respect to B—we should infer not that all As are B, but, at best, that all As that satisfy C are B.

Now, says the antirealist, let C be the condition of *being observable*. All observed As satisfy this condition. Indeed, one can never observe an A that fails to satisfy it. So, unless one can demonstrate that this does not bias the sample of As observed with respect to B, from the fact that all As observed have been B, all we can legitimately infer is that all observable As are B. The only way of demonstrating that "observability" does not bias the sample of As observed with respect to B is by collecting a suitable sample of unobservable As and showing that in this sample the unob-servable As are all B (or perhaps by showing that in other cases, samples of unobservables match observables with respect to some property). But, of course, one cannot do that! One cannot observe unobservables. So in order to exclude potential bias, we are restricted to making (inductive and causal) inferences to what is observable. This argument can be extended to cover all types of nondemonstrative inferences. That is why Duhem is right in claiming that we can discover nothing beyond appearances, and why van Fraassen is justified in claiming that experience can give us infor-mation only about what is observable.

Reply

An antirealist who argues in the previous manner looks at the situation as one involving so-called *stratified sampling*. The population of As is divided into two classes or strata: the observables and the unobservables (if any). To make inferences about the entire class of As with respect to a property B, the antirealist is claiming, one needs to select randomly members from both strata for observation. Since one cannot select unobservable mem-bers for observation, one cannot legitimately, without potential bias, make inferences about this stratum, but only about the observable stratum.

If this argument is derived from the general principle that to make an inductive inference about a class, samples must be taken from all strata of that class, then no inference from any observed sample will be possible. Let the stratifying condition C be 'has been observed' (or 'has been ob-served prior to 2500'). All the As observed satisfy condition C. We cannot (now) take a sample from the subclass satisfying not-C. Accordingly, if the general principle of stratification for any condition C is correct, then no generalizations are possible.

Assuming that the antirealist does not accept this general principle with respect to all stratifying conditions C, what reason can he offer for supposing that the specific stratifying condition "being observable" is a biasing condition? Does he have any *empirical* reason for supposing that, in general, when considering a class of *As*, the unobservable stratum of *As*, if any exist, is different with respect to *B* from the observable stratum? No, he does not, since, by his own admission, unobservables cannot be sampled. Nor does he have some a priori argument showing that the two strata are different with respect to *B*. All he has is the weak a priori claim that the strata *may* be different—a claim about a mere logical possibility. But this is not sufficient to justify the methodological injunction that to make a legitimate inductive inference about the entire class consisting of observables and unobservables one must sample both strata. Indeed, if it were sufficient, the antirealist would be prevented from making any generalizations from what has been observed to what is observable but never observed. If one stratifies the class of observable *As* into those which are or will be observed and those which never will be observed, then it is logically possible that these strata are different with respect to *B*.

The realist, who wants to make inferences about unobservables as well as observables, must also reject the general principle of stratification. Can he do so without rejecting the idea that sampling requires variation? Can the realist offer an argument that provides support for his claim that "observability" is not, in general, a biasing condition?

I suggest that here the realist has an advantage over the antirealist. The realist can offer an empirical argument that provides support for his claim. There is a type of variation that can be produced for the purpose of meeting the antirealist challenge. One can vary conditions or properties in virtue of which something is observable (or unobservable). For example, items can be observable (or unobservable) in virtue of their size, their distance from us in space or time, their duration, their interactions (or lack of them) with other items, and so on. Suppose that all physical bodies that have been observed have mass. Have we biased the observed sample with respect to mass by observing only bodies that are observable? Observed physical bodies are necessarily observable. Therefore, we cannot vary the physical bodies observed by observing unobservable as well as observable ones. But we can vary properties of physical bodies in virtue of which they are observable (or unobservable).

Suppose we do the latter and find that bodies have mass even when we observe bodies that have different sizes, different distances from us, different durations, and different numbers and kinds of interactions with other bodies. In the absence of any contrary empirical information, we can then infer that size, distance, duration, and numbers and kinds of interactions do not alter the situation: bodies observed with different sizes, distances, durations, and interactions all have mass. So we infer that differences in these properties—differences that make some bodies observable and others not—make no difference as far as having mass is concerned.[21] If we vary the conditions in virtue of which bodies are observable and find no differences in whether bodies have mass, and if we have no contrary empirical information, then we have offered an empirical argument to support the claim that the fact that all observed bodies are observable does not bias the observed sample with respect to the property of having mass. In so doing, we have provided empirical grounds for inferring that all bodies have mass, whatever their size, distance, duration, and so on, and hence, whether or not they are observable.[22]

An antirealist may vehemently repudiate this argument by insisting that the only way to vary a condition C that is satisfied by all observed As is to observe As that satisfy C and As that do not. The antirealist will then reject the claim that the types of variations noted (which do not do this) suffice. But the claim that this is the only type of variation that can eliminate bias needs an argument, especially since the antirealist should allow variations in size, distance, and so on to count as varying the conditions when making inferences about observables.

For example, suppose an antirealist makes an inference he considers legitimate from the fact that all observed bodies have mass to all *observable* bodies have mass. In doing so, in order to preclude bias, one might vary the size of the bodies examined, their distance from other bodies, and a host of other properties. More generally, some variations involve changing "qualitative" properties by examining As that have such properties and As that do not. But there are also variations that involve changing "quantitative"

21. This conclusion is subject to the restriction noted previously, namely, "in the absence of any contrary information." With mass, there is no such contrary information. But with many properties, there are; for example, observed bodies of various sizes, distances from us, durations, and interactions have temperatures. But we have other empirical information, including an empirically supported theory about the nature of heat, that prevents the inference that bodies of all sizes and so on have temperatures (for example, individual molecules). In such cases, however, it is not the unobservability of such bodies that prevents the inference that all bodies have temperature, but information about the nature of heat. More generally, with the addition of quantum-mechanical information, unknown of course to Perrin in 1908, various conclusions from observations made on observed macrobodies cannot be drawn to bodies of much smaller size such as electrons. But this is not because such bodies are unobservable but because bodies of that size exhibit quantum-mechanical properties.

22. This type of reasoning is analogous to what Philip Kitcher, in a perceptive article on realism, calls "the Galilean strategy"—"Real Realism: The Galilean Strategy," *Philosophical Review*, 110 (April 2001), 151–197, particularly pp. 177–180.

properties by examining *A*s with varying amounts of such properties. If the antirealist rejects this second type of variation for eliminating bias, he needs an argument for doing so. If he accepts it, but only for inferences to observables, again he needs an argument for this restriction. The claim that unobservable bodies *may* be different from the observed ones with respect to having mass—in the sense of logical possibility—cuts no ice, since exactly the same could be said for the observable (but not yet observed) bodies. Nor, again, does the antirealist have either an empirical or an a priori argument to show that the observed bodies are unrepresentative of the unobservable ones with respect to having mass.[23]

5. IS THIS SCIENTIFIC REALISM?

The final objection, possibly the most important, is that whatever Perrin proved in his argument, even if by means of his experiments he did prove that molecules exist, this is not scientific realism. An objection of this sort will be raised by anyone, realist or antirealist, with a more demanding view of what scientific realism requires. Various candidates for scientific realism have been suggested in recent years by proponents as well as critics; three prominent ones will be noted.

(1) Scientific realism is a view about truth and reference in scientific theories generally. For example, Richard Boyd[24] and Stathis Psillos,[25] defenders of scientific realism, and Larry Laudan,[26] a severe critic, all claim that scientific realism involves a number of central theses, including these:

(A) Scientific theories (at least in the "mature" sciences) are typically approximately true, and more recent theories are closer to the truth than other theories in the same domain.

(B) The observational and theoretical terms within the theories of a mature science genuinely refer (roughly, there are substances in the world which correspond to the ontologies presumed by our best theories).

(C) Successive theories in any mature science will be such that they "preserve" the theoretical relations and the apparent referents of

23. To be sure, there are variations that can be made to show that mass is not a constant but varies with velocity. But this fact about mass has nothing to do with the observability or unobservability of the bodies with mass.

24. "The Current Status of Scientific Realism," in Jarrett Leplin, ed., *Scientific Realism* (Berkeley: University of California Press, 1984), pp.41–82.

25. *Scientific Realism* (New York: Routledge, 1999), p. xix.

26. "A Confutation of Convergent Realism," in Leplin, pp. 218–249.

earlier theories (that is, earlier theories will be "limiting cases" of later theories).

(D) Acceptable new theories do and should explain why their predecessors were successful insofar as they were successful.

This is Laudan's formulation (pp. 219–20). To these theses Boyd adds:

(E) The reality which scientific theories describe is largely independent of our thoughts or theoretical commitments (p.42).

Thesis (E) relates scientific realism to a core idea of what is sometimes called *metaphysical realism*, namely, that there is a mind- and theory-independent way the world is; to this core idea it adds the claim that scientific theories describe such an independent world.[27]

Even if Perrin proved that molecules exist, he did not prove theses (A)–(E), or even make them probable. Nothing Perrin did establishes or makes probable claims about scientific theories generally, or even about ones in mature sciences. Nor did Perrin establish that there is a mind- and theory-independent world or that theories in the mature sciences describe such a world approximately correctly.

(2) Scientific realism is a view about the *aim* of science. Here is van Fraassen's formulation:

> Science aims to give us, in its theories, a literally true story of what the world is like; and acceptance of a scientific theory involves the belief that it is true. This is the correct statement of scientific realism.[28]

Van Fraassen distinguishes the aim of science, as a type of activity, from the aims of particular scientists, which may include fame and fortune.[29]

27. Psillos divides scientific realism into a "metaphysical" part that "asserts that the world has a definite and mind-independent natural-kind classification"; a "semantical" part that says that scientific theories are capable of truth values and that theoretical terms are capable of denoting unobservable entities in the world; and an "epistemic" part that claims that "mature and predictively successful scientific theories [are] well-confirmed and approximately true of the world" and that the theoretical terms they employ denote entities that exist.

28. *The Scientific Image*, p. 8. Van Fraassen's contrasting antirealism is this: "Science aims to give us theories which are empirically adequate, and acceptance of a theory involves as belief only that it is empirically adequate." Note that such an antirealism is compatible with the truth of theses (A), (B), (C), and (E) of the Boyd-Psillos-Laudan formulation of realism, though, van Fraassen would emphasize, it is not the aim of science to produce theories that satisfy these theses but only to produce theories that are empirically adequate.

29. Some realists insist on broader aims than the one van Fraassen assigns to realists. For example, Kitcher defends an account of realism that combines certain elements of van Fraassen's definition with that of the Boyd-Psillos-Laudan account—*The Advancement of Science* (New York: Oxford, 1993), chapter 5. Kitcher's realism, as expressed in this book, includes the idea that the aim of science is to recognize natural kinds and furnish a set of explanatory schemata that pick out dependencies in the world; it also includes the claim that various parts of the sciences achieve these aims. For his more recent account, see "Real Realism: The Galilean Strategy."

Now, proving that molecules exist does not establish that the aim of science is to provide a literally true story of the world (or to satisfy any other broad conditions, such as describing natural kinds and dependencies), not even if this were Perrin's aim in the case of molecules. One would need to show more than this to establish scientific realism in the present sense. (I shall return to this in section 7).

(3) The scientific realism of interest to philosophers is not itself an *internal* scientific question, to be settled by scientific reasoning, but an *external* one concerning the adequacy of the scientific representation of the world. It cannot be established by empirical means. Both Rudolf Carnap[30] and Arthur Fine[31] have defended a distinction between internal and external questions. Their views about internal questions are somewhat similar, although they take very different positions on external questions.

For Carnap, the question of whether molecules exist can be approached in two ways. First, it can be treated as an empirical question within what Carnap calls a "linguistic framework," which contains rules of language and of inference, including rules governing what counts as evidence for what. Considered as an internal question within a framework permitting "theoretical terms" for unobservable entities, the answer to whether molecules exist can be determined empirically by the sorts of arguments from experiments Perrin provided. But this is not what philosophers usually have in mind when they assert (or deny) scientific realism with respect to theoretical entities such as molecules. For these philosophers, the question is an external one concerning the adequacy of the "theoretical entity" framework within which molecular claims are made. For Carnap, the claim that the framework is adequate is not a claim about its relationship to a framework-independent world. It is a pragmatic claim about the employability of the framework based on features such as simplicity, ease of use, and familiarity. Accordingly, different frameworks can be adopted, some of which have no terms for unobservables such as molecules. Some frameworks may be more user-friendly than others, but none is "correct" or "incorrect."

Carnap's internal questions are part of what Fine calls the *natural ontological attitude* (NOA). So, Fine can agree, Perrin established the existence of molecules by means of his experiments. In this internal sense, an antirealist can agree with a realist about what Perrin accomplished scientifically. What a realist does, according to Fine, is to step outside of scientific activity and claim that theories correspond to reality. Fine does not endorse

---

30. "Empiricism, Semantics, and Ontology," in Carnap, *Meaning and Necessity* (Chicago: University of Chicago Press, 1956), pp. 205–221.
31. "The Natural Ontological Attitude," in Leplin, pp. 83–107.

Carnap's line that such a claim is pragmatic. Rather, he says simply that what the realist is doing when he steps outside of scientific activity is tantamount to pounding the table and saying "Molecules exist, really!" This adds only emphasis to the internal claim. Fine, then, advocates NOA, which he regards as different from both realism and antirealism but as something that realists as well as antirealists can accept.

Both Carnap and Fine could agree that Perrin proved empirically that molecules exist, where the latter claim is understood as one internal to science (as part of NOA). For Carnap and Fine, Perrin did not prove, nor could he, that a framework containing terms for molecules corresponds to reality in some external sense. So if, as is typical, scientific realism is construed as an external doctrine, Perrin did not establish scientific realism. For Fine, neither Perrin nor anyone else could establish realism in an external sense. For Carnap, Perrin showed, by using the framework he did, at best that it was useful; he did not show that it is the only or the most useful one for dealing with questions involving Brownian motion.

These three views about scientific realism represent a spectrum of positions. Perrin's arguments do not establish scientific realism in a sense of that term advocated by any of the philosophers noted. So is Salmon mistaken in his claim that Perrin provided a valid experimental argument for scientific realism? To answer, some history is relevant.

6. HISTORICAL REASONS FOR REJECTING ATOMISM

We need to consider reasons that certain scientists rejected atomic-molecular theory until the first decade of the twentieth century. These reasons were known to Perrin, who responded to them. Critics of atomic theory included Duhem, Ernst Mach, Friedrich Wilhelm Ostwald, Henri Poincaré, and Max Planck. Grounds cited for rejecting the theory were in part scientific.[32] But they also included important philosophical or methodological reasons. One was the claim that physicists such as James C. Maxwell and Ludwig Boltzmann, who proposed atomic-molecular theories, were employing an illegitimate "method of hypothesis." From unproved hypotheses about atoms and molecules, they were deducing observable consequences and claiming that from the truth of the latter, one could infer the truth of the hypotheses themselves.[33] While Mach, for example, did not repudiate the

---

32. For example, atomic theories, as proposed, were purely mechanical theories that should entail reversible processes, but the latter are incompatible with observed thermodynamic phenomena.

33. Whether Maxwell and Boltzmann were in fact doing this is questionable. For a discussion of Maxwell's reasoning, see my *Particles and Waves* and chapter 14 in this book.

use of hypotheses, he did reject the idea that one could infer their truth or probability from true observed consequences. He regarded the hypotheses of the atomic theory as provisional "mental artifices" for summarizing known observational facts and facilitating observational predictions.[34] Once such hypotheses have served their organizational and predictive purposes, they are to be discarded, not accepted as true or probable. Indeed, Mach championed an antirealist "sensationalist" view about observable matter, which he regarded as complexes of sensations.[35]

A related philosophical claim made by some of the critics of atomic theory (whether or not they were Machian reductionists) was that hypotheses about unobservables can never be established as true or probable by empirical means; such hypotheses can never be known to be true. For example, Poincaré[36] speaks of the atomic hypothesis as "indifferent," meaning that although it may be useful, it can never be empirically established or shown to be more probable than rival hypotheses that assert the continuity of matter (pp. 152–153). For Duhem,[37] as noted earlier, science can know only "sensible appearances and can discover nothing beyond them" (p. 304). Unlike Poincaré and Mach, Duhem does not even regard atomic hypotheses as useful devices for summarizing and predicting observable phenomena.

Like some of the critics of the atomic theory, and no doubt because of their criticism, Perrin offers his own general philosophical/methodological reflections on how to proceed with scientific investigations. He distinguishes two scientific methods, which he calls the *inductive method* and the *intuitive method*.[38] The former, associated with the critics of atomic theory previously noted, begins with what is observed and reasons only to statements about "objects that can be observed and to experiments that can be performed" (p. vii). The second method infers the existence of an unobservable mechanism:

> In studying a machine, we do not confine ourselves only to the consideration of its visible parts, which have objective reality for us only as far as

34. He writes: "However well fitted atomic theories may be to reproduce certain groups of facts, the physical inquirer who has laid to heart Newton's rules will only admit those theories as *provisional* helps, and will strive to attain, in some more natural way, a satisfactory substitute. The atomic theory plays a part in physics similar to that of certain auxiliary concepts in mathematics; it is a mathematical *model* for facilitating the mental reproduction of facts"—*The Science of Mechanics* (LaSalle, Ill.: Open Court, 1960), p. 589.

35. "ordinary 'matter' must be regarded merely as a highly natural, unconsciously constructed mental symbol for a complex of sensuous elements"—*Contributions to the Analysis of the Sensations* (LaSalle, Ill.: Open Court, 1890), p. 152.

36. *Science and Hypothesis* (New York: Dover, 1952).

37. "Physics of a Believer," in *Aim and Structure of Physical Theory*.

38. *Atoms*, p. vii.

we can dismount the machine. We certainly observe these visible pieces as clearly as we can, but at the same time we seek to divine the *hidden* gears and parts that explain its apparent motions.

To divine in this way the existence and properties of objects that still lie outside our ken, *to explain the complications of the visible in terms of invisible simplicity*, is the function of intuitive intelligence which, thanks to men such as Dalton and Boltzmann, has given us the doctrine of Atoms. This book aims at giving an exposition of that doctrine. (p. vii)

Perrin claims that in the times in which he is writing, the method of intuition has gone ahead of induction rejuvenating the doctrine of energy by the incorporation of statistical results borrowed from atomists (p. viii).

In these introductory passages, Perrin does not describe the intuitive method in detail other than to say that it is a method for inferring an invisible underlying reality from visible things and events in such a way that the former explains the latter. I suggest that we take his own arguments for molecules from experiments on Brownian motion as representing his use of the "intuitive method." If so, then that method is not simply a matter of speculating about an invisible realm. Nor is it a Machian provisional "mental artifice" for representing the facts, to be discarded once it has served its purpose. Nor is it a method simply for inferring the truth of claims about what can be observed (that is what he calls the inductive method). Nor, by contrast with Mach, does Perrin say or imply that assertions about ordinary matter are to be understood as claims about sensations, or (with later logical positivists) that assertions about an invisible realm of molecules are to be understood as claims about a visible realm such as that of Brownian motion, or that when he infers that molecules are real and that certain claims about them are true, by "real" and "true" he means "useful" or "saves the phenomena."

Finally, Perrin's intuitive method is not the method of hypothesis, which infers the truth or probability of a hypothesis simply from the fact that the hypothesis explains and predicts observable phenomena. To be sure, Perrin's full argument involves citing explanatory chemical reasons from combinations of elements and compounds. But in addition, it involves eliminative-causal reasoning of a sort indicated in section 2. It involves an appeal to similar determinations of Avogadro's number N from a variety of experiments on phenomena other than Brownian motion. And perhaps most important, it involves a calculation of N from Perrin's own experiments on Brownian motion and a demonstration that this number remains constant (proposition H' in section 2). The former arguments, according to Perrin, show that the molecular hypothesis is highly probable. The latter sustains and even increases this probability on the basis of new, precise, experimental results.

Now we are in a position to respond to Salmon's challenge.

7. DID PERRIN PROVIDE AN EXPERIMENTAL ARGUMENT FOR SCIENTIFIC REALISM?

Or did he merely furnish an answer to what Carnap calls an internal question? That is, Perrin's argument more than simply an empirical argument for the existence of a particular natural kind, namely, molecules—entities which had been previously postulated by scientists but not shown to exist? It is this and a good deal more. It is an argument to the existence of something that was regarded as dubious or objectionable on philosophical or methodological grounds. These grounds included the idea that from what is observed, one can make valid inferences only to what is observable, not to what is unobservable. Moreover, they are grounds for rejecting unobservables generally, not just molecules. (Duhem, for example, rejected a range of physical theories postulating unobservables.)

Perrin did not respond to these critics by making molecules observable. Rather, he claimed that there is a reasonable method or mode of reasoning (the intuitive method) that starts with observed experimental results and can be used to infer the existence of things that are unobservable (or "invisible," or "hidden," to use Perrin's terms). He showed in detail how this method could be used to infer the existence of invisible molecules from experimental observations on Brownian motion. And he clearly regarded this intuitive method as a general one, not restricted simply to molecules.[39] This is not just scientific business as usual. It is not simply an argument establishing (or rejecting) the existence of just one more type of physical entity. Nor did Perrin or his antirealist opponents take this as scientific business as usual.

The scientific realism implicit in Perrin's arguments can be put like this:

(1) There are unobservables (for example, molecules).
(2) Their existence and their properties can be inferred (only) on empirical grounds, in some cases from experiments, so that a claim to know they exist and have these properties is justified.[40]
(3) A legitimate mode of reasoning that can be used for this purpose involves two important components:

39. "The use of the intuitive method has not, of course, been used only in the study of atoms, any more than the inductive method has found its sole application in energetics"— *Atoms*, p. vii.

40. Statement (2) is close to what Leplin calls "minimal epistemic realism," a doctrine he defends in *A Novel Defense of Scientific Realism* (New York: Oxford, 1997).

(a) causal-eliminative reasoning to the existence of the postulated entity, and to certain claims about its properties, from other experimental results;

(b) an argument to the conclusion that the particular experimental results obtained are very probable given the existence of the postulated entity and properties.

Part (a) in (3) is intended to establish the high probability for the claim that the entity exists and has certain properties. Part (b) can be shown to sustain and possibly increase that probability on the basis of the new experiments. Reasoning involving (a) and (b) can be used to infer the existence of entities whether observable or unobservable.

The scientific realism reflected in points (1)–(3) does not say that theories about unobservables in mature sciences are (approximately) true and that the unobservables postulated exist, or that the aim of science is to obtain true theories about unobservables as well as observables. Nor does it adopt either some metaphysical viewpoint external to science, saying that there is a mind- and theory-independent way the world is and/or emphatically endorsing the adequacy of a scientific representation of this world, or a pragmatic viewpoint stressing the usefulness of scientific theorizing. It is not scientific realism *in these senses.*

Nor is it a restricted internal realism that says simply that molecules (electrons, or whatever) exist. It is much more general than this, and it has a methodological as well as an ontological component. It claims that there are unobservables (Perrin's realm of "invisible simplicity"), and that valid arguments can be used to infer their existence and properties; these are entities which, on philosophical and/or methodological grounds, anti-realists reject or understand in some nonrealistic way. It says, however, the arguments for these entities and claims about their properties are empirical ones, so that what entities exist in this realm and what properties they have are empirical questions. The particular empirical argument for a given unobservable will depend on, and vary with, the unobservable postulated. No *general* empirical argument can be given for all unobservables postulated. Nor can the issue of the existence of unobservables be settled a priori. Nevertheless, there is an a priori assumption that is essential to scientific realism so understood, namely, that a valid mode of reasoning can be employed (such as (a) and (b) in point (3)) which can justify a belief in the truth of propositions about the unobservable entities inferred.

Does this deserve the name "scientific realism"? Fine may answer "no," claiming that it does not go beyond what his neutral NOA permits. Fine says that NOA, and hence realism and antirealism, "accept(s) the results of scientific investigations as 'true' on par with more homely truths."[41] Hence, he will insist, since the results of scientific investigation include empirically based inferences to the existence of unobservables such as molecules, NOA, together with realism and antirealism, accepts both (1) and (2). Moreover, he may add that NOA, and hence both realism and antirealism, accepts point (3), since, he says, NOA sanctions "ordinary relations of confirmation and evidential support, subject to the usual scientific canons" (p. 98) (although he does not formulate any such canons, or indicate whether they include the type of inference in point (3)). But if NOA does endorse points (1)–(3), then, I suggest, *it endorses a form of scientific realism rejected by scientists of the sort Perrin was opposing who are generally classified as antirealists.*[42] These scientists, including Duhem, Mach, Ostwald, and Poincaré, claim either that point (1) is false or else that, if it is true, it is unknowable by empirical means. (They do not regard propositions about unobservables on a "par with more homely truths.") And they reject points (2) and (3), since they raise general methodological objections to inferences from what is observed to what is unobservable.

Moreover, if an antirealist says either that unobservables do not exist or that, if they do, they are empirically unknowable, and if he is an empiricist about science, then, as in the case of Duhem and van Fraassen, he is likely to deny that the aim of science is to provide true theories about unobservables. This is because he holds that such an aim cannot be satisfied at all or cannot be satisfied by empirical means. Although this position does not follow deductively from a denial of point (1)–(3), it is a natural claim to make if one wants to retain empiricism in science and hold that the aim of science can be achieved. Similarly, if one is a realist and states that unobservables do exist and that claims to know this in particular cases can be empirically justified, then it is natural to assert that the aim of science, or at least one of its aims, is to provide true theories about such unobservables.

The most important reason that antirealists such as Duhem and van Fraassen have for saying that the aim of science is (a) to provide theories that save the phenomena, rather than (b) to provide theories that are true, is that they regard (a) but not (b) as doable and empirically justifiable. By contrast, realists such as Perrin and Newton regard both (a) and (b) as doable and empirically justifiable. Since they do, and since they also regard unobservables (such as molecules and universal gravity, which Newton

41. Fine, "The Natural Ontological Attitude," p. 96.
42. Both Alan Musgrave—"NOA's Ark: Fine for Realism," *Philosophical Quarterly* 39 (1989), 383–398—and Psillos—*Scientific Realism*, chapter 10—make the general argument that Fine's NOA is not neutral, but a realist position that is incompatible with certain standard antirealist views.

considered a force extended to bodies "beyond the range of the senses") as causally responsible for observable phenomena (such as Brownian motion and motions of the planets), and since they regard particular causal claims of the latter sort as justifiable empirically, it would be natural for them to hold that:

> (4) One of the aims of science is to provide (approximately) true theories of what the world is like.

where truth applies to unobservables as well as observables. Point (4) is indeed strongly suggested by the methodological remarks of Newton (for example, in his Rules 1 and 4)[43] and Perrin (in his intuitive method). Accordingly, since it is not entailed by realist points (1)–(3), it is reasonable to consider it part of the realist position. Its truth is not demonstrated by Perrin's empirical argument for molecules, but it is plausible to say that Perrin presupposed its truth in conducting his investigation into the cause of Brownian motion.

The same cannot be said, however, for the doctrine of realism defended by Boyd and Psillos and attacked by Laudan. Points (1)–(4) make no claims about whether, in general, scientific theories in the mature sciences are true, contain terms that refer to objects that exist, and describe a mind- and theory-independent world; such a realism is much stronger than (1)–(4). Nor were any such general claims about theories in the mature sciences made or presupposed by Perrin in his investigation (or by Newton in his argument for the existence of a universal gravitational force).

For scientific realism *of the sort that was supported by scientists such as Perrin and rejected by his opponents*, points (1)–(4) suffice. These scientists claimed (or denied) that there is an empirically knowable realm of unobservables responsible for observable effects, and since there is, one of the aims of science is to provide true theories about this realm. Whether any particular theory is true is to be determined by empirical considerations specific to that theory. From the fact that the theory is part of a mature science one cannot infer that it is true or probable. Indeed, as Laudan has argued, historically many such theories have been empirically refuted. For scientific realism of the kind under attack by Duhem, Mach, and other scientists (as well as by van Fraassen), and defended by Perrin (and by Salmon), what is important is the idea that there is a realm of unobservables, claims

---

43. Rule 1 requires that causes postulated be "both true and sufficient to explain their phenomena"; Rule 4 requires that "propositions gathered from phenomena by induction should be considered either exactly or very nearly true . . . until yet other phenomena make such propositions either more exact or liable to exceptions." Newton applies both rules to unobservables as well as observables.

about which can be empirically justified as true. Whether unobservables do exist, and if so which ones, and what properties they have, are issues to be determined by empirical arguments of the sort Perrin provided for molecules. Accordingly, I regard Salmon's conclusion as justified. In a historically and conceptually important sense of "scientific realism" (though not in every sense assigned to that term), Perrin's experimental argument for molecules provides and empirical basis for scientific realism.

12

Jean Perrin and Molecular Reality

"Jean Perrin and Molecular Reality" is reprinted by permission from Perspectives on Science 2 *(1994), 396–427 (selected for Philosopher's Annual 1994). This chapter covers some of the same ground as chapter 11. I include it because it offers a more extensive account of Perrin's reasoning to molecules, as well as a criticism of alternative interpretations of this reasoning proposed by Wesley Salmon, Clark Glymour, and hypothetico-deductivists. Also, it relates Perrin's empirical argument to material on evidence in chapter 1.*

1. INTRODUCTION

In 1908 Jean Perrin conducted a series of experiments on Brownian motion from which he drew two conclusions of particular importance: (1) that molecules exist, and (2) that Avogadro's number, N, the number of molecules in a substance whose weight in grams equals its molecular weight, is approximately 6×10^{23}. Perrin's experimental work and conclusions were set forth in a series of articles published in 1908 and 1909, the most famous of which is his "Brownian Movement and Molecular Reality" (Perrin [1909] 1984). An expanded version of his results appeared four years later in his book *Atoms* (Perrin [1913] 1990).

In 1926 Perrin received the Nobel Prize in physics primarily for his work on Brownian motion. Despite his considerable success, philosophers and historians of science who read his articles and book should find some of his key arguments puzzling. For one thing, why in 1908, after nineteenth-century successes in the kinetic theory of gases and after the discovery of the electron in 1897 by J. J. Thomson, should Perrin have thought it necessary to argue that molecules exist?[1] Yet argue for this he did.

---

1. Indeed, Perrin in 1895 made an important contribution to the study of cathode rays by presenting experimental evidence that they are charged particles. This helped to facilitate Thomson's experiments, which determined, among other things, the ratio of mass to charge of these particles, and from which Thomson drew the conclusion in 1897 that they are smaller than, and constituents of, molecules and atoms. See Achinstein 1991, essays 10 and 11, and also chapter 15 in this book.

A second puzzling fact is that Perrin's argument for the reality of molecules seems circular. In brief, from assumptions in kinetic theory involving the existence of molecules, Perrin derives a formula, the "law of atmospheres," that governs a volume of gas. The law relates the number of molecules per unit volume of a gas at a height above some reference plane to Avogadro's number. He then assumes that a slightly modified version of this same law can be applied to the distribution of much larger, microscopic particles (Brownian particles) suspended not in a gas but in a fluid. With this assumption he proposes a formula that relates the number of suspended Brownian particles per unit volume at a height above a reference plane to Avogadro's number and to various experimentally measurable quantities of the visible particles, including their mass, density, and numbers at different heights. He performs experiments measuring these quantities, for different Brownian particles, different liquids, and different temperatures. Each of these measurements, when combined with the law of atmospheres, yields approximately the same value for Avogadro's number. From this fact he concludes that molecules exist. The apparent circularity is that to reach this conclusion Perrin begins by *assuming* that molecules exist. That is an assumption presupposed by the law of atmospheres.

In this article I will examine Perrin's reasoning to see whether it is in fact circular. I believe that it is not, and indeed that it conforms with a valid pattern of reasoning frequently used by scientists to infer the existence of "unobservables." I will show why, even in 1908, it was reasonable for Perrin to employ this pattern of reasoning in arguing for the existence of molecules. Finally, I will discuss the relationship between Perrin's reasoning and the debate between realists and antirealists regarding unobservable entities.

2. PERRIN'S DETERMINATION OF AVOGADRO'S NUMBER AND HIS ARGUMENT FOR MOLECULAR REALITY

Perrin's strategy is first to derive the law of atmospheres for gases.[2] He considers a volume of gas contained in a thin cylinder of unit cross-sectional area and very small elevation h. The density of molecules making up the gas will be greatest at the bottom of the cylinder and decreases exponentially with increasing height. The pressure p at the bottom of the cylinder is more than the pressure p' at the top (just as air pressure at the bottom of a mountain is greater than at the top). The very small difference in pressure p − p' balances the downward force of gravity gm_c on the mass m_c of gas in the cylinder. So

2. Here I follow the argument in Perrin 1990, pp. 90ff.; a briefer version is found in Perrin 1984, pp. 529–530.

$$p - p' = gm_c. \tag{1}$$

Now the mass m_c of the gas is to its volume $1 \times h$ as the gram molecular weight M (the mass in grams equal to the molecular weight of the gas) is to the volume v occupied by a gram molecular weight of the gas. That is,

$$\frac{m_c}{1 \times h} = \frac{M}{v}. \tag{2}$$

From equations (1) and (2) we get

$$p - p' = \frac{Mgh}{v}. \tag{3}$$

Now Perrin invokes the perfect gas law for one gram molecular weight of a gas,

$$pv = RT,$$

where R is the gas constant and T is absolute temperature, and substitutes RT/p for v in (3), obtaining

$$p - p' = \frac{Mgh}{RT} \cdot p,$$

or

$$\frac{p'}{p} = 1 - \frac{Mgh}{RT}. \tag{4}$$

The pressure of a gas is proportional to its density, and hence to the number of molecules per unit volume. So the ratio p'/p can be replaced by the ratio n'/n, where n' and n are the number of molecules per unit volume at the upper and lower levels, respectively. We obtain

$$\frac{n'}{n} = 1 - \frac{Mgh}{RT}. \tag{5}$$

If m is the mass of a molecule of gas and N is Avogadro's number, then

$$M = Nm; \tag{6}$$

that is, the gram molecular weight M of a gas is equal to the number of molecules in a gram molecular weight multiplied by the mass of a molecule. So from equations (5) and (6) we obtain

$$\frac{n'}{n} = 1 - \frac{Nmgh}{RT}, \tag{7}$$

in which Avogadro's number appears.[3]

---

3. A mathematically more rigorous derivation using differential calculus yields $n'/n = e^{-Nmgh/RT}$, where e is the natural log base. For tiny particles and small h the exponent becomes much smaller than 1, and the exponential factor can be expanded in a series whose first two terms are given on the right side of eq. (7). In his 1909 article, by contrast to his book, Perrin employs the more rigorous derivation.

Perrin proposes to use equation (7) to determine a value for Avogadro's number experimentally. The problem is that the molecular quantities n, n', and m are not directly measurable. So he makes a crucial assumption, namely, that visible particles making up a dilute emulsion will behave like molecules in a gas with respect to their vertical distribution. In 1827 the English botanist Robert Brown discovered that small, microscopic particles suspended in a liquid do not sink but exhibit rapid, seemingly haphazard motions—so-called Brownian motion. Following Leon Gouy, Perrin assumed that the motions of the visible particles are caused by collisions with the molecules making up the liquid in which the particles are suspended. He also made the assumption that just as a set of invisible molecules that make up a gas obey that gas laws, so do the visible particles exhibiting Brownian motion in a liquid. Among other things, he assumed that the law (eq. [7]) derived for molecules in a cylinder of gas could be extended to Brownian particles distributed in a dilute emulsion.

This means that just as the molecules making up a gas are all identical in mass and volume, so will the Brownian particles have to be. However, in the latter case, the gravitational force acting on a particle will not be its weight mg, but its "effective weight," that is, the excess of its weight over the upward thrust caused by the liquid in which it is suspended. This is

$$mg - \frac{mdg}{D} = mg\left(1 - \frac{d}{D}\right), \tag{8}$$

where D is the density of the material making up the particles and d is the density of the liquid. Replacing the weight mg in equation (7) by the expression in equation (8), we obtain

$$\frac{n'}{n} = 1 - \frac{Nmg(1 - d/D)h}{RT}. \tag{9}$$

In this equation, n' represents the number of Brownian particles per unit volume at the upper level and n the same at the lower level; m is the mass of a Brownian particle; N is Avogadro's number.[4] Equation (9) contains quantities for the suspended particles (not molecules) which Perrin attempted to determine experimentally.

This required the careful preparation of emulsions containing particles equal in size and determining the density of the material making up the particles, the mass of the particles, and (with microscopes) the number of

4. Strictly speaking, in eq. (9) N represents a number for Brownian particles; i.e., any quantity of these particles equal to their molecular weight will contain the same number N of particles. This number N will, according to Perrin's assumptions, be the same as Avogadro's number for molecules.

suspended particles per unit volume at various heights—all difficult procedures. Experiments were performed with different emulsions, particles of different size and mass, different liquids, and different temperatures. With various values obtained experimentally for the quantities n, n', m, h, and T in equation (9), Perrin could use equation (9) to determine whether Avogadro's number is really a constant, and if so what its value is. He writes, "In spite of all these variations, the value found for Avogadro's number N remains approximately constant, varying irregularly between 65×10^{22} and 72×10^{22} [i.e., 6.5×10^{23} and 7.2×10^{23}]" (Perrin 1990, p. 105).

Immediately after this sentence Perrin draws a broader conclusion: "Even if no other information were available as to the molecular magnitudes, *such constant results would justify the very suggestive hypotheses that have guided us*, and we should certainly accept as extremely probable the values obtained with such concordance for the masses of the molecules and atoms," (Perrin 1990, p. 105; italics his).[5]

Perrin's "suggestive hypotheses" include, of course, the assumption that molecules exist. He continues by noting that the values for Avogadro's number obtained through his experiments agree with the number (6.2×10^{23}) given by kinetic theory from considerations of viscosity of gases. And he concludes, *"Such decisive agreement can leave no doubt as to the origin of the Brownian movement.* . . . The objective reality of the molecules therefore becomes hard to deny" (Perrin 1990, p. 105; italics his).

Perrin's conclusions concerning the value of Avogadro's number and the reality of molecules are drawn form his experiments on Brownian particles suspended in a column of fluid. After drawing them Perrin goes on to consider the theory of Brownian motion developed by Einstein ([1905] 1956), which generates an equation relating Avogadro's number to the mean square of the displacement of the Brownian particles in a given direction during a given time. Perrin conducted experiments on such displacement, and using Einstein's equation he generated a value for N close to that achieved by his law-of-atmosphere experiments.[6]

At the end of his book Perrin notes that the value(s) he determined for Avogadro's number are approximately the same as ones obtained by a variety of different methods, including ones from experiments on radioactivity, blackbody radiation, and the motions of ions in liquids. And he writes, "Our wonder is aroused at the very remarkable agreement found

5. From Avogadro's number and the known molecular weights of substances the mass of molecules is readily determined: mass of a molecule of substance S is equal to the molecular weight of S divided by Avogadro's number.

6. A useful discussion of these experiments and the statistical reasoning involved is found in Mayo 1986 and 1988.

between values derived from the consideration of such widely different phenomena. Seeing that not only is the same magnitude obtained by each method when the conditions under which it is applied are varied as much as possible, but that the numbers thus established also agree among themselves, without discrepancy, for all the methods employed, the real existence of the molecule is given a probability bordering on certainty" (Perrin 1990, pp. 215–216; see also Perrin 1984, pp. 598–599).

3. IS THE ARGUMENT FOR MOLECULES CIRCULAR?

The basic structure of Perrin's reasoning seems to be this:

1. From various assumptions, including that molecules exist, and that gases containing them satisfy the ideal gas law, Perrin derives equation (7), which relates the number of molecules at a height h in a container of gas to Avogadro's number and to other quantities including the mass of a gas molecule and the temperature of the gas.
2. Perrin then claims that this formula, or a variation of it, can be applied to visible Brownian particles suspended in a fluid, yielding equation (9).
3. Next he devises ways to experimentally measure the quantities in equation (9) (other than Avogadro's number), and he conducts various experiments using different fluids and particles.
4. Each of these measurements, when combined with equation (9), yields approximately the value 6×10^{23} for N.
5. This approximate value for N is also obtained from experiments other than those involving particles suspended in a fluid.
6. From steps 4 and 5 Perrin concludes ("with a probability bordering on certainty") that molecules exist.

The apparent circularity consists in the fact that in step 1 Perrin is making the crucial assumption that molecules exist. Without this assumption he cannot derive equation (7), which gives a ratio of the number of molecules per unit volume at the height h to the number at the bottom of the cylinder. Is a charge of circularity warranted? In what follows I will consider some attempts to understand Perrin's reasoning so that circularity is avoided.

A. A Common-Cause Interpretation

Wesley Salmon (1984) urges that Perrin's reasoning to the reality of molecules is an example of a legitimate common-cause argument. The basic idea of such an argument is this. If very similar effects have been produced, and if it can reasonably be argued that none of these effects causes any of the others, then it can be concluded that these effects all result from a common cause. This, claims Salmon, is how Perrin argues for the reality of molecules: Perrin notes that experiments on various phenomena—including Brownian motion, alpha particle decay, X-ray diffraction, blackbody radiation, and electrochemical phenomena—all yield approximately the same value for Avogadro's number. Salmon asks us to imagine five different scientists engaged in experiments on the five phenomena mentioned. He writes, "These experiments seem on the surface to have nothing to do with one another [so that it is unlikely that one phenomenon studied causes the other]. Nevertheless, we ask each scientist to fill in the blank in this statement: On the basis of my experiments, assuming matter to be composed of molecules, I calculate the number of molecules in a mole [gram molecular weight] of any substance to be _____.When we find that all of them write numbers that, within the accuracy of their experiments, agree with 6×10^{23}, we are as impressed by the 'remarkable agreement' as were Perrin and Poincaré. Certainly, these five hypothetical scientists have been counting entities that are objectively real" (Salmon 1984, p. 221). He later says, "Remember, for instance, the victims of mushroom poisoning; their common illness arose from the fact that each of them consumed food from a common pot. Similarly, I think, the agreement in values arising from different ascertainments of Avogadro's number results from the fact that in each of the physical procedures mentioned, the experimenter was dealing with substances composed of atoms and molecules—in accordance with the theory of the constitution of matter that we have all come to accept. The historical argument that convinced scientists of the reality of atoms and molecules is, I believe, philosophically impeccable" (Salmon 1984, p. 223).[7]

Since Salmon claims Perrin's argument is philosophically impeccable, he would deny any circularity charge. According to him, the argument goes like this:

---

7. Nancy Cartwright (1983, pp. 82–85) offers a somewhat similar analysis of Perrin's reasoning. She takes it to be an argument to the "most probable cause." Experiments on seemingly unrelated phenomena all yield the same calculation for Avogadro's number. "Would it not be a coincidence if each of the observations was an artefact, and yet all agreed so closely about Avogadro's number? The convergence of results provides reason for thinking that the various models used in Perrin's diverse calculations were each good enough. It thus reassures us that those models can legitimately be used to infer the nature of the cause from the character of the effects" (pp. 84–85). For a criticism of Cartwright's account, see Mayo 1986.

1. If molecules exist, then from experiments on Brownian motion we get a value for Avogadro's number of $N = 6 \times 10^{23}$.
2. If molecules exist, then from Rutherford's experiments on alpha particle decay, we get a similar value for Avogadro's number. The same is true for experiments involving X-ray diffraction, blackbody radiation, and electrochemical phenomena.
3. There is no reason to suppose that Brownian motion's resulting in a value of $N = 6 \times 10^{23}$ causes alpha particle decay to yield the same value, nor vice versa. The same applies to other cases.
4. So probably each phenomenon's yielding a similar value for N has a common cause, namely, the existence of molecules.
5. So probably molecules exist.

This argument is not circular, since no assumption is made in premises 1 and 2 that molecules do in fact exist. All that is assumed is a conditional: if molecules exist, then. . . . Salmon himself recognizes this when he writes, "On the basis of my experiments, *assuming matter to be composed of molecules*, I calculate the number of molecules in a mole of any substance to be_____." This corresponds to premises 1 and 2. The problem, however, is that this conditional assumption is too weak to yield the strong conclusion 4. The most that premises 1, 2, and 3 warrant is the conditional

4′. *If molecules exist*, then probably each phenomenon's yielding a similar value for N has a common cause.

But 4′ is much less than Perrin himself claims. To generate the conclusion that Perrin wants, Salmon might alter the argument by adding an additional premise, namely, "Molecules exist." But now the argument becomes clearly circular. A more promising approach is to delete the antecedent "If molecules exist" from premises 1 and 2 and assert simply that on each of the varied experiments in question physicists calculated the value of N to be 6×10^{23}, where the latter claim does not presuppose that this is the correct value or even that molecules exist. On this interpretation, we have similar effects (similar calculations of a number that is supposed to represent a number of molecules); and these effects do not cause one another. So by the common-cause principle, we may infer a common cause (without the antecedent assumption that molecules exist). The problem is that a common-cause argument by itself (even assuming its validity)[8] does not permit us to infer what that common

8. For a general criticism of common-cause arguments, see van Fraassen 1980 and Arntzenius 1992.

cause is but only that there is one. Additional facts must be cited to show that it is the existence of molecules, and not something else, that is the common cause.[9]

One strategy for doing so would be to argue for two points: (*a*) that the existence of molecules can cause, or be a causal factor in producing, similar calculations of *N* from experiments on Brownian motion, alpha particle decay, X-ray diffraction, and so on (this could be done by showing how molecular processes can be involved in, or related to, the phenomena in question); and (*b*) that other possible causes do not produce these effects. Both before and after giving his common-cause argument involving the five hypothetical scientists, Salmon in fact goes some way toward arguing for points (*a*) and (*b*). He considers how *N* is related to the five phenomena cited. And he discusses one rival to molecular theory, namely, energeticism, which, he argues, is incapable of explaining the experimental results. But if indeed it is possible to defend points (*a*) and (*b*), then a common-cause argument is both unnecessary and unproductive. It is unnecessary because if (*a*) and (*b*) can be successfully defended then the existence of molecules is shown to be probable without invoking a common-cause argument. It is unproductive because a common-cause argument does not by itself make probable the existence of molecules, contrary to what Salmon claims is shown by his "five hypothetical scientists" argument.

B. A Hypothetico-Deductive Interpretation

A different interpretation is to suppose that Perrin is engaging in a form of hypothetico-deductive reasoning: From the hypothesis that molecules exist and have the properties he attributes to them he draws deductive conclusions regarding observable phenomena, including Brownian motion. He tests these conclusions experimentally and finds they are correct. From this he infers that his molecular hypotheses are probable,

9. In explicating the idea of a common cause, Salmon employs Reichenbach's notion of a conjunctive fork defined probabilistically in terms of these four conditions: (i) $p(A\&B/C) = p(A/C) \times p(B/C)$; (ii) $p(A\&B/-C) = p(A/-C) \times p(B/-C)$; (iii) $p(A/C) > p(A/-C)$; (iv) $p(B/C) > p(B/-C)$. These conditions are satisfied, Salmon argues, if A and B represent experimental results from two different phenomena yielding the same value for Avogadro's number, and C includes the assumption that molecules exist. But as Salmon himself recognizes (1984, pp. 167–168), these are not sufficient conditions for C to be a common cause of A and B. Nor, indeed, does the satisfaction of these conditions make it highly probable that C is a common cause of A and B. Incompatible C's could satisfy these conditions. (For an example, see my coin-tossing case, in nn. 23 and 24). Yet Perrin (as well as Salmon) wants to conclude that, in all probability ("bordering on certainty"), molecules exist. The satisfaction of the conjunctive fork conditions will not yield such a conclusion.

or at least that they are confirmed or supported by observations. This is no more circular than any use of hypothetico-deductive reasoning. In its simplest form it is just this: O is derivable from T; O is true; hence T is confirmed or probable. Proposition T is not being assumed to be true or probable at the outset.

From what hypothesis or set of hypotheses is Perrin supposed to have derived observational conclusions, and what observational conclusion(s) does he derive that he takes to confirm the hypothesis? The following hypothesis is clearly among those from which Perrin derives consequences:

> h. Chemical substances are composed of molecules, the number N of which in a gram molecular weight of a substance is the same for all substances.

A claim (indeed the most important one) that Perrin establishes experimentally that he takes to confirm h is this:

> C. The calculation of N done by means of Perrin's experiments on Brownian particles, using equation (9), is 6×10^{23}, and this number remains constant even when values for n', n, and so on, in equation (9) are varied.

Proposition C might well be called "observational." But it is not something that Perrin derives from his theoretical hypothesis h, nor from h together with other hypotheses he employs about molecules and Brownian particles. What Perrin does is to derive equation (9), not proposition C, deductively from such hypotheses. Then he uses equation (9) *together with results from various carefully designed experiments* to establish C, which he regards as confirming molecular theory.[10] But this is not the procedure advocated by hypothetico-deductivists. Contrary to the hypothetico-deductive view, the conclusion whose establishment is being claimed to confirm the theory is not derived from that theory.

Even if Perrin does not derive C from his theory, could he have done so? Is C derivable from the theoretical assumptions Perrin in fact makes? No, because even though one of the hypotheses Perrin was using is that N is a constant, he did not begin with any theoretical postulate concerning the numerical value of this constant. As noted, there were experiments on phenomena other than Brownian motion from which N was calculated to be approximately 6×10^{23}. But C is not derivable from this fact. Nor, in order to obtain his result C, did Perrin assume that these other experimental values for N were correct.

Finally, and perhaps most important, as I will argue in section 4, Perrin's approach to confirming molecular theory is much richer than that

----

10. See Achinstein 1991, pp. 304ff., for an analogous case in which Thomson arrives at a number representing the ratio of mass to charge of the electron.

suggested by a hypothetico-deductive approach. He does not in fact defend this theory simply on the grounds that it entails true "observational" conclusions (whether or not these include C). Nor, therefore, is he subject to criticisms of the dubious hupothetico-deductive view of confirmation, according to which if h entails e, then e confirms h (see Achinstein 1983a, chap. 10).

C. Bootstrapping

Clark Glymour's idea of bootstrapping looks more promising than the hypothetico-deductive account because it uses experimental results together with hypotheses in a theory to confirm those hypotheses (Glymour 1980). To invoke Glymour's own simple example, consider the ideal gas law expressed as

$$PV = kT, \tag{10}$$

where P represents the pressure of a gas, V its volume, T its absolute temperature, and k an undetermined constant. We suppose that we can experimentally determine values for P, V, and T, but not for k. Equation (10) can be "bootstrap confirmed" by experimentally obtaining one set of measurements for P, V, and T and then employing equation (10) itself to compute a value for k. Using this value for k, together with a second set of values for P, V, and T, we can instantiate this equation.

Glymour himself cites Perrin's reasoning in determining a value for Avogadro's number as an example of this type of confirmation (Glymour 1975; in Achinstein 1983b, p. 30, n. 12). Although he does not spell out the Perrin example, presumably what Glymour will say is this: Perrin's equation (9) relates Avogadro's number to measurable quantities n', n, m, and so on. Using one set of measurements for these quantities, Perrin employed equation (9) itself to compute a value for N. Using this value for N, together with a second set of values for n', n, m, and so on, Perrin instantiated, and thus bootstrap confirmed, equation (9).

In *The Nature of Explanation* (Achinstein 1983a) I criticize Glymour's general account of bootstrap confirmation on the grounds that it allows the confirmation of equations containing completely undefined or obviously meaningless terms. This objection is related to the point I now want to make.

When the ideal gas equation $PV = kT$ gets confirmed in the manner indicated by Glymour—simply by experimentally determining two sets of values for P, V, and T—the term k (at least in Glymour's example) simply represents a constant—that is, a number. This constant can be given a molecular interpretation.[11] But it need not be; it can simply be construed as a constant of proportionality—that is, that number by which T needs to be multiplied to yield the same number as the product PV. This is the way that Glymour seems to be treating it. The value of that constant is to be determined experimentally.

Now in Perrin's equation (9) the constant N can be construed in a manner exactly analogous to the way Glymour seems to be treating k in equation (10), that is, as a numerical constant relating the other, physical quantities in equation (9). Indeed, nothing in Glymour's theory of confirmation requires us to interpret N in equation (9) as a number *of anything*, let alone a number *of molecules*.[12] (The other quantities in equation [9] are physically interpreted.) Equation (9) would be bootstrap confirmed by two sets of measurements of the quantities n, n', and so on, if N represented the number of angels on the head of a pin, or if N were just like a constant of proportionality. So bootstrap confirming equation (9), or any other equation (e.g., equation [7]) containing the constant N, does not confirm the existence of molecules. (No one, not even Glymour, takes bootstrap confirming the ideal gas equation—equation [10]—to be confirming the existence of molecules, even though k in equation (10) can be given a molecular interpretation.) But when Perrin determined Avogadro's number from his experiments using equation (9) he took his results to

---

11. When Glymour writes eq. (10) he does not make clear which constant he has in mind by k. Perhaps he means what physicists usually call R, the universal gas constant, which is experimentally determined in the manner he notes. Perhaps he means Boltzmann's constant k, which is equal to R divided by Avogadro's number. In either case, Glymour's k in eq. (10) can be related to molecular quantities.

12. It is instructive to look at an example which Glymour does work out involving six equations: (1) $A_1 = E_1$; (2) $B_1 = G_1 + G_2 + E_2$; (3) $A_2 = E_1 + E_2$; (4) $B_2 = G_1 + G_2$; (5) $A_3 = G_1 + E_1$; (6) $B_3 = G_2 + E_2$. The As and Bs are directly measurable quantities, the Es and Gs are "theoretical" quantities whose values can be determined indirectly through the theory by determining the values of the As and Bs. (Glymour identifies none of these quantities.) According to Glymour, here is how we can confirm hypothesis (1). We determine a value for A_1 directly by experiment; since this quantity is directly measurable. We obtain a value for the theoretical quantity E_1 by obtaining values for the observables B_1, B_3, and A_3, and then by using hypotheses (2), (5), and (6), mathematically computing a value for E_1. If this value is the same as the one determined for A_1 directly by experiment, then we have confirmed hypothesis (1). Note that we can confirm (1) without assigning any physical meaning to E_1. Only the observable quantities (the As and Bs) need be given any physical meaning. In a simple counterexample to Glymour's system I develop in Achinstein 1983a, chap. 11, let A = the total force acting on a particle; B = the product of the particle's mass and acceleration; C = the quantity of God's attention focused on a particle. The theory consists of two equations: (i) A = C; (ii) B = C. On Glymour's account, these equations can be bootstrap-confirmed by measuring A and B using eqq. (i) and (ii) in the manner Glymour proposes. Surely one cannot conclude that anything about God has been confirmed by such a procedure!

confirm the existence of molecules. Either he was mistaken in doing so, or else Glymour's bootstrap confirmation of equation (9) does not capture, at least not completely enough, the logic of Perrin's reasoning.

In this section I have noted three ways of construing Perrin's reasoning to the reality of molecules from his experimental determination of Avogadro's number on the basis of Brownian motion. Salmon's common-cause idea, as he formulates it, is not sufficient or necessary to yield the desired conclusion. The hypothetico-deductive account does not adequately represent Perrin's reasoning, since his calculation of N, from which he infers the existence of molecules, is not derived or derivable from the theoretical assumptions he makes. Nor does Glymour's bootstrapping approach to equation (9) permit us to see how Perrin legitimately could have inferred the existence of molecules.

4. A SOLUTION

I will now suggest a way to understand Perrin's reasoning that avoids circularity and yields an argument free from problems of the previous interpretations.

At the beginning of section 3, I took the first step in Perrin's reasoning to be (in part) this: From various assumptions, including that molecules exist, and that gases containing them satisfy the ideal gas law, Perrin derives equation (7). This certainly is part of Perrin's reasoning, but it is not his first step. Both in his 1909 article and in his 1913 book, long before he begins to derive equations (7) and (9), he offers a general discussion of the atomic theory and the existence of atoms and molecules making up chemical substances. In his book 82 pages are spent developing atomic theory and giving chemical evidence in its favor before he turns to a discussion of Brownian motion in chapter 3 (Perrin 1990, p. 83). In his article he begins with a description of Brownian motion and then offers arguments that Brownian motion is caused by the agitation of molecules and hence that molecules exist. (This is also how he begins chap. 3 of his book.) Let me briefly mention two such arguments.

First, he writes, "It was established by the work of M. Gouy (1888), not only that the hypothesis of molecular agitation gave an admissible explanation of the Brownian movement, but that no other cause of the movement could be imagined, which especially increased the significance of the hypothesis" (Perrin 1984, pp. 510–511). Perrin notes that Gouy's experiments established that known "external" causes of motion in a fluid, including vibrations transmitted to the fluid by external causes, convection currents, and artificial illumination of the fluid, do not produce the

Brownian motion. When each of these known causes was reduced or eliminated the Brownian motion continued unabated. So, Perrin concludes, "It
was difficult not to believe that these [Brownian] particles simply serve
to reveal an internal agitation of the fluid, the better the smaller they [the
Brownian particles] are, much as a cork follows better than a large ship
the movements of the waves of the sea" (1984, p. 511).

Perrin offers a second argument that he regards as even stronger than
the first. When a fluid is disturbed, the relative motions of its small but
visible parts are irregular. (This can be seen when colored powders are
mixed into the fluid.) However, this irregularity of motion does not continue as the visible parts get smaller and smaller. At the level of Brownian
motion an equilibrium is established between what Perrin calls "coordination" and "decoordination": if certain Brownian particles stop, then
other Brownian particles in other regions assume the speed and direction of the ones that have stopped. From this Perrin draws the following
conclusion:

> Since the distribution of motion in a fluid does not progress indefinitely,
> and is limited by a spontaneous recoordination, it follows that the fluids are
> themselves composed of granules or *molecules*, which can assume all pos-
> sible motions relative to one another, but in the interior of which dissemi-
> nation of motion is impossible. If such molecules had no existence it is not
> apparent how there would be any limit to the de-coordination of motion.
>
> On the contrary if they exist, there would be, unceasingly, partial
> re-coordination; by the passage of one near another, influencing it (it may
> be by *impact* or in any other manner), the speeds of these molecules will
> be continuously modified, in magnitude and direction, and from these same
> chances it will come about sometimes that neighboring molecules will have
> concordant motions. (1984, pp. 514–15; italics his)

Perrin is arguing that irregular motions of the parts of a fluid become
regular at the level of Brownian particles, in such a way that the total
momentum of these particles is conserved. This strongly suggests that the
Brownian particles (which are not responsible for their own motion) are
being subjected to the influence of smaller particles still—molecules—
which exhibit an equilibrium between coordination and de-coordination
of motion. He concludes, "In brief the examination of Brownian movement alone suffices to suggest that every fluid is formed of elastic molecules animated by a perpetual motion" (1984, p. 515).

In both arguments Perrin appears to be using eliminative-causal reasoning of the following sort:

A. (1) Given what is known, the possible causes of effect E (e.g., Brownian
   motion) are C, C_1, . . . , C_n (e.g., the motion of molecules, external vibrations, convection currents).

(2) $C_1, \ldots, C_n$ do not produce effect E.
So, probably,
C produces E.

A premise of type 1 may be defended by appeal to the fact that similar known observed effects are produced by and only by one of the types of causes on the list. Alternatively, it may be defended by appeal to more general established principles mandating one of these causes for an effect of that type. (Such principles may also provide a mechanism by means of which E can be produced by one or more of these causes.) A premise of type 2 may be defended by appeal to the fact that effect E is achieved in the absence of $C_1, \ldots, C_n$, or even when these causes are varied. In the first argument, for example, Perrin claims that Gouy's experiments take into account known external causes of motion in a fluid, and that molecular motion can in principle produce Brownian motion, since "the incessant movements of the [postulated] molecules of the fluid, which striking unceasingly the observed [Brownian] particles, drive about these particles irregularly through the fluid, except in the case where these impacts exactly counterbalance one another" (1984, p. 513). This causal possibility, he obviously believes, can be defended by appeal to more general mechanical principles.[13] In addition, in the first argument Perrin defends premise 2 by appeal to the fact that the motion of the Brownian particles exists whether or not there is external agitation, convection currents, or the like.

Although causation is invoked in these arguments, this is different from Salmon's version of the common-cause argument. For one thing, a common cause of different phenomena is not inferred here. For another, in a common-cause argument no premises of types 1 and 2 need appear. Nor do they in Salmon's "five hypothetical scientists" argument cited earlier. (Nor are they required by the conjunctive fork conditions; see n. 9.)

---

13. At this point, however, Perrin does not present such principles or show quantitatively exactly how molecular motion can cause Brownian motion. This is important because some earlier investigators claimed that Brownian motion was incompatible with standard assumptions of the kinetic-molecular theory. One objection, first raised by Karl Nageli in 1879, is that kinetic theory calculations show that the velocity that would be imparted to a Brownian particle by a collision with molecules would be much too small to observe, contrary to what is the case. A second objection is that Brownian motion, if produced by molecular collisions, would violate the second law of thermodynamics. (For a discussion of the validity and impact of these objections see Nye 1972, pp. 25–27, 101–102; Brush 1968, pp. 10ff; Maiocchi 1990, pp. 261ff.) Although Perrin in the qualitative discussion of Gouy does not present a quantitative mechanical explanation of Brownian motion, he does later in his article when he gives the theoretical explanation offered by Einstein in 1905. He responds to the second objection by defending a statistical, by contrast to a universal, interpretation of the second law of thermodynamics—one that he regards as established by Clausius, Maxwell, Helmholtz, Boltzmann, and Gibbs (see Perrin 1984, p. 512).

Even if arguments of type A do not establish the existence of molecules with certainty—since other possible causes cannot be precluded with certainty—Perrin believes that his arguments make it likely that Brownian motion is caused by the motion of molecules that make up the fluid. Accordingly, before any discussion of his own experimental results leading to his determination of Avogadro's number, and then to his claim that molecules exist, Perrin presents preliminary reasons to believe that latter claim. (In his article, as well as in his book, chemical arguments are also presented, e.g., from combinations of elements and compounds.) In addition, he presents reasons for believing that Avogadro's number exists—that is, that the number of molecules in a substance whose weight in grams is its molecular weight is the same for all substances (1984, pp. 515–516; 1990, pp. 18ff.). Finally, as Perrin notes, values for Avogadro's number determined by experiments on phenomena other than Brownian motion yield approximately 6×10^{23} (1990, pp. 105, 215; 1984, pp. 521–524, 583–598). Accordingly, independently of his own experimental results with granules in an emulsion, Perrin clearly believed that there was information (call it background information b) available to him and to other physicists and chemists that supported the following theoretical proposition:

T. Chemical substances are composed of molecules, the number N of which in a gram molecular weight of any substance is (approximately) 6×10^{23}.[14]

Perrin believed that the probability of T on information b alone was reasonably high, or, using probability notation, he believed that

$$p(T/b) > k, \tag{i}$$

where k represents some threshold of high probability. He gives arguments (some noted previously) to support claim (i)

Now, as indicated earlier, the experimental result achieved by Perrin on the basis of which he most firmly concludes that molecules exist is

C. The calculation of N done by means of Perrin's experiments on Brownian particles, using equation (9), is 6×10^{23}, and this number

14. Note that T, unlike h in section 3, gives a specific value for Avogadro's number (h is simply "Chemical substances are composed of molecules, the number N of which in a gram molecular weight of a substance is the same for all substances"). The point of the difference is this. Perrin's derivation of eq. (7), and then of eq. (9), proceeds from h, not from the stronger T (which contains a specific value for N). Otherwise, in eqq. (7) and (9) he could have substituted a specific value for N. So from the perspective of the hypothetico-deductive account, which considers what theoretical hypotheses Perrin starts with, from which he derives eqq. (7) and (9), it is appropriate to choose h rather than T. However, my point in the present section is not to consider Perrin's initial theoretical hypotheses, but rather hypotheses he takes to be proved or made likely by his arguments. Clearly the stronger hypothesis T (which entails the weaker h) is what Perrin seeks to establish.

remains constant even when values for n', n, and so on, in equation (9) are varied.

Proposition C is not a deductive consequence of T. Even if T is true, C could be false, since the particular experimental assumptions and conditions introduced by Perrin are not required by T to be appropriate to test T. To be sure, we might add experimental assumptions to T that would yield C as a deductive consequence. Such assumptions would include that the Brownian particles of gamboge employed by Perrin all have the same mass and volume, that such particles can be treated like large molecules obeying the standard gas laws, and that Stokes's law is applicable to Brownian particles. Perrin gave empirical arguments for each of these and other assumptions he made.[15] But suppose that instead of adding these assumptions to T, we simply add to the background information b Perrin's experimental results which do not deductively entail these assumptions but (Perrin believed) make them probable. If so, then, even if T together with all the information we are now counting as part of the background information b (including other determinations of N) does not entail the experimental result C, it does make C probable. At least C becomes more probable given the truth of T than without it. That is, it is more likely that Perrin's experiments will yield $N = 6 \times 10^{23}$ given the assumption that there are molecules whose number $N = 6 \times 10^{23}$ than it is without such an assumption. So

$$p(C/T\&b) > p(C/b) \qquad \text{(ii)}$$

The following is a theorem of probability (proof in appendix):

$$\begin{aligned} &\text{If } p(C/T\&b) > p(C/b), \\ &\text{and if } p(T/b) > 0 \text{ and } p(C/b) > 0, \qquad \text{(iii)}\\ &\text{then } p(T/C\&b) > p(T/b). \end{aligned}$$

Theorem (iii) states that if T increases C's probability on b, and if both T's and C's probabilities on b are greater than zero, then C increases T's probability on b.

Now, from claim (i), T's probability on b is not zero. And, since b contains the information that other experimental determinations of N yield approximately 6×10^{23}, C's probability on b is also not zero. So, it follows from claim (ii) and theorem (iii) that Perrin's experimental result C increases the probability of the theoretical assumption T, that is,

---

15. For example, in Perrin 1908, pp. 147 ff., he gives experimental arguments for the applicability of Stokes's law. For a discussion and criticism of these arguments, see Maiocchi 1990, pp. 278–279.

$$p(T/C\&b) > p(T/b) \qquad\qquad\qquad\qquad \text{(iv)}$$

Finally, if T's probability on b alone is high—that is, if claim (i) is true—then we can conclude that T's probability on C&b is at least as high, and hence that

$$p(T/C\&b) > k. \qquad\qquad\qquad\qquad \text{(v)}$$

Result (iv) will be of interest to those philosophers of science who consider increase in probability as sufficient (as well as necessary) for evidence. According to a standard view,

e is evidence that h, given b,
if and only if $p(h/e\&b) > p(h/b)$. $\qquad\qquad$ (11)

On this conception of evidence, Perrin's experimental result C concerning the calculation of Avogadro's number from experiments on Brownian motion counts as evidence in favor of his theoretical assumption T, which postulates the existence of molecules. Moreover, the greater the boost in probability that T gives to C in claim (ii), the greater the boost in probability that C gives to T in result (iv). Assuming these boosts in probability are high, on the standard conception of evidence expressed in proposition (11), we can conclude that Perrin's experimental result C provides strong evidence for his theoretical assumption T. (In section 5, I discuss Perrin's reasons for believing that his evidence was so strong.)

Elsewhere (see chapter 1), I criticize the increase-in-probability account of evidence (proposition [11]), arguing that it provides neither a necessary nor a sufficient condition for evidence. In its place I advocate this definition

(PE) e is potential evidence that h, given b, if and only if
(a) e and b are true;
(b) e does not entail h;
(c) $p(h/e\&b) \times p$ (there is an explanatory connection between h and e/h&e&b) > $\frac{1}{2}$.(This is equivalent to p (there is an explanatory connection between h and e/e&b $> \frac{1}{2}$).

On this conception of evidence, what is important is result (v), not (iv). Increase in probability is neither necessary nor sufficient for evidence. But it follows from condition (c) in (PE) that high probability is necessary. (c) also requires the high probability of an explanatory connection between h and e, given the truth of h&e&b. But this is also satisfied in the case of Perrin. Given T, that chemical substances are composed of molecules, the number N of which in a gram molecular weight of a substance is 6×10^{23}, and given C, that the calculation of N from Perrin's experiments using Eq. (9) is 6×10^{23}, and given the information noted in b, the probability is high that the reason C obtains is that T is true. The probability is high that Perrin's experimental calculation yielded 6×10^{23} because chemical substances are composed of molecules, the number N of which in a gram molecular weight is 6×10^{23}. So

(vi) p(there is an explanatory connection between T and $C/T \& C \& b) > \dfrac{1}{2}$.

If, as seems reasonable, we may also suppose that the probabilities in (v) and (vi) are sufficiently high to allow their product to be greater than $\frac{1}{2}$, then condition (c) in (PE) is satisfied. Assuming that C is true, as are the facts reported in b, and that C does not entail T, it follows that Perrin's experimental result C is potential evidence for his theoretical claim T. Since T is true, and since there is an explanatory connection between T and C, the experimental result C is also veridical evidence that T.

Perrin's reasoning, so represented, reaches the conclusion that his experimental result from Brownian motion constitutes evidence for the truth of a theoretical claim involving the existence of molecules. It does so on the conceptions of potential and veridical evidence I defend. Moreover, it does so without circularity. There is no undefended assumption at the outset that molecules exist. The claim in (i) that molecules probably exist is based on reasons for their existence cited in the background information b in (i). Perrin does not begin by assuming without argument that molecules probably exist. He begins by providing a basis for this assumption that includes experiments other than the one of concern to him in C.[16]

The pitfalls of the three interpretations in the previous section are avoided. Unlike the common-cause and bootstrap accounts, we end up by confirming a claim entailing that molecules exist. Unlike the hypothetico-deductive account, we need not suppose that Perrin's experimental result expressed in C is a deductive consequence of his theoretical assumptions about molecules. Nor need we accept the dubious hypothetico-deductive view of evidence.

5. WHY ARGUE FOR MOLECULES IN 1908?

Suppose we agree that Perrin's reasoning has been adequately represented and that it is not circular. Why in 1908, eleven years after the discovery of the electron, let alone in 1913, when his book appeared, should Perrin

---

16. As indicated in note 13, it also includes the theoretical assumption, later justified, that a quantitative mechanical explanation of Brownian motion can in principle be obtained from kinetic theory assumptions.

have thought it necessary or even useful to present an argument for the existence of molecules?

To begin with, extending into the first decade of the twentieth century, serious opposition to any atomic-molecular theory had been expressed by some physicists and chemists. French and German positivists, including Mach, Duhem, and Poincaré, for whom unobservable entities underlying the observed phenomena were anathema, rejected any realist interpretation of atomic theory. At best, atoms and molecules, if invoked at all, were to be construed simply as instrumental, conceptual devices. The German physical chemist Friedrich Wilhelm Ostwald until at least 1908 rejected atomic theory in favor of the doctrine of "energetics". His grounds for doing so were partly philosophical (a repudiation of any form of unverifiable materialism) and partly based on scientific reasons (including the belief that atomic theories, being purely mechanical, should always entail reversible processes, something incompatible with observed thermodynamic phenomena). Indeed, in the preface to his book *Atoms*, Perrin explicitly mentions Ostwald's rejection of hypotheses about unobserved atomic structure. He describes Ostwald as advocating the "inductive method," which he (Perrin) takes to be concerned only with inferring what is observable from what is observed. By contrast, Perrin is employing what he calls the "intuitive method," which attempts *"to explain the complications of the visible in terms of invisible simplicity"* (1990, p. vii; his italics).

Although Ostwald rejected atomic theories well into the first decade of the twentieth century, he changed his views by 1909, as a result of the work of Thomson and Perrin.[17] At the end of his 1913 book Perrin refers to the recent controversy over atomic theory and boldly claims that as a result of his (and other) determinations of Avogadro's number "the atomic theory has triumphed. Its opponents, which until recently were numerous, have been convinced and have abandoned one after the other the sceptical position that was for a long time legitimate and no doubt useful" (Perrin 1990, p. 216). Perrin was very conscious of the controversies over atoms extending into the twentieth century and felt the need to settle the issue on the side of the atomists.[18]

---

17. *"I have convinced myself that we have recently come into possession of experimental proof of the discrete or grainy nature of matter, for which the atomic hypothesis had vainly been sought for centuries, even millenia.* The isolation and counting of gas ions on the one hand ... and the agreement of Brownian movements with the predictions of the kinetic hypothesis on the other hand, which has been shown by a series of researchers, most completely by J. Perrin— this evidence now justifies even the most cautious scientist in speaking of the *experimental* proof of the atomistic nature of space-filling matter" (Ostwald 1909; quoted in Brush 1968; italics Ostwald's).

18. For a very informative extended discussion, see Nye 1972.

As noted earlier, independently of his 1908 experiments, Perrin believed that available information provided at least some support for the existence of atoms and molecules. Yet he regarded his own experimental results as particularly important in this connection. Why?

Although he considered previous arguments to be supportive, he believed that they did not provide sufficiently direct evidence for molecules. Interestingly, in 1901 he regarded the evidence for the existence of electrons—evidence he himself had helped to develop (see Achinstein 1991, essay 10)—to be more direct than that for molecules: "It is remarkable that the existence of these corpuscles [following Thomson, Perrin used this term for electrons], thanks to the strong electric charges which they carry, is demonstrated in a more direct manner than that of atoms or molecules, which are much larger" (Perrin 1901, p. 460; quoted in Nye 1972, pp. 83–84). In 1901, although neither molecules nor electrons were visible as discrete particles observable with a microscope, the effects of electrons were more directly observable than those of molecules. Cathode rays, that is, streams of negatively charged electrons produced in cathode tubes, were observed to produce fluorescence in the glass of the tube as well as on zinc sulfide screens and to be deflected by magnetic and electric fields. Neutral molecules and atoms were not known to have these or analogous observable effects. Prior to his experiments, or at least prior to the study of Brownian motion, Perrin regarded the evidence for molecules to be less direct, based as it was in chemistry on the regularities of chemical composition and proportion, and in physics, especially in the kinetic theory of gases developed by Maxwell, on phenomena of heat transfer, on the success of mechanical theories in general, and on the ability of chemical theory as well as the kinetic theory to explain a range of observable phenomena.[19] For Perrin, Brownian motion was for molecules what cathode rays were for electrons. Both phenomena provided a relatively direct link between the postulated entities and their observable effects.

Second, Perrin regarded his evidence for molecules as providing more precise and certain quantitative information about molecules than was previously available. He considered his determination of Avogadro's number and of the masses and diameters of molecules and atoms to be more accurate than previous estimates. He writes, "This same equation [one corresponding to eq. (9)] affords a means for determining the constant N, and the constants depending on it, which is, it appears, *capable of an unlimited precision*. The preparation of a uniform emulsion and the determination

---

19. For Maxwell's arguments for molecules, see Achinstein 1991, essays 7 and 8, and chapter 14 in this volume.

of the magnitudes other than N which enter into the equation can in reality be pushed to whatever degree of perfection [is] desired. It is simply a question of patience and time; nothing limits *a priori* the accuracy of the results, and the mass of the atom can be obtained, if desired, with the same precision as the mass of Earth" (Perrin 1984, pp. 555–556).

Finally, Perrin regarded his experimental results on Brownian motion as important in the confirmation of atomic theory for another reason as well. These results included not only a determination of Avogadro's number from law-of-atmosphere experiments—which has been the focus of attention in this article. They also included such a determination from Einstein's theory of Brownian motion, which from kinetic theory assumptions generates a formula relating the displacement of Brownian particles to N. Perrin considered Einstein's theory crucial in providing what he called a "mechanism" by which an equilibrium is reached in molecular situations such as those governed by the law of atmospheres. Prior to his 1908 experiments Perrin considered Einstein's theory to be experimentally unverified.

Let us return now to the probabilistic reconstruction of Perrin's reasoning from his law-of-atmosphere experiments. We formulated his major experimental result as proposition C; a theoretical claim for which C is supposed to provide evidence is theoretical assumption T (see section 4). Perrin believed that T's probability is increased by establishing C; that is,

$$p(T/C\&b) > p(T/b). \tag{iv}$$

Indeed, because of two of the facts noted above concerning the evidence reported in C—its directness and precision—by contrast to other evidence for molecules contained in b, Perrin believed that C gave a substantial boost to the probability of T. If this is right, then for those who adopt account (11) of evidence, according to which increase in probability is sufficient for evidence, the bigger the increase, the stronger the evidence, Perrin's experimental result C provided substantial evidence for the theoretical claim T. More precisely, on this account of evidence, C and b together count as stronger evidence for T than b by itself if and only if claim (iv) obtains.[20] So on this view of evidence, we can understand at least one reason why Perrin regarded his experimental result C as important. Not only did it, together with b, provide evidence for T, but also it provided stronger evidence for T than b alone, that is, than information available before Perrin's experiments.

---

20. On a standard view, e_1 provides stronger evidence than e_2 for h if and only if $p(h/e_1) - p(h) > p(h/e_2) - p(h)$, that is, if and only if $p(h/e_1) > p(h/e_2)$.

Matters are not so simple on the account of evidence represented in (PE). Although the latter sanctions the conclusion that, given b, Perrin's experimental result C is evidence for theoretical claim T, the question of the strength of that evidence is not settled by (PE). Nevertheless, at least this much can be said. If, in accordance with (PE) both e_1 and e_2 are evidence for h, given b, and if e_1 reports a higher frequency of the property in question than does e_2, or if e_1 contains a larger, more varied, or more precisely described sample than e_2, or if it describes items more directly associated with those in h than does e_2, and so on, then e_1, is stronger evidence for h than e_2 *in one or more of these respects*. In Perrin's case, I have argued, definition (PE) is satisfied. His experimental result C counts as evidence for T, given the background information b in question. It can also be argued that b itself contains evidence for T. But C is stronger evidence for T than b in several respects, including precision and directness. This is among the reasons why Perrin believed his evidential claim was worth making in 1908.

6. PERRIN AND REALISM

Salmon urges that Perrin's argument is an argument for scientific realism. Moreover, unlike the usual philosophical arguments for realism, it is empirical rather than a priori. He writes, "In an effort to alleviate this intellectual discomfort [produced by philosophical arguments between realists and antirealists], I decided to try an empirical approach to the philosophical problem. Since it seemed unlikely that scientists would have been moved by the kinds of arguments supplied by philosophers, I felt that some insight might be gained if we were to consider the evidence and arguments that convinced scientists of the reality of unobservable entities" (Salmon 1984, pp. 213–214). Salmon believes that Perrin's argument to the reality of molecules provides a "clear and compelling example" of a scientific argument for the existence of unobservable entities. As noted, he considers Perrin's argument to be of the common-cause variety. Even if we reject this interpretation, the question remains as to whether Perrin's argument is, or is best construed as, an argument for scientific realism, and whether Perrin himself understood it in this way.

An antirealist might provide a very different interpretation of Perrin's conclusion. Instead of claiming that the theoretical proposition T is true, all that Perrin is doing, or at least all that he is entitled to do, is infer that T is empirically adequate, that it "saves the phenomena." Assumption T can accomplish the latter without being true. This suggests two questions, one philosophical, one historical. First, is the antirealist correct in supposing that it is possible to have a valid argument to the probable conclusion that some theory saves the phenomena that is not also a valid argument to the probable conclusion that the theory is true? Second, even if it is possible, is it historically plausible to construe Perrin's reasoning in this way?

The answer to the first question is yes. To show this, let me speak of a theory as "potentially saving" some putative phenomenon described by e. We might think of this in terms of explanation: T potentially saves e if it potentially explains it (explains it in a sense that does not require T to be true). We might suppose that the potential explanation is deductive, so that T entails e.[21] With this notion as basic, let us adopt the following:

DEFINITION 1. T saves e if and only if (a) T potentially saves e, and (b) e is true.

Introducing probability, from definition 1 we can say that if T potentially saves e, then it is probable to degree r that T saves e, if and only if $p(e) = r$. More generally,

DEFINITION 2. If T potentially saves e, then, given $e_1, \ldots, e_n$, it is probable to degree r that T saves e if and only if $p(e/e_1 \ldots e_n) = r$.

Now the following is provable from probability theory:[22]

THEOREM 1. If T together with b entails $e_1, e_2, \ldots$, and if $p(T/b) > 0$, then

$$\lim_{m,n \to \infty} p(e_{n+1} \ldots e_{n+m} / e_1 \ldots e_n \& b) = 1.$$

From theorem 1 and definition 2, we get

THEOREM 2. If T potentially saves $e_1, e_2, \ldots$ in such a way that T together with b entails $e_1, e_2, \ldots$ (e.g., T explains the e's by derivation), and if $p(T|b) > 0$, then

$$\lim_{m,n \to \infty} p(\text{T saves } e_{n+1} \ldots e_{n+m}/e_1 \ldots e_n \& b) = 1.$$

From theorem 2, it follows that it can be the case that

$$\lim_{m,n \to \infty} p(\text{T saves } e_{n+1} \ldots e_{n+m}/e_1 \ldots e_n) = 1, \tag{13}$$

21. This is stronger than van Fraassen's 1980 account of "saving," which requires only that e be consistent with T. My point here is not to attack but rather to defend one antirealist claim, namely, that it is possible to construct a valid argument to the conclusion that a theory saves the phenomena that is not also a valid argument to the truth of the theory. To do so I employ the present concept of "saving".

22. For a proof, see Earman 1985.

even though $p(T/b)$ is very small, so long as it is not zero. Could equation (13) obtain even if, for any n, $p(T/e_1 \ldots e_n \& b)$ is very small? Yes, it could. Suppose some incompatible theory T' also potentially saves the e's in such a way as to entail them, but that the probability of T' on b is very high. Then no matter how many e's T entails, the probability of T on the e's will be and remain very low.

More precisely, suppose that the rival theory T' is such that $p(T'/b) = r$. If T' together with b entails the e's, then for any n, $p(T'/e_1 \ldots e_n \& b)$ is greater than or equal to r. If the original theory T is incompatible with T', then for any n, $p(T/e_1 \ldots e_n \& b) < 1 - r$. So if the rival theory T' is initially very probable, say $p(T'/b) = .95$, then, no matter how many e's the original theory T saves, its probability $p(T/e_1 \ldots e_n \& b)$ will be and remain less than or equal to .05, for any n. This can be true even if equation (13) obtains, that is, even if the probability that T saves the e's gets larger and larger, approaching 1 as a limit.[23]

Accordingly, it is indeed possible for it to be highly probable that a theory saves the phenomena while it is highly improbable that the theory is true. So, to answer our earlier question, their can be a valid argument to the probable conclusion that a theory saves the phenomena that is not also a valid argument to the probable conclusion that the theory is true.[24]

Now let us apply this to Perrin's reasoning. Perrin conducted a series of experiments on Brownian motion with different values for n', n, and

---

23. Here is an example. Suppose that our background information b tells us that one side of a certain coin marked tails is magnetized but the other is not, and that a powerful magnetic field exists under the spot on which the coin will land. The coin is tossed and lands heads each time. Let $e_1, \ldots, e_n$ describe the results of the first n tosses. Now consider two incompatible hypotheses designed to save the phenomena: T, when the coin is tossed God intervenes (not the magnetic field) and causes the coin to land heads; and T', when the coin is tossed the magnetic field (not God) causes the coin to land heads. Let us suppose that the initial probability of each theory is not zero. Then, since both theories entail $e_1, e_2, \ldots$, it follows from theorem 2 that the probability that each theory saves the phenomena approaches 1 as a limit, i.e., eq. (13) obtains for both theories. Let us also suppose that the probability of T' on b alone is very high, say .95. It follows that, for any n, $p(T'/e_1 \ldots e_n \& b)$ is greater than or equal to .95, and so, for any n, $p(T/e_1 \ldots e_n \& b)$ is less than or equal to .05. That is, the probability that the God-intervention theory is true is and remains low, no matter how many coin-tossing phenomena it saves. Yet the probability that the God-intervention theory saves the phenomena gets higher and higher, approaching 1 as a limit.

24. Recall the four conjunctive fork conditions in n. 9. For the God-intervention example discussed in n. 23, let A include the results of the first 100 tosses (all heads). Let B include the results of the second 100 tosses (same). Let C be the condition the God almost always intervenes to cause the coin to land heads. (We need to weaken the God-intervention theory a bit to satisfy Salmon's [1984, p. 160] requirement that none of the four probabilities for a conjunctive fork be 1.) Then A, B, and C satisfy the conjunctive fork conditions, even though C is an extremely unlikely cause of A and B.

so on, in equation (9). Let C_i be the proposition that the calculation of N done by means of Perrin's ith experiment on Brownian particles using equation (9) is (approximately) 6×10^{23}, and let proposition T be as stated before. In section 4, I noted the possibility of taking Perrin's background information b to contain assumptions that together with T entail C.[25] On an antirealist interpretation, Perrin could be arguing that it is highly probable that T saves the C phenomena without arguing that T is probably true. That is, Perrin could be arguing that

$$\lim_{m,n \to \infty} p(\text{T saves } C_{n+1} \cdots C_{n+m} / C_1 \cdots C_n \& b) = 1 \tag{14}$$

without supposing that $p(\text{T}/C_1 \ldots C_n \& b)$ is high, or that

$$\lim_{m,n \to \infty} p(\text{T}/C_1 \cdots C_n \& b) = 1. \tag{15}$$

Accordingly, an antirealist has a way of understanding Perrin's reasoning that does not commit the antirealist, or Perrin, to drawing the conclusion that the theory itself is true or highly probable, hence to drawing the conclusion that molecules are real.

Although such a reconstruction is possible, is it historically plausible? Admittedly, Perrin makes some remarks which may suggest antirealism. For example, near the end of his article he writes, "Lastly, although with the existence of molecules or atoms the various realities of number, mass, or charge, for which we have been able to fix the magnitude, obtrude themselves forcibly, it is manifest that we ought always to be in a position to express all the visible realities without making any appeal to the elements still invisible. But it is very easy to show how this may be done for all the phenomena referred to in the course of this Memoir" (Perrin 1984, p. 599). Perrin argues that one can take various laws that relate Avogadro's number to measurable quantities and derive a new equation containing only measurable quantities. If the two laws governing different phenomena are expressible as $N = f(A,B,C)$ and $N = g(D,E,F)$, where A–F are measurable quantities, we can write $f(A,B,C) = g(D,E,F)$, in which (as Perrin puts it) "*only evident realities occur*" (1990, p. 600; his italics). But Perrin does not conclude from this that the most we can say is that the molecular hypothesis is empirically adequate or has only instrumental value. His main point seems to be that by expressing an equation of the last form here we obtain a result that "expresses a profound connection between two phenomena at first sight completely

---

25. Although this possibility was noted, in that section I supposed only that T increases C's probability on b.

independent, such as the transmutation of radium and the Brownian movement" (p. 600).

Most of his comments strongly suggest an attitude of realism. For example, "the real existence of the molecule is given a probability bordering on certainty" (1990, p. 216). Elsewhere, he writes, "Thus the molecular theory of the Brownian motion can be regarded as experimentally established, and, at the same time, *it becomes very difficult to deny the objective reality of molecules*" (1984, p. 554; italics his). These are more typical passages.

Finally, Perrin's argument as I have reconstructed it probabilistically in steps (i)–(v) in section 4 is not an antirealist argument. It is not an argument simply to the conclusion that T saves the phenomena, or to equation (14), a probabilistic version of this. Step (v) asserts the high probability of T itself.

Accordingly, an antirealist must show not simply that Perrin's reasoning *can* be reformulated in an antirealist way to the conclusion (equation [14]), but that such a reformulation is required or desirable for historical or logical reasons. The historical grounds for such a reformulation are dubious at best. On logical grounds, considering my probabilistic reconstruction, the antirealist would need to show that there are invalid steps in the argument that can be removed only by adopting an antirealist conclusion such as equation (14) rather than a stronger realist conclusion such as equation (15). He must show that Perrin's preliminary arguments leading to step (i)—for example, eliminative-causal arguments of type A in section 4 from Brownian motion (not appealing to his own experimental results), arguments from chemical combinations, from kinetic theory, and from other determinations of Avogadro's number—do not give T a high probability. The antirealist needs to show not simply that these arguments *can* be reformulated as arguments to the conclusion that T saves the phenomena, but that something is faulty with these arguments themselves—that they fail to confer high probability on T or that they fail to establish step (i). He must show that Perrin's scientific reasoning is erroneous. Perhaps it is. But this is not demonstrated by showing simply that the antirealist conclusion "T saves the phenomena" is possible, or even that it is more probable than T itself, since it commits one to much less than T. In the absence of arguments against specific steps in Perrin's reasoning, one can conclude, with Salmon, that Perrin supplies a reasonable empirical argument for the reality of molecules.[26]

---

26. For a discussion of other antirealist arguments, see chapter 11 in this book.

APPENDIX

Proof of Theorem (iii)

1. According to Bayes's theorem,

$$p(\text{T}/\text{C}\&\text{b}) = \frac{p(\text{T}/\text{b}) \times p(\text{C}/\text{T}\&\text{b})}{p(\text{C}/\text{b})}.$$

2. Let $p(\text{T}/\text{C}\&\text{b}) = a$; $p(\text{T}/\text{b}) = b$; $p(\text{C}/\text{T}\&\text{b}) = c$; $p(\text{C}/\text{b}) = d$.
3. Then, from 1, $a = bc/d$.
4. Now, by hypothesis, $c > d$, so $c = d + h$, where $h > 0$.
5. So, from 3 and 4, where $d > 0$, $a = b(d + h)/d = b(1 + h/d)$.
6. From 5, since $b > 0$, $a/b = 1 + h/d$.
7. But $h/d > 0$, so $a/b > 1$, so $a > b$.
8. From 2 and 7, $p(\text{T}/\text{C}\&\text{b}) > p(\text{T}/\text{b})$. Q.E.D.

REFERENCES

Achinstein, Peter (1983a), *The Nature of Explanation*. New York: Oxford University Press.

Achinstein, Peter, ed. (1983b), *The Concept of Evidence*. Oxford: Oxford University Press.

Achinstein, Peter (1991), *Particles and Waves*. New York: Oxford University Press.

Achinstein, Peter (1994), "Stronger Evidence," *Philosophy of Science* 61, 329–350.

Arntzenius, Frank, (1992), "The Common Cause Principle," *PSA* 1992, 2, 227–232.

Brush, Stephen G. (1968), "A History of Random Processes," *Archive for History of the Exact Sciences* 5, 1–36.

Cartwright, Nancy (1983), *How the Laws of Physics Lie*. Oxford: Oxford University Press.

Earman, John (1985), "Concepts of Projectibility and Problems of Induction," *Nous* 19, 321–335.

Einstein, Albert (1905) 1956, *Investigations on the Theory of Brownian Movement*. New York: Dover.

Glymour, Clark (1975), "Relevant Evidence." *Journal of Philosophy* 72, 403–426. Reprinted in Peter Achinstein, ed. (1983), *The Concept of Evidence*. Oxford: Oxford University Press, pp. 124–144.

Glymour, Clark (1980), *Theory and Evidence*. Princeton, N.J.: Princeton University Press.

Maiocchi, Roberto (1990), "The Case of Brownian Motion," *British Journal for the History of Science* 23, 257–283.

Mayo, Deborah (1986), "Cartwright, Causality, and Coincidence," *PSA 1986* 1, 42–58.

Mayo, Deborah (1988), "Brownian Motion and the Appraisal of Theories." In *Scrutinizing Science*, edited by Arthur Donavan, Larry Laudan, and Rachel Lauden. Dordrecht: Kluwer, pp. 219–243.

Nye, Mary Jo (1972), *Molecular Reality: A Perspective on the Scientific Work of Jean Perrin*. London: Macdonald.

Ostwald, Friedrich Wilhelm (1909), *Grundrib der allgemeinen Chemie*. Leipzig: Engelmann.

Perrin, Jean. (1901), "Les Hypotheses Moleculaires," *Revue Scientifique* 15, 449–461.

Perrin, Jean. (1908), "Stokes Law and Brownian Motion," *Comptes Rendus*.

Perrin, Jean. (1909) 1984, "Brownian Movement and Molecular Reality." In *The Question of the Atom*, edited by Mary Jo Nye. Los Angeles: Tomash, pp. 507–601.

Perrin, Jean. (1913) 1990, *Atoms*. Woodbridge, Conn: Ox Bow.

Salmon, Wesley, (1984), *Scientific Explanation and the Causal Structure of the World*. Princeton, N.J.: Princeton University Press.

van Fraassen, Bas C. (1980), *The Scientific Image*. Oxford: Oxford University Press.

13

The Problem of Theoretical Terms

"The Problem of Theoretical Terms" is reprinted by permission from American Philosophical Quarterly 2 *(1965), 1–11. Although this chapter appeared earlier than the others, I include it because it was among the first group of articles published by philosophers skeptical of the sort of noncontextualized observable-unobservable distinction central to antirealism. There is an addendum showing how problems raised in my article are present in van Fraassen's version of antirealism and how my own defense of realism avoids these problems.*

Philosophers with quite different viewpoints have considered it important to distinguish two sorts of terms employed by scientists. While various labels have been suggested I shall use the expressions *theoretical* and *nontheoretical* to represent the intended distinction. Those who propose it provide examples of terms which fall into these respective categories, and, although there is by no means general agreement on all classifications, there is substantial accord on many examples. What follows is a list of some of the illustrations cited:

theoretical terms

electric field	mass
electron	electrical resistance
atom	temperature
molecule	gene
wave function	virus
charge	ego

nontheoretical terms

red	floats
warm	wood
left of	water
longer than	iron
hard	weight
volume	cell nucleus

The author is indebted to the National Science Foundation for support of research.

Some philosophers base this distinction on a concept of "observability." Others appeal to a notion of "conceptual organization" or "theory dependence." My purpose here is to examine this distinction and suggest reasons for doubting the claim that there is some unique criterion or set of criteria which underlies it. Rather, I shall argue, the notions of "observability," "conceptual organization," and "theory dependence" introduced by these authors generate many distinctions which result in a number of different ways of classifying terms on these lists. Since the alleged distinction between theoretical and nontheoretical terms has played an important role in the philosophy of science, as well as epistemology, an examination of its basis may show the need for reformulating some rather persistent issues and indicate the sort of steps which might profitably be taken.

1

The proposal first to be considered is that the classification rests upon a distinction between entities or properties which are observable and those which are not. Thus, according to Carnap, we have on the one hand "terms designating observable properties and relations," and on the other, "terms which may refer to unobservable events, unobservable aspects or features of events."[1] Carnap does not go on to explain what he means by "observable" and "unobservable" and presumably believes that his readers will understand in at least a general way the distinction intended. Unfortunately the situation is more complex than he seems willing to admit, since the terms "observable" and "unobservable" can be employed for the purpose of making a substantial number of different points.

Consider the case of visual observation. Just what it is that I can appropriately claim to have observed depends very importantly on the particular context in which the claim is made.[2] Suppose that while sitting by the roadside at night I am asked what I observe on the road ahead. I might, in one and the same situation, reply in a number of different ways; for example: a car, the front of a car, a pair of automobile headlights, two yellowish lights, and so on. Or, when driving on a dirt road in the daytime I might, in one and the same situation, claim to be observing a car, a trail

---

1. Rudolf Carnap, "The Methodological Character of Theoretical Concepts," in Herbert Feigl and Michael Scriven, eds., *Minnesota Studies in the Philosophy of Science*, vol. 1(Minneapolis, 1956), pp. 38–76.

2. This is emphasized by J. L. Austin in *Sense and Sensibilia* (Oxford, 1962), pp. 97ff., in a discussion in which he is concerned with criticizing the doctrine that verbs of perception have different senses.

produced by a car, or just a cloud of dust. Two points deserve emphasis here. First, in each case what I will actually say that I have observed
depends upon a number of factors, such as the extent of my knowledge
and training, how much I am prepared to maintain about the object
under the circumstances, and the type of answer I suppose my questioner to be interested in. Second, in both examples I might claim to have
observed a car ahead, though in the first the only visible parts of the car
are its headlights, and in the second I see none of its parts at all, not even
a speck in the distance which *is* the car. Nor must such claims necessarily
be deemed imprecise, inaccurate, ambiguous, or in any way untoward.
In the particular circumstances it may be perfectly clear just what I am
claiming, though someone ignorant of the context might misconstrue my
claim and expect me to know more than I do, such as the color, the shape,
or even the make of the car.

Both of these points can be illustrated by reference to scientific contexts. Suppose that an experimental physicist, acquainted with the sorts
of tracks left by various subatomic particles in cloud chambers, is asked
what he is now observing in the chamber. He might reply in a number
of ways, e.g., electrons passing through the chamber, tracks produced by
electrons, strings of tiny water droplets which have condensed on gas ions,
or just long thin lines. Similarly, to the question "What does one observe in
a cathode-ray experiment?" the physicist might answer: Electrons striking
the fluorescent zinc sulfide screen, light produced when molecules of zinc
sulfide are bombarded, bright spots, and so forth. In each case what the
physicist actually claims to have observed will depend upon how much
he knows and is prepared to maintain, the knowledge and training of
the questioner, and the sort of answer he thinks appropriate under the
circumstances. Furthermore, just as in the previous automobile examples,
there are situations in which the physicist, concerned mainly with indicating the occurrence of certain events and with proper identification, will
report observing various particles pass through the chamber—electrons if
the tracks are long and thin, alpha particles if they are shorter and heavier.
Whether he chooses to describe the situation in this way will depend
upon the sort of factors just noted.

Analogous considerations hold for other terms on the "theoretical" list.
Thus the physicist may report having observed the electric field in the
vicinity of a certain charge, or he may describe what he did as having
observed the separation of leaves in an electroscope; he may report to
be observing the rise in temperature of a given substance, or simply the
increase in length of the column of mercury in the thermometer, and so
on. Accordingly, those who seek to compile a list of "observational" terms
must not do so on the basis of an assumption to the effect that there

exists some unique way of describing what is observed in a given situation. Nor can a classification of electrons, fields, temperature, and the like, as *un*observable be founded simply on a claim that one cannot ever report observing such items. Or, at least, if such a claim is made it will need to be expanded and defended in a manner not attempted by Carnap.

Suppose then, Carnap were to acknowledge that scientists often describe what they have observed in different ways, and that physicists do speak of observing such things as subatomic particles in cloud chambers and electric fields in the vicinity of charges, when the main concern is to report the occurrence of a certain event or the presence of a certain type of entity. Still, he might urge, contextual considerations of the sort mentioned will be irrelevant when we consider, strictly speaking, what is really observed in such cases. For what the physicist (really) observes is not the electron itself (but only its track, or a flash of light), just as in the automobile examples, what is (really) observed is not the car itself (but only its headlights, or a dust trail). And when the physicist detects the presence of an electric field, what he observes is not the field itself, but (say), only the separation of leaves in the electroscope. In general, it might be said, the distinction desired can be drawn on the basis of the claim that items on the "theoretical" list are not themselves (really) observable.[3]

I do not want to deny that electrons, fields, temperature, and so on can be described in this way. Indeed, such a description may be invoked when the physicist begins to explain just what claims he is making when he speaks of observation in each of these cases. However, as will presently be indicated, when an expression such as "not itself (really) observable" is employed it makes sense only with reference to a specific context of observation and some particular contrast. And I want to show that this fact precludes that general sort of distinction desired.

Suppose that in the second automobile example I report that I cannot (really) observe the car itself. What claim am I making? I might be saying that all I can observe is a dust trail and no speck in the distance which I can identify as the car; or that I can observe only a speck, but not the body of the car; or again, that I can see the car in the mirror but not with the naked eye. And obviously other contrasts could be cited which would make the point of my assertion clear.

Consider now the case of a virus examined by means of an electron microscope. Suppose I say that the microbiologist does not (really)

3. Cf. R. B. Braithwaite, "Models in the Empirical Sciences," in E. Nagel, P. Suppes, and A. Tarski, eds., *Logic, Methodology, and Philosophy of Science* (Stanford, Calif., 1962), p. 227: "in all interesting cases the initial hypotheses of the theory will contain concepts which are . . . not themselves observable (call these theoretical concepts); examples are electrons, Schrödinger wave functions, genes, ego-ideals."

observe the virus itself. What am I claiming? I might be saying that since (let us suppose) he employs a staining technique, he sees not the virus but only the staining material known to be present in certain parts of the specimen. Or I might simply be saying that what he observes is the image of the object as presented by the microscope, and not the object itself. On the other hand, comparing electron microscopy with X-ray diffraction, I might claim that in the former case he is able to observe the virus itself, whereas in the latter case he observes only the effect of X rays on the virus. On different occasions any one of these contrasts, and others, could underlie the claim that the virus itself cannot (or can) really be observed.

Similar considerations are relevant in understanding a corresponding claim regarding electrons. In the context of a cloud chamber experiment, if I assert that electrons themselves cannot (really) be observed I might be saying that though a track is visible there is no speck which can be identified as the electron, in the way that if a jet airplane is close enough, one can see not only its trail but identify a certain speck in the distance as the airplane itself. On the other hand, I might wish to contrast the case of the electron with that of the neutron and claim that whereas electrons themselves *can* be observed in a cloud chamber, neutrons cannot. The point of this contrast is that neutrons, being neutral in charge, cannot cause ionization in their passage through the chamber, and hence will not produce a track, the way electrons will.[4]

In general, then, it is not sufficient simply to refer to the previous list of so-called theoretical terms and claim that the distinguishing feature of the items designated by these terms is that they are not themselves (really) observable. What must be done is to indicate for each item the point of such a classification, and this is most readily accomplished by contrasting the sense in which it is said to be (really) unobservable itself with the sense in which something else is claimed to be observable. Now I do not deny that one could supply a context for each item on the list in which it would be appropriate to speak of that item in the manner proposed. The important point is simply that these contexts, and the sorts of contrasts they may involve, will in general be quite different and will yield different classifications. Here are a few contrasts, some of which have already been noted, namely, those between:

---

4. Another contrast sometimes invoked in atomic physics has to do with objects such as electrons for which (in accordance with the Heisenberg uncertainty relationships) the product of the uncertainties in position and simultaneous velocity is much greater than that for objects of considerably larger mass such as atoms and molecules. A particle of the former sort may be classified as (itself) unobservable where it is this particular contrast which is intended.

(a) objects such as electrons and alpha particles which are detected by means of their tracks, and objects such as cars and airplanes which can be seen together with or apart from their tracks.

(b) objects such as neutrons and neutrinos which do not leave tracks in a cloud chamber, and those such as electrons and alpha particles which do.

(c) objects such as smaller molecules which it is necessary to stain in order to observe with the electron microscope, and larger objects for which staining is unnecessary.

(d) objects such as individual atoms which are too small to scatter electrons appreciably and hence cannot be seen with the electron microscope, and larger objects such as certain molecules which have significant scattering power and hence can be observed.

(e) objects requiring illumination by electron beams which then must be transformed into light via impact with a suitable screen, and objects visible with ordinary light.

(f) objects which can only be observed by the production of images in microscopes, and those which can be seen with the naked eye.

(g) properties such as electrical resistance whose magnitudes must be (or are generally) calculated on the basis of measuring a number of other quantities, and those properties for which this is usually not necessary.

(h) properties such as temperature for which some instrumentation is usually required (for determining differences), and those such as color for which it is not.

(i) objects such as electric fields which are not the sorts of things to which mass and volume are ascribed, and objects such as solids to which they are.

Each of these contrasts, as well as others which could readily be cited, *might* be used to generate some sort of observational distinction. Yet the same item would be classified differently depending upon the particular distinction invoked. Electrons would be unobservable under (a) and (d) but observable under (b); heavy molecules would be unobservable under (e) and (f) but observable under (c) and (d); temperature would be unobservable under (h) but observable under (g). Also, under certain contrasts some items cannot be classified at all—electrons under (c), (e), and (f); heavy molecules under (a) and (b); temperature under (a)–(f). Accordingly, if contrasts of the type cited must be invoked to provide significance for the claim that a certain entity or property is itself (really) unobservable, then the sort of distinction required by Carnap seems difficult if not impossible to draw.

2

I want now to consider two qualifications which some authors place on the notion of observation. The first is that one should not speak simply of observability, but of *direct* observability. Hempel, e.g., writes:

> In regard to an observational term it is possible, under suitable circumstances, to decide by means of direct observation whether the term does or does not apply to a given situation. . . . Theoretical terms, on the other hand, usually purport to refer to not directly observable entities and their characteristics.[5]

In offering this criterion, Hempel, like Carnap, mentions no special or technical sense which he attaches to the phrase "direct observation." Nor does he elaborate upon its meaning, except to cite a few examples.[6] He admits that his characterization does not offer a precise criterion and that there will be borderline cases. Yet the problem involved is more complex than Hempel seems willing to allow and, contrary to his suggestion, does not just turn on the question of drawing a more precise "dividing line." For the expression "(not) directly observable," like "(un)observable itself," is one whose use must be tied to a particular context and to some intended contrast. Thus, if the physicist claims that electrons cannot be observed directly, he may simply mean that instruments such as cloud chambers, cathode-ray tubes, or scintillation counters are necessary. Here direct observability has to do with observation by the unaided senses. Or he might mean that when one observes an electron in a cloud chamber one sees only its track but not, e.g., a speck which one would identify as the electron itself. Again the nuclear physicist might claim that particles such as neutrons and neutrinos are not directly observable, meaning that such particles cannot themselves produce tracks in a cloud chamber, unlike electrons and alpha particles, which, under this contrast, would be deemed directly observable. Another type of situation in which the expression "direct observation" might be invoked involves a contrast between properties, such as electrical resistance, whose magnitudes must be calculated by first measuring other quantities, and those, such as length or temperature, for which this is often not necessary.[7]

---

5. Carl G. Hempel, "The Theoretician's Dilemma," in H. Feigl, M. Scriven, and G. Maxwell, eds., *Minnesota Studies in the Philosophy of Science*, vol. 2 (Minneapolis, 1958), pp. 37–98.

6. Observations of "readings of measuring instruments, changes in color or odor accompanying a chemical reaction, utterances made. . . ."

7. Indeed, it is for this very reason that in thermodynamics pressure, volume, and temperature are frequently called directly observable properties of a thermodynamic system, whereas other thermodynamic properties such as internal energy and entropy are not.

In short, many contrasts can be invoked by the notion of direct observation,[8] and a given item will be classified in different ways depending upon the particular one intended. An appeal to direct observation by itself does little to advance the cause of generating a unique distinction, and when such an appeal is spelled out in individual cases various distinctions emerge.

The second qualification sometimes placed on observability concerns the *number* of observations necessary to correctly apply a term or expression. Thus, in "Testability and Meaning," Carnap writes:

> A predicate '*P*' of a language *L* is called *observable* for an organism (e.g., a person) *N*, if, for suitable argument, e.g., '*b*', *N* is able under suitable circumstances to come to a decision with the help of a few observations about the full sentence, say '*P(b)*', i.e., to a confirmation of either '*P(b)*' or '*–P(b)*' of such high degree that he will either accept or reject '*P(b)*'.[9]

Carnap does not, however, explain his qualification in sufficient detail and leaves some important questions unanswered. Is the number of observations to mean the number of times the object must be observed (or, if an experiment is in question, the number of times the experiment needs to be repeated) before a property can definitely be ascribed to the object? Or does Carnap perhaps mean the number of different characteristics of the object which need to be observed? Again, he may be thinking of the amount of preliminary investigation necessary before a final observation can be made.[10] Or perhaps all of these considerations are relevant.

Yet whether an observation or experiment will need to be repeated, or many different characteristics of the item in question examined, or considerable preliminary investigation undertaken, depends not only on the nature of the object or property under examination but also on the particular circumstances of the investigator and his investigation. One relevant factor will be the type of instrument employed and how easily the scientist has

8. Somewhat simpler ones may of course be presupposed when the expression "directly observable" is employed in more everyday situations. For example, a contrast between an object such as the bank robber's coat which is readily accessible to view and his revolver which is hidden under it during the robbery; or between an item such as this side of the moon's surface which can readily be observed and the far side which from our vantage point is always hidden from view.

9. Reprinted in Herbert Feigl and May Brodbeck, eds., *Readings in the Philosophy of Science* (New York, 1953), pp. 47–92. Quotation from p. 63. Similar qualifications on observability have been expressed more recently by Grover Maxwell, "The Ontological Status of Theoretical Entities," in H. Feigl and G. Maxwell, eds., *Minnesota Studies in the Philosophy of Science*, vol. 3 (Minneapolis, 1962), and by Israel Scheffler, *The Anatomy of Inquiry* (New York, 1963), p. 164.

10. According to Carnap when instruments are used we have "to make a great many preliminary observations in order to find out whether the things before us are instruments of the kind required" ("Testability and Meaning," p. 64.)

learned to manipulate it. The physicist familiar with electroscopes need make few, if any, repetitions of an experiment with this instrument to determine the presence of an electric charge and hence of an electric field. Nor need he observe many characteristics of the field (e.g., its intensity and direction at a certain point) in order to determine its presence. And he will not always need to make extensive preliminary observations on the instrument but only a few. Yet, charges and electric fields are alleged to be unobservable. Another factor determining the facility with which an observer will identify an object or property is the extent of his knowledge regarding the particular circumstances of the observation. If the physicist knows that a certain radioactive substance has been placed in a cloud chamber he may readily be able to identify the particles whose tracks are visible in the chamber. Whereas, if he knows nothing about the circumstances of the experiment, and he is simply shown a photograph of its results, successful identification may be a more complicated task. Rapid classification, then, depends in considerable measure upon particular features of the context of observation and the knowledge of the investigator. Under certain "suitable circumstances" (to use Carnap's phrase), quite a number of terms classified by him as nonobservational can be correctly applied "with the help of [just] a few observations."

Furthermore, if nonobservability in Carnap's sense is held to be sufficient for a *theoretical* classification additional difficulties emerge. For many fairly ordinary expressions are such that in numerous circumstances more than a "few observations" might well be required before correct application is possible; for example, "is chopped sirloin," "is a bridge which will collapse," "was composed by Corelli." Yet these do not really seem to be the sorts of expressions the authors in question wish to call theoretical. On the other hand, if, following Scheffler,[11] Carnap's criterion for "nonobservability" is to be construed simply as a necessary but not a sufficient condition for being classified as theoretical, then unless further criteria are proposed (which they are not either by Carnap or Scheffler) we will have no general basis for separating theoretical from nontheoretical terms.[12] And if this criterion concerning the number of observations is to be construed as a sufficient one for a *non*theoretical classification (as Carnap and Scheffler suggest), then, as we have seen, many terms classified by these authors as theoretical will, in numerous situations, require reclassification.

11. Ibid., pp. 164ff.

12. Scheffler concludes (ibid., p. 164) that the only thing left to do is simply specify an exhaustive list of primitive terms to be called "observational" (and presumably a corresponding list of those to be called "theoretical"). But this leaves the question of the basis for this separation unanswered.

3

I have considered attempts to base a theoretical-nontheoretical distinction upon some notion of observation. Generally speaking, the thesis that a list of "observational" terms can be compiled is defended by those envisaging the possibility of an "empiricist language." One of the underlying assumptions of this program appears to be that there exists a unique (or at least a most suitable) way of describing what is, or can be (really, directly) observed—a special "physical object" or "sense datum" vocabulary eminently fit for this task. Yet, as emphasized earlier, there are numerous ways to describe what one (really, directly) observes in a given situation, some more infused with concepts employed in various theories than others. This does not, of course, preclude the possibility of classifying certain reports as observational in a given case. The point is simply that there is no special class of terms which must be used in describing what is observed. Words from the previous "theoretical" list, such as "electron," "field," and "temperature," are frequently employed for this purpose.

Still, it might be urged, even though terms on both lists can be used in descriptions of what is (really, directly) observed, those on the first list are more "theory-dependent" than those on the second. And while it may not be possible to draw the intended large-scale distinction on the basis of observation, it is nevertheless feasible and important to separate terms on the basis of their "theoretical" character. It is to the latter position, which has been defended by Hanson and Ryle, that I now wish to turn.

According to Hanson a distinction should be drawn between terms which "carry a conceptual pattern with them" and terms which "are less rich in theory and hence less able to serve in explanations of causes,"[13] or, in Ryle's words, between expressions which are "more or less heavy with the burthen of [a particular] theory . . . [and those which] carry none [of the luggage] from that theory."[14] As an example of a term which carries with it a conceptual pattern Hanson cites the word "crater":

> Galileo often studied the Moon. It is pitted with holes and discontinuities; but to say of these that they are craters—to say that the lunar surface is craterous—is to infuse theoretical astronomy into one's observations. . . . To speak of a concavity as a crater is to commit oneself as to its origin, to say that its creation was quick, violent, explosive. . . .[15]

---

13. N. R. Hanson, *Patterns of Discovery* (Cambridge, England, 1958), p. 60.
14. Gilbert Ryle, *Dilemmas* (Cambridge, England, 1956), pp. 90–91.
15. Hanson, p. 56.

"Crater," then, carries with it a conceptual pattern not borne by (non-theoretical) terms such as "hole," "discontinuity," or "concavity."

Two notions underlie these suggestions, one stressed more by Hanson, the other by Ryle. The first is that a theoretical term is one whose application in a given situation can organize diffuse and seemingly unrelated aspects of that situation into a coherent, intelligible pattern; terms which carry no such organizing pattern Hanson sometimes calls "phenomenal." The second notion is that theoretical terms are such that "knowing their meanings requires some grasp of the theory" in which they occur.[16] "The special terms of a science," Ryle asserts, "are more or less heavy with the burthen of the theory of that science. The technical terms of genetics are theory-laden, laden, that is, not just with theoretical luggage of some sort or other but with the luggage of genetic theory."[17]

Despite the fine examples Hanson cites, and the use he makes of the notion of "organizing patterns" in supplying trenchant criticisms of various philosophical positions, surely the first proposal fails to provide a sufficient characterization of those terms Hanson calls "theory-laden" (or "theory-loaded"). For almost any term can be employed in certain situations to produce the type of pattern envisaged. Indeed, Hanson himself offers many examples of this; quite early in his book, for instance, he presents a drawing whose meaning is incomprehensible until it is explained that it represents a bear climbing a tree. In this context, the expression "bear climbing a tree" is one which organizes the lines into an intelligible pattern. Moreover, one could describe contexts in which Hanson's "phenomenal" terms such as "hole," "concavity," and "solaroid disc" might be employed to organize certain initially puzzling data. Conversely, there are situations in which terms such as "crater," "wound," "volume," "charge," and "wave-length," which Hanson calls "theory-loaded," are used to describe data which are initially puzzling and require "conceptual organization." Hanson, at one point, grants that terms can have this dual function:

> It is not that certain words are absolutely theory-loaded, whilst others are absolutely sense-datum words. Which are the data words and which are the theory-words is a contextual question. Galileo's scar may at some times be a datum requiring explanation, but at other times it may be part of the explanation of his retirement.[18]

Yet this admission is a large one. For it means that the rendering of "conceptual organization" is not a special feature of terms on the "theoretical" list which sets them apart from those on the "nontheoretical" list.

16. Ryle, p. 90.
17. Ryle, p. 90.
18. Hanson, pp. 59–60.

Whether a term provides an organizing pattern for the data depends on the particular situation in which it is employed. In some contexts, the use of the term "electron" will serve to organize the data (e.g., tracks in a cloud chamber); in others the term "electron" will be employed to describe certain data requiring organization (e.g., the discontinuous radiation produced by electrons in the atom). But even a presumably nontheoretical expression such as "(X is) writing a letter" can be used in certain contexts to organize data thereby explaining a piece of behavior, and in others to describe something which itself demands explanation.

Hanson does make reference to the "width" of terms, claiming that some expressions are "wider" theoretically than others and hence presumably "carry a [greater] conceptual pattern with them."[19] So despite the fact that most terms are capable of serving explanatory functions, distinctions might still be drawn on the basis of "width." Yet it is not altogether clear how this metaphor should be unpacked. Sometimes the suggestion appears to be that one term will be "wider" than another if it can be used to explain situations whose descriptions contain the latter term. Thus, referring to the Galileo example quoted earlier, the term "scar" would be wider than the term "retirement" because it can be used to explain something designated by the latter. Yet this is not altogether satisfactory since we might imagine a case in which a man's retirement constituted part of an explanation of a scar he incurred. Again, the term "electron" can be employed in explanations of magnetic fields, yet the presence of a magnetic field can explain motions of electrons.

Perhaps, however, the reference to "width" should be understood in connection with the thesis, proposed by Ryle (and shared by Hanson), that certain terms depend for their meaning upon a particular theory, whereas others do not, or at least are much less dependent. By way of explanation Ryle cites as an analogy the situation in games of cards. To understand the expression "straight flush" one must know at least the rudiments of poker, whereas this is not so with the expression "queen of hearts," which is common to all card games and carries with it none of the special "luggage" of any of them. In a similar manner certain terms used by scientists are such that to understand them one must have at least some knowledge of the particular theory in which they appear. These are the "theory-laden" terms.[20] Other expressions utilized by scientists can be understood without recourse to any specific theoretical system.

19. See Hanson, p. 61.
20. Cf. Hanson, pp. 61–62: "'Revoke,' 'trump,' 'finesse' belong to the parlance system of bridge. The entire conceptual pattern of the game is implicit in each term. . . . Likewise with 'pressure,' 'temperature,' 'volume,' 'conductor,' 'charge'. . . in physics. . . . To understand one of these ideas thoroughly is to understand the concept pattern of the discipline in which it figures."

Before examining this proposal some preliminary points should be noted. First, Ryle often seems to be suggesting that a theory-laden term is one which "carries the luggage" of one particular theory. Yet quite a few of the terms which he and Hanson classify as "theory-laden"—terms such as "temperature," "wave-length," "electron"—appear in, and might be thought to be infused with the concepts of, *many* scientific theories. Such terms are not restricted to just one theory, as with respect to games, "straight flush" is to poker. Second, it is certainly not a feature characteristic only of terms Ryle calls "theory-laden"—or only of such terms and those from card games—that they must be understood by reference to some scheme, system of beliefs, or set of facts. Following Ryle's lead one might draw up many different sorts of classifications, such as "university-laden" terms ("hour examination," "credit," and "tutorial") which cannot be understood without some knowledge of universities and their procedures; or, referring to scientific contexts, "instrument-laden" terms, such as "dial," "on," "off," which presumably would not appear on the "theoretical" list, yet require at least some knowledge of instruments and their uses. Thus Ryle's proposal must not be construed simply as a criterion for distinguishing terms which must be understood in the context of a set of beliefs from those which can be understood independently of any such set, though Hanson's "theory-laden" versus "sense-datum" labels might misleadingly suggest this. Third, one must always specify the theory with respect to which a given term is or is not "theory-laden." And, it would appear, a term might receive this classification with reference to one theory but not another, though it occurs in both. For in one theory its meaning might not be understood unless the principles of the theory are known, whereas this would not necessarily be so in the case of the other theory (or at least there could be significant differences of degree). For example, "mass" might be considered "theory-laden" with respect to Newtonian mechanics but not with respect to the Bohr theory of the atom in which it also appears, since it can be understood independently of the latter. Thus, presumably, not every term occurring in a given theory will be "theory-laden," just as not every term found in standard formulations of the rules and principles of poker—such as "sequence" and "card"—will be "poker-laden," to use Ryle's expression. But if a theory must always be specified with respect to which a given term is deemed "theory-laden," and if a term can be classified in this way with reference to one theory and not to another in which it appears, then lists of the sort compiled at the beginning of this chapter cannot be legitimately constructed. The most that could be done would be to cite particular theories and for each one compose such lists indicating which terms are to be considered theoretical and which not *for that theory*.[21]

Yet even this task may be deemed incapable of fulfillment once we examine Ryle's claim that expressions are theory-laden if they are such that "knowing their meanings requires some grasp of the theory." For there are many different ways in which terms might be said to be dependent upon principles of a given theory, and it is not altogether clear whether any or all of these should be classified as cases of "meaning-dependence." Since, we have already seen, the issue of whether a term is "theory-laden" must be considered always with reference to a specific theory, let us suppose that we are given such a theory. Within it we could expect to encounter the following sorts of terms or expressions which might be considered theory-dependent in some sense:

(1) A term or expression whose *definition* cannot be stated without formulating some law or principle of the theory in question. For example, "Newton's gravitational constant" could only be defined by invoking the law of universal gravitation. The expression "Bohr atom," frequently employed in atomic physics, is defined as one satisfying the postulates of the Bohr theory. "Electrical resistance" is defined by reference to Ohm's law, and so forth.

(2) A term or expression whose definition can be stated without formulating laws of the theory, but whose use must be *justified* by invoking some of these laws. In electrostatics an "electrostatic unit charge" (esu) is defined as one which when placed in a vacuum one centimeter away from a like equal charge will repel it with a force of one dyne. Such a definition proves useful provided that the force with which like charges repel each other in a vacuum depends upon their distance, which it does according to Coulomb's law.

(3) A term whose definition can be stated without formulating laws of the theory, yet which denotes some more or less complex expression which appears in a formula whose *derivation* in the theory will not be understood unless certain laws of that theory are known. Quite often various expressions utilized in the theory will not be considered thoroughly understood unless one knows "where they come from," i.e., how certain

---

21. Ryle at many points does seem to be pressing for a distinction between terms appearing within the context (broadly speaking) of a given theory (or system) which are "theory-laden" and those which may also appear in the same general context but are not. This is evidenced by the sorts of examples he chooses ("light wave" vs. "blue"; "straight flush" vs. "Queen of Hearts"), and also by the questions he raises ("How are the special terms of Bridge or Poker [e.g., "trump"] logically related to the terms in which the observant child describes the cards that are shown to him [e.g., "hearts"]?"). So, relativizing the distinction to terms employed in the context of a particular theory is not completely foreign to Ryle's thought, though on some occasions he does suggest that he intends a broader distinction, as between terms "laden" with some theory or other and those dependent on no theory whatever.

formulas containing these expressions are derived from more fundamental principles of the theory. This is true, for example, of the term "enthalpy" in thermodynamics, which is defined as "$U + pV$," where U is the internal energy of a system, p its pressure, and V its volume. One standard method for introducing this term is by considering a process of constant pressure and applying the first law of thermodynamics, arriving at an expression containing "$U + pV$."

(4) A term or expression referring to something x which the theory is designed to describe and explain in certain ways, and for which the question "What is (an) x?" could be answered, at least in part, by considering principles of that theory. Very often this question, rather than "What does the term 'x' mean?" will be asked, and an answer given not by reference to some formal definition of 'x' (if indeed one exists) but to principles of the theory which characterize features of x. For example, suppose one were to ask, "What are electrons?" Many sorts of replies could of course be given depending upon the knowledge and interests of the inquirer. Part of the answer might involve references to the Bohr or quantum theories which describe the various energy states of electrons within the atom; to the band theory of solids which uses quantum mechanical results in describing properties which electrons manifest in conductors; to the theory of the chemical bond which describes the sharing of electrons by atoms, and so forth. By characterizing various properties of electrons, theories such as these provide answers to the question "What are electrons?" and in this sense the term "electron" might be considered theory-dependent with respect to each.

(5) A term or expression whose *role* in the theory can only (or best) be appreciated by considering laws or principles in which it appears.[22] In most theories the roles of constituent terms can be examined from several points of view. One might simply consider whether and how a given term is needed for the purpose of *formulating* some of the principles of the theory (for example, how 'h' (Planck's constant) is used in the formulation of two fundamental postulates of the Bohr theory). Once a theory has been stated one might ask whether and how a certain term affords a *simplification* or *concise expression* of other principles (as how the term 's' (entropy) facilitates the formulation of an equation combining the first and second laws of thermodynamics); or how it is used in *proofs* of important theorems. From a wider viewpoint, the role of a term might also be studied by considering how principles in which it functions serve to *explain* various phenomena (as how "resonance potential" in the Bohr theory is used in the explanation of electron transitions to different

---

22. Cf. Ryle, "The Theory of Meaning," in Max Black (ed.), *The Importance of Language* (Englewood Cliffs, N.J., 1962), p. 161.

energy levels). Conversely, one might consider the manner in which principles of the theory are used to explain various phenomena which the term itself designates.[23] Thus, the role played by the expression "discrete spectral lines" in the Bohr theory might be specified by showing how the postulates of that theory serve to explain the sort of phenomenon referred to by this expression.

The five sorts of theory-dependence mentioned reflect various factors which may be relevant in understanding a given term and represent at least some of the ways in which expressions employed by a theory might be deemed "theory-laden" in Ryle's sense, i.e., dependent (at least in part) on the theory for their meaning. No doubt others could be listed and within those already mentioned further distinctions drawn. Yet each type of dependence cited, if employed to generate a classification of terms, might well yield different results. On the basis of the first sort of dependence noted we could distinguish (a) terms whose definitions are usually given by reference to laws of the theory in question, from (b) terms usually defined independently of such laws. (With respect to thermodynamics, "entropy" might be considered an expression of the former sort, whereas "enthalpy" would be placed in the latter category.) On the basis of the second dependence we could distinguish (a) terms (such as "electrostatic unit charge") whose definitions require justification by appeal to some of the principles of the theory, from (b) terms (such as "electrostatic force") which are not specifically defined in that theory, or whose definitions require no special defense by reference to principles of the theory. And so forth. . . .

For these reasons a criterion of theory-dependence of the sort proposed by Ryle and Hanson not only precludes the construction of theory-*independent* lists of the type given at the beginning of this paper, but, even with respect to a specific theory, can give rise to various distinctions under which terms may be classified differently. On the other hand if all the various senses in which a term might be dependent upon a given theory are lumped together and a term classified as "theory-laden" if it conforms to any of these, then such a label would become useless for distinguishing between terms in a given theory since it would be applicable to almost all of them.

---

23. Hanson, it might be noted, suggests at one point that terms referring to something explained by a given theory are dependent in meaning upon that theory. (Thus, he claims, Tycho and Kepler, because they had different theories about the movement of the sun, attached different meanings to "sun." *Op cit.*, p. 7.) This thesis is also defended by P. K. Feyerabend, "Explanation, Reduction, and Empiricism," in H. Feigl and G. Maxwell (eds.), *Minnesota Studies in the Philosophy of Science*, vol. III (Minneapolis, 1962).

Our conclusions here are relevant also for those seeking to draw the broader distinction between terms laden with the concepts and principles of some theory or other and terms dependent upon no theory whatever. Since there are many sorts of theory-dependence, various distinctions become possible. And should any one of the criteria outlined earlier be considered sufficient to render a term "theoretical," few if any terms will escape this classification.[24]

4

We have been considering the doctrine that expressions employed by scientists can be divided into two sets. On one view the principle of division rests upon observation; on the other, upon conceptual organization or theory-dependence. What has been shown is not that divisions are impossible to make, but rather that the proposed criteria are capable of generating distinctions of many different sorts, each tied, in most cases rather specifically, to a particular context of observation or to a particular theory. Questions such as "Does the term refer to something which can be observed?" and "Does its meaning depend upon some theory?" are too nebulous to provide illuminating classifications.

This means that certain problems raised by philosophers need serious rethinking. For example, authors of logical empiricist persuasion introduce the following issue: If theoretical terms in science do not refer to what is observable, how can they be said to have meaning? The type of answer given consists in treating such terms as uninterpreted symbols which gain meaning in the context of a theory by being related via "correspondence rules" to observational terms. The problem is then to make this idea precise by providing a "criterion of meaningfulness" for theoretical terms.[25] Yet in the absence of some definite basis for drawing the intended large-scale distinction between theoretical and observational terms such problems cannot legitimately be raised, at least not in this form. Again Ryle, beginning with the question, "How is the World of Physics related to the Everyday World?" suggests the need to restate it in a clearer way as, in effect, "How are the 'theory-laden' concepts of physics related to others?" Yet unless his notion of theory-dependence is made precise and

---

24. Especially if, following Hanson, a term which refers to something explained by a theory is to be considered "theory-laden."

25. See, e.g., Carnap, "The Methodological Character of Theoretical Concepts"; Hempel, "The Theoretician's Dilemma"; William W. Rozeboom, "The Factual Content of Theoretical Concepts," in *Minnesota Studies in the Philosophy of Science,* vol. 3.

is shown to generate some rather definite distinction one will be in doubt about which terms he is referring to and what special characteristic he is attributing to them. This by no means precludes questions concerning the manner in which terms employed by scientists are tied to observation and to theories. Such questions, however, should not be raised about observation *in general*, or theories *in general*, but about particular sorts of observations and about terms in specific theories.

The concept *electron*, for instance, is tied to observation in a manner different from that of *temperature, field,* or *molecule*. And while there are some similarities there are also important differences, so that epithets such as "not directly observable" are bound to prove unhelpful. The philosopher of science genuinely concerned with the relation between theory and observation must begin by examining individual cases. Taking a clue from earlier discussion, one illuminating procedure consists in invoking a series of contrasts. How, for example, is the observation of electrons similar to and also unlike the observation of high-flying jets, large molecules, neutrons, chairs and tables? Each such contrast can be invoked to bring out some quite definite point concerning the relation between electrons and observation. This constitutes one important way of dealing with certain questions raised by logical empiricists, though obviously in a much more specific form than they envisage. Employing a series of contrasts we can also proceed to discover how given concepts are theory-dependent, thus turning our attention, though again in a specific way, to issues raised by Ryle and Hanson.

It is important to consider the manner in which entities studied by the physicist are tied to observation and to theory. Yet the philosopher of science must not at the outset assume that items on the "theoretical" list constructed earlier are related to observation (or theory) in the same way, or even in the same *general* way. Some items can be grouped together as similar in certain observational respects (for instance, electrons and neutrons as being too small to observe with electron microscopes), though in other such respects there will be important differences (e.g., ionizing effects). If categories are invoked to mark the similarities which do exist they will need to be a good deal more specific than the "theoretical" and "nontheoretical" classifications too often presupposed by epistemologists and philosophers of science.

ADDENDUM

Philosophy of science in the 1950s and early 1960s was dominated by philosophers who believed that to make sense of science an important distinction needs to be drawn between two sorts of terms that appear in scientific theories: "theoretical" and "observational." Various questions became important, including these: How can one confirm or provide evidence of theoretical claims in science (ones expressed using "theoretical terms") on the basis of observational results (ones described using "observational terms")? Indeed, if theories make claims about a realm of unobservables, then if one is to be an empiricist in the sciences, how can one even make sense of such claims? One prominent answer to both questions was to say that for a theory to be genuinely empirical, the theory must explicitly formulate relationships between its theoretical and its observational terms using sentences called "correspondence rules" or "bridge principles." These confer empirical meaning on the theory and also allow a theory to be tested by permitting purely observational claims to be derived from the theory, which can then be confirmed experimentally. This chapter offers a range of criticisms of the distinction drawn between theoretical and observational terms.

In 1980 Bas van Fraassen published *The Scientific Image*, which became very influential because it offered a new defense of an antirealist position in science that he called "constructive empiricism." His idea is that it is not the aim of science to give theories that provide true descriptions of what the unobservable world is like. Rather it is to provide theories that are "empirically adequate," that is, that make true claims about the observable parts of the world. Accordingly, van Fraassen's view depends on a fundamental distinction between what is observable and what is not observable. He emphasized that this is not the earlier distinction between terms in a theory but between objects, events, and processes in the world. Some are observable; some are not. Despite van Fraassen's claims to the contrary, I believe that some of the problems with the earlier distinction between observational and theoretical *terms* are present also with the distinction between observable and unobservable *things* in the world. This is particularly evident in the first part, in which I discuss the distinction between entities or properties in the world that are observable and those that are not. My claim still holds that there are many different distinctions and contrasts that can be made by saying that electrons are (or are not) observable—depending on features of the context of assertion. (Electrons seem to be van Fraassen's favorite example of unobservables.)

How, if at all, is my own defense of scientific realism in chapter 11 affected by the conclusions of this chapter? There I defend the idea that, despite antirealist claims to the contrary, Perrin offered a valid experimental argument for the existence of molecules. (Similarly, in chapter 15 I argue, among other things, that J. J. Thomson offered a valid experimental argument for the existence of electrons.) Now, on my view, there are different claims one might be making in calling molecules or electrons "unobservable." Pick any of these you like. The realism of my view is that scientists can and do present valid empirical arguments for entities they (or philosophers) call "unobservable" (in whatever sense or contrast they have in mind); that the arguments being used to establish their existence are not at all impugned or affected by the fact that such entities are called "unobservable"; and that (as van Fraassen's realist says) it is one of the aims of science to provide true theories of what the world is like, no matter whether, or in what sense, or with what contrast, the objects being referred to are classified as observable or unobservable. Accordingly, the scientific realist does not have to pick out some preferred sense of, or contrast to be made with, the terms "observable" and "unobservable." His view applies to all entities, events, or processes postulated by theories. He wants his theories to make true claims about all of them. By contrast, the antirealist does have to select some preferred sense or contrast to be made with these terms. This is because the antirealist wants theories to "save the phenomena," that is, the observable parts of the universe. But on my view, what parts are selected as "observable" vary contextually with the contrast intended, and no one contrast has pride of place. The antirealist offers no general epistemic or ontological principle for deciding whether electrons, for example, are or are not the sorts of things that theories are supposed to "save."

14

What to Do if You Want to Defend a Theory You Can't Prove

A Method of "Physical Speculation"

"What to Do if You Want to Defend a Theory You Can't Prove" is reprinted by permission from The Journal of Philosophy, *January 2010. I formulate a method employed by James Clerk Maxwell in 1875 to argue for the truth of molecular theory without any experimental proof that molecules exist. I generalize that method to a broad class of microtheories, and I defend it against potential critics.*

In 1875 the theoretical physicist James Clerk Maxwell published a paper in *Nature* entitled "On the Dynamical Evidence of the Molecular Constitution of Bodies."[1] In it he argues for the existence of molecules and for various claims of the molecular theory that he and others had been developing, including that molecules satisfy dynamical principles of classical physics. He does so without any experimental proof for his fundamental claims. Since he regards this as contrary to a prominent methodological view that the defense of a theory requires experimental proof, at the outset he announces that he will employ a different scientific method. It is designed for developing and defending theories that postulate objects that, at the time, cannot be observed, and that make claims about such objects that, at the time, cannot be demonstrated to be true by observation and experiment.

Two questions are of special interest to Maxwell. First, can you use the method to develop and defend a theory about unobservables in a way that can make it possible to be justified in believing the theory (or at least the set of its central and distinctive assumptions) to be true, without being

---

1. Reprinted in *The Scientific Papers of James Clerk Maxwell*, vol. 2, W. D. Niven, ed. (Dover, 1965), 418–438.

able to experimentally prove that it is true?[2] Second, can you do so in a way that is sufficiently precise and complete to answer a range of questions about the unobservables postulated, even if you have no epistemic warrant for some of these answers? Maxwell gives an affirmative answer to both questions. He refers to his method as a "method of physical speculation." He takes it to be different from an inductive method of a sort espoused by Newton and Mill, which he regards as too demanding for his purposes, and from "the method of hypothesis" (or hypothetico-deductivism), which he deems too weak.

Maxwell gives only a very brief general description of his method, leaving his readers the task of understanding what it is from seeing how he actually employs it in defending his molecular theory. Whether it is worthy of being called a "method" at all, or just a general strategy, or something else, I believe that it is important for philosophers to consider. It is, indeed, different from standard scientific methods advocated not only in the nineteenth century but today as well, including hypothetico-deductivism, inductivism, and inference to the best explanation (IBE). It is a method that many scientists (whether knowingly or not) have employed in developing and defending a theory they could not prove. Maxwell's position is not that following the method will necessarily yield truth, or justified belief, or even a theory worth considering, but that it can do so if the development and defense are sufficiently good, and that it is a reasonable and useful strategy to follow when experimental proof is not available. I propose to formulate and illustrate the method, see how it differs from the others noted previously, and explore and defend its virtues. I begin with a characterization of the contrasting methods.

1. CONTRASTING METHODS OF DEFENSE

The Newton-Mill-Whewell Tradition of Proof

Within the empiricist tradition of the sort with which Maxwell was familiar, especially in the works of Newton, Mill, and Whewell, is the

---

2. Maxwell, as well as other authors to be considered here (including Newton, Mill, and Whewell), were scientific realists who believed that in principle empirical arguments could be given that prove the existence of unobservables. Accordingly, my discussion will be conducted within a realist framework. (For my own defense of scientific realism, see chapter 11 in this book. However, the issue to be treated here does not depend on what attitude one takes about realism. Antirealists can substitute some version of "saving the phenomena" for "truth" and then raise Maxwell's question by asking how to defend a theory when you can't prove that it "saves the phenomena."

view that one defends a scientific theory by attempting to prove that it is true. For these writers "proving" a theory in empirical science consists in giving arguments involving appeals to experiments and observations that allow one to conclude, beyond reasonable doubt, that the theory is true. Inductivists such as Newton and Mill advocate doing so by offering causal-inductive arguments from experiments and observations to universal causal laws. According to Newton, one constructs such arguments on the basis of his four "Rules for the Study of Natural Philosophy." The first two of these rules allow one to infer a single cause from the same type of observed effects; and the third and fourth rules allow one to infer the truth of an inductive generalization that such a cause operates within the entire class of phenomena in question.[3] Newton speaks of propositions derived using these rules as being "deduced from the phenomena and made general by induction," and he regards them as having "the highest evidence a proposition can have in this [experimental] philosophy."[4]

For Mill, using his "Four Methods of Experimental Inquiry," we vary circumstances under which phenomena of one type follow those of another, and by doing so we can determine whether causation exists and how general it is.[5] As in the case of Newton, such causal-inductive arguments should establish these laws with as much certainty as is possible in empirical science. Mill speaks of arguments of these sorts as providing "proof" of the propositions. Indeed, in his initial definition of "induction" he defines it as "the operation of discovering and proving general propositions." In cases typical in the theoretical sciences where effects are explained by reference to multiple causes, Mill introduces his "deductive method," which requires three steps in order to infer the truth of a theoretical system: causal-inductive generalizations from observations to a set of causal laws comprising the system; "ratiocination," which involves inferences showing how this set, if true, can explain and predict various observable effects; and verification of new effects predicted. Only if these three steps are followed, and not simply the last two, can one infer the truth of the theoretical system and regard it as proved.

By contrast, Whewell, who rejects the inductive methodology of Newton and Mill, advocates a robust form of IBE. If the universal causal

---

3. Newton, *The Principia: Mathematical Principles of Natural Philosophy*, trans. I. Bernard Cohen and Anne Whitman (Berkeley: University of California Press, 1999), 794–796. For a discussion of these rules, see my *Particles and Waves* (New York: Oxford University Press, 1991), chapter 2; also chapter 4 in this book.

4. From a letter to Cotes in 1713. Reprinted in H. S. Thayer, ed., *Newton's Philosophy of Nature* (New York, 1953), p. 6.

5. John Stuart Mill, *A System of Logic*, 8th ed. (London: Longmans, 1872), Book 3, chapter 8.

laws in question not only explain the phenomena used to generate them, but explain and predict phenomena of types different from those that generated the laws to begin with, then Whewell says there is a "consilience of inductions," and we have no basis for any reasonable doubt.[6] If this continues over time as new phenomena are discovered, and does so in such a way that the theory is simple and coherent, then one can infer with the highest possible certainty that the theory is true.

Newton, Mill, and Whewell do recognize that propositions are introduced into science without proof. Newton calls them "hypotheses," and although in the *Principia* he claims that they "have no place in experimental philosophy," he does in fact employ them, clearly labeling them as such. Overall his view seems to be that you can introduce them and consider their implications, but you are not justified in inferring that they are true, even if the implications are experimentally verified, since conflicting hypotheses may be equally successful. Mill has a very similar view. According to Whewell, if the theory explains known phenomena and predicts new ones only of the same type, you can conclude that the theory is "valuable," or even (so far at least) "verified" by positive instances. But this is not sufficient for proof, which is what Whewell seeks in "testing," since such theories often turn out to be false.

For purposes of contrast with Maxwell, then, I shall understand these "proof-demanding" writers to be claiming (a) that it is one of the principal aims of scientists to provide empirical proof of a theory; (b) that scientists are justified in believing a theory only if they have such proof; and (c) that merely showing that observations constitute positive instances of the theory, or are entailed or explained by it, or even (following contemporary Bayesians) that the probability of the theory is increased by these observations, is not sufficient for proof. While Maxwell agrees with (a) and (c), he rejects (b).

The Method of Hypothesis

What can you do to defend a theory in the absence of experimental proof? One standard approach is to employ some version of the "method of hypothesis."

Maxwell writes:

The method which has been for the most part employed in conducting such inquiries is that of forming an hypothesis, and calculating what would

6. William Whewell, *The Philosophy of the Inductive Sciences, Founded upon Their History* (London: Parker, 1840; reprinted London: Routledge/Thoemmes, 1996), vol. 2, chapter 5, section 10.

happen if the hypothesis were true. If these results agree with the actual phenomena, the hypothesis is said to be verified, so long, at least, as someone else does not invent another hypothesis which agrees still better with the phenomena.[7]

Maxwell rejects this "method of hypothesis" on grounds that apply to even more sophisticated versions, namely, that its users have no empirical basis from which to generate their hypotheses. Because of this, either they leave "their ideas vague and therefore useless" or else they engage in an "illegitimate use of the imagination." By the former Maxwell means that one thing users of the method of hypothesis sometimes do is invent very general hypotheses that are not sufficiently precise or developed to be tested. By the latter he means that the fact that hypotheses accommodate the phenomena by itself constitutes insufficient empirical warrant for those hypotheses, since there may be other conflicting hypotheses that accommodate the phenomena at least as well, if not better.[8] Even if Maxwell were to agree (which he does not) that the type of "verification" claimed by the method of hypothesis provided some support for a hypothesis, it cannot provide enough to justify a belief in the hypothesis. Maxwell wants a method that can do the latter when proof by "methodized experiment and strict demonstration" is not available. He also seeks a method that will enable one to provide a set of hypotheses that are not "vague and therefore useless." This is the entering point for the "method of physical speculation."

2. WHAT IS MAXWELL'S METHOD?

In very general terms, it is a method, or strategy, or procedure to be used when developing and defending a theory about "unobservables," when whatever experimental evidence exists is not sufficient to establish the theory. It is a method designed for, or at least particularly appropriate for,

7. *Scientific Papers*, vol. 2, p. 419.

8. This is implied in the passage quoted, and even more explicitly in Maxwell's book *Matter and Motion* (New York: Dover, first published 1877), p. 122. The "method of hypothesis" that Maxwell is here rejecting is much more basic than the more sophisticated IBE espoused by Whewell. The latter requires agreement not only with "actual phenomena" (presumably observed phenomena) but also with predicted ones, especially ones of a type different from those used to generate the hypothesis in the first place, and it requires simplicity and coherence over time in the face of new observations. However, Maxwell, like Mill before him, would find these (additional) Whewellian criteria neither necessary nor sufficient justification for an inference to the truth of a hypothesis. Maxwell never mentions Whewellian "predictivity" or "coherence" as being required by his "method of physical speculation." And while he cites the ability of the kinetic theory to explain a variety of different observed facts as counting in favor of that theory, this by itself is not sufficient for him to conclude that the theory is true.

theories in which the "unobservables" comprise a microsystem of which some observable macrosystem is claimed to be composed, and in which the claim is that the behavior of the microsystem causes or determines that of the macrosystem. In what follows I will offer a general characterization of the method that goes well beyond what Maxwell himself provides. In doing so I will distinguish four components and illustrate each by reference to what Maxwell actually does in his "physical speculations" about molecules.

Independent Warrant

First, whatever reasons one can offer should be given in favor of the existence of the postulated unobservables that determine macrobehavior, in favor of the central and distinctive principles introduced, and in favor of supposing that such principles are applicable to these unobservables. Such reasons can be of different sorts and may include: (a) appeals to experimental results and observations, arrived at independently of the theory in question, usually from other domains; these may provide a causal-inductive or an analogical basis for supposing that the macrosystem is composed of some type of unobservables that produce some of the observed behavior of the macrosystem;[9] (b) a methodological appeal to the "fundamental" character and simplicity of the principles being applied to those unobservables; and (c) an inductively based appeal to the success of these principles in other domains when applied to objects with the same or similar properties as those attributed to the unobservables. The reasons offered may vary in their strength, but they are not of the form "if we make these assumptions then we can explain and predict such and such phenomena," and they are not sufficiently strong to prove that the theory is true. In other writings I have said that such reasons supply "independent warrant."[10] They provide some epistemic reasons for believing the hypotheses in question that are independent of the explanatory and predictive power of the assumptions.

Maxwell seeks to develop and defend a general molecular theory of gases and liquids that governs, relates, and interprets properties and phenomena such as pressure, volume, temperature, density, specific heat, and diffusion. In accordance with the "method of physical speculation," the

---

9. In his 1855 paper "On Faraday's Lines of Force," Maxwell defends a "method of physical analogy" for dealing with "electrical science" so as to produce a "simplification and reduction" of the known laws of electricity and magnetism. He constructs an analogy between the electromagnetic field and a purely imaginary incompressible fluid. The analogy enables him to offer a physical representation of the field while at the same time avoiding speculations about unobservable constituents of the field. This is very different from Maxwell's later "method of physical speculation," which insists on such speculations, and allows analogical arguments if they provide some warrant for them. For extended discussions of these issues, see *Particles and Waves*.

10. See *Particles and Waves*.

first thing he wants to provide are some reasons for making the molecular assumptions he does, including, most important, the assumption that
bodies are composed of molecules, and that these satisfy classical principles of dynamics. He offers three different sorts of reasons.

A reason he proposes for assuming that bodies are composed of molecules of the sort postulated is that "whatever may be our ultimate conclusions as to molecules and atoms, we have experimental proof that bodies
may be divided into parts so small that we cannot perceive them" and that
by "particle" he means a small, possibly unobservable, part of a body, not
some ultimate or indivisible "atom." In his 1875 paper Maxwell does not
say what such "experimental proof" is, but it is likely that he is thinking of
various claims, made in his book *Theory of Heat* (first published in 1871),
starting with the idea that it has been experimentally established that heat
is not a substance (caloric) but a form of energy.[11] The energy of a body, he
continues in that book, is either kinetic energy due to motion, or potential
energy due to the body's position with respect to other bodies. But, he
claims, heat cannot be the latter, because the presence of another body is
not necessary for heat radiation. So it is due to motion, but not that of the
body as a whole, since a body radiates heat even when stationary. He concludes: "The motion which we call heat must therefore be a motion of parts
too small to be observed separately. . . . We have now arrived at the conception of a body as consisting of a great many small parts, each of which is in
motion. We shall call any one of these parts a molecule of the substance."[12]

Maxwell offers two sorts of reasons for applying dynamical principles
to the postulated set of unobservables. The first, which is empirical, is that
such principles have been successful in astronomy and electrical science.
Maxwell does not explicitly draw the inductive inference from this that
such methods will therefore be successful for the kinds of phenomena he
is concerned with. But this does seem implicit in his thought. The second
involves claims that are methodological or conceptual. One is that, on his

11. By the mid-nineteenth century, the experiments of Rumford and Davy, at the end
of the eighteenth century, showing that if caloric exists it must be weightless, and showing
that mechanical work can produce an indefinite quantity of heat, were considered decisive
against the caloric theory. Also, experiments by Joule in the 1840s on heat produced by the
friction of bodies established a quantitative relationship between mechanical work and heat.
Maxwell is thinking of the latter when near the beginning of his book he writes:

> Such evidence [as to the nature of heat] is furnished by experiments on friction, in
> which mechanical work, instead of being transmitted from one part of a machine to an-
> other, is apparently lost, while at the same time, and in the same place, heat is generated,
> the amount of heat being in an exact proportion to the amount of work lost. We have,
> therefore, reason to believe that heat is of the same nature as mechanical work, that is, it
> is one of the forms of Energy. (*Theory of Heat*, 10th ed. (London: Longmans), p. 7)

12. *Theory of Heat*, 311–312.

view, and that of most nineteenth-century physicists, dynamical explanations of phenomena are complete so that no further explanations are "necessary, desirable, or possible." Another is at least an implicit appeal to simplicity, when he says that "of all hypotheses as to the constitution of bodies, that is surely the most warrantable which assumes no more than that they are material systems, and proposes to deduce from the observed phenomena just as much information about the conditions and connections of the material system as these phenomena can legitimately furnish."[13] Here the idea is that the basic molecular assumptions he is and will be making will satisfy a standard of simplicity by explaining macrosystems composed of bodies in terms of microsystems composed of bodies, and so introduce no new ontological category.

Having presented some reasons in support of the assumption that gases and liquids are composed of molecules and that they are subject to dynamical principles, Maxwell proceeds by formulating a virial equation derived by Clausius from classical mechanics as applied to a system of particles constrained to move in a limited region of space, and whose velocities can fluctuate within certain limits. The equation relates the pressure and volume of a gas or fluid to the total kinetic energy of the system of particles of which it is composed, the forces of attraction or repulsion between the particles, and the distances between them. Maxwell writes the equation as follows:

$$pV = 2/3T - 2/3\Sigma\Sigma(1/2Rr).[14]$$

In using this equation, Maxwell and Clausius are *assuming* that gases and fluids are composed of unobservable particles; this is not something which is proved by proving the equation itself. (In his discussion Maxwell uses the terms "particle" and "molecule" interchangeably.) Since the equation is derived from classical mechanics, support for which comes from observations of the behavior of observable bodies, he is also supposing that such observations provide some independent warrant for the claim that if the postulated particles exist they satisfy the virial equation as well. (As we will see next in

13. *The Scientific Papers of James Clerk Maxwell*, vol. 2, p. 420.
14. The quantity on the left represents the pressure of the gas or fluid multiplied by the volume of its container and can be directly measured; T is the kinetic energy of the total system of particles; R is the force of attraction or repulsion between two particles; and r is the distance between two particles. The quantity 1/2Rr Clausius calls the virial of the attraction or repulsion. The sum is double since the virial for each pair of particles must be determined and then the entire sum of these is taken. Clausius's paper was published in German in 1870, with an English translation in *Philosophical Magazine*, vol. 40, pp. 122–127 (1870). The latter is reprinted in Stephen G. Brush, *Kinetic Theory*, vol. 1 (Oxford: Pergamon, 1965), pp. 172–178. The general theorem yields the result that the mean value of the kinetic energy of such a system of material particles equals the mean value of the virial. In the special case of a gas, considered to be composed of such material particles, where the gas is acted on by an external pressure p and confined to a volume V, the theorem can be expressed in the form Maxwell gives it, as shown previously.

considering the second part of Maxwell's method, he uses this equation to explain and give molecular interpretations of known gaseous phenomena.)

None of the facts Maxwell cites as independent warrant, separately or together, *establishes* Maxwell's initial hypothesis that gases are systems of particles or molecules satisfying the Clausius virial equation. But they do constitute at least some reason in favor of such a hypothesis. In Maxwell's own terms, such a hypothesis cannot "be derided as mere guess-work."

Derivations and Explanations of Known Phenomena

Second, known properties, laws, and experimentally established deviations from these laws of the macrosystem should be explained by invoking properties of, and principles governing, the unobservables that comprise the postulated microsystem. More specifically, known properties of the macrosystem should be characterized as determined by, or identical with, certain properties attributed to the microsystem. And laws governing the macrosystem, and deviations from them, should be derived from assumptions regarding the microsystem defended in the first component. If they are so derived, then whatever justification for the assumptions is claimed can be claimed not just on the basis of the independent warrant but also on the basis of known laws and phenomena that are derivable from those assumptions.[15]

Maxwell considers a gas with observable properties of temperature, volume, pressure, specific heat, and the like, which is subject to known laws and known deviations from them, and explains these properties, laws, and deviations using known properties and laws governing dynamical systems in general involving bodies in motion. Employing Clausius's virial equation, and assuming that the pressure and volume of a gas are simply the pressure and volume of the postulated molecular system and that the temperature of the gas is proportional to the mean kinetic energy of the molecules, Maxwell derives Boyle's law for gases; and using the virial equation, he explains why known deviations from the law occur at low temperatures and high densities (see the appendix to this chapter). He considers the derivation of Boyle's law, and of deviations from that, to count in favor of the theory, even to provide at least some reason (or part thereof) for thinking the theory is true. But this is so only if there is some independent warrant for basic assumptions in the theory.

15. A formal probabilistic representation of this idea is as follows: Let h be a hypothesis or set of hypotheses, let i be the independent warrant for h, and let e describe a set of known laws and other phenomena derived from h. Then $p(h/i\&e) \geq p(h/i)$. So if h's probability on the independent warrant is high, it will remain at least as high on additional data e if e is derived from h. For more discussion of this probabilistic representation, see *Particles and Waves*.

Theoretical Development

The postulation of the set of unobservables satisfying the properties and principles introduced will suggest a range of questions about what properties and principles in addition to those introduced in components 1 and 2 these unobservables satisfy. To the extent possible, the theorist should attempt to develop the theory further by formulating and answering these questions. Doing so will usually require the introduction of new theoretical assumptions about the unobservables for which there may or may not be independent warrant, and derivations of new results that may or may not be testable by known means. Judging from the amount of time Maxwell devotes to it, this "theoretical development" of the theory—which can go well beyond what is contained in the two components discussed here—is a crucial part of Maxwell's idea. Its focus is on providing more and more information about the postulated microsystem, whether or not this yields testable predictions and explanations of properties of the macrosystem.

Maxwell introduces a series of questions about the unobservable molecules he postulates, including these: What is the mean distance traveled by a molecule before striking another molecule (the mean free path)? What is the motion of molecules after collision? Are all directions of rebound equally likely? What is the distribution of molecular velocities? He introduces various new assumptions which enable him to answer these and many other questions.[16] In the case of the last question, Maxwell derives a distribution law, now bearing his name, that relates the number of molecules with velocities between given limits to the total number of molecules in the sample of gas and to the velocities themselves. In doing so he makes various new assumptions about molecules, including that molecular components of velocity in different directions are independent, and that the fraction of molecules in a unit volume does not depend on their direction but only on their speeds. He had no way of experimentally verifying these assumptions, or experimentally determining any of the quantities in the law, and hence no way of experimentally verifying the law.[17] It is a "purely theoretical" conclusion.[18]

---

16. In an earlier 1860 paper on kinetic theory, Maxwell sets out all of these questions as tasks to perform, and making various new assumptions, he derives a set of "propositions" that provide answers to them.

17. Direct experimental tests of Maxwell's law became possible only in the twentieth century with molecular beam experiments. In the 1875 paper under discussion, Maxwell gives only a qualitative account of the law, which he had formally derived in his 1860 paper. For an account of that derivation, see my *Particles and Waves*, 171–173.

18. Another derived conclusion is one that gives actual numerical values for mean velocities of molecules of oxygen, nitrogen, and hydrogen at 0 degrees centigrade. Although these are derived using experimentally measurable values for volume, pressure, and mass of a gas, these velocity values could not themselves be checked experimentally by Maxwell.

Unsolved Problems

In addition to formulating, defending, and developing the theory in accordance with the three points noted previously, problems with the theory should be noted. These can include a reference to known laws and properties of the macrosystem that have not yet been explained, as well as to experimental results that are not in accord with certain consequences of the theory. This, of course, is not a way of defending the theory. But it is a way of suggesting aspects of the theory that need further development, and of defending the "theorist" by showing that he is aware of these aspects.

Maxwell derives some conclusions from his theoretical assumptions that are contradicted by experiments. The most important of these he considers to be a derivation (first done in 1860) of the ratio of the specific heat of a gas at constant pressure to its specific heat at constant volume. According to theoretical calculations, in the best case, assuming that molecules are mere material points incapable of rotation, the ratio is 1.66, whereas the observed value is 1.4. This difference Maxwell considers "too great for any real gas." And if we suppose that molecules can vibrate, so that there are at least six degrees of freedom, the theoretical calculation of specific heat ratios will be a maximum of 1.33, which is too small for hydrogen, oxygen, nitrogen, and several other gases. Maxwell says that he considers this "to be the greatest difficulty yet encountered by the molecular theory."[19] In addition to this problem Maxwell mentions several properties of gases, including electrical ones, that neither he nor anyone else had explained in molecular terms.

3. WHAT CAN ONE CONCLUDE ABOUT A THEORY DEVELOPED USING MAXWELL'S METHOD?

Let us divide the assumptions made by a theory postulating unobservables into two sorts: those for which there are independent warrant arguments and those for which there are not. In Maxwell's method the most fundamental assumptions of the theory should be of the first sort. If they are, and if the arguments supplied are sufficiently strong, then one can claim to be justified in believing them to be true, even if the assumptions postulate unobservables, and even if the assumptions cannot at the time be proved experimentally. And if a range of observed phenomena is explained by derivation from these assumptions, then justification for the assumptions can be claimed not only on the basis of the independent warrant but also on the basis of the explained phenomena.[20]

19. *Papers*, vol. 2, 1875, p. 433.
20. See note 15.

The assumptions for which no independent warrant is given are ones for which conditional claims are usually made: if we assume such and such, then we can derive the following result, which may or may not be testable. If it is not testable, then we certainly cannot conclude that we are justified in believing the assumptions leading to that result, or the result itself (e.g., Maxwell's assumptions leading to his distribution law). If the result is testable and determined to be true but there is no warrant for the assumptions, then, since Maxwell explicitly rejects the method of hypothesis, he will not conclude that one is justified in believing the explanatory assumptions. What, then, can one conclude about such assumptions?

For Maxwell, nothing epistemic. Yet an important way of defending a theory is by showing how it can be developed theoretically. According to Maxwell this involves formulating assumptions precisely, often mathematically; adding new theoretical assumptions about the unobservables postulated in response to questions about the properties and behavior of those entities; and deriving consequences. Frequently in such a development new theoretical assumptions are introduced for which no independent warrant is given, and theoretical consequences are drawn that are not testable. In response to questions he posed regarding molecular velocities, Maxwell developed his theory by adding (unargued for) assumptions about the independence of component molecular velocities, leading to a derivation of his (untestable) molecular distribution law. In doing so he did not provide any new or increased epistemic reason to believe his general molecular assumptions or the specific ones needed for the derivation. Nor is such theoretical development what some have called an "aesthetic" criterion of goodness that adds beauty or simplicity to the theory. (A particular theoretical development may be quite complex and unbeautiful.[21]) Nor is a theoretical development of this sort engaged in simply to show that the theory is "worthy of pursuit." In telling us much more about the entities and properties introduced than is done in central assumptions, its purpose is to add some measure of completeness to theory by answering a range of questions that might be prompted by considering the fundamental assumptions, and to do so with precision. Completeness and precision are nonepistemic virtues Maxwell regards as valuable for their own sake and not just for leading to conditional explanations and predictions of phenomena (if they even do so) or for leading to tests of the theory (again

---

21. This was Duhem's criticism of Kelvin's theoretical development of the wave theory of light in the latter's *Baltimore Lectures* (reprinted in Robert H. Kargon and Peter Achinstein, eds., *Kelvin's Baltimore Lectures and Modern Theoretical Physics* (Cambridge, Mass.: MIT Press, 1987)). Kelvin developed the theory by proposing conflicting theoretical models of the ether to interpret various optical phenomena. He developed the theory by answering a series of questions about the structure of the ether, but the development lacked coherence.

if they do), or just for providing reasons to pursue the theory.[22] Without a theoretical development, he suggests, the basic assumptions are "vague," in the sense of being underdeveloped and imprecise.

Accordingly, in using "the method of physical speculation" one may be able to conclude that a theory is defensible both epistemically and nonepistemically. It has the epistemic virtue that its fundamental assumptions and perhaps others have independent warrant; and, depending on the strength of this warrant and on the known phenomena derived from them, this may be enough for one to be justified in believing those assumptions. It has the nonepistemic virtue of being developed with some measure of completeness and precision.

4. IS THIS REALLY A NEW METHOD?

Is Maxwell correct in claiming that there are genuine differences between his method and more standard ones mentioned earlier? It is clearly different from the "method of hypothesis," as formulated by Maxwell, since the latter, unlike the former, requires no independent warrant at all for its hypotheses. As a result, unless it can be shown that any competing system is less probable, the most that one can conclude from the fact that the hypotheses explain or predict observational facts is that these hypotheses are "possible," or even "confirmed" or "verified" by the facts, but not that these facts justify believing that the hypotheses are true.

There are two important differences between Maxwell's method and those of Newton, Mill, and Whewell. One pertains to "theoretical development." To be sure, the methods of Newton, Mill, and Whewell involve producing derivations of observable phenomena from the basic assumptions. And Whewell, like Maxwell, emphasizes the idea of developing a theory over time by adding new assumptions in response to phenomena not yet explained. However, Maxwell is also concerned, very importantly, with developing new theoretical assumptions about the unobservable entities postulated, *whether or not those assumptions are actually employed in explaining observable phenomena or are even capable of being verified at*

---

22. It would be misleading to say that for Maxwell, the "theoretical development" constitutes simply what some philosophers have called a "logic of pursuit." Maxwell's aim is to employ a method that can be used to show both epistemic and nonepistemic virtues of a theory without proving it. He wants more than simply giving reasons for pursuing the theory or taking it seriously. He wants reasons for believing it to be true, and for concluding that it is a good theory. The "theoretical development" may provide part of one's reasons to pursue a theory, but so will the other components of the method; and, as I have emphasized, that is not the raison d'etre of this component.

the time. And unlike Whewell's idea of "coherence," which is an epistemic criterion supposed to guarantee the highest measure of justified belief, Maxwell's "theoretical development" idea does not guarantee any measure of justified belief but nevertheless contributes to a defense of the theory by exhibiting nonepistemic virtues of the theory.

A second difference between Maxwell's method and those of Newton, Mill, and Whewell is that the latter, but not the former, are based on the idea that inference to the truth of a scientific proposition or theory requires proof, which these methods are designed by their proponents to enable scientists to provide. Newton and Mill draw a sharp distinction between proof and possibility. Whewell recognizes that there are situations in which you have less than proof (which requires "consilience") but more than mere possibility—for example, when your hypothesis predicts as well as explains phenomena of the same type as those prompting the hypothesis in the first place. By contrast, Maxwell's method is based on the idea that although proof is always desirable, a range of situations exists in which you have less than proof and more than possibility, or Whewellian success in explaining and predicting phenomena of the sort that prompted the theory. In such situations, depending on the strength of the independent warrant and of the explanations offered, you may be able to infer that your theory (or at least its set of fundamental assumptions) is true, while at the same time recognizing that more theoretical development and experimental support are needed and that unsolved problems remain.

Is there a difference between Maxwell's method and those of Newton, Mill, and Whewell over the *types* of epistemic arguments that can be employed in defense of a theory? Maxwell is clearly denying Whewell's claim that "consilience" is sufficient for inference; independent warrant—warrant other than the explanatory and predictive success of the theory—is also necessary. This is something with which Newton and Mill would agree. (It is Mill's first step in his "deductive method.") The relevant difference here is over the strength of the arguments required, not over types. Unlike Newton and Mill, Maxwell has in mind cases in which none of the arguments, individually or collectively, suffice to prove the assumptions. Why do they fail to do so?

Recall just the two empirical arguments Maxwell gives for assuming that molecules exist and that they obey laws of dynamics. The first is a causal-eliminative argument from the theory of heat (in his 1871 book), which starts with the claim that experiments show that heat is a form of energy, not a substance; then it moves to the claim that it must be kinetic energy rather than potential, since observations show that heat radiation doesn't depend on relative positions of bodies (which potential energy does); then, since hot bodies do not necessarily exhibit observable motion, it concludes that the motion must be that of parts of the body too small to observe, parts Maxwell will call molecules. The argument is certainly not decisive, since it makes assumptions that could be, and indeed were, questioned, e.g., that energy of motion requires bodies in motion—an assumption denied by "energeticists" who rejected molecular theory, such as Ostwald later in the nineteenth century.[23]

The second empirical argument Maxwell offers is one for supposing that molecules in motion obey laws of dynamics. The argument is simply an inductive generalization from the fact that such laws have been successful in astronomy and electrical science. In the absence of conflicting information, although this gives some reason for supposing these laws hold for domains both large and small, it is by no means decisive, since the phenomena in the domains cited are so different; and, of course, its conclusion was abandoned in the twentieth century with the advent of quantum mechanics.

What Maxwell is saying is that despite the lack of certainty in such cases, we provide what empirical and methodological arguments we can. Furthermore, he is saying, we don't need to base our belief in the assumptions of a theory on such "independent warrant" arguments alone but on these together with the fact that the assumptions can be used to explain known laws and deviations. And he is saying that a theory can be defended not only on epistemic grounds but also on nonepistemic ones, including the precision and completeness of its theoretical development.

5. A MAXWELLIAN BELIEF STATE; EPISTEMIC IMPLICATIONS AND OBJECTIONS

Despite the lack of proof, Maxwell's own belief state with regard to his kinetic-molecular theory was a quite confident one, which might be characterized as follows:

1. He believed that molecules exist and that the independently warranted dynamical assumptions about them were true.
2. He believed that he was justified in so believing.
3. He believed that neither he nor anyone else had sufficient experimental evidence to demonstrate that the assumptions he was making in the theory are true.

23. Friedrich Wilhelm Ostwald, "Emancipation from Scientific Materialism" (1895), reprinted in Mary Jo Nye, ed., *The Question of the Atom* (Los Angeles: Tomash, 1986), 337–354. This essay contrasts with Ostwald's later 1908 conversion to atomic theory, which is discussed in section 6.

Claims (1) and (2) about Maxwell can be supported by examining many of his published and unpublished writings in the 1870s, and not just the 1875 paper in question.[24] Claim (3) is clearly made in his 1875 paper.[25]

Let's call a belief state of the sort Maxwell was in (one satisfying (1)–(3)) a "confident but less than perfect one" with respect to a hypothesis h (which I will abbreviate as CLP(h)). Now admittedly one can be in such a state without being justified in believing h. But my claim is that one can also be in such a state and be justified in believing that h is true. Suppose I own 85 percent of the tickets in a fair lottery, one ticket of which will be drawn at random, and I believe that I will win because I own 85 percent of the tickets. I am justified in believing this even if I haven't proved or demonstrated that I will win. Or suppose that I am a detective trying to solve a crime, and that I have a good deal of information that suspect number one is the perpetrator: the motive, means, and opportunity all fit, as do the descriptions of some witnesses. On the basis of these facts, I come to believe that this suspect is guilty— even though, let's say, not all the evidence fits exactly, and even though I need more direct and positive evidence for a court of law. In the sort of case I am imagining, I am justified in believing what I do, even if I cannot yet prove it. In relevant respects, in 1875 Maxwell's belief state with regard to molecular theory was analogous to these. Now for some objections.

---

24. Here is a passage from an 1875 article he wrote on atoms for the *Encyclopedia Britannica*: "Having thus justified the hypothesis that a gas consists of molecules in motion, which act on each other only when they come very close together during an encounter, but which, during the intervals between their encounters which constitute the greater part of their existence, are describing free paths, and are not acted on by any molecular force, we proceed to investigate such a system." This contrasts with Maxwell's much more skeptical epistemic state around 1860, during the time of his first kinetic theory paper. In that period Maxwell took his theory to be, as he described it, "an exercise." Writing to Stokes in 1859, he says,

> I do not know how far such speculations may be found to agree with facts . . . and at any rate as I found myself able and willing to deduce the laws of motion of systems of particles acting on each other only by impact, I have done so as an exercise in mechanics. Now do you think there is any so complete a refutation of this theory of gases as would make it absurd to investigate it further so as to found arguments upon measurements of strictly "molecular" quantities before we know whether there be any molecules?

25. *Scientific Papers*, vol. 2, p. 420. In an 1873 lecture titled "Molecules," Maxwell divides various claims of molecular theory into "three ranks," which vary with degree of certainty and completeness of the knowledge about the molecular assumptions. In the first rank are assumptions about relative molecular masses and velocities; in the third (yielding what he calls only "probable conjecture") are assumptions about absolute molecular masses and diameters. *Scientific Papers*, vol. 2, p. 371.

Objection 1

In the lottery and detective cases, as well as in Maxwell's case, we need to distinguish what justification a person offers for his belief, on the one hand, from whether his belief is really justified, since (the opponent might say) in these cases the person in question doesn't really have sufficient evidence to be justified in his belief. One has this only if the justification is sufficient for knowledge. Although CLP(h)-states are possible, and someone in such a state may offer a justification for believing h, this is not sufficient for knowledge that h is true. Such a position has in fact been taken in epistemology by Jonathan Sutton, who distinguishes a "loose" and a "strict" sense of justification.[26] In a case such as my lottery example, he argues that although in a "loose" sense (which is used colloquially and is championed by most epistemologists) I am justified in believing that I will win, in a "strict" sense I am not, because I don't know that I will win. In a strict sense I am justified in believing only that I will *probably* win.

Reply

To do justice to Sutton's position one would need to carefully examine each of the epistemic arguments and advantages he offers for employing his "strict" sense of justification. Elsewhere I have drawn a distinction somewhat similar to his between "veridical" and "nonveridical" senses of expressions such as "good reason to believe," "evidence," and "sign or symptom of," in which the veridical sense requires the truth of the hypothesis in question, and the nonveridical does not.[27] For purposes of this chapter it suffices to say that the claims about justified belief in the lottery, detective, and Maxwellian cases are being made in my "nonveridical" sense. They can also be made in Sutton's "loose" sense, which does not require either truth or knowledge of the truth.[28] Maxwell's general epistemic position with respect to molecular theory

26. Jonathan Sutton, *Without Justification* (Cambridge, Mass.: MIT Press, 2007).

27. *The Book of Evidence* (see chapter 1). The distinction I draw is not exactly Sutton's, since for my "veridical" sense it is required that the hypothesis (which is justified, for which there is evidence, etc.) be true, not that anyone know this, which is what Sutton requires in addition to truth.

28. If we do the latter, then we would reformulate these claims by saying that ("strictly speaking") in the lottery, detective, and Maxwellian cases, one is justified in believing that the claims made are probably true. And we would reformulate Maxwell's aim in employing his method of physical speculation to be one of showing how one can develop and defend a theory without experimental proof by showing that one is justified in believing it is probably

fits both descriptions. It is one that other theoretical scientists are frequently in.[29]

Objection 2

As has been noted, even in 1875 Maxwell recognized problems with the theory, including theoretical derivations of specific heat values that were incompatible with observed values, and the inability of the theory to explain various known properties of gases. Since there were such problems and since they caused Maxwell to have some doubts concerning the theory, how could Maxwell believe the theory, let alone have confidence in his beliefs?

Reply

Maxwell did not doubt that the theory, in its essentials, is true. He doubted that all the assumptions he was making were true, without being able to point to specific ones as being particularly dubious. And he believed that the theory had not yet been sufficiently developed to deal with the inconsistencies or with unanswered questions concerning electrical and certain other known properties of gases. But doubts of these sorts were not enough to shake his confidence that the fundamental ideas are correct and that these problems would be worked out.

Objection 3

Maxwell's 1875 paper is titled "On the Dynamical Evidence of the Molecular Constitution of Bodies." Evidence need not provide proof. It

---

29. Although in the *Principia* Isaac Newton demands "deductions from the phenomena," which require the satisfaction of his four methodological rules, and, he believes, yield the kind of certainty he seeks, in several queries in the *Opticks* he gives arguments in favor of the particle theory of light and against the competing wave theory, that by his own admission do not furnish such certainty. Yet Newton believed that light consists of unobservable particles, and pretty clearly he believed he was justified in so believing. For example, Query 29 begins as follows: "Are not the Rays of Light very small Bodies emitted from shining Substances. For such Bodies will pass through uniform Mediums in right Lines without bending into the Shadow, which is the Nature of the Rays of Light." (Newton continues to show how various known properties of light can be explained on the particle theory.) Newton is giving arguments for the particle theory that put him in the same epistemic position as Maxwell was in with respect to molecular theory. These arguments, he thought, justify his belief in the particle theory without giving decisive proof.

Although I will not argue for it here, I think that quite similar things can be said about Darwin's reasoning in *The Origin of Species* for natural selection as the mechanism for evolution. Darwin believed his hypotheses, believed he was justified in so believing, and yet explicitly recognized that he lacked decisive proof.

need not even provide reasons sufficient for belief. All it has to do is supply some reasons for increasing one's degree of belief in the theory. And that is all that Maxwell was in fact doing or was justified in claiming to do.

Reply

This objection presupposes an increase-in-degree-of-belief (or probability) position on evidence, which I have criticized elsewhere[30] and will not pursue here. Suffice it to say that, on Maxwell's view, one can give evidence that is strong enough to justify belief, and goes beyond simply increasing one's degree of belief, without giving proof; and that is precisely what he was trying to do in his 1875 paper and in other writings during this period.

6. TWO "DECISIVE" EXPERIMENTS

Given that Maxwell's "evidence" for his molecular assumptions was not decisive, what sort of evidence would be? For proof of the existence of molecules Maxwell was not demanding experiments making molecules "directly observable," but only experimental results from which their existence and properties could be inferred with certainty. Let me begin by noting two different experimental results that were regarded as decisive not only by many who were believers already but also by at least some initially skeptical scientists. The arguments presented, one for the existence of molecules, the other for electrons, were of the same general type. I want to ask what such arguments possessed that Maxwell's did not that, at least in some cases, made believers out of skeptics. Neither of the experimental results I will mention made the postulated unobservables "observable," nor did they need to do so to be decisive.

For an initially skeptical scientist I choose Friedrich Wilhelm Ostwald, Professor of Physical Chemistry at the University of Leipzig, and winner of the Nobel Prize in chemistry in 1909. In 1896 Ostwald published a paper titled "Emancipation from Scientific Materialism,"[31] in which he lays out his fundamental objections to atomism.[32] For our purposes here, the most important is his claim that no way had yet been found to experimentally measure, with any degree of certainty, quantities associated with atoms or molecules; this measurement criterion Ostwald took to be necessary and sufficient for proving the existence of a postulated unobserved entity.

---

30. *The Book of Evidence* (see chapter 1).
31. See note 23.
32. For a discussion of these objections, see my "Atom's Empirical Eve: Methodological Disputes and How to Evaluate Them," *Perspectives on Science* 15 (2007), 359–390.

However, in 1908 Ostwald was converted by experiments of two physicists: those of Jean Perrin in 1908 on Brownian motion, which Ostwald claims "justify the most cautious scientists in now speaking of the experimental proof of the atomic nature of matter," and experiments of J. J. Thomson (in the mid-1890s) on the counting of gas ions and (in 1897) on cathode rays, leading to Thomson's discovery of the electron. In other writings I have discussed both sets of experiments at length.[33] Here I will very briefly outline the arguments based on Perrin's experiments for the existence of molecules in order to indicate, first, the type of reasoning involved; second, why the argument was so convincing to Ostwald and to many (though not all) scientists; and third, how it differed from Maxwell's "evidence" for molecular theory.

Perrin's argument contains two stages. In the first, he offers a general qualitative causal-eliminative argument from experiments on Brownian motion, the haphazard motion exhibited by small microscopic particles suspended in a liquid. In the 1880s various experiments had been performed, principally by Leon Gouy, to determine whether this observed Brownian motion was caused by forces external or internal to the fluid in which the motion occurred. Gouy examined a range of possible external causes. When these were reduced or eliminated, the Brownian motion continued unabated. Perrin concluded that the motion of the observable Brownian particles is caused internally by their bombardment with unobservable molecules comprising the fluid.[34]

The second stage of Perrin's argument invoked experimental results that completely convinced Ostwald of the existence of molecules. (The first stage by itself Ostwald would probably have regarded as no more convincing than Maxwell's "independent warrant" arguments.) In 1908 Perrin conducted a series of experiments in which he prepared tiny ("Brownian") particles visible through a microscope, each of which had the same mass and density, and inserted them into a cylinder containing a dilute liquid of known density and temperature. He derived an equation containing terms for the number of microscopic Brownian particles per unit volume at the upper and lower levels of the cylinder, the mass and density of the particles, the density of the liquid, the height of the cylinder, the temperature of the liquid, and, most important, Avogadro's number N (the number of molecules in a gram molecular weight of a substance). All of these quantities except the last were experimentally measurable. When Perrin performed various experiments with different types of microscopic particles and different fluids, he determined that Avogadro's number was

33. See chapters 12 and 15 in this book.
34. Jean Perrin, *Atoms* (Woodbridge, Conn.: Ox Bow, 1990).

the same in all cases, approximately 6×10^{23}. He concluded from this that molecules exist.[35]

J. J. Thomson's argument for the existence of electrons (or "corpuscles," as he called them) is in important respects parallel to Perrin's arguments for molecules.[36]

In the first stage of their arguments both physicists cite experiments yielding results that purport to show the existence of the object postulated without providing any measurements of the object's properties. Their arguments are of a causal-eliminative type. They begin with an observed phenomenon: Brownian motion, in the case of Perrin, and cathode rays, in the case of Thomson, which, it is claimed, given the background information, is likely to have one of several different types of causes that are specified. Then it is asserted that experiments make it very probable that all but one of these causes are eliminated, leaving the hypothesis which postulates the unobservable entity in question as the probable cause of the phenomenon. In the second stage of the argument, experiments yielding other effects of the inferred entity are cited, from which certain magnitudes associated with these causes are derived and experimentally measured to be approximately the same in various different types of experiments performed. In neither case did the experimenters make the entities inferred "observable."

It is not my claim that arguments containing both of these stages are in general necessary to decisively establish claims of the existence of unobservable entities, but only that in the cases in question there were arguments of these types, and they did in fact convince not only the experimenters themselves but also at least some initial skeptics. Nor is it my claim that all arguments of these types are in fact decisive (whether or not they are deemed to be so), since it depends on how well the premises, or other assumptions implicitly made, are themselves established.[37]

35. Jean Perrin, *Atoms*, p. 105. Once an experimental value for Avogadro's number is obtained, then an experimental value for a weight in grams of a given molecule is determined by dividing this by the gram molecular weight.

36. See *Particles and Waves*, chapters 10–11.

37. Although the arguments of Thomson and Perrin were considered decisive by many, there were some skeptics. For example, in Thomson's case, there were some who questioned whether (in the first stage of the argument) Thomson was right in supposing that the most probable cause of electrical deflection in cathode tubes was the passage of charged particles with (classical) mass. (George FitzGerald, e.g., thought that it was at least as probable that they were "aetherial" free charges.) In the second stage of the argument in which Thomson experimentally determines a constant mass to charge ratio, some questions might be raised, since the experimental values Thomson actually obtained had a significant range in both sets of experiments he performed to obtain this ratio. For these and other issues pertaining to the decisiveness of Thomson's argument, see George E. Smith, "J. J. Thomson and the Electron, 1897–1899," in Jed Z. Buchwald and Andrew Warwick, eds., *Histories of the Electron* (Cambridge, Mass.: MIT Press, 2001), 21–76.

What is the difference between these cases in which experiments for the postulated entities are decisive, or considered to be so, and Maxwell's empirical arguments for molecules, which he himself did not characterize as decisive? In all three cases, appeals are made to experiments, and in all three cases numerical values associated with the postulated entities are given. The difference is in the strength of the empirical arguments. Maxwell's causal-eliminative argument for the existence of molecules from experiments on heat makes it probable that bodies contain "parts too small to be observed separately," which Maxwell called molecules. But it didn't make it probable enough to be decisive since it did not decisively preclude other possible causes of heat phenomena. Nor was his inductive argument decisive from the success of dynamical principles in other domains to their applicability to the inferred molecules, since, as he notes, such principles have been successfully applied only to macrobodies. And although Maxwell gives some theoretical estimates for various molecular speeds, he had no experimental way to verify these calculations. Accordingly, in the 1870s, although Maxwell had some empirical arguments for the existence of molecules and for assumptions he was making about them, even if these arguments provided a reasonable basis for believing the theory true, they were by no means conclusive, or regarded by Maxwell as so.

Had he lived then, what Maxwell might have said in response to Ostwald's late conversion to the molecular theory in 1908 is this: True, in the 1870s "methodized experiments" that provide a "strict demonstration" of molecular theory did not exist. Nevertheless, in accordance with the "method of physical speculation," epistemic arguments were given that furnished a reasonable basis for believing the central assumptions of the theory, and in addition nonepistemic ones were presented showing how the theory can be developed theoretically. One doesn't need "strict demonstration" to accomplish these purposes.

APPENDIX: AN EXAMPLE OF MAXWELL'S EXPLANATORY STRATEGY

Examining the Clausius equation given in section 2, we may conclude that the pressure of a gas depends on the kinetic energy T of the system of molecules, which is due to the motion of the molecules and to the quantity $1/2Rr$, which depends on the forces between them. Maxwell now argues that the pressure of a gas cannot be explained by assuming repulsive forces between molecules. He shows that if it were due to repulsion, then the pressure of a gas with the same density but in different containers would be greater in a larger container than in a smaller one, and greater in the open air than in any container, which is contrary to what is observed. If we suppose that the molecules of the gas do not exert any forces on each other, then the Clausius virial equation reduces to $pV = 2/3T$. Then since T is the kinetic energy of the system of particles, where M is the mass of the gas, i.e., the mass of the system of molecules, and since $T = 1/2Mc^2$, where c is the mean velocity of a molecule, Maxwell derives the equation $pV = 1/3Mc^2$. The latter is Boyle's law, on the assumption that the temperature of a gas is proportional to the mean kinetic energy of the molecules.

Now, continues Maxwell, it is known that real gases deviate from Boyle's law at low temperatures and high densities. And he asks whether the second factor in Clausius's equation dealing with forces between molecules, which was ignored in deriving Boyle's law, can be invoked to explain actual deviations from that law found in experiments. These experiments show that as the density of a gas increases, its pressure is less than that given by Boyle's law. Hence, the forces between the molecules must on the whole be attractive rather than repulsive. In the virial equation this is represented by a positive virial. Experiments also show that as the pressure of a gas is increased, it reaches a state in which a very large increase in pressure produces a very small increase in density, so that the forces between molecules are now mainly repulsive.[38]

ACKNOWLEDGMENT   For sharp criticisms and very helpful suggestions, I am indebted to Linda S. Brown, Victor DiFate, and Richard Richards.

38. In the paper Maxwell goes on to give mechanical interpretations, analyses, explanations, and calculations involving other gaseous phenomena, using probabilistic ideas first introduced by Clausius and developed by Maxwell and Boltzmann. For example, he derives a theoretical estimation of the speeds of molecules. In a highly rarefied gas, as noted, where the second term in the Clausius equation can be ignored, we can derive $pV = 1/3Mc^2$ in which p (pressure), V (volume), and M (mass of the gas) are measurable quantities, and c = mean velocity of a gas molecule. Maxwell proceeds to give some calculations: at 0 degrees centigrade, the average velocity of a molecule of oxygen is 461 meters per second, that of nitrogen is 492, and that of hydrogen 1,844. Of course, these are theoretical calculations, not experimental results.

15

Who Really Discovered the Electron?

"Who Really Discovered the Electron?" is reprinted by permission from Jed Buchwald and Andrew Warwick, eds., Histories of the Electron: The Birth of MicroPhysics *(MIT Press, 2001). Written for a conference at MIT commemorating the 100th anniversary of the discovery of the electron. I provide a general account of what it means for someone to discover something and distinguish a weak and a strong sense of "discovery." In terms of this account, I consider historically whether J. J. Thomson, who is generally regarded as the discoverer of the electron, deserves that title.*

TWO PROBLEMS WITH IDENTIFYING J. J. THOMSON AS THE DISCOVERER

Heroes are falling in this age of revisionist history. Thomas Jefferson, according to one recent authority, was a fanatic who defended the excesses of the French Revolution. Einstein was not the saintly physicist we were led to believe but was mean as hell to his first wife. And, more to the present purpose, J. J. Thomson really didn't discover the electron. So claim two authors, Theodore Arabatzis, in a 1996 article on the discovery of the electron,[1] and Robert Rynasiewicz, at a February 1997 A.A.A.S. symposium in honor of the 100th anniversary of the discovery.

I am indebted to Wendy Harris for helping me express the views I want, to Robert Rynasiewicz and Kent Staley for stimulating discussions in which they tried their best to dissuade me from expressing those views, to Ed Manier who, when I presented an earlier version of this paper at Notre Dame, raised the question that forms the tide of section 6, and to Jed Buchwald and Andrew Warwick for helpful organizational suggestions and for convincing me to tone down my anti-social-constructivist sentiments.
    1. Theodore Arabatzis, "Rethinking the 'Discovery' of the Electron." *Studies in History and Philosophy of Science* 27B (December 1996), 405–435. See also his later work *Representing Electrons: A Biographical Approach to Theoretical Entities* (Chicago: University of Chicago Press, 2006).

I would like my heroes to retain their heroic status. However, my aim in this chapter is not to defend Thomson's reputation but to raise the more general question of what constitutes a discovery. My strategy will be this. First, I want to discuss why anyone would even begin to doubt that Thomson discovered the electron. Second, I want to suggest a general view about discovery. Third, I will contrast this with several opposing positions, some of which allow Thomson to retain his status, and others of which entail that Thomson did not discover the electron; I find all of these opposing views wanting. So who, if anyone, discovered the electron? In the final part of this chapter I will say how the view I develop applies to Thomson and also ask why we should care about who discovered the electron, or anything else.

Let me begin, then, with two problems with identifying Thomson as the discoverer of the electron. The first is that before Thomson's experiments in 1897 several other physicists reached conclusions from experiments with cathode rays that were quite similar to his. One was William Crookes. In 1879, in a lecture before the British Association at Sheffield, Crookes advanced the theory that cathode rays do not consist of atoms, "but that they consist of something much smaller than the atom—fragments of matter, ultra-atomic corpuscles, minute things, very much smaller, very much lighter than atoms—things which appear to be the foundation stones of which atoms are composed."[2]

So eighteen years before Thomson's experiments, Crookes proposed two revolutionary ideas essential to Thomson's work in 1897: that cathode rays consist of corpuscles smaller than atoms, and that atoms are composed of such corpuscles. Shouldn't Crookes be accorded the title "discoverer of the electron"?

Another physicist with earlier views about the electron was Arthur Schuster. In 1884, following his own cathode ray experiments, Schuster claimed that cathode rays are particulate in nature and that the particles all carry the same quantity of electricity.[3] He also performed experiments on the magnetic deflection of the rays, which by 1890 allowed him to compute upper and lower bounds for the ratio of charge to mass of the particles comprising the rays. Unlike Thomson (and Crookes in 1879), however, Schuster claimed that the particles were negatively charged gas molecules.

2. William Crookes, "Modern Views on Matter: The Realization of a Dream" (an address delivered before the Congress of Applied Chemistry at Berlin, 5 June 1903): 231. *Annual Report of the Board of Regents of the Smithsonian Institution* (Washington D.C., Government Printing Office, 1904). In this paper Crookes quotes the present passage from his 1879 lecture.

3. See Arthur Schuster, *The Progress of Physics* (Cambridge: Cambridge University Press. 1911), 61.

Philipp Lenard is still another physicist with a considerable claim to be the discoverer of the electron. In 1892 he constructed a cathode tube with a special window capable of directing cathode rays outside the tube. He showed that the cathode rays could penetrate thin layers of metal and travel about half a centimeter outside the tube before the phosphorescence produced is reduced to half its original value. The cathode rays, therefore, could not be charged molecules or atoms, since the metal foils used were much too thick to allow molecules or atoms to pass through.

Other physicists as well, such as Hertz, Perrin, and Wiechert, made important contributions to the discovery. Why elevate Thomson and say that he discovered the electron? Why not say that the discovery was an effort on the part of many?

The second question is: Even assuming that Thomson discovered something, was it really the *electron*? How could it be, since Thomson got so many things wrong about the electron? The most obvious is that he believed that electrons are particles or corpuscles (as he called them), *and not waves*. In a marvelous twist of history, Thomson's son, G. P. Thomson, received the Nobel Prize for experiments in the 1920s demonstrating the wave nature of electrons. Another mistaken belief was that electrons are the only constituents of atoms. Still others were that the charge carried by electrons is not the smallest charge carried by charged particles, and that the mass of the electron, classically viewed, is entirely electromagnetic, a view Thomson came to hold later. Why not deny that Thomson discovered anything at all, since nothing exists that satisfies his electron theory? To deal with these issues something quite general needs to be said about discovery.

WHAT IS DISCOVERY?

The type of discovery with which I am concerned is discovering some thing or type of thing (for example, the electron, the Pacific Ocean), rather than discovering that something is the case (for example, that the electron is negatively charged). Later I will consider a sense of discovering some thing X that requires a knowledge that it is X, as well as a sense that does not.

My view has three components, the first of which is ontological. Discovering something requires the existence of what is discovered. You cannot discover what doesn't exist—the ether, the Loch Ness monster, or the fountain of youth—even if you think you have. You may discover the *idea* or the *concept* of these things. Everyone may think you have discovered the things corresponding to these ideas or concepts. They may honor you and give you a Nobel Prize, but if these things don't exist, you haven't discovered them.

The second component of discovery is *epistemic*. A certain state of knowledge is required. If you are to be counted as the discoverer of something, not only must that thing exist but also you must know that it does. Crookes in 1879 did not discover electrons because he lacked such knowledge; his theoretical claim that cathode rays consist of subatomic particles, although correct, was not sufficiently established to produce the knowledge that such particles exist. Not just any way of generating knowledge, however, will do for discovery. I may know that something exists because I have read that it does in an authoritative book. Discovery, in the sense we are after, requires that the knowledge be firsthand.

What counts as "firsthand" can vary with the type of object in question. With physical objects such as electrons one might offer this rough characterization: knowledge that the objects exist is generated, at least in part, by observing those objects or their direct effects. This knowledge may require rather strenuous inferences and calculations from the observations. (Scientific discovery is usually not like discovering a cockroach in the kitchen or a nail in your shoe.) As noted, discovery involves not just any observations that will produce knowledge of the object's existence, but observations of the object itself or its direct effects. I may come to know of the existence of a certain library book by observing a computer screen in my office which claims that the library owns it. I may discover that the book exists by doing this. But I may never discover the book itself if I can't find it on the shelf. In discovering the book at least among the things that make me know that it exists is my seeing it. Finally, for discovery, the knowledge in question involves having as one's reason, or at least part of one's reason, for believing that X exists the belief that it is X or its direct effects that have been observed. My knowledge that electrons exist may come about as a result of my reading the sentence "Authorities say that electrons exist" on my computer screen. What is on my screen is a direct effect of electrons. But in such a case, I am supposing, my reason for believing that electrons exist does not include the belief that I have observed electrons or their direct effects on the screen.[4]

Putting together these features of the second (epistemic) component of discovery, we can say that someone is in an *epistemic state necessary for discovering* X if that person knows that X exists, observations of X or its direct effects caused, or are among the things that caused, that person to

---

4. I am indebted to Kent Staley for this example and this point.

believe that X exists, and among that person's reasons for believing that X exists is that X or its direct effects have been observed. More briefly, I will say that such a person knows that X exists from observations of X or its direct effects.

The third component of discovery is priority. If I am the discoverer of something, then the epistemic state I have just described must be a "first." I put it this way because it is possible to relativize discovery claims to a group or even to a single individual. I might say that I discovered that book in the library last Tuesday, meaning that last Tuesday is the first time for me. It is the first time I knew the book existed by observing it, even though others knew this before I did. I might also make a claim such as this: I was the first member of my department to discover the book, thereby claiming my priority over others in a certain group. Perhaps it is in this sense that we say that Columbus discovered America, meaning that he was the first European to do so. And of course, the relevant group may be the entire human race. Those who claim that Thomson discovered the electron mean, I think, that Thomson was the first human to do so.

There is a rather simple way to combine these three components of discovery, if we recognize that knowing that something exists entails that it does, if we confine our attention to discovering physical objects (rather than such things as facts, laws, or proofs), and if we employ the previously introduced concept of an epistemic state necessary for discovery. The simple way is this: P discovered X if and only if P was the first person (in some group) to be in an epistemic state necessary for discovering X. That is, P was the first person (in some group) to know that X exists, to be caused to believe that X exists from observations of X or its direct effects, and to have as a reason for believing that X exists that X or its direct effects have been observed.

Before contrasting this with opposing views, and applying this to Thomson and the electron, some points need clarification.

First, on this account, to discover X, you don't need to observe X directly. It suffices to observe certain causal effects of X that can yield knowledge of X's existence. If I see a cloud of dust moving down the dirt road that is obviously being produced by a car approaching, then I can discover a car that is approaching even though I can't see the car itself, but only the cloud of dust it is producing as it moves. It is not sufficient, however, to come to know of X's existence via observations of just any sort. If I read a letter from you saying that you will be driving up the dirt road to my house at noon today, and I know you to be someone who always keeps his word, that, by itself, does not suffice for me to say that I discovered a car that is approaching at noon, even if I know that the car is approaching. Discovering the car requires observations of the car or its direct effects.

Second, this will prompt the question "What counts as observing direct effects?" Some physicists want to say that the tracks produced by electrons in cloud chambers are direct effects, because electrons, being charged, ionize gas molecules around which drops of water condense, forming the tracks. By contrast, neutrons, being neutral, cannot ionize gas molecules and hence do not leave tracks. They are detected by bombarding charged particles that do leave tracks. More recently detected particles, such as the top quark, involve many different effects that are less direct than these.[5] This is a complex issue that cannot be quickly settled.[6] What appears to be involved is not some absolute idea of directness, but a relative one. Given the nature of the item whose effects it is (for example, if it is a neutron it cannot produce a track but must interact with charged particles that do produce tracks), this degree of directness in detecting its effects not only yields knowledge that the item exists but also furnishes the best, or one of the best, means at the moment available for obtaining that knowledge.

Third, on this account, the observations of X or its effects need not be made by the discoverer, but by others. What is required is only that the discoverer be the first to know that X exists from such observations. The planet Neptune was discovered independently by Adams and Leverrier from observations of the perturbations of Uranus caused by Neptune. These observations were made by others, but complex calculations enabled these astronomers to infer where the new planet could be observed in the sky. The first actual telescopic observation of Neptune was made not by either of these astronomers but by Johann Galle at the Berlin Observatory. Although Galle may have been the first to see Neptune, he is not its discoverer, because he was not the first to come to know of its existence from observations of Neptune or its effects.

Fourth, to discover X it is not sufficient simply to postulate, or speculate, or theorize that X exists. In 1920 Rutherford theorized that neutrons exist, but Chadwick in 1932, not Rutherford in 1920, is the discoverer of these particles. There were before 1932 no experimental results that allowed the existence of this particle to be known.

In connection with the electron, there are two physicists whose names I have not mentioned so far: Larmor and Lorentz. Both had theories about what they called electrons. Setting aside questions about whether they were referring to what we call electrons, one reason these physicists are

---

5. For an illuminating discussion, see Kent Staley, *The Evidence for the Top Quark* (Cambridge: Cambridge University Press, 2004).

6. For more discussion, see my *Concepts of Science* (Baltimore: Johns Hopkins University Press, 1968), chapter 5, and chapter 13 in this book.

not the discoverers of electrons is, I think, epistemic. Although their theories explained experimental results, such results were not sufficiently strong to justify a knowledge-claim about the electron's existence. Their claims about electrons were primarily theory driven.

Fifth, this view allows there to be multiple discoverers, as were Adams and Leverrier. They came to be in the appropriate epistemic states at approximately the same time. It allows a cooperative group of scientists, rather than the scientists individually in that group, to be the discoverers—as in the case of the top quark. And it allows scientists to make contributions to the discovery of X without themselves being discoverers or part of a group that discovered X. Plucker did not discover the electron, though in 1859 he made a crucial contribution to that discovery—the discovery of cathode rays.

Sixth, we need to distinguish two ways of understanding the phrase "knowing that X exists" in my definition of discovery and hence two senses of discovery. Suppose that while hiking in the Rockies, I pick up some shiny stones. You inform me that I have discovered gold. This could be true, even if I don't know that it is gold. In this case by observing the stones I have come to know of the existence of something that, unknown to me, is gold. That is one sense in which I could have discovered gold. Of course, I might also have come to know that these objects are gold. That is another sense in which I could have discovered gold.[7]

The same applies to discovering the electron. To say that Thomson discovered the electron might mean only that by suitable observations he came to know of the existence of something that happens to be the electron, even if he didn't realize this. Or it might mean something stronger to the effect that he came to know that the thing in question has the electron properties (whatever those are). I shall speak here of the latter as the "stronger" sense of discovery and the former as the "weaker."

CONTRASTING VIEWS OF DISCOVERY

The present view of discovery will now be contrasted with several others, including ones suggested by two historians of science who have discussed the history of the discovery of the electron. Although the primary focus

---

7. In philosophical jargon this distinction corresponds to that between referential transparency and opacity in the expression "discovering X" (and in "knowing that X exists"). In the referentially transparent sense, but not the referentially opaque sense, if I have discovered X, and if X = Y, then it follows that I have discovered Y.

of these authors is historical and not philosophical, what they claim about Thomson suggests more general views about what counts as a discovery. These more general views provide sufficient conditions for discovery, or necessary ones, or both. I want to indicate how these views conflict with mine, and why I reject them both as generalizations about discovery and as particular views about what made, or failed to make, Thomson the discoverer of the electron.

Manipulation-and-Measurement View

At the end of her important 1987 paper on Thomson, Isobel Falconer writes:

> In the light of this reinterpretation of Thomson's work is there any sense remaining in which he can be said to have "discovered the electron"? Arriving at the theoretical concept of the electron was not much of a problem in 1897. Numerous such ideas were "in the air." What Thomson achieved was to demonstrate their validity experimentally. Regardless of his own commitments and intentions, it was Thomson who began to make the electron "real" in Hacking's sense of the word. He pinpointed an experimental phenomenon in which electrons could be identified and methods by which they could be isolated, measured, and manipulated.[8]

Several things are suggested here, but one is that Thomson discovered the electron because he was the first to design and carry out experiments in which electrons were manipulated and measured. We might recall that, on Hacking's view, to which Falconer alludes, "if you can spray them they are real."[9] On the more sophisticated version suggested by Falconer in this passage, if you can manipulate them in such a way as to produce some measurements they are real; and if you are the first to do so, you are the discoverer. Such a view needs expanding to say what counts as "manipulating" and "measuring." I will not try to do so here, but will simply take these ideas as reasonably clear. It appears obvious that Thomson manipulated electrons by means of magnetic and electric fields and that he measured their mass-to-charge ratio.

Important Classification View

This view is suggested by an earlier passage in Falconer's paper. Discussing the experimental work of Wiechert, she writes:

---

8. Isobel Falconer, "Corpuscles, Electrons and Cathode Rays: J. J. Thomson and the 'Discovery of the Electron,'" *British Journal for the History of Science* 20 (1987), 241–276: quotation on 276.

9. Ian Hacking, *Representing and Intervening* (Cambridge: Cambridge University Press, 1983), 23.

Wiechert, while realizing that cathode ray particles were extremely small and universal, lacked Thomson's tendency to speculation. He could not make the bold, unsubstantiated leap, to the idea that particles were constitutents of atoms. Thus, while his work might have resolved the cathode ray controversy, he did not "discover the electron."[10]

This suggests that, despite the facts that both Wiechert and Thomson manipulated the electron in such a way as to obtain a mass-to-charge ratio and that both physicists claimed that cathode particles were "extremely small and universal," Thomson, and not Wiechert, is the discoverer of electrons because Thomson but not Wiechert got the idea that cathode particles are constituents of atoms. Although Falconer does not say so explicitly, perhaps what she has in mind is that Thomson's identification of cathode particles as universal constituents of atoms is what is important about electrons. Generalizing from this, you are the discoverer of X when you are the first to arrive at an important (and correct) classification of X. The question remains as to what counts as an "important" classification—a major lacuna, as I will illustrate in a moment. However this is understood, it should include Thomson's classification of electrons as constituents of atoms.

Social Constructivist View

Social constructivism is a broad viewpoint pertaining to many things, including the reality of scientific objects themselves such as electrons (they are "socially constructed" and have no reality independently of this). There is, however, a much narrower social constructivist view that is meant to apply only to scientific discovery. On this view, whether some scientist(s) discovered X depends on what the relevant scientific community believes. This view is adopted by Arabatzis prior to his historical discussion of the work of Thomson and others on the electron. He writes:

A final approach [to discovery]—and the one I favour—takes as central to the account the perspectives of the relevant historical actors and tries to remain as agnostic as possible *vis-à-vis* the realism debate. The criterion that this approach recommends is the following: since it is the scientific community (or its most eminent representatives) which adjudicates discovery claims, an entity has been discovered only when consensus has been reached with respect to its reality. The main advantage of this criterion is that it enables

---

10. Falconer, "Corpuscles, Electrons and Cathode Rays," 251. I would take issue with Falconer here. In a paper of January 1897 Wiechert does indeed claim that cathode particles are constituents of atoms. Emil Wiechert, *Physikalisch-Ökonomischen Gesellschaft*, Königsberg, 7 January 1897, 3–16.

the reconstruction of past scientific episodes without presupposing the resolution of pressing philosophical issues. For historical purposes, one does not have to decide whether the consensus reached by the scientific community is justifiable from a philosophical point of view. Furthermore, one need not worry whether the entity that was discovered (in the above weak sense) can be identified with its present counterpart.[11]

Although in this passage Arabatzis claims that there is a discovery only when the community believes there is, he also says that the main advantage of his criterion is that it avoids the issue of whether the consensus reached is justified, and the issue of whether the entity that was discovered is the same as the one scientists now refer to. Accordingly, the view suggested is a rather strong one, to the effect that consensus is both necessary and sufficient for discovery. (At least, that is the social constructivist view about discovery that I will consider here.) Thomson discovered the electron if he is generally regarded by physicists as having done so. The physicists who so regard him may have different reasons for doing so, but these reasons do not make him the discoverer: simply their regarding him as such does. Even if the reasons are false (in some "absolute," nonconsensual sense), he is still the discoverer, unless the physics community reaches a different consensus.

Different Contributions View

According to this idea, there are discoveries in science, including that of the electron, that are not made by one person, or by several, or by any group, but involve various contributions by different people. We need to replace the question "who discovered the electron?" with more specific questions about who made what contributions to the discovery. We might note that in 1855 Geissler contributed by inventing a pump that allowed much lower gas pressures to be produced in electrical discharge tubes; that in 1859 using this pump, Plucker found by experiment that when the pressure is reduced to 0.001 mm of mercury, the glass near the cathode glows with a greenish phosphorescence and the position of the glow changes when a magnetic field is introduced; that in 1869 Plucker's student Hittorf found that if a solid body is placed between the cathode and the walls of the tube it casts a shadow, from which he concluded that rays are emitted from the cathode that travel in straight lines. This story could be continued with experimental and theoretical contributions by Crookes, Larmor, Lorentz, Hertz, Goldstein, Schuster, and so forth, culminating with the experiments of Thomson—or well beyond if you like.

11. Arabatzis, "Rethinking the 'Discovery' of the Electron," 406.

Now, it is not that all the people mentioned, or even several of them, or a group working together, discovered the electron. Plucker didn't discover the electron, nor was he one of several people or a group that did. Still the electron was discovered, but it was not the sort of discovery made by one individual, or several, or a group. Rather it was the sort of discovery that involved different contributions by different persons at different times. Thus, Arabatzis writes:

> Several historical actors provided the theoretical reasons and the experimental evidence which persuaded the physics community about its [the electron's] reality. However, none of those people discovered the electron. The most that we can say is that one of those, say Thomson, contributed significantly to the acceptance of the belief that "electrons" denote real entities.[12]

True Belief View

According to this view, you have discovered something only if what you believe about it is true or substantially true. Despite Lord Kelvin's claim to know various facts about the luminiferous ether,[13] that entity was not discovered by nineteenth-century wave theorists (or by anyone else), since what was believed about it, including that it exists and that it is the medium through which light is transmitted, is false. Similarly, in this view, Thomson did not discover the electron since quite a few of his core beliefs about electrons (or what for many years he called corpuscles) were false. His corpuscles, he later thought, were entirely electrical, having no inertial mass; they were arranged in stationary positions throughout the atom; they were the only constituents of atoms; they were not waves of any sort; and they were not carriers of the smallest electric charge. So, if he discovered anything at all, it was not the electron.

Now, I reject each of these five views about discovery, both in the generalized forms I have given them and as ones applicable to the case

---

12. Arabatzis, 432. Is Arabatzis's "different contributions" view about the electron compatible with what I take to be his more general social constructivist position about discovery? I believe so. The combined view would be that in general someone is the discoverer of something when and only when there is consensus about who discovered what; in the electron case, however, there is no such consensus about any one person, only (at most) about who made what contributions toward the discovery.

13. Kelvin wrote: "We know the luminiferous ether better than we know any other kind of matter in some particulars. We know it for its elasticity; we know it in respect to the constancy of the velocity of propagation of light for different periods." *Kelvin's Baltimore Lectures and Modern Theoretical Physics*, ed. Robert Kargon and Peter Achinstein (Cambridge, Mass.: MIT Press, 1987), 14.

of Thomson and the electron. Although manipulation and measurement are frequently involved in a discovery, they are neither necessary nor sufficient. Galileo discovered mountains and craters on the moon without manipulating or measuring them (in any reasonable sense of these terms). Moreover, the manipulation and measurement view would too easily dethrone Thomson. Many physicists before Thomson in 1897 manipulated electrons in the sense that Thomson did; that is, they manipulated cathode rays, and did so in such a way as to produce measurements. As noted, in 1890 Schuster conducted experiments involving magnetic deflection of electrons in which he arrived at upper and lower bounds for their ratio of mass to charge. Lenard's experiments manipulated cathode rays out of the tube and measured the distance they traveled. Perhaps one can say that Thomson's manipulations yielded better and more extensive measurements. But why should that fact accord him the title "discoverer"? Manipulations and measurements after Thomson by Seitz in 1901 and by Rieger in 1905 gave even more accurate measurements of the mass-to-charge ratio. Yet none of these physicists is regarded as having discovered the electron.

The second view—"important classification"—fails to provide a sufficient condition for discovery since you can arrive at an important classification of Xs without discovering them. You can postulate their existence on largely theoretical grounds, and describe important facts about them, without "confronting" them sufficiently directly to count as having discovered them. In the early 1930s Pauli hypothesized the existence of a neutral particle, the neutrino, in order to account for the continuous distribution of energy in beta decay. But the neutrino was not discovered until there was a series of experiments, beginning in 1938, that established its existence more directly.

Whether the important-classification view fails to provide even a necessary condition for discovery is more difficult to say because of the vagueness in the notion of important classification. Roentgen discovered x-rays in 1895 without knowing that they are transverse electromagnetic rays. Although he speculated that they were longitudinal vibrations in the ether, he did not claim to know this (nor could he know this) and for this reason, and to distinguish them from other rays, he called them x-rays. Did he fail to arrive at a sufficiently important classification? Or shall we say that the fact that he discovered that x-rays are rays that travel in straight lines, that have substantial penetrating power, that cannot be deflected by an electric or magnetic field, and so forth, is sufficient to say that he arrived at an important classification?

Similarly, in the case of the electron, isn't the fact that the constituents of cathode rays are *charged particles smaller than ordinary ions* an important classification? If so, then Crookes in 1879 deserves the title of discoverer. Is it that the classification "constituent of all atoms" is more important than "being charged particles smaller than ordinary ions," and so Thomson rather than Crookes deserves the honor? Crookes, indeed, claimed that he, not Thomson, first arrived at the classification "constituent of all atoms." Moreover, why choose this classification rather than something more specific about how these constituents are arranged in atoms? If so, then Rutherford or Bohr should be selected, not Thomson, whose plum-pudding model got this dead wrong.

The crucial question concerning the present view is whether you could know that X exists from observations of X without knowing an important classification of X. In the weaker sense of discovery I distinguished earlier, one could discover X without knowing very much about X, including that it is X. (Recall my discovering gold.) The stronger sense involves knowing that it is X. But what important classification one needs to know to know that something is X I'll leave to important classification theorists.

The view I propose also contradicts the social constructivist account of discovery, since in my view there is, or at least can be, a fact of the matter about who discovered what that is independent of who the scientific community regards as the discoverer. This is because there is, or can be, a fact of the matter about who was the first to be in an epistemic state necessary for discovery. Being regarded by the scientific community as the discoverer of X is neither necessary nor sufficient for being the discoverer of X. No doubt scientific discoverers wish to be recognized by the scientific community for their discovery. Perhaps for some a discovery without recognition is worthless. But this does not negate the fact of discovery itself. Nor is this to deny that a discovery that is and remains unknown except to the discoverer will have little chance of advancing science, which depends on public communication. That is one reason scientists make their discoveries public. Although publicity helps to promote the discovery and the recognition for it, neither publicity nor recognition creates the discovery. Finally, one can relativize discovery claims to a group. I can be the first in my department to discover a certain book in the library, Columbus the first European to discover America, and so forth. This is not social constructivism, however, since there is a fact of the matter about discovery within a group that is independent of the beliefs of the members of the group. Either I was or I wasn't the first in my department to discover that book, no matter what views my colleagues have about my discovery.

Two of the views of discovery that contrast with mine deny the claim that Thomson discovered the electron: the "different-contributions" view and the "correct-belief" view. Briefly, my response to these views is this. The fact that various people made contributions to the discovery of the electron does not, on my account, necessarily preclude the fact that Thomson discovered the electron. All this means is that various people helped make it possible for Thomson to be the first to achieve an epistemic state necessary for discovery. Nor, finally, does getting into that epistemic state about some X require that all or most of your beliefs about X be true. Suppose that while walking along a road I discover a person lying in the ditch beside the road. Suppose that, after observing the person, I come to believe that the person is a woman, quite tall, at least fifty years old, with blond hair, and wearing a gray jacket. Suppose, finally, that I am quite wrong about these beliefs. The person in the ditch is actually a man, five feet tall, thirty years of age, with dark hair, and wearing no jacket at all. I can still be said to have discovered the person in the ditch, despite the fact that what I believe about the person in the ditch is substantially false. So I reject the general rule that you have discovered X only if what you believe about X is true or substantially true.

DID THOMSON DISCOVER THE ELECTRON?

Having proposed an account of discovery and disposed of some others, we are now in a position to take up this question. To begin with, I think my account helps us to see why we refrain from attributing this discovery to some of the other physicists mentioned. For example, claims made about the electron by Crookes, Larmor, and Lorentz, even if many were correct, were primarily theory-driven, not experimentally determined. This is not to say that Thomson had no theoretical beliefs about electrons. Falconer and Feffer[14] claim that he probably believed that they are not discrete particles with empty spaces between them, but certain configurations in an all-pervading ether. But that is not enough to put him in the same category as some of the more theoretically driven physicists. The question is whether Thomson was the first to know that electrons exist from observations of them or their direct effects.

Let me divide this question into three parts. First, in 1897 did Thomson know that electrons exist? Second, if he did, did he know this from observations of electrons or of their direct effects? Third, was he the first to know this from such observations? If the answer to all three questions is "yes," then Thomson retains the honor usually accorded to him.

14. Stuart M. Feffer, "Arthur Schuster, J. J. Thomson and the Discovery of the Electron," *Historical Studies in the Physical and Biological Sciences* 20 (1989), 33–51.

In 1897 did Thomson know that electrons exist? Well, what did he claim to know in 1897? Here is a well-known passage from his October 1897 paper:

> As the cathode rays carry a charge of negative electricity, are deflected by an electrostatic force as if they were negatively electrified, and are acted on by a magnetic force in just the way in which this force would act on a negatively electrified body moving along the path of these rays, I can see no escape from the conclusion that they are charges of negative electricity carried by particles of matter.[15]

Thomson continues: "The question next arises, What are these particles? Are they atoms, or molecules, or matter in a still finer state of subdivision. To throw some light on this point, I have made a series of measurements of the ratio of the mass of these particles to the charge carried by it" (384).

Thomson then proceeds to describe in some detail two independent experimental methods he employed to determine the mass-to-charge ratio. At the end of this description he concludes: "From these determinations we see that the value of m/e is independent of the nature of the gas, and that its value 10^{-7} is very small compared with the value 10^{-4}, which is the smallest value of this quantity previously known, and which is the value for the hydrogen ion in electrolysis."

He continues:

> Thus, for the carriers of electricity in the cathode rays m/e is very small compared with its value in electrolysis. The smallness of m/e may be due to the smallness of m or the largeness of e, or to a combination of these two. That the carriers of the charges in the cathode rays are small compared with ordinary molecules is shown, I think, by Lenard's results as to the rate at which the brightness of the phosphorescence produced by these rays diminishes with the length of the path travelled by the ray. (392)

After a little more discussion of Lenard's experimental results, Thomson concludes: "The carriers, then, must be small compared with ordinary molecules."

In sum, in 1897 Thomson claimed to know these facts:

1. That cathode rays contain charged particles. (This he claimed to know from his experiments showing both the magnetic and the electrostatic deflection of the rays.)

---

15. J. J. Thomson, "Cathode Rays," *Philosophical Magazine and Journal of Science* (October 1897), reprinted in Mary Jo Nye, ed., *The Question of the Atom* (Los Angeles: Tomash, 1986), 375–398; quotation on 384.

2. That the ratio of mass to charge of the particles is approximately 10^{-7}, which is much smaller than that for a hydrogen atom. (The 10^{-7} ratio he claimed to know from experiments of two different types involving magnetic and electrical deflection.)

3. That the particles are much smaller than ordinary molecules. (This he claimed to know from his own experiments yielding a mass-to-charge ratio smaller than that for the hydrogen atom, together with Lenard's experiments on the distance cathode rays travel outside the tube, which is much greater than that for hydrogen ions.)

Did he know these facts? He certainly believed them to be true: he says so explicitly. Are they true? True enough, if we don't worry about how much to pack into the notion of a particle. (Clearly Thomson had some false beliefs about his particles, in particular that they lacked wave properties.) Was he justified in his beliefs? His experimental reasons for claims 1 and 2 are quite strong, that for the smallness of the particles is perhaps slightly less so (but I think better than Heilbron alleges in his article on Thomson in the *Dictionary of Scientific Biography*, 367). A reasonable case, I think, can be made that Thomson knew the facts in question in 1897.

To be sure, there are other claims Thomson made in 1897 concerning which one might not, or could not, attribute knowledge to him. Perhaps one of the former sort is the claim that the charged particles are constituents of all atoms. Indeed, Thomson's explicit argument here appears a bit more tentative and less conclusive than those for the three other claims. It is simply an explanatory one to the effect that if atoms are composed of the particles whose existence he has already inferred, then this would enable him to explain how they are projected from the cathode, how they could give a value for m/e that is independent of the nature of the gas, and how their mean free path would depend solely on the density of the medium through which they pass. In general, explanatory reasoning does not by itself establish the claims inferred with sufficient force to yield knowledge. And finally, there are the claims that the particles are the only constituents of atoms and are arranged in accordance with a model of floating magnets suggested by Mayer. Both claims, being false, are not claims that Thomson or anyone else could know to be true.

Like knowing that there is a person in the ditch, however, not every belief about that person needs to be true or known to be true. If in 1897 Thomson knew that cathode rays contain charged particles, whose ratio of mass to charge is 10^{-7} and that are much smaller than ordinary molecules, then I think it is reasonable to say that in 1897 he knew that electrons exist at least in the weaker of the two senses discussed earlier. He knew of the existence of things that happen to be electrons.

Electrons are the charged particles in question. Knowing these particular facts about them entails knowing that they exist. Whether he knew that electrons exist in the stronger sense is a question I will postpone for a moment.

The second of my three questions is whether Thomson knew what he did from observations of electrons or their direct effects. I suggest the answer is clearly "yes." Those were electrons in his cathode tubes, and they did produce fluorescent effects and others that he observed in his experiments. Despite various theoretical assumptions, his conclusions about electrons are primarily experiment driven.

The final of the three questions concerns priority. Was Thomson the first to be in the appropriate epistemic state? Was he the first to know that electrons exist in the weaker sense of this expression? Was he the first to know of the existence of things that happen to be electrons? He was clearly not the first to know of the existence of cathode rays which happen to be, or to be composed of, electrons. But that is not the issue here. Was he the first to know, by experimental means, of the existence of the things that happen to be the constituents of cathode rays, that is, electrons? That would be a more important question, albeit a question of discovery in the weaker sense. How do you demonstrate the existence of the constituents of cathode rays? Not simply by showing that cathode rays exist. Thomson demonstrated their existence by showing that charged particles exist comprising the rays, and he did so by means of experiments involving the direct effects of those charged particles. Was he the first to do so?

The answer I would offer is a less than decisive "maybe." Other physicists, including Schuster, Perrin, Wiechert, and Lenard, had conducted experiments on cathode rays which yielded results that gave support to the claim that the constituents of cathode rays are charged particles. Moreover, these experiments involved observing the electron's direct effects. It might be argued that although these other physicists provided such experimental support, that support was not strong enough to produce knowledge. One might claim that Thomson's refinements of Perrin's experiment, and more important, his achievement of producing electrostatic deflection of the rays, and his determination of m/e, showed conclusively, in a way not shown before, that cathode rays contain charged particles. (This is what Thomson himself claims in his October 1897 paper.) If this is right, then one can say that, in the weaker sense of discovery, Thomson discovered the electron. Although others before him had produced experimental evidence of its existence, he was the first to produce evidence sufficient for knowledge.

This, however, is a controversial priority claim. It was vehemently denied by Lenard, who claimed that his own experiments prior to Thomson's conclusively proved the existence of electrons.[16] It was also denied, albeit less vehemently, by Zeeman, who claimed that he determined the ratio of mass to charge before Thomson.[17] Finally, Emil Wiechert makes claims about the constituents of cathode rays that are fairly similar to Thomson's in a paper published in January 1897, before Thomson's papers of April and October of that year.[18] In this paper Wiechert explicitly asserts that cathode rays contain charged particles that are much smaller than ordinary molecules, and from experiments involving magnetic deflection of cathode rays he determines upper and lower bounds for the mass-to-charge ratio of the particles. Unlike Thomson, however, Wiechert did not produce electrostatic deflection, he did not obtain two independent means for arriving at his determination of mass to charge, and he did not produce precise values. The issue, as I have defined it, is simply this: even though others had provided some experimental evidence for the existence of charged particles as the constituents of cathode rays, were Thomson's experiments the first to *conclusively* demonstrate this? Were they the first on the basis of which knowledge of their existence could be correctly claimed? If so, he discovered the electron. If not, he didn't.

One might make another claim. Relativizing discovery to the individual, one might say that Thomson first discovered the electron (for himself) in 1897, whereas others had done so a bit earlier. One might then say that Thomson was among first to discover the electron (for himself). Perhaps this is what Abraham Pais has in mind when, as reported in the *New York Times* (April 29, 1997), he claims that Thomson was a, not the, discoverer of the electron. The others Pais mentions are Wiechert and Kaufmann.

STRONG DISCOVERY

What about the stronger sense of discovery, the sense in which if I discover gold, then I know it is gold? To those seeking to deny the title "discoverer of the electron" to Thomson, one can concede that he did not know that the constituents of cathode rays have all the properties that electrons do. If this is required, the electron has yet to be discovered, since presumably no one knows all the properties of electrons. Obviously, this is not required for knowledge in the stronger sense. I can know that I have

---

16. Philipp Lenard, *Wissenschaftliche Abhandhangen*, vol. 3 (Leipzig: S. Hirzel, 1944), I.
17. See Arabatzis, "Rethinking the 'Discovery' of the Electron," p. 423.
18. Wiechert, *Physikalisch-Ökonomischen Gesellschaft*.

discovered gold without knowing all the properties of gold. Indeed, I can know that I have discovered gold without knowing any of the properties of gold. If an expert, after examining it, tells me it is gold, then I think I know it is. Clearly, however, Thomson did not know *in this way* that the constituents of cathode rays are electrons. So what must one know to know that the items in question are electrons? That is a problem. (A similar problem was raised concerning the "important classification" view.)

There is a further problem here with the question of whether Thomson knew that the constituents of cathode rays are electrons. Putting the question that way presupposes some established concept of electron. And the question appears to be whether what Thomson discovered (in the weaker sense) fits that concept and whether Thomson knew this. By analogy, to ask whether I discovered gold (in the stronger sense) is to presuppose that these objects satisfy some established concept of gold and whether I know that they do. Which concept of electron is meant in the question about Thomson? In 1897 there was no established concept. Stoney, who introduced the term "electron," used it to refer to an elementary electric charge, but Thomson was not talking about this. Nor was his claim that the constituents of cathode rays are Lorentz's electrons, which in 1895 Lorentz claimed were ions of electrolysis. (In fact, Thomson never used the term "electron" until well into the twentieth century.) Nor did Thomson claim that the cathode ray constituents have the properties we currently attribute to electrons.

So the question "did Thomson know that the constituents of cathode rays are electrons?" is, I think, ambiguous and misleading. Instead, I suggest, it is better simply to ask what facts, if any, about the constituents of cathode rays Thomson knew, when he knew them, and when others knew them.

Briefly, let's take four central claims that Thomson made about cathode ray constituents in his October 1897 paper: first, they are charged particles; second, their ratio of mass to charge is approximately 10^{-7}; third, they are much smaller than ordinary atoms and molecules; and fourth, they are constituents of atoms. Earlier I said that it is reasonable to suppose that Thomson knew the first three of these facts in 1897, but not the fourth. He came to know them during that year as a result of his experiments with cathode rays. I also said that one might claim that Thomson was the first to demonstrate conclusively that the constituents of cathode rays are charged particles, though this is controversial. At least he was among the first to do so.

With regard to the second claim—that the ratio of mass to charge of these particles is approximately 10^{-7}—Wiechert had arrived at upper and lower bounds before Thomson. In defense of Thomson, one might say that his determinations were more precise and were based on two independent experimental methods.

With respect to the third claim—that the cathode particles are much smaller than atoms and molecules—perhaps Lenard is correct in claiming knowledge of this prior to Thomson. Indeed, Thomson made important use of Lenard's absorption results in his own arguments that cathode particles are smaller than atoms. And if Wiechert's arguments are sufficiently strong, he too has some claim to knowledge before Thomson.

Finally, the fourth claim—that cathode particles are constituents of atoms—is, it is probably fair to say, one that Thomson did not know the truth of in 1897, although he gave explanatory arguments in its favor.

WHAT IS SO IMPORTANT ABOUT WHO DISCOVERED THE ELECTRON (OR ANYTHING ELSE)?

Was there a discoverer of the electron? Was it Thomson? Have I needlessly complicated the issue with recondite distinctions that permit no definitive answers, as philosophers are wont to do? I think the issue is complicated, much more so than when I first began to think about it. The complications arise for two reasons. The concept of discovery itself is complex, requiring philosophical attention. And the historical facts about who knew what and when are complex. So who discovered the electron is usefully addressed by joint efforts of philosophers and historians of science. Before turning to the question raised in the title of this concluding section, let me summarize and simplify what I have said so far.

First, the philosophical account of discovery that I propose involves three factors: ontological (the thing discovered must exist); epistemic (the discoverer must be in a certain knowledge-state with respect to it); and priority (this state must be a first). Second, contrary to the opposing views mentioned, discovery does not require either manipulation and measurement of the item discovered or the idea of an important classification, or group recognition or consensus; nor is any of these sufficient. Furthermore, one can be the discoverer of some entity even if one's beliefs about it are substantially false and even if many persons contributed to making that discovery possible.

Third, my account distinguishes a weak and a strong sense of discovery. In the weak but not the strong sense one can discover X even if the discoverer does not know it is X that has been discovered.

Fourth, in virtue of Thomson's magnetic deflection experiments, which were better than Perrin's, his electrostatic deflection experiments, which had not been achieved before, and his two independent determinations of

m/e (better and more precise than the results produced by Wiechert), some case might be made that Thomson discovered the existence of charged particles that are electrons. Relativizing discovery to the individual, we can at least say that, in the weak sense of discovery, he was among the first to discover them. As far as the strong sense is concerned, it may be better to replace the question "did Thomson know that the constituents of cathode rays are electrons?" with the question "what facts about the constituents of cathode rays did Thomson know and when?" A case can be made that Thomson was the first to demonstrate, from experimental results, in a way producing knowledge, that the constituents of cathode rays are charged particles and that their mass-to-charge ratio is 10^{-7}.

Now, why do, or should, we care about who discovered the electron, or any other entity? The question arises especially for my account of discovery. On that account, the fact that something has been discovered by someone does not by itself imply that what is discovered, or by whom, is important or interesting, even to the discoverer. (I may have discovered yet one more paperclip on the floor.) The importance of the discovery will depend on the item discovered and on the interests of the discoverer and of the group or individual to whom the discovery is communicated. Discovering a universal particle such as the electron, which is a constituent of all atoms, is obviously more important, especially to physicists, than discovering yet one more paperclip on the floor is to them or to me.

Not only can the object discovered be of importance, but so can the method(s) employed. In his discovery of the electron (at least for himself) Thomson discovered a way to produce electrostatic deflection of the cathode rays, which had not been achieved before. Using this he devised a new independent way to obtain a fundamental measurement of mass-to-charge.

There is another point worth emphasizing about discoveries of certain entities, particularly those that are too small, or too far away, or otherwise too inaccessible to be observed directly. Scientists may have theoretical reasons for believing that such entities exist. These theoretical reasons may be based on observations and experiments with other entities. Sometimes such reasoning is sufficiently strong to justify a claim to know that the entity exists. Yet there is still the desire to find it, to discover it, by observing it as directly as possible. (Although the case of the electron does not illustrate this, one that does fairly closely is that of the top quark, whose existence was inferred from the "standard model" before it was detected experimentally.[19]) This need not increase the degree of confidence in its existence significantly if at all over what it was before. So why do it?

19. See Staley, *Over the Top*.

One reason may simply derive from a primal desire or curiosity to "see" or detect something by confronting it more or less directly. Another more important reason is to discover new facts about it, which is usually facilitated by observing it or its effects, and which may allow the theory that entailed its existence to be extended. It will also provide additional support for that theory without necessarily increasing the degree of probability or confidence one attaches to that theory.[20]

Why should we care about who, if anyone, was the discoverer, that is, about who was the first to be in an appropriate epistemic state for discovery with respect to some entity? It depends on who the "we" is and on what is discovered. As noted, not all discoveries and discoverers are of interest to all groups; some may be of interest to none. If what is discovered is important to some community, and if there was a discoverer, whether a person or a group, then simply giving credit where credit is due is what is appropriate and what may act as a spur to future investigations. In this regard discovery is no different from other achievements. If accomplishing something (whether flying an airplane, or climbing Mt. Everest, or discovering the electron) is valuable to a certain community, and some person or group was the first to do it, or if several persons independently were the first, then such persons deserve to be credited and perhaps honored and rewarded by the community, especially to the extent that the accomplishment is important and difficult. Generally speaking, more credit should be given to such persons than to those who helped make the achievement possible but did not accomplish it themselves.

Whether Thomson deserves the credit he received for being the (or a) discoverer of the electron is, of course, of interest to him and to other contemporaries such as Lenard, Zeeman, and Crookes, who thought they deserved more credit. It should also be of interest to subsequent physicists, historians of physics, and authors of textbooks who write about the discovery. The answer to the question of who discovered the electron, and hence who deserves the credit, is, I have been suggesting, not so simple. Part of that answer depends upon establishing who knew what, when, and how, which in the electron case is fairly complex. The other part depends on establishing some reasonably clear concept of discovery. In this chapter I have attempted to contribute to each task, particularly the latter.

Finally, credit is deserved not only for discovering the existence of an important entity, but for other accomplishments with respect to it as well. Even if Lenard has some claim to priority for the discovery that cathode ray constituents are smaller than atoms, and even if in 1897 Thomson's

20. For arguments that evidence can provide support for a theory without necessarily increasing its probability, see chapter 1 in this book.

arguments that his corpuscles are constituents of all atoms are not conclusive, we can admire and honor Thomson, among other reasons, for the experiments leading to the conclusions he drew, for the conclusions themselves, and for proposing and defending a bold idea that revolutionized physics: that the atom is not atomic.